This book represents a significant contribution to the growing interest from both academics and practitioners alike in developing collaborative academic-practitioner partnerships that can yield dual benefits of rigorous research with internationally excellent publications, and strong organizational impact. This book also represents a departure from others in the area with its focus on developing how we think about academic-practitioner partnerships and the skills and capabilities to carry them out, providing a set of stimulating examples involving creative ways of collaborating that lead to successful partnerships. Both academics and practitioners who are either engaging, or considering engaging, in collaborations can gain a lot from this book.

Professor Julia Balogun, *Director University of Liverpool Management School, UK*

Academic–Practitioner Relationships

While executives are keen to harness organizational knowledge and improve business performance, the topic of how academics can produce rigorous and relevant theory in working relationships with practitioners is a much contested topic. Many aspects of this knowledge co-creation can create tensions, and the ways in which research is conducted and published can affect academic credibility and practitioner acceptance, as well as its consequent uptake and use in different contexts.

Expertly compiled by Jean Bartunek and Jane McKenzie, with contributions from global thinkers in the field, this book offers a concise and up-to-date review of the essential analysis and action underlying scholarly engagement with the world of business. It discusses the sorts of capability academics need to collaborate effectively with practitioners and illustrates good practice through international case studies drawn from acknowledged centers of excellence. These show how to negotiate different constituencies with different priorities, values, and practices to work together to produce research of rigor and relevance.

It will be a key reference and resource for all researchers who are engaged with practitioners, for practitioners who wish to engage with researchers and an invaluable tool for training academics to develop research with impact.

Jean M. Bartunek is the Robert A. and Evelyn J. Ferris Chair and Professor of Management and Organization at Boston College.

Jane McKenzie is Professor of Management Knowledge and Learning at Henley Business School, University of Reading, UK.

Routledge Studies in Organizational Change & Development
Series Editor: Bernard Burnes

Academic–Practitioner Relationships

Developments, Complexities and Opportunities

Edited by Jean M. Bartunek and Jane McKenzie

LONDON AND NEW YORK

First published 2018 by Routledge

2 Park Square, Milton Park, Abingdon, Oxfordshire OX14 4RN
52 Vanderbilt Avenue, New York, NY 10017

Routledge is an imprint of the Taylor & Francis Group, an informa business

First issued in paperback 2019

British Library Cataloguing in Publication Data
A catalogue record for this book is available from the British Library

Library of Congress Cataloging in Publication Data
Names: Bartunek, Jean, editor. | McKenzie, Jane, editor.
Title: Academic practitioner relationships : developments, complexities and opportunities / [edited by] Jean M. Bartunek, Jane McKenzie.
Description: Abingdon, Oxon ; New York, NY : Routledge, 2017. |
Includes bibliographical references and index.
Identifiers: LCCN 2017003075 (print) | LCCN 2017020528 (ebook) |
ISBN 9781315657530 (eBook) | ISBN 9781138100695 (hardback : alk. paper)
Subjects: LCSH: Management–Study and teaching (Higher) |
Management–Research. | Academic-industrial collaboration.
Classification: LCC HD30.4 (ebook) | LCC HD30.4 .A27 2017 (print) |
DDC 378.1/035–dc23
LC record available at https://lccn.loc.gov/2017003075

ISBN: 978-1-138-10069-5 (hbk)
ISBN: 978-0-367-87500-8 (pbk)

Typeset in Times New Roman
by Wearset Ltd, Boldon, Tyne and Wear

Contents

Figures

Tables

Contributors

Benjamin N. Alexander is an assistant professor of management at the Orfalea College of Business at California Polytechnic State University, San Luis Obispo. He received his PhD from the A.B. Freeman School of Business at Tulane University and his MA from George Mason University. His research focuses on social entrepreneurship, corporate social responsibility, and organizational institutionalism. In particular, he explores for-profit organizations that incorporate core social objectives and the legal structures designed to accommodate these multi-faceted firms. His interest in the institutional forces with which organizations contend has also led to research on family firms and the broader interface between business, business education, and society.

Elena P. Antonacopoulou is Professor of Organizational Behaviour at the University of Liverpool Management School, where she leads GNOSIS, a research initiative advancing impactful collaborative research in management and organization studies. Her principal research expertise lies in the areas of Organizational Change, Learning, and Knowledge Management with a focus on the Leadership implications. Her research continues to advance cutting edge ideas and thought leadership, as well as new methodologies for studying social complexity, and is strengthened by her approach. Elena also works with leading international researchers, practitioners and policy makers collaboratively. Her current study on "Realizing Y-Our Impact" is one example of the approach that governs her commitment to pursuing scholarship that makes a difference through actionable knowledge. Elena's work is published widely in leading international journals and edited books. She has Editorship and Associate Editor roles for a range of journals including *Management Learning*, *British Journal of Management*, and *Emergence: Complexity and Organizational Journal*, and is on the editorial board of several journals such as *Organization Science*, *Group and Organization Management*, *Society, Business and Organization Journal*, and the *Irish Journal of Management*. She is a regular assessor of Research Grant Applications and sits on commissioning panels of research councils in the UK, the USA, Australia and elsewhere in Europe. As one of only 16 Senior Fellows appointed to lead the prestigious Advanced Institute of Management Research, she has fostered the development of innovative, international, interdisciplinary, and interactive modes of research. In addition Elena has held several other leadership roles (at Board, Council and Executive level leading special committees such as Ethics, Management Practice) in the top international professional bodies in her field including the Academy of Management (USA), the European Group for Organizational Studies, the British Academy of Management, and the Society for the Advancement of Management Studies. Elena is actively engaged in collaborative consulting projects with leading businesses and frequently delivers keynote presentations and master classes in practitioner fora on topical themes such as Crisis and Strategic Learning, Change and the Dynamics of Management Practice, Impactful Learning and Knowing, Dynamic Capabilities in Leadership, and Practising for Innovation and Growth.

Jean M. Bartunek is the Robert A. and Evelyn J. Ferris Chair and Professor of Management and Organization at Boston College, where she has taught since 1977. Her Bachelor's degree in psychology and sociology is from Maryville University (St. Louis), and her PhD is in social and organizational psychology from the University of Illinois at Chicago. She is a past president and fellow of the Academy of Management. In 2009 she won the Academy of Management's Career Distinguished Service Award. Jean has published over 125 journal articles and book chapters, as well as five books. Her primary research interests center around organizational change and academic–practitioner relationships. Jean is currently an associate editor of the *Academy of Management Review* as well as an associate editor of the *Journal of Applied Behavioral Science*. She was previously an associate editor of the Academy of Management Learning and Education.

Guillaume Carton is an assistant professor in management at Institut Supérieur de Gestion (Paris). He holds a PhD from PSL Université Paris-Dauphiné he obtained in 2015, for which he was awarded a prize by the foundation of PSL Université Paris-Dauphiné. His research deals with the production of management knowledge that he analyzes through a science and technology studies stance. He focuses on what happens at the research–practice interface, either concepts, people, or organizations. He is also interested in the topic of business schools (and management education) as well as management consulting. His work has been published in a number of book chapters, both in English and in French. He is involved in different academic circles, including the Association Internationale de Management Stratégique (AIMS), the Academy of Management (AOM), the European Group of Organization Studies (EGOS), the European Academy of Management (Euram), and the Strategic Management Society (SMS). He has also been involved in the Société Française de Management (SFM), an academic circle that contributes to shaping the institutional setting of the academic field. Guillaume teaches management classes and has been a management consultant for over three years.

David Coghlan is Professor Emeritus and Fellow Emeritus at the Trinity Business School, Trinity College Dublin, Ireland. He specializes in organization development and action research and is active in both communities internationally. He has published over 150 articles and book chapters. Recent books include: *Inside Organizations* (Sage), *Organizational Change and Strategy* (Routledge), *Doing Action Research in Your Own Organization* (4th ed., Sage), *Collaborative Strategic Improvement through Network Action Learning* (Edward Elgar). He is co-editor of *The Sage Encyclopedia of Action Research* and of the four-volume sets *Fundamentals of Organization Development* (Sage) and *Action Research in Business & Management* (Sage). He serves on the editorial advisory boards of *Journal of Applied Behavioral Science, Action Research, Action Learning: Research and Practice, Systemic Practice and Action Research,* and *The OD Practitioner,* among others.

Claire Collins is Associate Professor of Leadership Development and Behaviour, Deputy Head of School and Director of the DBA Programme at Henley Business School, University of Reading. She researches and teaches leadership and leadership development with a special interest in coaching leaders, leadership diversity, leadership derailment and women in leadership. She teaches on a number of post-experience, postgraduate programmes, such as the MBA, full-time, executive and flexible modes, and the newly accredited MA in Leadership. She also teaches business research methods on the MSc in Business and Management Research, both at Henley and at the Rotman School of Management, University of Toronto. Claire chairs the Chartered ABS DBA Steering Group, is an active member of BAM and regularly presents at the Academy of Management. She holds a number of external examiner positions and has supervised and examined several doctoral candidates. She has experience of working with a variety of organizational and academic clients from the private and public sectors. Claire enjoyed a significant career outside academia before joining Henley Business School in 2007. She has 20 years' experience in the NHS, initially in a scientific role and then in senior management in a large acute Trust, following which she became CEO of a London law firm. She has also enjoyed some years as an independent consultant and coach, and combined this with being a Research Fellow at the Royal College of Nursing Institute before joining the faculty at Henley Business School. As part of her portfolio, Claire is an accredited and experienced business coach working with a wide variety of senior clients.

Stéphanie Dameron is Professor of Strategy at Paris Dauphine University where she runs the Chair of Strategic and Competitive Intelligence. Her research topics include cooperative relationships within or between organizations and the participation of various stakeholders in the decision-making process. She also has a special interest in management education systems. Her work has been published in international journals including the *Journal of Management Studies* and the *British Journal of Management.* She is one of the chair leaders at the Strategic Management Society. She is also the former elected chair of the French Academy of Management and the former chair of the Advisory Board of EM Normandie Business Schools. She is regularly invited as a keynote speaker and teaches strategic management and organization theory in Executive Education in France and elsewhere.

Kali Demes is a consultant and Head of Research at Glowinkowski International Ltd. Kali is a graduate of the University of Essex, with a research background in social, cultural, and occupational psychology. Kali has extensive experience of survey design and associated data handling and data analytic techniques. Over the course of her PhD, Kali project managed an especially innovative research study funded by the Economic and Social Research Council, in which over 2,000 intercultural exchange students were followed during their year abroad, via a series of online surveys. Following the completion of her thesis in 2014, Kali joined Glowinkowski International Ltd (GIL) to develop a new consultancy metric aimed at assessing an organizations values culture. Having been trialed in a number of organizations internationally, this tool proves to produce data that can be used to guide practical change strategies in organizations wishing to more fully embed values in their work culture. This work has resulted in GIL's values alignment and quotient survey methodology. Moving forward in her role at GIL, Kali will be involved in the ongoing development of the GIL consultancy toolkit as well as in the delivery of accreditation and training in the use of these methodologies. Kali retains strong ties to the University of Essex and is a visiting scholar at the Essex Business School.

Laura Empson is Professor in the Management of Professional Service Firms and Director of the Centre for Professional Service Firms. She has dedicated more than two decades to researching professionals and professional service firms. Her current research focuses on leadership dynamics in professional service firms and has been funded by a major grant from the Economic and Social Research Council of Great Britain. Her previous ESRC-funded study explored the survival of the partnership "ethos" within alternative governance structures and alongside more rigorous methods of performance management. Her research into professional service firms has also covered themes such as mergers and acquisitions, the professionalization of management, organizational and identity change, knowledge management, and diversity. At Cass Business School, as well as being Director of the Centre for Professional Service Firms, she teaches the Cass MBA elective "Succeeding in Professional and Financial Services" and the core MBA module on "Organizational Behaviour." She has published numerous articles in leading international academic journals and is lead editor of the recently published *Oxford Handbook of Professional Service Firms* (Oxford University Press). She is committed to translating her academic research for a practitioner audience, most notably in her 2007 book *Managing the Modern Law Firm* (Oxford University Press) which was described by *The Times* as marking a "seminal moment in the development of management theory in this sector." She is Senior Research

Fellow at Harvard Law School, a Member of the Editorial Boards of the *Journal of Management Studies, Organization Studies*, and the *Journal of Professions and Organizations*. She is also a member of the ESRC's Peer Review College. In 2013 she was honored by the *Financial Times* for her research and teaching on professional service firms. She was previously a reader at the University of Oxford's Said Business School and remains a Supernumerary Fellow of St Anne's College, Oxford. Before becoming an academic, Laura worked as an investment banker and strategy consultant. She acts as an adviser to many of the world's leading professional service firms in the areas such as accounting, law, investment banking, actuarial and management consulting. Through her consultancy work she translates her scholarly research into actionable insights into a range of issues that challenge leaders in professional service firms.

Kristy Faccer is an independent researcher and consultant, currently completing her PhD at the University of Cape Town Graduate School of Business. She has worked as a sustainability practitioner and, since 2014–15, as Knowledge Manager with NBS-SA.

Steve Glowinkowski is Professor, Managing Director and Founder, Glowinkowski International Ltd. Steve's initial background included a series of management/director roles within the chemicals and financial services sectors. This involved a raft of work in the fields of leadership, talent management, change, and safety. This included developing and implementing behavioral frameworks and leading culture change programs. In the early 1990s Steve established Glowinkowski International. The organization now operates internationally across sectors, providing consultancy and research-based services within the fields of behavior, culture change, and performance improvement. Steve has experience in the assessment/development of senior executives. He has conducted extensive research into the question of what differentiates outstanding performance at the level of the individual and organization, which has been implemented in a wide range of organizations globally. Steve has published as an author and co-author in numerous academic and business publications. He is an Honorary Professor at the University of Essex Business School and a Visiting Research Professor at Glyndŵr University. Steve is also co-founder and chairman of the Gillson Partnership, which is a consulting and talent analytics firm based in Southern California. Steve is a Chartered and Research Psychologist by background and over the past 20 years has developed a series of frameworks which both define and measure/assess individual values, motives, predisposition, and culture. In addition to his consultancy activities Steve spends considerable time accrediting and licensing fellow change and HR practitioners in the use of these methodologies.

Ralph Hamann is Professor and Research Director at the University of Cape Town Graduate School of Business. He is also Academic Director of the

Network for Business Sustainability (South Africa) and Chair of the Advisory Board of the Southern Africa Food Lab.

Paula Jarzabkowski is Professor of Strategic Management at Cass Business School, City University London. Her research focuses on strategy-as-practice in complex contexts, such as regulated firms, third-sector organizations, and financial services, particularly insurance and reinsurance. Her work has appeared in a number of leading journals including *Academy of Management Journal, Organization Science, Strategic Management Journal*, and *Journal of Management Studies and Organization Studies*. Her most recent book is *Making a Market for Acts of God: The Practice of Risk-Trading in the Global Reinsurance Industry* (Oxford University Press).

Jennifer Kurkoski manages Google's People Innovation Lab (PiLab), an applied R&D lab in Google's People Operations (aka Human Resources) department. Her work has been featured in the *New York Times*, the *Wall Street Journal, Fast Company*, and *Slate*, as well as on the BBC and ABC's Nightline. Prior to Google, Jennifer was a product manager and senior community manager at Excite@Home and consulted with nonprofit organizations on leadership development. Jennifer holds a PhD in Business Administration (Organizational Behavior) from UC Berkeley's Haas School of Business.

Todd Landman is Professor of Political Science and Pro Vice Chancellor of Social Sciences at the University of Nottingham. He was Professor of Government (2009–15) and Executive Dean of the Social Sciences at the University of Essex (2013–15), and has held a variety of academic and leadership roles at the University of Essex since 1993. He is author of *Human Rights and Democracy: The Precarious Triumph of Ideals* (Bloomsbury), *Protecting Human Rights* (Georgetown University Press), *Studying Human Rights* (Routledge), and *Issues and Methods in Comparative Politics* (Routledge), and co-author of *Measuring Human Rights* (Routledge), *Assessing the Quality of Democracy* (International IDEA), *Governing Latin America* (Polity Press), and *Citizenship Rights and Social Movements* (Oxford University Press). He was editor of *Human Rights*, Vols I–IV (Sage), and co-editor of the *Sage Handbook of Comparative Politics* (Sage) and *Real Social Science: Applied Phronesis* (Cambridge University Press). He has numerous articles published in *International Studies Quarterly, The British Journal of Political Science, Human Rights Quarterly, Democratization, Political Studies, The Journal of Human Rights, The British Journal of Politics and International Relations, Electoral Studies, Human Rights and Human Welfare, Public Law*, and *The California Western International Law Journal*. He has carried out a large number of international consultancies in the areas of development, democracy, and human rights, and is engaged in values measurement, change management, and leadership work for large organizations in the public and private sectors. He is an associate of the Inner Magic Circle with Silver Star (AIMC) and Fellow of the Royal Society for the Arts (FRSA).

Marianne W. Lewis is Dean of the Cass Business School, City University of London Her research explores leadership paradoxes in managing tensions, conflicts, and contradictions. Her paper "Exploring Paradox: Toward a More Comprehensive Guide" received the *Academy of Management Review* Best Paper Award in 2000. Her work also appears in such journals as the *Academy of Management Journal, Organization Science*, the *Journal of Operations Management*, and *Harvard Business Review.* As a dean, she consistently applies her theories and theorizes the applications.

Robert MacIntosh is Professor of Strategic Management at Heriot-Watt University where he is also Head of the School of Management and Languages. He has a PhD in Engineering and researches the development of strategy in senior teams as well as organizational change. He sits on the councils of the British Academy of Management, the Chartered Association of Business Schools, and the board of Turning Point Scotland, and is the co-founder of Stridesite, which provides on-line resources for those developing strategy.

Donald MacLean received a BSc in Physics from the University of Strathclyde, a PhD in Optoelectronics from the University of Cambridge and an MBA from Kingston University. He spent ten years working in the global optoelectronics industry before joining the University of Glasgow in 1993 where he is now a professorial research fellow in the Adam Smith Business School. He has published extensively on strategy, transformation, and complexity theory in a range of international journals including the *Strategic Management Journal, The Journal of Management Studies, Organization Studies*, and *Human Relations.* His latest book *Strategic Management: Strategist at Work* (Palgrave) is aimed particularly at practitioners.

Richard McBain is currently an Associate Professor in the School of Leadership, Organisation and Behaviour at Henley Business School and Head of Post-Experience Postgraduate Programmes, having previously undertaken Programme Director roles for the DBA and Distance Learning and consortium MBA programmes. Prior to joining Henley Richard had 17 years' experience of working in the financial services sector in various operational, business development, and training and development roles. His experience includes project managing the merger of two financial services organizations, the setting up of an offshore banking subsidiary, and implementing competence development and coaching and mentoring programs. His interest in learning and development has continued at Henley, where Richard teaches on the human resources and managing people modules on the MBA. He contributes to teaching on the Henley coaching programs and has run coaching and mentoring development programs for a number of clients. Richard also teaches research methods on the Henley MSc/DBA prgramme. He is currently researching in the areas of management and leadership development, employee engagement and organizational commitment, and he retains a long-standing research interest in coaching and mentoring. He has also completed doctoral research into the impact of mentoring on self-efficacy, emotional intelligence and academic progression.

Jane McKenzie is Professor of Management Knowledge and learning at Henley Business School, University of Reading. Until 2016, she was Director of the Henley Forum for Organisational Learning and Knowledge Strategies, a research center with the Business School. The Henley Forum is funded entirely by large organizations interested in learning how to harness organizational knowledge, improve business performance, and increase value. Jane has been actively researching with the Forum since 2000, and with her colleague Christine van Winkelen has produced two books and many papers from the research, as well as practical guidance for the practitioners. She is on the editorial board of the *Journal of Knowledge Management*. Jane joined Henley in 1997, having previously worked as an accountant in industry and an independent consultant. She has worked at the academic–practitioner interface since 1990, when she started her PhD (completed in 1994) working for Henley to deliver research to large UK consultancy clients in relation to technology-enabled business transformation.

Susan Albers Mohrman is a Senior Research Scientist at the Center for Effective Organizations (CEO) in the Marshall School of Business at the University of Southern California. Her research is in the areas of organization design and effectiveness. She has published papers in professional journals and books on the topics of: organization design for the global knowledge economy; organization development, learning, and change; high technology organizations; the design of teams and other lateral approaches to organizing; design for growth; the design of sustainable business systems; and designing for complexity. Susan has been actively involved as a consultant and/or researcher to a wide variety of organizations instituting innovative management systems and organizational designs. She is Faculty Director of the Certificate Program in Organization Design at the Center for Effective Organizations in the Marshall School, and principal investigator in CEO's Design for Sustainability Program.

Richard P. Nielsen is Professor, Management and Organization Department, Carroll School of Management, Boston College. He works in the areas of organizational ethics, politics, conflict transformation, and political economy. He has served as President and Executive Board Member of the Society for Business Ethics and as Senior Editor for ethics- and social responsibility-related articles of *Organization Studies*. Currently, he is serving on the editorial board of *Business Ethics Quarterly*, the *Journal of the Society for Business Ethics*, as well as the editorial boards of the *Journal of Academic Ethics, Finance, Ethics and Regulation* and the *Sustainability, Accounting, Management and Policy Journal*. His publications include *The Politics of Ethics: Methods for Acting, Learning, And Sometimes Fighting, With Others In Addressing Ethics Problems In Organizational Life* (Oxford University

Press). He has published more than 100 articles in journals such as *Academy of Management Review*, *Academy of Management Executive*, *American Business Law Journal*, *Business Ethics Quarterly*, *Business Ethics: A European Review*, *Business and Society*, *Human Resources Management*, *Journal of Applied Behavioral Science*, *Journal of Business Ethics*, *Journal of Management Inquiry*, *Labor Law Journal*, *Organization Studies*, and *Strategic Management Journal*. He has consulted and done executive and MBA education work internationally with many organizations, including Carrefour, Citigroup, Eurobank, the European Union, IBM, the Krannert Center for the Performing Arts, Neochemiki, New York City, Novo Nordisk, the Peace Research Institute of Oslo, Piraeus Bank, Titan, the United Nations and the U.S. Office of Education.

Sara Rynes is the Tippie–Rollins Chair in Excellence at the University of Iowa's Tippie College of Business. Her research interests are the academic–practice gap, evidence-based management, management education, compensation, and social movements. She is a Fellow of the Academy of Management, the American Psychological Association, the Management Education Research Institute, and the Society for Industrial and Organizational Psychology. She received the Academy of Management's Herbert Heneman Career Achievement Award for Research in Human Resource Management in 2006, the Dutch HRM Network Research Award in 2011, and the 2011 Society of Human Resource Management's Michael Losey Human Resource Management Research Award. In 2013 she received the University of Iowa's Regents Award for Faculty Excellence and was the University of Iowa's Presidential Lecturer. She and her co-authors won the 2003 Ulrich & Lake Award for Excellence in Human Resource Management Scholarship and the 2004 Moskowitz Prize for the best quantitative research in the field of social investment. She was the editor-in-chief of the *Academy of Management Journal* in 2005–7 and has served on the editorial boards of *Academy of Management Review*, *Personnel Psychology*, *Journal of Applied Psychology*, *Academy of Management Learning & Education*, *Academy of Management Discoveries*, and *Human Resource Management*. She has consulted for Corning, CIGNA, Citibank, Pearson, 3M, IBM, AT&T, Merrill Lynch, General Foods, World at Work, and the American Arbitration Association. Prior to joining the University of Iowa, she taught at the University of Minnesota and Cornell University. She received her PhD in industrial relations from the University of Wisconsin-Madison.

Abraham B. (Rami) Shani is Associate Dean for Faculty and Research and Full Professor of Management at the Orfalea College of Business, California Polytechnic State University, San Luis Obispo. He held Visiting Professor appointments at The Stockholm School of Economics, Tel Aviv University and Politecnico Di Milano. His research interests include organizational change and development, creativity, collaborative research methodologies, learning in and by organizations, sustainability, and sustainable effectiveness.

He is the author, co-author, or co-editor of many books and articles including *The Collaborative Management Research Handbook, Collaborative Research in Organizations*, annual research series *Research in Organization Change and Development*, and *Organizing for Sustainable Effectiveness* with Emerald. His articles have appeared in journals such as *Academy of Management Journal, Journal of Applied Behavioral Science, Human Relations, Organizational Dynamics, Sloan Management Review*, and *California Management Review*.

Wendy K. Smith is Associate Professor of Management in the Lerner College of Business and Economics at the University of Delaware, and Research Fellow of the Cambridge Centre for Social Innovation. Her research explores how leaders and their organizations manage strategic paradoxes. She has published articles on strategic paradoxes in journals such as the *Academy of Management Review, Organization Science*, and *Harvard Business Review*.

Ramkrishnan (Ram) V. Tenkasi is Professor with the PhD program in Organization Development and Change at Benedictine University. He started his academic career as an assistant professor with the Marshall School of Business, University of Southern California. His research broadly covers the topics of organizational change, learning, and knowledge, and approaches the study of these issues from both interpretive and positivist frameworks typically combining these traditions to draw on the unique strengths of both. An enduring and strong interest is the integration of theory and research knowledge to inform practice and the role of the scholar–practitioner in enabling these integration dynamics. He has received multiple grants from federal agencies such as the National Science Foundation and corporations and serves on editorial boards such as the *Journal of Organizational Change Management* and is Associate Editor of the *Journal of Applied Behavioral Sciences*. He was awarded the Fulbright Senior Research Scholar and was past chairperson of the Organization Development and Change Division of the Academy of Management.

Andrew H. Van de Ven is Professor Emeritus of Strategic Management, Entrepreneurship, Work, and Organizations in the Carlson School of Management at the University of Minnesota. He received his PhD from the University of Wisconsin-Madison in 1972 and taught at Kent State University (1972–5) and the Wharton School of the University of Pennsylvania (1975–81). Van de Ven directed the Minnesota Innovation Research Program, which tracked a wide variety of innovations from concept to implementation during the 1980s and 1990s. In addition to organizational innovation and change, Andrew's research has dealt with the Nominal Group Technique, program planning and problem solving, organization assessment, inter-organizational relationships, and engaged scholarship. He teaches courses on the management of innovation and change, organizational behavior, and engaged scholarship. Andrew has published over 100 research papers and is a co-author of 13 books, including *The Innovation Journey* (1999, 2008), *Organization Change and Innovation Processes: Theory and Methods for Research* (2000), *Handbook of Organizational Change and Innovation* (2004), *Engaged Scholarship* (2007, which won the 2008 Terry Book Award from the Academy of Management), and *Managing Knowledge Integration Across Boundaries* (2017). He was the president of the Academy of Management in 2000–2001, a founding senior editor of *Organization Science*, and now serves as the founding editor of Academy of Management Discoveries.

Sandra Waddock is Galligan Chair of Strategy, Carroll School Scholar of Corporate Responsibility, and Professor of Management at Boston College's Carroll School of Management. Author of some 140 papers and 11 books, she received the 2016 Lifetime Achievement Award from Humboldt University in Berlin for contributions in corporation sustainability and responsibility, the 2015 award for Leadership in Humanistic Management, and the 2014 Lifetime Achievement Award in Collaboration Research (CSSI Symposium and Partnership Resource Center, Erasmus U.), among others. Current research interests are largely systems change, the role of memes in change processes, developing a new narrative for business in society, stewardship of the future, corporate sustainability responsibility, the problem of growth, wisdom, management education, and intellectual shamans. Her latest book is *Intellectual Shamans* (Cambridge University Press), and she blogs at www.intellectual-shaman.com. Other recent books include: *Building the Responsible Enterprise*, with Andreas Rasche (2012), *SEE Change: Making the Transition to a Sustainable Enterprise Economy*, with Malcolm McIntosh (2011), and *The Difference Makers* (2008, Social Issues in Management Division Best Book Award, 2011).

Christine van Winkelen has worked with Henley Business School since 1999. She has been part of the management team of the Henley Forum since its formation in 2000 (then known as the Henley Knowledge Management Forum) and was the director for five years. She has project managed and been the research lead for many Forum research projects. This research broadly relates to managing knowledge and organizational learning to improve performance and has been undertaken with a wide range of public and private sector organizations. She regularly speaks at conferences and has published extensively in academic and practitioner journals and books.

1 Reviewing the state of academic practitioner relationships

Jean M. Bartunek and Jane McKenzie

Overview introduction

Welcome to this book—a combined presentation by all the authors and editors—that showcases the contemporary vitality of academic–practitioner relationships and partnerships and suggests future steps.

We begin our introduction with a value proposition. As social scientists who focus on management and organizations our role is to deliver research that makes a positive difference to business, to an array of organizations and to the wider society. But this cannot be done except in partnership with those (typically referred to by academics as practitioners) who carry out the kinds of work that organizational research addresses. To put it another way, organizational and management research should deliver the broadest value to society when theory and research are useful for improving organizational practice *and* the reality of practice truly informs theorizing.

This is not a new claim: Kurt Lewin (1951: 169) made a similar argument for psychology more than six decades ago:

> Many psychologists working today in an applied field are keenly aware of the need for close cooperation between theoretical and applied psychology. This can be accomplished in psychology, as it has been accomplished in physics, if the theorist does not look toward applied problems with high-brow aversion or with a fear of social problems, and if the applied psychologist realizes that there is nothing so practical as a good theory.

But what such an accomplishment means in management practice and academia has not been adequately recognized in either theory or practice. Rather, scholarly practice for producing rigorous and relevant theory in working relationships with practitioners has been a contested topic within the halls of academe (e.g., Banks, Pollack, Bochantin, Kirkman, Whelpley & O'Boyle, 2016; Bartunek & Rynes, 2014; Bennis & O'Toole, 2005; Daft & Lewin, 2008; Empson, 2013; Kieser & Leiner, 2009; Rynes, Bartunek & Daft, 2001). Some academics (e.g., Daft & Lewin, 2008) have argued strongly against it; others (e.g., Bennis & O'Toole, 2005) have argued strongly for it. As a signal of its importance, it has recently been recognized as one of the grand challenges of our current age (Banks et al., 2016).

The importance of the metaphor of interfaces for academic–practitioner relationships

In discussions of academic–practitioner relationships terms such as "gap" and "divide" are the metaphors most used to describe them. Further, some suggest that the gap is widening (Banks et al., 2016). Many who label themselves scholar–practitioners feel caught in the middle of the gap, without an adequate sense of community on either side (Empson, 2013; Kram, Wasserman & Yip, 2012). For many, consideration of the possibility of academic–practitioner relationships has evoked considerable ambiguity and anxiety. It has even generated rival tribes of academics (Gulati, 2007).

Outside of academe, executives, middle managers, consultants, change agents, and other practitioners are less interested in the debate, but much more interested in timely, reliable, and accessible work that helps them deliver better outcomes. Some practitioners are baffled by the gap, do not label themselves as practitioners, and see such discussions as irrelevant. For them, the way research is conducted, published, and conveyed—how new important knowledge is developed—shapes their perspective on its value and consequent utility and uptake.

However, during the past decade, helped considerably by Van de Ven's (2007) conception of "engaged scholarship" and by multiple initiatives undertaken by a variety of academics and practitioners in many countries, there has also come to be much more optimism about the possibilities and potentials in academic–practitioner relationships, a greater awareness of the possibilities and potentials of them, and how important and productive these may be for both constituencies and their larger societies. Shani, Mohrman, Pasmore, Stymne and Adler's (2008) *Handbook of Collaborative Research* provided a comprehensive guide to the tools and techniques in use in collaborative research. Mohrman and Lawler (2011) edited a book on *Useful Research: Advancing Theory and Practice* which discussed a number of dimensions of research that are useful for practice. It includes discussions of books, organization development practice, collaborative research and some illustrative collaborations. And, of course, there are several older books that have helped set directions for collaboration.

This work makes evident that the often used metaphor of a gap, despite its continuing ubiquity (e.g., Banks et al., 2016), is, in some ways at least, outmoded. Given the advances that have been taking place, the image it presents is no longer adequate. The term "interface" is probably much more appropriate (Rau, Möslein & Neyer, 2016); it refers not only to a gap or a wall separating groups, but an interconnection between them (Kulik, 2016). According to the Oxford English Dictionary, for example, while the term *interface* originally referred to "A surface lying between two portions of matter or space, and forming their common boundary," it has also come to refer to "a means or place of interaction between two systems, organizations, etc.; a meeting-point or common ground between two parties, systems, or disciplines; also, interaction, liaison, dialogue." The term conveys great energy for relationships between parties such as academics and practitioners. In fact, a good deal of work has gone into creating a range of interactions, meeting points, and common ground between academics and practitioners (e.g., Bartunek, 2007). We suggest here that the term *interface* is a much better metaphor than gap for links between academics and practitioners.

What this book contributes

However, there have been very few occasions for presenting a full portrait of the progress being made in *thinking* about academic–practitioner partnerships, in *developing the skills* to carry them out successfully, and in showcasing a wide range of *successful examples* of such partnerships. Presenting these is the purpose of this book. In it we offer a concise and up-to-date review of scholarly engagement with the world of management, one which builds on engaged scholarship, and connects it to the capabilities and practical experience of creating productive collaborative relationships.

The chapters in this book examine how understandings of collaborative academic–practitioner relationships have evolved in recent years, elaborate conceptual challenges that create tensions in academic–practitioner relationships, discuss the sorts of capability academics need to collaborate effectively with practitioners given the conflicting expectations and constraints inherent in their different worlds, and illustrate good practice through case studies occurring at acknowledged centers of excellence.

For whom might this book be helpful?

This book is an important contribution to the mounting interest in such collaborations. It responds to the growing number of universities that have recognized that they need scholars with the capabilities necessary to operate effectively in two worlds: successfully building a solid academic track record in publication and a reputation for high-quality theoretically grounded empirical research, along with sustainable collaborative relationships with organizational practitioners to enhance the relevance and impact of their research (for which others have argued, cf. Banks et al., 2016). It also speaks to governments, work organizations, community agencies, and others that may be interested in creating collaborations with academics who might be able to help them achieve their purposes more effectively, that may, in other words, contribute to the impact of academic work (MacIntosh, Beech, Bartunek, Mason, Cooke & Denyer, 2017). The initiative for collaboration can come from managers and other practitioners, not just academics.

This book is also a provocation and guide for individual scholars learning to navigate the complexity involved in academic–practitioner interfaces, as well as a reference book for interested practitioners who want to learn more about how working more closely with academics can enhance their effectiveness. Many students and faculty working in DBA or other types of practitioner doctoral programs may find it particularly helpful.

At the same time, this book does not present a finished product. At the beginning of this millennium there was a good deal of excitement about Mode 2 approaches to research (e.g., Gibbons et al., 1994; Starkey & Madan, 2001; Tranfield & Starkey, 1998) and some treated Mode 2 as a panacea for academic–practitioner relationships. However, that did not turn out to be the case (Bartunek, 2011). While Mode 2 is still in some use (Shani et al., Chapter 2 in this volume), especially in practitioner-based doctoral programs, many approaches to academic–practitioner relationships do not refer to it at all, and it has not been anywhere as influential as expected. Instead, there is considerable ingenuity and creativity in the development of academic–practitioner partnerships, in the types of issue they address, in the ways academics and practitioners collaborate, and in the development of skill in the ability to collaborate. We see this book as a step on the path. We are introducing some of what is salient now, in the hopes that future developments will move far beyond what is present today. We invite readers to use this book to stimulate your own creativity.

Crucial characteristics and challenges of successful academic–practitioner partnerships and relationships

As this book makes evident, and as we have indicated above, there is a wide range of forms that academic–practitioner partnerships might take. However, there are some characteristics many have in common, characteristics that often are not recognized or appreciated.

In particular, successful academic–practitioner relationships necessarily involve contradictory yet inter-related priorities that exist simultaneously and persist throughout the life of a partnership. These likely include differing (and possibly contradictory) logics, temporal perspectives, communication practices, emphases on rigor and relevance and interests and incentives (Bartunek & Rynes, 2014; McKenzie, Van Winkelen & Bartunek, 2014). Consequently the field of activity is inherently filled with tension and paradox (Smith & Lewis, 2011). Holding these in tension, appreciating that both sides of these dilemmas are simultaneously crucial, rather than one better than the other, is necessary for the partnerships to succeed, in large part because they signal the presence of underlying paradoxes. This is inadequately appreciated by many, but is crucial.

Some paradoxical features of academic–practitioner relationships have been suggested already (Bartunek & Rynes, 2014), and some others will be highlighted by the editors, through editorial commentary on the chapters in the book. Yet others are included in some of the individual chapters. The crucial issue here is that, without appreciating tensions and paradox, it is impossible to appreciate the dynamics of successful academic–practitioner partnerships.

Despite the tensions surrounding such relationships, the potential loss if academics and practitioners cannot make them work well is substantial. For example, in an interconnected, rapidly changing and increasingly unpredictable business environment, separating theory creation from the constantly evolving context for use has several limitations. It can result in incomplete framing of the profound nature of important problems (Mitroff & Featheringham, 1974), neglect of relevant but either relatively weak or previously unrecognized forces shaping systems, difficult translation problems in applying the thinking in the real world setting (Carlile, 2004; Van de Ven, 2007) and delayed recognition of research value and impact.

The recognition of crucial paradoxical features highlights ways that thinking about academic–practitioner partnerships has been evolving. It also highlights how, as the practice of relating is explored at a more granular level, new challenges have emerged.

For example, to overcome acknowledged problems of knowledge transfer, Van de Ven (2007) reframed the research process as a knowledge production problem. His heuristic model for co-creating knowledge demands iterative reconsideration of the fit between problem formulation, theory building, research design and problem solving to satisfy the different criteria of each constituency in the academic–practitioner relationships. Yet, because academics largely develop their praxis in relation to other academics and the internal priorities of academe (Bartunek & Rynes, 2014), while executives and managers develop their praxis through working together on different priorities, the meaningful experiences for each community create distinct identities (Ibarra & Barbulescu, 2010).

Being and doing, intention and action, are mutually informative in the sense that an individual's identity is formed by the dynamics of these experiences in their context (Golsorkhi, Rouleau, Seidl & Vaara, 2010). This can undermine the sustainability of the relationship if each constituency follows their natural inclination to gravitate to their familiar "tribe," because common knowledge foundations make communication and building new and relevant insights less taxing (Knorr Cetina, 1999). Indeed research projects that begin using more collaborative Mode 2 (Gibbons et al., 1994) approaches have sometimes reverted over time to Mode 1 approaches, because of the relationship challenges (Swan, Bresnen, Robertson, Newell & Dopson, 2010). Learning from one another and engaging in knowledge co-production (Van de Ven, 2007; Van de Ven & Johnson, 2006) requires building bridges between deeply held epistemological and ontological positions.

Others have expanded upon what that might mean in practice, including but also going beyond research, and encompassing joint action on issues of concern (Bansal, Bertels, Ewart, MacConnachie & O'Brien, 2012; Banks et al., 2016; Bartunek, 2007). Further, the influence of contradictory expectations from business schools about what academics should contribute to practice (Bennis & O'Toole, 2005; Flickinger, Tuschke, Gruber-Muecke & Fielder, 2014) has been increasingly acknowledged.

Certainly there are similarities as well as differences between the worlds of academia and practice. Business and management practitioners immersed in changing patterns of employment, more extensive use of inter-organizational partnerships and collaborative working combined with the use of social technologies are challenged to pay attention to more heterogeneous perspectives in making sense of the complexity, despite the fact that increasing the intricacy of relationships (in their case with customers, employees, and other influencers), makes it harder to produce meaningful agreement on direction and action. Scholars now face similar challenges when seeking to produce research that satisfies multiple stakeholders. Each may have something to learn from the other. Satisfying diverse stakeholder priorities, perspectives, and requirements, starts with recognizing and acknowledging the practical differences between each world, then negotiating courses of action that are mutually beneficial without compromising any key requirements. Van de Ven calls this art "arbitrage."

The construction of this book

In this edited book we draw on and arbitrage the experience of both well-respected academics who have successfully navigated the rich variety of tensions and paradoxes that occur when two constituencies with different priorities, values, and practices work together to produce research that has rigor and relevance in equal measure, and managers and leaders from commercial, public, and non-profit sectors who have worked in relationships of knowledge co-creation. We are fortunate in having been able to attract a large number of highly regarded authors discussing work that is likely to be new to many readers and important for those already familiar with the work. Through the book's three major sections our aim is to unpack what is involved in academic–practitioner relationships that are productive and sustainable and produce research and practice outcomes that meet the needs of all parties in academic–practitioner collaboration.

We will introduce each of the sections of this book in more detail at the beginning of the section. Here, however, we give an overview of the sections.

Part I of this book addresses the topic of academic–practitioner relationships conceptually. The various chapters in the section explore philosophical foundations for academic–practitioner relationships from Aristotle (Shani et al., Nielsen), to contemporary philosophical theorizing (Coghlan). Other chapters lay foundations in Shamanic thought (Waddock) and induce theory from contemporary research on such relationships (Bartunek and Rynes). These foundations help in understanding more broadly what is going on in developing skills in academic–practitioner collaboration and in conducting successful collaborative efforts.

In Part II we outline some of the necessary capabilities for translating theory into practical value, as well as how these capabilities may be developed. Van de Ven describes the flipped classroom he has developed to teach engaged scholarship. Jarzabkowski et al. discuss how they have learned to work with paradox in multiple types of academic–practitioner relationships. MacIntosh and Maclean present a narrative of history of how they developed the personal abilities to collaborate with practice. Collins and McBain present how they develop skills in such collaboration at Henley, and Antonacopolou describes these processes in terms of the development of praxis, a contribution that links with the scholarly descriptions in the first section.

In Part III, we present a range of examples of the living practice of academics working *with* practitioners, or, in one important case, working as a practitioner, Laura Empson's description of her combination practitioner/academic experience, and the challenges she has faced. The examples of academics working with practitioners include the Henley Management Forum (Van Winkelen and McKenzie), the development of concepts based on academic–practitioner interactions (Carton and Dameron), the International Network for Business Sustainability (Hamann and Faccer), an academic–practitioner collaboration to produce a new tool to measure values (Landman et al.), the Center for Effective Organizations at the University of Southern California (Mohrman) and the kinds of academic–practitioner collaboration that regularly take place at Google (Kurkoski). These illustrations highlight the range of activities in which academics and practitioners might engage together as well as the global scale of such collaborations.

In summary, in this book our authors uniquely explore both conceptually and practically what it takes to understand, develop and sustain engaging and fruitful knowledge creating interfaces that are mutually beneficial, further the advance of theory, and provide expositions of the praxis of those who have been successful in sustaining these productive relationships. Such work should help us accomplish the value proposition with which we began our introduction.

At the same time, as we noted, we hope very much that this book is a marking point along a broad journey that spurs the ongoing development, understanding, and appreciation of such developments. We believe that they are vital to progress in a number of important areas that will benefit business, a wide array of organizations, and our broader society.

We are grateful to a number of people who have provided crucial support in the development of this book. First, we thank all of our authors, who have participated fully with us in realizing this book. It has been a joy to work with you. We thank Jacqueline Curthoys, our commissioning editor at Routledge, who has been a constant help throughout the process. We thank Michael Smith and Victoria Fisher at Boston College, both of whom have provided needed administrative support.

This book grew out of Jane's leadership of the Henley Forum for Organisational Learning and Knowledge Strategies. We got to know each other when Jane invited Jean to speak at one of the sessions of the Forum. We are very grateful to Christine van Winkelen, who brought the possibility of this book to our attention and laid the solid foundations for the sustainability of the Henley Forum for many years. We thank Marina Hart and all the staff at the Forum for all the work they have done enabling its ongoing work.

We also thank the Carroll School of Management at Boston College and its Dean Andy Boynton, who is a strong believer in the type of work described in this book. We are also grateful for the support Jean has received from the Robert A. and Evelyn J. Ferris chair that enabled a good deal of her travel. Finally, we thank her fellow members of the Religious of the Sacred Heart, who have enabled her to be at home in both the US and the UK during the time of our work on this book.

References

Banks, G., Pollack, J., Bochantin, J., Kirkman, B., Whelpley, C. & O'Boyle, E. (2016). Management's science-practice gap: a grand challenge for all stakeholders. *Academy of Management Journal*, 59(6), 2205–31.

Bansal, P., Bertels, S., Ewart, T., MacConnachie, P. & O'Brien, J. (2012). Bridging the research–practice gap. *Academy of Management Perspectives*, 26(1), 73–92.

Bartunek, J. M. (2007). Academic–practitioner collaboration need not require joint or relevant research: Toward a relational scholarship of integration. *Academy of Management Journal*, 50(6), 1323–3.

Bartunek, J. M. (2011). What has happened to Mode 2? *British Journal of Management*, 22(3), 555–8.

Bartunek, J. M. & Rynes, S. L. (2014). Academics and practitioners are alike and unlike: The paradoxes of academic–practitioner relationships. *Journal of Management*, 40(5), 1181–201.

Bennis, W. G. & O'Toole, J. (2005). How business schools lost their way. *Harvard Business Review*, 83(5), 96–104.

Carlile, P. R. (2004). Transferring, translating and transforming: An integrative framework for managing knowledge across boundaries. *Organization Science*, 15(5), 555–68.

Daft, R. L. & Lewin, A. Y. (2008). Rigor and relevance in organization studies: Idea migration and academic journal evolution. *Organization Science*, 19(1), 177–83.

Empson, L. (2013). My affair with the "other": Identity journeys across the research–practice divide. *Journal of Management Inquiry*, 22(2), 229–48.

Flickinger, M., Tuschke, A., Gruber-Muecke, T. & Fielder, M. (2014). In search of rigor, relevance and legitimacy: What drives the impact of publications. *Journal of Business Economics*, 84(1), 99–128.

Gibbons, M., Limoges, C., Nowotny, H., Schwartzman, S., Scott, P. & Trow, M. (1994). *The New Production of Knowledge: The Dynamics of Science and Research in Contemporary Societies*. London: Sage Publications.

Golsorkhi, D., Rouleau, L., Seidl, D. & Vaara, E. (2010). *Cambridge Handbook of Strategy as Practice*. Cambridge: Cambridge University Press.

Gulati, R. (2007). Tent poles, tribalism, and boundary spanning: The rigor–relevance debate in management research. *Academy of Management Journal*, 50(4), 775–82.

Ibarra, H. & Barbulescu, R. (2010). Identity as narrative: Prevalence, effectiveness, and consequences of narrative identity work in macro work role transitions. *Academy of Management Review*, 35(1), 135–54.

Kieser, A. & Leiner, L. (2009). Why the rigour–relevance gap in management research is unbridgeable. *Journal of Management Studies*, 46(3): 516–33.

Knorr Cetina, K. (1999). *Epistemic Cultures: How Sciences Made Knowledge*. Cambridge, MA: Harvard University Press.

Kram, K. E., Wasserman, I. C. & Yip, J. (2012). Metaphors of identity and professional practice: Learning from the scholar–practitioner. *Journal of Applied Behavioral Science*, 48(3), 304–41.

Kulik, C. (2016). 77th Annual meeting of the Academy of Management theme: At the Interface. Retrieved April 7, 2017 from http://aom.org/annualmeeting/theme/.

Lewin, K. (1951). *Field Theory in Social Sciences*. New York: Harper & Row.

MacIntosh, R., Beech, N., Bartunek, J. M., Mason, K., Cooke, B. & Denyer, D. (2017). Impact and management research: exploring relationships between temporality, dialogue, reflexivity and praxis. *British Journal of Management*, 28(1), 3–13.

McKenzie, J., Van Winkelen, C. & Bartunek, J. M. (2014). Elaborating from practice on the theoretical model of engaged scholarship. Paper presented at the Academy of Management Conference, Philadelphia, PA, August.

Mitroff, I. I. & Featheringham, T. R. (1974). On systemic problem solving and the error of the third kind. *Behavioral Science*, 19(6), 383–93.

Mohrman, S. A. & Lawler, E. E. (Eds.). (2011). *Useful Research: Advancing Theory and Practice*. San Francisco, CA: Berrett-Koehler.

Rau, C., Möslein, K. M. & Neyer, A. K. (2016). Playing possum, hide-and-seek, and other behavioral patterns: Knowledge boundaries at newly emerging interfaces. *R&D Management*, 46(2), 341–53.

Rynes, S. L., Bartunek, J. M. & Daft, R. L. (2001). Across the great divide: Knowledge creation and transfer between practitioners and academics. *Academy of Management Journal*, 44(2), 340–55.

Shani, A. B. R., Mohrman, S. A., Pasmore, W. A., Stymne, B. & Adler, N. (Eds.) (2008). *Handbook of Collaborative Management Research*. Thousand Oaks, CA: Sage Publications.

Smith, W. K. & Lewis, M. W. (2011). Towards a theory of paradox: A dynamic equilibrium model of organizing. *Academy of Management Review*, 36(2) 381–403.

Starkey, K. & Madan, P. (2001). Bridging the relevance gap: aligning stakeholders in the future of management research. *British Journal of Management*, 12(Special Issue), S3–S26.

Swan, J., Bresnen, M., Robertson, M., Newell, S. & Dopson, S. (2010). When policy meets practice: Colliding logics and the challenges of "Mode 2" initiatives in the translation of academic knowledge. *Organization Studies*, 31, 1311–40.

Tranfield, D. & Starkey, K. (1998). The nature, social organization and promotion of management research: towards policy. *British Journal of Management*, 9(4), 341–53.

Van de Ven, A. H. (2007). *Engaged Scholarship: A Guide for Organizational and Social Research*. Oxford: Oxford University Press.

Van de Ven, A. H. & Johnson, P. E. (2006). Knowledge for theory and practice. *Academy of Management Review*, 31(4), 802–21.

Part I

Conceptual challenges

Introduction to Part I

In this first part the authors lay a conceptual foundation for academic–practitioner partnerships. They present some of the philosophical history pertinent to these relationships, some current philosophical thinking about them, and illustrations of academic–practitioner links in practice, including introducing some academics who are particularly adept at creating such links. The section concludes with theorizing that derives from the small amount of empirical work that already exists in this area.

Taken together, the chapters make evident that there is much more to academic–practitioner collaboration than simple interaction or particular techniques or skills. Such collaboration may be developmental; it has the potential for fostering in participants a profound understanding of themselves and of what joint work entails. Such collaboration also benefits from deep commitment and the willingness to develop relational skills. Perhaps part of the reason for some of the difficulties sometimes written about in academic–practitioner collaboration arise from the unwillingness and/or lack of capacity of partners in such collaboration to engage it and themselves very fully and to learn from their interactions.

Shani et al. present in Chapter 2 an intellectual history of knowledge and/vs. practice. While some management school academics might see this topic as somewhat relatively new, in fact it has an ancient heritage (Stokes, 2011). Shani et al. start with Aristotle's original and later thinking. Originally Aristotle separated theory and practice, but later on he concluded that they had to be joined, in *phronesis*, or practical wisdom (Bartunek & Trullen, 2007). But it was Aristotle's first way of thinking that had primary impacts on the development of Western thinking, especially through universities.

Several philosophers such as Hume, Kant, Comte, and, especially, Karl Popper extended Aristotle's early thinking. Popper (1972) in particular claimed that it is not possible to learn solely from experience, which is bound to be limited. It is only by testing experience against theory that one can learn. It was the test of theory that, augmented by Vanevar Bush's work establishing the US National Science Foundation, came to dominate the kinds of theorizing that found its way into US business schools starting in the mid-twentieth century (Stokes, 2011).

However, Shani et al. see movements now that move more towards possibilities of *phronesis*, Aristotle's second way of thinking. They focus in particular on Mode 2 research and, more broadly, collaborative research involving both academics and practitioners, as modes consistent with Aristotle's later ways of thinking.

Chapter 3, by Coghlan, introduces a contemporary philosophical focus that sheds light on collaboration. Just as Popper's work was the foundation for many contemporary approaches to theory–practice separation, Coghlan introduces the much more recent work of twentieth-century philosopher Bernard Lonergan as a model for academic–practitioner links.

Coghlan begins with a vignette of a successful academic–practitioner collaboration. He uses this example as a foundation for introducing the philosophical work of Lonergan and, related to this, the work of Reg Revans, a professor and consultant who developed action learning, a process that involves considerable self-reflection that is consistent with Lonergan's philosophy.

Lonergan's philosophy emphasizes characteristics he considers true of all human beings, operations of inquiry and knowing, insight, and reflection. For Lonergan, knowing is a three-step process involving experience, understanding, and judgment. In other words, quite contrary to positivist philosophies, experience is considered a crucial starting point. Further, experience is both external and internal, including knowledge from both the senses and internal processes. Insight based on such experience requires deep reflection, and authentic knowledge requires attention, intelligence, reasonableness, and responsibility. These characteristics likely make a substantial difference in the kinds of collaborative research Shani et al. discuss, but are typically not recognized in discussions of these relationships.

For Coghlan, action learning is an elegant exemplar of Lonergan's philosophy on a group level. In this approach learning begins with a big question, and, importantly, includes a "metalogue," a structured conversation in a group in which participants—academics and practitioners alike—reflect on their questions and processes together, in ways that lead them to greater insight. Thus, this chapter adds to earlier insights appreciation of the importance of the individual experience of both academics and practitioners, as well as experiences that foster deeper insight on the part of participants about their action.

Nielsen (Chapter 4) addresses the question of what characteristics individuals must have to be able to participate well in the type of insightful processes Coghlan discusses. He emphasizes the importance of reflexivity for individuals, as well as the need for individual development into such reflexivity. Such development occurs, for Nielsen, through three moments in a dialectical, developmental process. These are inductive attention to experience-based data, theory-based interpretation, reflection, and ethical action, and, finally, developmental ethical practice, learning, and theory-building. He notes that too many actions—including too much academic–practitioner collaboration—reflect simply technique. But what is crucial is developing the capability to understand underlying assumptions of one's actions, and be able to change them when appropriate.

Nielsen introduces several academics who have been able to do this, and he emphasizes the example of Adam Curle, an academic and peace activist. Curle was originally a social psychologist who also did a considerable amount of work in mediation and peacemaking. As he did more and more work with practitioners, he came to realize that, while some social science theory helped his work, reflection-in-practice, something emphasized by Schön (1983) (and Lonergan) was also crucial. As Curle developed his work over time, he came to recognize it as transformational of both the situation and of himself. He came to see links between science and ethics in a much larger light. Further, he came to realize the importance of both friendship and love in work with practitioners, a topic that is not addressed at all in academic–practitioner literature.

Waddock's chapter (Chapter 5) also emphasizes important personal characteristics of those capable of linking academics and practitioners, and the profound impacts they may have. She writes about intellectual shamans (Waddock, 2015), academics who, following in the paths of shamans of old, develop the ability to ask big questions, think holistically, and work in ways that may heal the world.

She describes three practices in which intellectual shamans engage that in their hands can have transformative impacts on academic–practitioner relationships. The first is creating networks that involve getting a wide range of stakeholders involved and that involve creating connections with deep levels of consciousness. The second is engaged scholarship across such borders, in which academics and practitioner engage together in joint scholarly inquiry. The third is engaging academics and practitioners in ongoing learning that includes experiences of paradox and ambiguity as crucial elements of their connecting.

The final chapter in this section, Chapter 6, by Bartunek and Rynes, is based on the scholarly research of academics engaged in writing about academic–practitioner relationships. Bartunek and Rynes analyze the small body of empirical studies that explore such relationships to understand the kinds of common themes discussed in the studies. They find in their exploration a number of contradictory findings, such as:

- Academics and practitioners can both benefit from joint contact.
- Human Resources practitioners and Human Resources academics have very different interests.
- Practitioner journals have much more impact on academia than academic journals have on practitioners.
- The cultures of academia and practice differ considerably.
- Academics and practitioners judge articles the same ways as each other and in diametrically opposed ways.

In other words, taken together, the empirical literature on academic–practitioner relationships suggests considerable underlying contradiction and paradox (Bartunek & Rynes, 2014), and this contradiction and paradox make evident how much identity dynamics that center around sameness and difference from each other are at the heart of academic–practitioner relationships. Without recognizing this fundamental paradox, it will be difficult to fully appreciate academic–practitioner relationships and the processes underlying their joint work. This difficulty is applicable not only to academics studying such relationships, but also to academics and practitioners involved in enacting them.

Despite some expectations that academic–practitioner relationships should be fairly straightforward and successful (Augier & March, 2007; Bennis & O'Toole, 2005), this has not always happened. Together the chapters in this section suggest several underlying reasons. Personal characteristics and capabilities matter and so does the capability of engaging individually and together in profoundly developmental learning processes. Expectations of what should happen when academics and practitioners engage in depth should include ambiguity, contradiction, and paradox.

But the possibilities of what might happen when academics and practitioners are willing and able to participate with each other in common experiences and journeys and have adequate guidance from wise people who have traveled this journey are quite profound. Thus, Part I launches a book that describes both how academics and practitioners learn about and carry out interactions that may be transformative for both.

References

Augier, M. & March, J. G. (2007). The pursuit of relevance in management education. *California Management Review*, 49(3), 129–46.

Bartunek, J. M. & Rynes, S. L. (2014). Academics and practitioners are alike and unlike: The paradoxes of academic–practitioner relationships. *Journal of Management*, 40(5), 1181–201.

Bartunek, J. M. & Trullen, J. (2007). The virtue of prudence. In Kessler, E. & Bailey, J.R. (Eds.) *Handbook of Organizational and Managerial Wisdom* (pp. 91–108). Thousand Oaks, CA: Sage Publications.

Bennis, W. G. & O'Toole, J. (2005). How business schools lost their way. *Harvard Business Review*, 83(5), 96–104.

Popper, K. R. (1972). *The Logic of Scientific Discovery*. London: Hutchinson.

Schön, D. A. (1983). *The Reflective Practitioner: How Professionals Think in Action*. New York: Basic Books.

Stokes, D. E. (2011). *Pasteur's Quadrant: Basic Science and Technological Innovation*. Washington, DC: Brookings Institution Press.

Waddock, S. (2015). *Intellectual Shamans*. New York: Cambridge University Press.

2 Knowledge and practice

A historical perspective on collaborative management research

Abraham B. (Rami) Shani,
Ramkrishnan (Ram) V. Tenkasi,
and Benjamin N. Alexander

Management scholars have long addressed tensions between basic knowledge production and practice. This separation, which emerged in business schools during the first half of the twentieth century, divides management scholars and practitioners, rigor and relevance, knowledge and action. More recently, some management scholars have re-examined this division, recognizing the potential of research paradigms that combine basic research with practice to solve problems of organizational, societal and scientific concern (Lawler, Mohrman, Mohrman, Ledford & Cummings, 1985; Astley & Zammuto, 1993; Gibbons, Limoges, Nowotny, Schwartzman, Scott & Trow, 1994; Nowotny, Scott & Gibbons, 2001). Collaborative management research (CMR), which draws on the spirit of early management scholarship, provides a paradigm for bridging the production of basic knowledge with practice (Shani, Mohrman, Pasmore, Stymne & Adler, 2008).

Through clarifying the philosophical and historical foundations of the separation between knowledge and practice and more recent calls for integration, we can better mark the way forward towards more balanced management scholarship that addresses both basic knowledge and practice. In this chapter, we trace the origins of different philosophies of science in Aristotle's writings and briefly follow the application and development of those ideas in European learning centers. We then turn our attention to the instantiation of different modes of knowledge production in university-based business schools and management scholarship. We conclude by characterizing how, through CMR and similar paradigms, the re-emergence of Aristotle's second, less-celebrated legacy offers a significant opportunity for management scholarship.

Aristotle's legacies and philosophies of science

Interestingly, both the legacy of separating theory and practice and subsequent calls for their integration emanate from Aristotle's work more than 2,300 years ago. Inspired by his mentors Plato and Socrates, Aristotle initially distinguished the spheres of scientific knowledge, and of craft and experience as two separate domains in Book VI of the *Nicomachean Ethics* (Parry, 2003). His reasoning was that scientific knowledge, *episteme theoretike*, concerns the underlying rules and principles governing why and how something happens, whereas craft, *techne*, deals with everyday practice. Deriving *episteme theoretike* required scholars, who, through their careful and systematic inquiry, clarify universal truths and "causal laws that are universally applicable to events and situations" (Tenkasi & Hay, 2008: 51).

However, Aristotle would later re-examine this division in his reflections on the nature of knowledge in the classic work *Metaphysics*. Here, Aristotle shifts his attention from the pursuit of generalizable knowledge as the ultimate end to consider practical action or "actionable knowledge," *phronesis*, which can both solve practical problems and, in turn, inform generalizable knowledge. He argues that the bedrock of true understanding emanates from, and appropriate action is guided through, the creative integration of experience and craft, and theory. As Nielsen discusses in Chapter 4 of this volume, Aristotle argued that true knowledge of events and situations, especially as it concerns practical action, involves knowledge of both the experience and the craft, *empeiria* and *techne*, derived from those experiences, as well as universal principles, or *episteme theoretike* (Dunne, 1993), that may apply to those settings. Aristotle further contrasts individuals with *empeiria, techne,* and *episteme* with the scholar, the *lógios*, who has only *episteme* and relies on the rational accounting of why things happen without a basis in experience or craft. According to Aristotle, *lógios* are ineffective in producing *phronesis* (Parry, 2003). Aristotle explains:

> experience, like action or production, deals with things severally as concrete individuals, whereas art deals with them generally.... If then someone lacking experience, but knowing the general principles of the art [of medicine], sizes up a situation as a whole, he will often, because he is ignorant of the individuals within that whole, miss the mark and fail to cure; for it is the individuals who must be cured.
>
> (Aristotle, 1961: 981)

Though *phronesis* was highly valued in certain non-Western spheres, it was Aristotle's first legacy of separation that most subsequent Western philosophers and scientists carried forward through recent decades (Tenkasi & Hay, 2008). Greek philosophers such as Plotinus found little use for *techne*, because it did not reveal underlying rules and principles governing why and how something happens beyond a single event or instance (Parry, 2003). Later philosophers such as John Locke, David Hume, Auguste Comte, and, more recently, Karl Popper, also perpetuated Aristotle's legacy of separation (Chalmers, 1999), an orientation which eventually became institutionalized in Western universities and the construct of science.

The rise of Western universities, rationalism, and empiricism

Western universities, which emerged after 1000 CE, such as the University of Bologna, the University of Paris, and the University of Oxford, strictly adhered to Aristotle's first legacy. The rediscovery of Aristotle's early works fueled a spirit of inquiry applying Aristotelian logic and deduction towards understanding the natural world and natural processes. Drawing on Aristotle's ideas, a community of scholars, communicating primarily in Latin, explored a reconciliation between the deductive works of Greek antiquity, particularly ideas related to understanding the natural world, with those of the church (Shapin, 1996). Scholars characterized this period as a "turning point in the history of Western thought" (Rubenstein, 2003; Grendler, 2004).

During the early modern period (late 1500s to 1800s) and the age of enlightenment, Europe's universities saw tremendous growth, producing enormous quantities of research (Grendler, 2004). Promoted by René Descartes, Baruch Spinoza, and Gottfried Leibniz, rational deduction came into use in numerous disciplines including natural philosophy, medicine, theology, mathematics, astronomy, and law (Rüegg, 1996). Formally, rationalism is a methodology or a theory "in which the criterion of the truth is not sensory but intellectual and deductive. Rationalists believe reality has an intrinsically logical structure ... that the intellect can directly grasp these truths" (Bourke, 1962: 263).

This period was also characterized by the rise of empiricism, through which *phronesis* initially retained a place in scholarship. Empiricism focuses on the role of experience and evidence in the formation of ideas, especially as discovered in experiments, over the notion of innate ideas. As a part of the scientific method, empiricism required that theories were tested against observations, instead of relying on only reason or intuition. John Locke, considered the father of empiricism, proposed the influential view that the *only* knowledge humans can have is a posteriori, i.e., based on experience (Chalmers, 1999). Locke held, like Aristotle, that the human mind is a *tabula rasa*, a "blank tablet" on which experiences derived from sensory impressions are written. He maintained that there are two sources of ideas: sensation and reflection.

However, in contrast to Aristotle's second legacy, which called for the integration of scholarly *episteme theoretike* with the *empeiria and techne* of the practitioner, Locke viewed the scientist/scholar as the objective producer of knowledge on the basis of experience rather than innate thoughts (Chalmers, 1999; Tenkasi & Hay, 2008). Similarly, the Scottish philosopher David Hume maintained that all knowledge, even the most basic beliefs about the natural world, could not be conclusively established by reason (Chalmers, 1999). Rather, he maintained that beliefs are more a result of accumulated habits, developed in response to sensory experiences. Hume argued that induction is problematic as a method for developing science because the future may not resemble the past. John Stuart Mill argued that that knowledge is not from direct experience but an inference from direct experience.

Later thinkers would critique both rationalist and empiricist orientations. Immanuel Kant, a modern philosopher, argued that both reason and experience are necessary for human knowledge (Baird & Kauffman, 2008). He proposed that while experience is fundamentally necessary for human knowledge, reason is necessary for translating that experience into coherent ideas. Auguste Comte, much like Immanuel Kant, observed that, "If it is true that every theory must be based upon observed facts, it is equally true that facts cannot be observed without the guidance of some theories" (Comte, 2003 [1855]). Comte, one of the founders of sociology and the doctrine of positivism, emphasized quantitative, mathematical foundations for knowledge production.

Popper's theory of falsification

Sir Karl Popper, one of the twentieth century's most influential philosophers of science, rejected classical inferential views on the scientific method in favor of empirical falsification. In his influential book, the *Logic of Scientific Discovery*, Popper (1972) derided the value of learning from experiences which he viewed as an inherently fallible source of *episteme theoretike*. The notion that "all swans are white, or all ravens are black, can be logically refuted by the observation of one swan that is black, or one raven that is white" (Chalmers, 1999: 60). Instead, Popper argued for the construction of theories that could be subjected to rigorous testing. He asserted that while theories can never be proven, they can be falsified. True to Aristotle's first legacy, Popper believed that only carefully constructed theories derived from prior theories can generate scientific knowledge. By implication, Popper holds the scholar as the objective producer of knowledge (Chalmers, 1999).

Philosophers of science and eventually management scholars perpetuated the separation of theory from experience and practice on the basis of Popper's ideas. This separation would also eventually characterize university-based business schools, which emerged in the nineteenth century and later became the institutional home of most management scholarship. In the following sections, we narrow our focus to management scholarship and the expression and elaboration of Aristotle's legacies in business schools.

Business schools and management scholarship

As business schools took shape as a formal academic space, the role of collaboration shifted and flexed. In this section, we explore the evolution of management scholarship from its early practical (*techne*) orientation, to a focus on producing *episteme theoretike* in the mid-twentieth century and to more recent methodological diversity and renewed interest in *phronesis*.

Business schools (1850–1950)

Business schools began to evolve from for-profit vocational programs towards full-fledged university-based professional schools in the nineteenth century (Khurana, 2007; Kaplan, 2014). The earliest business schools were in France and Germany, with the latter leading the integration with formal theory and larger university systems (Kaplan, 2014). However, American business schools would powerfully influence business schools across the world after WWII (Kaplan,

2014). Their rise, beginning with the Wharton School in 1881, mirrored the ascension of modern corporations during the late nineteenth and early twentieth centuries during which enrollment grew from less than 100 students in 1895 to over 47,000 in 1924 (Bossard & Dewhurst, 1931).

Business schools contentiously sought legitimacy by pursuing universities' plural goals of teaching, research, and public service (Wiebe, 1967; Khurana, 2007). In pursuit of these goals, their proponents positioned business as a tool for social order in alignment with contemporary progressive values. Like their for-profit forebears, early university-based business schools offered a variety of vocationally oriented courses including transportation, finance, accounting, lumbering, printing, and publishing (Pierson, 1959: 40). However, these early schools were widely criticized during this period on several accounts. Social scientists denigrated management scholars' lack of scientific rigor (e.g., Donham, 1922), arguing that business schools did not belong in universities (Khurana, 2007). Contrariwise, many business leaders saw the training as impractical and at times rejected business schools' dissemination of progressive values.

Largely, business schools forged deep ties with business leaders and retained a practical focus. Over time this practical angle shifted, stimulated by Harvard Business School (HBS), from individual vocations to the perspective of general managers (Pierson, 1959). Several schools increasingly emphasized graduate programs alongside or at the exception of undergraduate studies. During this period, practitioners made up a substantial proportion of instructional faculties, the ranks of which included engineer Frederick Taylor at Dartmouth's Tuck School and accountant George O. May of Price Waterhouse & Co. at HBS (Fourcade & Khurana, 2013; Pierson, 1959). Many scholars, such as Elton Mayo, had close ties to industry and were deeply engaged with the organizations they studied.

As such, management scholarship entailed significant collaboration with industry and focused primarily on immediate, practical issues (Gordon & Howell, 1959; Pierson, 1959). Research was strongly influenced by Taylor's scientific management and systems engineering, which were deployed through a progressive lens to address various labor issues (Bateman, 2008; Shenhav, 1995; Fourcade & Khurana, 2013). The director of the first business school research center (at Wharton), for example, "worked mainly through cooperative studies with selected local industries to develop new labor relations techniques that, he hoped, would help improve the social environment of business" (Fourcade & Khurana, 2013: 132). Taylor's work and the later Hawthorne studies, jointly conducted by HBS and AT&T, exemplified these collaborative achievements (Pasmore, Woodman & Simmons, 2008b). In accordance with the general management perspective, HBS (and later others), poured significant resources into case research (Pierson, 1959).

However, despite several enduring achievements, the sum of early management scholarship was widely criticized. Two comprehensive reports on the state of business education, commissioned by the Carnegie and Ford Foundations in the 1950s, denounced the scientific rigor, quantity, and practical impact of research conducted in business schools (Pierson, 1959; Gordon & Howell, 1959). First, the reports suggested that research produced in business schools was largely descriptive and lacked the scientific rigor characteristic of the social/behavioral sciences. Even case research, which engendered some praise from the reports' authors, reduced management to art rather than established more general principles. Management scholars, argued the reports, also produced relatively little research, regardless of quality, and their research had little impact on business practice (Pierson, 1959; Gordon & Howell, 1959; Wheeler, 1965). The reports found that far more impactful research had been produced by scholars in the underlying social science disciplines (Gordon & Howell, 1959), which reflected the orientations of Comte and Popper. Herbert Simon later wrote that business schools at this time were "a wasteland of vocationalism that needed to be transformed into science-based professionalism" (Simon, 1991: 139).

The scientization of business schools (1950–90)

In the 1950s, rationality, in accordance with the mode of knowledge production predominant in the sciences, roared from the administrative and technical conquests of WWII (e.g., Bateman, 2008). It became a societal value to be deployed in the war against Communism through economic management and business. Marginalized by host universities, business schools rushed to embrace their role in the Cold War, modeling themselves after the prevailing social science-based construct of science (Ross, 1991). The Ford and Carnegie Foundations, backing their reports, funded business schools willing to better integrate the social sciences in curricula, faculty, and research (Khurana, Kimura & Fourcade, 2011; Fourcade & Khurana, 2013; Wheeler, 1965). Later, the AACSB (Association to Advance Collegiate Schools of Business) reinforced and legitimized many of these practices in new accreditation standards (Irwin, 1966).

Though the reports broadly advocated the integration of the social sciences, economists (particularly of the Chicago school) were hired in disproportionately large numbers (Fourcade, 2009; Fourcade & Khurana, 2013). These scholars spread the seeds of neoclassical theory and reinforced the deployment of quantitative analysis and mathematical modeling to develop *episteme theoretike*. As economics grew to shape functional areas from finance to marketing (e.g., Pieters & Baumgartner, 2002), business schools shifted away from a general manager focus to emphasize financial markets and shareholder primacy (Bateman, 2008; Fligstein 1990, 2002; Fourcade & Khurana, 2013). With massive enrollment increases, the rise of large conglomerate corporations, and new theories (e.g., agency theory, transaction cost economics), business schools increasingly shaped the business world, rather than described it.

Though a focus on the business context initially persisted (Simon, 1991), the new scholarly regime eventually diverged from business schools' applied origins and progressive foundations (Bernstein, 2001; Fourcade, 2009; Fourcade & Khurana, 2013). Under the supremacy of financial markets, managers were disciples of a rational body of knowledge. In scholarship, they were Greek characters in an equation, not essential collaborators in knowledge production. Practitioners were culled in large numbers from many faculties and, though a few prominent scholars advocated for academics to have practical experience (and some engaged management practice via practitioner journals and consulting), basic knowledge production became increasingly abstract and decoupled from practical impact (Bennis & O'Toole, 2005; Fourcade & Khurana, 2013; Kay, 1992; Khurana & Spender, 2012; Porter & McKibbin, 1988; Simon, 1967; Stern, Jacobs & Chew, 2003). According to Spender (2007: 1), "history suggests we [business schools] finally parted company with managers after the 1959 Ford and Carnegie reports, as we presumed rationality alone was the sufficient basis for understanding them and their doings."

Nonetheless, management scholarship retained a practical flavor in isolated pockets and new collaborative methodologies slowly evolved in the social sciences. HBS and a few others persisted in case-focused research and teaching, and several business leaders published practical tomes, albeit often without explicit academic collaborators (Pasmore et al., 2008b). Several "new" knowledge production approaches, including grounded theory and action research, sharpened as a counterforce to the prevailing conception of science and alienation from practice (Glaser & Strauss, 1967; Argyris, Putnam & Smith, 1985; Coghlan & Brannick, 2003). Though long marginalized, these methodologies had deep roots and their pioneers sought to redefine the "canons of good science" (e.g., Corbin & Strauss, 1990) by implicitly or explicitly embracing collaboration. New meta-theories, such as Eric Trist and Ken Bamforth's sociotechnical theory, nurtured these methods, which soon found a small and devoted following among management scholars. In addition, the partial "(re)emancipation" of European business schools in the 1980s and 1990s from American influence offered new life to methodological diversity and conversations on the nature of science (Kaplan, 2014; Welter & Lasch, 2008; Hessels & Lente, 2008). This context fertilized today's vibrant global discourse on CMR and Mode 2 scholarship, on which we focus in the remainder of this chapter (Gibbons et al., 1994; Huff, 2000; Huff & Huff, 2001; MacLean, MacIntosh & Grant, 2002; Tranfield & Starkey, 1998; Pettigrew, 2001).

The scientization of business schools, beginning in the mid-twentieth century, yielded massive scholarly productivity, legitimacy, and influence. However, the apparent chasm between business school scholarship, business education, and business practice (e.g., Hambrick, 1994; Mintzberg, 2004; Bennis & O'Toole, 2005; AACSB, 2008) compels greater methodological diversity and the embrace of scholar–practitioner collaboration. Though much of the practical and collaborative activity that typified early management research was decidedly unscholarly, returning to the essence of early business schools offers a path to *phronesis* and practical relevance (Mohrman, Pasmore, Shani, Stymne & Adler, 2008).

Collaborative management research

Gibbons et al.'s (1994) distinction between Mode 2 and Mode 1 knowledge production frames the exploration of CMR. The authors describe Mode 2 knowledge production as a "socially distributed," system-based process with five characteristics that distinguish it from Mode 1. Mode 2 knowledge production:

- is generated in the *context of application*. Results diffuse to problem contexts and practitioners during the process of knowledge production;
- is *transdisciplinary* in that theoretical plurality cannot easily be reduced to disciplinary parts;
- occurs in many settings including universities, private industry, government agencies, think-tanks, and consultancies. This diversity results in *heterogeneous conduct*;
- is *reflexive* as a dialogic process that incorporates multiple views and is explicitly sensitive to broad social consequences; and
- requires *quality control* extending beyond traditional peer review systems to address economic, political, social, and cultural criteria.

Nielsen's chapter in this volume (Chapter 4) provides an interesting lens through which to understand the ethical complexities Mode 2 researchers contend with in achieving quality.

The Mode 2 knowledge producer, as described by Gibbons and others (Gibbons et al., 1994; Brunet, Hickey & Humphries, 2014; Hardeman, Frenken, Nomaler & Ter Wal, 2014), combines theoretical knowledge with practical knowledge to solve particular scientific and organizational problems. In the manner of Mode 2 knowledge production, CMR is a potent method for developing *phronesis*, both advancing basic science, *episteme theoretike*, and bringing about change in organizations, in *techne*. Pasmore, Stymne, Shani, Mohrman and Adler (2008a: 20) defined CMR as:

> an effort by two or more parties, at least one of whom is a member of an organization or system under study and at least one of whom is an external researcher, to work together in learning about how the behaviour of managers, management methods, or organizational arrangements affect outcomes in the system or systems under study, using methods that are scientifically based and intended to reduce the likelihood of drawing false conclusions from the data collected, with the intent of both proving performance of the system and adding to the broader body of knowledge in the field of management.

CMR rests on the assumption that collaboration between managers and scholars advances work in creativity, innovation, organizational growth, change, effectiveness, and sustainable development (and many more areas) beyond what either can achieve separately (Shani et al., 2008).

As we discussed earlier in this chapter, collaboration is not new to management research. Early studies, such as those by Frederick Taylor and Elton Mayo, involved managers, non-management organizational members, and external researchers who collaborated to study issues of mutual interest (Fourcade & Khurana, 2013; Shani et al., 2008). In accordance with the standards of Mode 2 knowledge production, CMR echoes early research collaborations and Aristotle's *phronesis*, drawing their spirit into a rigorous program for contemporary management scholarship.

Collaboration, management, and research

CMR has three core pillars: collaboration, management, and research. *Collaboration* encompasses a full range of partnerships and relationships among individuals and organizations. In the context of CMR, collaboration implies research efforts which include the active engagement of managers and researchers in the framing of the research agenda, the selection and pursuit of methods, and the development of actionable implications. Collaboration requires collective inquiry, the joint pursuit of answers to questions of mutual interest through dialogue, experimentation, the review and integration of knowledge, or other means (Shani & Coghlan, 2014). Management engages in collective inquiry in order to better understand a certain issue or phenomenon using scientifically valid knowledge and methods. Scientists engage in collective inquiry in order to better understand a certain issue or phenomena using practically valid knowledge from practitioners. Collaboration does not impose the requirement of an equal partnership in each of these activities, although we posit that a more equal partnership better supports the fulfillment of CMR's multiple objectives.

CMR's second pillar, management, is multidimensional. *Management* means an individual or group of actors who aspire to influence the behavior or performance of a system. Management (or managing) also refers to the practice of those actors (i.e., what formal or informal managers actually do to achieve their intentions). In addition, management refers to an art or practice, what managers tacitly or explicitly know and believe about how to guide an organization or complex system (Pasmore et al., 2008a). In CMR, the multidimensional matrix of management includes a dimension for different types of managerial actors (individual, organizational, systemic), the setting (a single organization, networks of organizations, systems, regions or communities) and the *aspect* of management studied (specific managerial actions, systems of management processes affecting organizational culture or performance, coordinating mechanisms among networks of organizations, etc.). Additional dimensions could be added to this matrix such as managerial roles. Thus, the construct of management under CMR is open to elaboration.

Research is CMR's third pillar. At the most fundamental level, all research tries to understand something important through means that limit the likelihood of reaching false conclusions. Researchers aspire to provide "objective" data to clarify an important issue, to bolster beliefs characterized elsewhere with observations gathered through more rigorous methods, and to arrive at conclusions through the application of more formalized logic and observation than one would casually use in forming an opinion (Shani & Docherty, 2004).

The collaborative management research process

The CMR process is a complex composition of interrelated context, collaborative relationships, phases, and outcomes (Cirella, Guerci & Shani, 2012). The context and collaborative relationships are shaped by the different phases of the research process. The process affects the possible outcomes, which a priori and continuously inform other aspects of the CMR process. Below, we illustrate the CMR process using a 13-month CMR effort in the ReBUILD company (Canterino, Shani, Coghlan & Brunelli, 2016).[1]

Context. The CMR *context* includes the nature of the external business context (macroeconomic conditions, industry characteristics, regional and national institutions), key organizational features (e.g., strategy, structure, key routines, technology, the social system, performance indicators, management systems, dynamics) and initial research activities (preliminary dialogue with top management about common interests, perceived legitimacy and added value of a collaborative orientation, past experiences in collaborative research). The context is partially exogenous to collaborative relationships, phases, and outcomes, in that some aspects pre-exist the actual conduct of CMR. It also shapes these elements, such as possible outcomes, and is affected by the CMR process if, for example, organizational routines are adjusted in response to collected data.

Collaborative relationships. The nature and quality of *collaborative relationships* have the most significant impact on the phases of knowledge production and its outcomes. Collaboration between scholars and practitioners through CMR enhances management decision-making, generating new and relevant knowledge about emerging issues and possible future business directions by integrating insights from organizational members in a scientific way. The quality of collaboration depends upon the collaborative mechanisms that are designed and managed. Thompson, Perry and Miller (2009) suggest that higher levels of reciprocal autonomy and mutuality yield opportunities for more intense collaboration. Indeed, in the ReBUILD study, the study team was given autonomy to design and implement the study to meet both organizational and research needs. The team's decision to conduct three cycles of data sense-making, as described above, is a key example.

Mohrman and Shani (2008) theorized that collaborative relationships depend on four factors:

- institutional and resource contexts of collaboration;
- alignment of purpose between the different actors (namely academics and practitioners);
- mechanisms that enable learning in collaborative relationships; and
- convergence of the languages of practice and theory.

While the institutional and resource contexts in which collaboration takes places are partially exogenous and thus less under the control of CMR partners, collaborators actively strive to create a common definition of critical issues and to agree on the scope of research. In Chapter 3 of this volume, Coghlan describes metalogue to capture this overarching conversation. An organization does not simply seek help and researchers do not simply impose studies; collaboration on a topic of mutual interest is co-determined through metalogue between the researchers and management.

During early dialogue, collaborators typically explore different ways to undertake a project including the composition of a project steering group and/or study teams that fit the organization and topic. The steering group develops processes to guide itself and the study team(s), determines how collaborators interact with organizational members that are not directly involved in the research, identifies appropriate coordination mechanisms, and develops mechanisms to address unanticipated challenges. In the ReBUILD study, the top management team served as the steering group that sanctioned the study as it evolved. Following an assessment of current practices to identify the major challenges faced by the company, the sense-making processes among the steering group and the study team yielded a consensual focus on culture and subcultures and the dynamics between them that influenced firm performance for in-depth study.

Collaborators must consider the make-up of the study team(s) including diversity (e.g., demographics, motivation, personality), the number of organizational and academic members, the structure and roles of the team(s) and individual members, necessary resources, and the further development of a shared vision. In the ReBUILD company the study team was composed of members of the organization, who were by design a microcosm of the company, and external researchers from varied disciplinary backgrounds that led the project. The study team also included a vice president who was part of the company's top management team (and the project's steering group). Throughout the research process, the study team jointly designed and implemented the different phases of the study, developed the protocols and research tools, and engaged in collaborative sense-making and sense-giving activities. Sense-making of the data collected occurred in three cycles and through structured process and generated both insight and actions.

The climate is also an integral part of collaborative relationships. Nurturing a collaborative climate requires modeling concern, a learning orientation, trust, openness, and mutual respect. Furthermore, the collaborators must foster the development and maintenance of skills and competencies needed to fulfill the goals of a CMR project. CMR's complex nature suggests the need for sensitive structural configurations and processes that sustain the academic–practitioner partnerships (Shani & Docherty, 2004). According to a design perspective, CMR partners create a tapestry of cognitive, structural, and procedural learning mechanisms (Docherty & Shani, 2008) to fit a particular collaboration. For example, the complex nature of the ReBUILD company required academic expertise in different disciplines that included real estate, public finance, business strategy, organization design, information systems, and organization development and change. As such, faculty with the needed expertise were recruited onto the study team.

CMR phases. The CMR process includes several phases or sub-processes. We organize them based on those that have to do with the *design* of the research process, those that have to do with the actual *inquiry*, and those that have to do with *results-implementation*. Though we delineate these phases linearly, CMR phases often unfold in cycles:

- *Design* concerns the establishment of scope, resources, timelines, further mutual learning about the issue(s), and the identification of possible research methods. Both theoretical and methodological pluralism are essential. In fact, because different theories inform different methodologies, methodological pluralism (drawing upon methods from different paradigms) becomes an easy partner to theoretical pluralism. As described in the previous section, design includes mutual education and learning about the research topic. Design also pertains to the shaping and management of ongoing communications with organizational members about the study.
- *Inquiry*, the second phase, is the operative core of the CMR process and is jointly guided by the steering group and study team(s), if formed. Typically, inquiry includes exploring alternative data collection methods and processes, finalizing data collection approaches, training study team(s) in data collection, systematic data collection, initial data analysis, and developing mechanisms for creating shared meaning and data interpretations.
- *Results-implementation*, the third phase, rests on shared understandings and typically occurs iteratively. It includes developing possible managerial implications and actions, identifying possible additional research actions, presenting possible actions for change to top management, top management decisions about next actions and steps, and the actual implementation of these decisions. Implementation can yield significant organizational changes and influence the quality of CMR's ultimate outcomes. As change actions continue to take place, and ideally become integral routines of organizational life, implications for additional changes can be sharpened and/or reformulated. The collaborative process itself is influenced by the quality of the collaboration, developed and transformed through the evolution of the process. Similarly, the CMR process has a direct influence on its outcomes.

Outcomes. CMR is directed towards four possible outcomes:

- organizational change including specific learning on studied phenomena, improvements in work-life balance, the development of learning competencies, etc.;
- creation of new scientific knowledge that pertains to either the topic studied and/or research group development (in terms of knowledge and skills, both on the studied topic and on the collaborative processes);

- creation of evaluative systems. A post-study review and/or a continuous monitoring program can assess the collaborative processes and organizational change actions; and
- finally, the fourth outcome is the creation of new CMR protocol(s) and tool(s) that can stimulate new processes for scientific discovery.

This reflexivity is essential because it allows CMR to address a void in basic knowledge regarding the synthesis of management knowledge and practice (e.g., Kieser, Nicolai & Seidl, 2015).

The ReBUILD CMR study generated outcomes of each type. The study generated a new organization structure, the redesign of key processes, and the institutionalization of the study as an integral part of ongoing organizational learning. Second, new scientific knowledge was created and published. Third, a continuous monitoring program to assess collaborative processes and organizational change actions was established. Finally, a new CMR protocol and processual paths for rotation of study team members were determined to enable continuous learning and the diffusion of knowledge throughout the organization.

CMR outcomes are influenced by context, relationships, and phases, factors which evolve throughout the course of the CMR process. Outcomes are influenced by the development of the CMR process, which, in turn, is influenced by the quality of the collaboration and CMR phases, which themselves are influenced by contextual factors. To add to this complexity, outcomes later influence the process, the quality of collaboration and, at times, even contextual factors, such as organizational features. Coghlan (Chapter 3) in this volume further examines the plurality of outcomes and interdependencies in the CMR process. CMR's dynamic nature and its orientation with Mode 2 knowledge production demand the consideration of a variety of processual paths and outcome assessments.

Knowledge and practice: CMR's role in translation

Calls to close the gap between management scholarship and management practice have persisted for several decades. Though mainstream methods of knowledge production align more with Popper's construction of Aristotle's first legacy, *phronesis* underlies widespread calls to address management scholarship's limited relevance. CMR, among Mode 2 knowledge production paradigms, represents an important avenue towards reconciliation. In fostering knowledge production through academic–practitioner collaborations, basic knowledge is more tightly coupled with practice, and changes in practice are deployed with a consideration of basic knowledge.

Kieser et al. (2015), in summarizing the considerable and diverse discourses castigating management scholarship for its limited practical value, suggest that the continued failure to address the relevance gap reflects the absence of a directed research program examining the actual utilization of management research. CMR, in explicitly addressing the translation of data between collaborators, is positioned to contribute to such a program in several ways, including the generation of theoretical frameworks and the continuous refinement of methodologies that capture the bidirectional influence between scientific knowledge and its utilization. Indeed, it is hard to imagine the advancement of such a research program without true collaboration (Shani & Coghlan, 2014).

CMR is positioned to draw basic knowledge and practice closer together in management scholarship in general, and by facilitating a clearer understanding of how scientists and practitioners translate their perspectives across professional domains. As captured in this chapter, CMR, as a research paradigm, is imperfect and requires additional clarification. Some claim that it fails to resolve communication challenges among collaborators and that it cannot manage inevitable tradeoffs between rigorous, generalizable knowledge production and local practical relevance (Kieser & Leiner, 2011; Kieser et al., 2015). However, the evolution of management inquiry is characterized by a range of methods with different degrees of basic scholarship, action, and collaboration which vary in generating scientific knowledge and local practical relevance in accordance with early philosophies of science (Radaelli, Guerci, Cirella & Shani, 2014; Van de Ven, 2007; Mohrman & Lawler, 2011). The scholarly debate continues to be anchored in seeking a balance between relevance, scientific rigor, and reflectiveness. Those engaged in collaborative research must continue to address these challenges, improving the paradigm for broader application. CMR, embedded within the Mode 2 research domain and among a diverse set of knowledge production paradigms and approaches, promises to nurture the recoupling of management knowledge and practice.

Note

1 These illustrations are brief to clarify processual features. The reader is encouraged to read the complete account in the original article to understand that CMR effort.

References

AACSB (2008). *Final Report of the AACSB International Impact of Research Task Force.* Tampa, FL: AACSB International. Retrieved April 15, 2016 from www.aacsb. edu/publications/researchreports.

Argyris, C., Putnam, R. & Smith, D. (1985). *Action Science.* San Francisco, CA: Jossey-Bass.

Aristotle. (1961). *Metaphysics.* (H. Tredennick, Trans.) Loeb Classical Library (Vol. 1, Bks. 1–9; Vol. 2, Bks. 10–14). Cambridge, MA: Harvard University Press.

Astley, W. & Zammuto, R. (1993). Organization science, managers, and language games. *Organization Science,* 3(4), 443–60.

Baird, F. E. & Kaufman, W. (2008). *From Plato to Derrida.* Upper Saddle River, NJ: Pearson Prentice Hall.

Bateman, B. W. (2008). American Economics: 1885–1945. *New Palgrave Dictionary of Economics.* London: Palgrave.

Bennis, W. G. & O'Toole, J. (2005). How business schools lost their way. *Harvard Business Review,* 83(5), 96–104.

Bernstein, M. (2001). *A Perilous Progress: Economists and Public Purpose in Twentieth Century America*. Princeton, NJ: Princeton University Press.

Bossard, J. & Dewhurst, J. F. (1931). *University Education for Business*. Philadelphia, PA: University of Pennsylvania Press, cited in Khurana, 2007: 89.

Bourke, V. J. (1962). Rationalism. In Runes, D. (Ed.) *Dictionary of Philosophy* (p. 263). Totowa, NJ: Littlefield.

Brunet, N. D., Hickey, G. M. & Humphries, M. M. (2014). The evolution of local participation and the mode of knowledge production in Arctic research. *Ecology and Society*, 19(2), 69.

Canterino, F., Shani, A. B., Coghlan, D. & Brunelli, M. (2016). Collaborative management research as a modality of Action Research: Learning from a merger-based study. *Journal of Applied Behavioral Science*, 52(2), 157–86.

Chalmers, A. F. (1999). *What Is This Thing Called Science?* Indianapolis, IN: Hackett.

Cirella, S., Guerci, M. & Shani, A. B. (2012). A process model of collaborative management research: The study of collective creativity in the luxury industry. *Systemic Practice and Action Research*, 25(3), 281–300.

Coghlan, D. & Brannick, T. (2003). Kurt Lewin: The "practical theorist" for the 21st century. *Irish Journal of Management*, 24(2), 31.

Comte, A. (2003 [1855]). *Positive Philosophy of Auguste Comte* (1855) (Harriet Martineau. Trans.). Whitefish MT: Kessinger Publishing.

Corbin, J. M. & Strauss, A. (1990). Grounded theory research: Procedures, canons, and evaluative criteria. *Qualitative Sociology*, 13(1), 3–21.

Docherty, P. & Shani, A. B. (2008). Learning mechanisms as means and ends in Collaborative Management Research. In Shani, A. B., Mohrman, S. A., Pasmore, W. A., Stymne, B. & Adler, N. (Eds.) *Handbook of Collaborative Management Research* (pp. 163–81). Thousand Oaks, CA: Sage Publications.

Donham, W. B. 1922. Essential groundwork for a broad executive theory. *Harvard Business Review*, 1(1), 1–10.

Dunne, J. (1993). *Back to the Rough Ground: "Phronesis" and "Techne" in Modern Philosophy and in Aristotle*. Notre Dame, IN: University of Notre Dame Press.

Fligstein, N. (1990). *The Transformation of Corporate Control*. Cambridge, MA: Harvard University Press.

Fligstein, N. (2002). *The Architecture of Markets*. Princeton, NJ: Princeton University Press.

Fourcade, M. (2009). *Economists and Societies: Discipline and Profession in the United States, Britain and France*. Princeton, NJ: Princeton University Press.

Fourcade, M. & Khurana, R. (2013). From social control to financial economics: the linked ecologies of economics and business in twentieth century America. *Theory and Society*, 42(2), 121–59.

Hambrick, D. C. (1994): What if the academy really mattered? *Academy of Management Review*, 19(1), 11–16.

Gibbons, M., Limoges, C., Nowotny, H., Schwartzman, S., Scott, P. & Trow, M. (1994). *The New Production of Knowledge*. London: Sage Publications.

Glaser, B. G. & Strauss, A. L. (1967). *The Discovery of Grounded Theory: Strategies for Qualitative Research*. New York: Aldine.

Gordon, R. A. & Howell, J. E. (1959). *Higher Education for Business*. New York: Columbia University Press.

Grendler, P. F. (2004). The Universities of the Renaissance and Reformation. *Renaissance Quarterly*, 57, 2–8.

Hardeman, S., Frenken, K., Nomaler, Ö. & Ter Wal, A. L. J. (2014). Characterizing and comparing innovation systems by different "modes" of knowledge production: A proximity approach. *Science and Public Policy*, 42(4), 530–48.

Hessels, L. K. & Lente, H. V. (2008). Re-thinking new knowledge production: A literature review and a research agenda. *Research Policy*, 37(4), 740–60.

Huff, A. S. (2000). Changes in organizational knowledge production: Presidential Address. *Academy of Management Review*, 25(2), 288–93.

Huff, A. & Huff, J. (2001). Refocusing the business school agenda. *British Journal of Management*, 12 (Special Issue), S49–S54.

Irwin, R. D. (1966). *The American Association of Collegiate Schools of Business, 1916–1966.* Homewood, IL: American Association of Collegiate Schools of Business.

Kaplan, A. (2014). European management and European business schools: Insights from the history of business schools. *European Management Journal*, 32(4), 529–34.

Kay, I. (1992). *Value at the Top: Solutions to the Executive Compensation Crisis*. New York: Harper Collins.

Khurana, R. (2007). *From Higher Aims to Hired Hands: The Social Transformation of Business Schools and the Unfulfilled Promise of Management as a Profession*. Princeton, NJ: Princeton University Press.

Khurana, R. & Spender, J. C. (2012). Herbert A. Simon on what ails business schools: More than "a problem in organizational design." *Journal of Management Studies*, 49(3), 619–39.

Khurana, R., Kimura, K. & Fourcade, M. (2011). *How foundations think: The Ford Foundation as a dominating institution in the field of American business schools*. Working Paper 11–070, Harvard Business School. Retrieved December 11, 2014 from www.hbs.edu/faculty/Publication%20Files/11-070.pdf .

Kieser, A. & Leiner, L. (2011). Collaborate with practitioners: But beware of collaborative research. *Journal of Management Inquiry*, 21(1), 14–28.

Kieser, A., Nicolai, A. & Seidl, D. (2015). The practical relevance of management research: Turning the debate on relevance into a rigorous scientific research program. *The Academy of Management Annals*, 9(1), 143–233.

Lawler, E., Mohrman, A., Mohrman, S. Ledford, G. & Cummings, T. (Eds.) (1985). *Doing Research that is Useful for Theory and Practice*. San Francisco CA: Jossey Bass.

MacLean, D., MacIntosh, R. & Grant, S. (2002). Mode 2 management research. *British Journal of Management*, 13(3), 189–207.

Mintzberg, H. (2004). *Managers Not MBAs: A Hard Look at the Soft Practice of Managing and Management Development*. San Francisco, CA: Berrett-Koehler.

Mohrman, S. & Lawler, E. (2011). *Useful Research: Advancing Theory and Practice*. San Francisco, CA: Berrett-Koehler.

Mohrman, S. A. & Shani, A. B. (2008). The multiple voices of collaboration. In Shani, A. B., Mohrman, S. A., Pasmore, W. A., Stymne, B. & Adler, N. (Eds.) *Handbook of Collaborative Management Research* (pp. 531–8). Thousand Oaks, CA: Sage Publications.

Mohrman, S. A., Pasmore, W., Shani, A. B., Styme, B. & Adler, N. (2008). Toward building a collaborative research community. In Shani, A. B., Mohrman, S. A., Pasmore, W. A., Stymne, B. & Adler, N. (Eds.) *Handbook of Collaborative Management Research* (pp. 615–33). Thousand Oaks, CA: Sage Publications.

Nowotny, H. P., Scott, P. & Gibbons, M. (2001). *Rethinking Science: Knowledge and the Public in an Age of Uncertainty*. London: Polity Press.

Parry, R. (2003). *Episteme* and *Techne*. In Zalta, E. N. (Ed.) *The Stanford Encyclopedia of Philosophy.* Retrieved from http://plato.stanford.edu/archives/sum2003/entries/episteme-techne.

Pasmore, W. A., Stymne, B., Shani, A. B., Mohrman, S. A. & Adler, N. (2008a). The promise of collaborative management Research. In Shani, A. B., Mohrman, S. A. Pasmore, W. A., Stymne, B., and Adler, N. (Eds.) *Handbook of Collaborative Management Research*. Thousand Oaks, CA: Sage Publications.

Pasmore, W., Woodman, R. & Simmons, A. (2008b). Toward a more rigorous, reflective, and relevant science of collaborative management research. In Shani, A. B., Mohrman, S. A., Pasmore, W. A., Stymne, B. & Adler, N. (Eds.) *Handbook of Collaborative Management Research*. Thousand Oaks, CA: Sage Publications.

Pettigrew, A. (2001). Management research after modernism. *British Journal of Management*, 12(Special Issue), 61–70.

Pierson, F. C. (1959). *The Education of American Businessmen*. New York: McGraw-Hill.

Pieters, R. & Baumgartner, H. (2002). "Who talks to whom?" Intra- and interdisciplinary communication of economics journals." *Journal of Economic Literature*, 40(2), 483–509.

Popper, K. R. (1972). *The Logic of Scientific Discovery*. London: Hutchinson.

Porter, L. W. & McKibbin, L. E. (1988). *Management Education and Development: Drift or Thrust into the 21st Century?* New York: McGraw-Hill.

Radaelli, G., Guerci, M., Cirella, S. & Shani, A. B. (2014). Intervention research as management research in practice: Learning from a case in the fashion design industry. *British Journal of Management*, 25(2), 335–51.

Rubenstein, R. E. (2003). *Aristotle's Children: How Christians, Muslims, and Jews Rediscovered Ancient Wisdom and Illuminated the Dark Ages* (1st ed.). Orlando, FL: Harcourt.

Rüegg, W. (1996). Themes. In H. de Ridder-Symoens (Ed.) *A History of the University in Europe, Vol. 2: Universities in Early Modern Europe, 1500–1800* (pp. 33–9). Cambridge: Cambridge University Press.

Ross, D. (1991). *The Origins of American Social Science*. Cambridge: Cambridge University Press.

Shani, A. B. & Coghlan, D. (2014). Collaborate with practitioners: An alternative perspective. *Journal of Management Inquiry*, 23(4), 433–7.

Shani A. B. & Docherty, P. (2004). *Learning by Design*. Malden, MA: Blackwell Publishing.

Shani, A. B., Mohrman, S. A., Pasmore, W. A., Stymne, B. & Adler, N. (Eds.) (2008). *Handbook of Collaborative Management Research*. Thousand Oaks, CA: Sage Publications.

Shapin, S. (1996). *The Scientific Revolution*. Chicago, IL: University of Chicago Press.

Shenhav, Y. (1995). From chaos to systems: The engineering foundations of organization theory 1879–1932. *Administrative Science Quarterly*, 40(4), 557–85.

Simon, H. A. (1967). The business school: A problem in organizational design. *Journal of Management Studies*, 4(1), 1–16.

Simon, H. A. (1991). *Models of my Life*. Cambridge, MA: MIT Press.

Stern, J. M., Jacobs, L. H. & Chew, D. H., Jr. (Eds.) (2003). *The Revolution in Corporate Finance*. New York: Wiley-Blackwell.

Tenkasi, R. V. & Hay, G. W. (2008). Following the second legacy of Aristotle: The scholar–practitioner as an epistemic-technician. In Shani, A. B., Mohrman, S. A.,

Pasmore, W. A., Stymne, B. & Adler, N. (Eds.) *Handbook of Collaborative Management Research*. Thousand Oaks, CA: Sage Publications.

Thompson, A. M., Perry, J. & Miller, T. (2009). Conceptualizing and measuring collaboration. *Journal of Public Administration Research and Theory*, 19(1), 23–56.

Tranfield, D. & Starkey. K. (1998). The nature, social organization and promotion of management research: Towards policy. *British Journal of Management*, 9(4), 341–53.

Van de Ven, A. H. (2007). *Engaged Scholarship: A Guide for Organizational and Social Research*. Oxford: Oxford University Press.

Welter, F. & Lasch, F. (2008). Entrepreneurship research in Europe: Taking stock and looking forward. *Entrepreneurship Theory and Practice*, 32(2), 241–8.

Wiebe, R. H. (1967). *The Search for Order, 1877–1920*. Chicago, IL: Macmillan.

Wheeler, J. (1965). *Changes in Collegiate Business Education in the United States 1954–64 and the Role of the Ford Foundation in these Changes*. Ford Foundation Archives.

3   Insight and reflection as key to collaborative engagement

David Coghlan

In a collaborative research project that sought to create sustainable networks of small to medium-sized traditional food-producing firms, the central deliverables were: innovation, knowledge transfer, transfer of technology to upgrade processes and technologies, and the provision of training in technical areas such as supply chain management, packaging, labeling, and health and safety. The integrating process across these activities was a focus on action and on learning through action learning research. The actual learning experience of the participating firms in their desires and efforts to implement improved business practices and technological processes were grounded in each firm's individual capabilities. After a year and a half, the academic scholars who were guiding the action learning research had the insight that inviting the practitioners to write short cases (4–5 pages) describing their experience in the project would enable them to articulate the stories of the firms, question the insights, and consolidate the learning through participating in the project. The invitation was accepted enthusiastically and up to 40 cases were written and circulated within the project. The stories of each firm and of their engagement in the project enabled the advancement of the technical agenda of the project and the generation of scholarly output about the creation of sustainable networks in this subsector of the food industry.

This vignette opens up themes for this chapter. The setting was a collaborative research project where the aim was to form and develop a practitioner network conducted by means of action learning. In this project participants (traditional food producers in the dairy, meat, and bakery sectors in nine hubs across eight European countries) and academics worked together to establish learning networks that would provide economic, business, and social support to these small businesses in this food subsector. In the project there was engagement between the practitioners in the firms and academic scholars. Both communities engaged with the learning of the participants, one through a science-based orientation (food technology) and a social science (organization development), and the other through a business-focused orientation. This engagement took place in the present tense as the project unfolded and was constructed around the learning formula, $L = P + Q$, where P stands for programmed learning (i.e., current knowledge in use, already known, what is in books, etc.) and Q for questioning insight (Revans, 2011). The learning formula provides a facility to hold both the P of the science-based knowledge with the practical Q of the business experience and to frame the engagement in terms of the operations of human knowing and learning. This chapter is a philosophical reflection that explores the common foundation in the operations of human knowing that both academics and practitioners share and how exploring insight and reflection are the foundations of collaboration between them. In the context of this volume and chapter it is explored in order to build common ground across both communities and to provide a framework that can enhance collaborative engagement. The chapter is structured as follows. After a brief location of the challenges of academic–practitioner engagement, I describe the invariant structure of human knowing as framed by the philosopher–theologian Bernard Lonergan. This structure comprises operations of experiencing, understanding, and judging, and forms the basis for a general empirical method for ways of holding different realms of knowing as interiority. I then introduce action learning as a theory of practice and the learning formula $L = P + Q$, alluded to in the vignette, and located it in the operations of human knowing. From the focus on the operations of knowing and learning, I suggest Bateson's notion of metalogue as an approach to conversing about academic–practitioner engagement. Finally I offer a framework for academic–practitioner engagement based on the common operations of human knowing.

Academic–practitioner engagement

In the context of the ever-growing literature on academic–practitioner engagement the differences between them are expressed frequently in terms of a gap or divide (Anderson, Herriot & Hodgkinson, 2001; Empson, 2013), for example, that academics are interested in scientific knowing and practitioners in practical knowing. Bartunek and Rynes (2014) discuss a number of tensions between academics and practitioners that are identified in this literature: different logics, time dimensions, communication practices, rigour and relevance, interests and incentives. They suggest that these tensions be explored in terms of dialectics and paradox. This chapter suggests a complementary approach, one that builds on what is common across all human beings, namely the operations of human inquiry and knowing, particularly the activities of insight and reflection. Scolari, Coghlan and Shani (2015) argue that attending to knowing how we know, i.e., being aware that knowing comprises operations of experience, understanding and judgment, is critical in collaborative management research.

The dynamic structure of human knowing

Bernard Lonergan (1992 [1957]) presents the structure of knowing as a dynamic, heuristic three-step process: experience, understanding, and judgment. Experience takes place at the empirical level of consciousness and is an interaction of outer and inner events, or data of sense and data of consciousness. We not only experience external data through our five senses but we also experience internal data as we think, feel, remember, and imagine. We also experience ourselves as seeing, hearing, thinking, feeling, remembering, and imagining. Sensory data are what we experience but do not yet understand. What was that noise? Is it raining? So we ask questions, and the answers come in the form of insights which are acts of understanding, of grasping and formulating patterns, unities, relationships, and explanations in response to questions posed to our experience. The noise sounded like a plate being dropped on the floor. The water running down the window means it is raining. While we might not know yet if a particular current search is intelligent, we anticipate intelligent answers. Insight or understanding occurs at the intellectual level of consciousness as we move beyond description to explanation. Yet, while insights are common they are not always accurate, correct, or satisfactory answers to our questions. The question then is, is the insight correct or does it provide a satisfactory answer to the question posed to experience? This opens up a question for reflection. Is it so? Yes or no? Maybe. I don't know. I can affirm that the noise was a plate being dropped on the floor. I can affirm that it is raining and the water on the window is not due to a leak overhead. So we move to a new level of the cognitional process, where we marshal and weigh evidence and assess its sufficiency. We are at the rational level of consciousness. We do not merely know; we also make decisions and act (the responsible level of consciousness). At this level we ask what courses of action are open to us and we review options, weight choices, and decide. The responsible level of consciousness is added to the empirical, intellectual, and rational levels. This pattern is invariant in that it applies to all settings of cognitional activity, whether solving an everyday problem or engaging in scientific research. To reject or dismiss this pattern involves experience, understanding, and judging and, paradoxically, confirms it.

Of course this is not all that simple. We know that there are such things as obtuseness, narrow-mindedness, confusion, stupidity, divergent views, bias, lack of attention, and a general lack of intelligence. We may not bother to ask questions about our experience. An understanding may not come quickly enough, and we may be impatient and not question further. Many insights may be wrong. Interpretations of data may be superficial, inaccurate, or biased. Judgments may be flawed. We may have unconscious fears which censor, block, or divert questioning. We can be egotistical where we use our intelligence to figure out how to exploit people. We can be blind to the limitations of our culture, race, and gender, and of the groups with which we identify. Accordingly, we need to gain insight into these negative manifestations of knowing, what Lonergan refers to as "flights from understanding" by the same threefold process of knowing.

Lonergan's work focusing on the central role of insight in human knowing, while mainly discussed in the fields of philosophy and theology, has been brought to and explored in such diverse arenas as science education (Marroum, 2004; Roscoe, 2004), health science (Daly, 2009), nursing theory and research (Perry, 2004), interdisciplinary engagement (Sawa, 2005; Kane, 2014), conflict management (Melchin & Picard, 2008), housing research (McNelis, 2014), organization development (Coghlan & Shani, 2013) and action research (Coghlan, 2008, 2010a; Coghlan & Brannick, 2014), to name a few applications. Here it is extended to encompass the dynamics of academic–practitioner engagement.

Lonergan states that his concern is not with the existence of knowledge or with what is known but with the structure of knowing and with the personal appropriation of the dynamic and recurrent operative structure of cognitional activity as a method of coming to terms with oneself as a knower (McCarthy, 1990, Flanagan, 1997; Meynell, 1998). Appropriating our intellectual activities means becoming aware of them, being able to identify and distinguish them, grasping how they are related, and being able to make the process explicit.

General empirical method and authenticity

Lonergan presents authenticity as being at the heart of being human, as being human means to be experiencing, understanding, judging and deciding/acting. He frames four transcendental precepts that are *imperatives*, in that they point to what "ought" to be. As Coghlan (2008) describes it, as we experience data so we ought to *be attentive*. Therefore, avoiding issues, turning a blind eye, refusing to inquire into some matter diminish human authenticity. As we ask questions and seek answers, we ought to *be intelligent*. Refusing to question or wonder, uncritically or sheepishly following the party line, and suppressing curiosity destroy authenticity. We wonder if our ideas are correct so we ought to have sound reasons for what we hold and base our judgments on evidence. So the imperative is, *be reasonable*. Suppressing discussion and obscuring evidence destroy authenticity. We wonder what we ought to do, so we ought to be sensitive to value and choose what we believe to be right. The imperative, therefore, is, *be responsible*. Cheating, lying, and being unjust destroy authenticity. In this chapter the notion of authenticity (referring to how we are attentive, ask questions, form judgments, and take responsibility for our actions) provides the ground for framing how academics and practitioners may engage in conversation.

The operations of experience, understanding, judgment, and deciding/acting form a general empirical method, which requires:

- attention to observable data;
- envisaging possible explanations of that data;
- preferring as probable or certain the explanations which provide the best account for the data; and
- deliberating, deciding, and taking action.

These require the dispositions to perform the operations of attentiveness, intelligence, and reasonableness, and their responsible enactment constitutes authenticity.

The general empirical method underlies the specific modes of inquiry across the natural sciences, critical scholarship, social sciences, and practical living in asking intelligent questions about experience, and providing and verifying reasonable answers to those questions (Table 3.1). For Lonergan, the general

Table 3.1 Operations of human cognition and doing

Operations of human knowing	Level of consciousness	Activities	Examples of questions	Authenticity
Experiencing	Empirical	Seeing, hearing, smelling, tasting, touching, remembering, imagining, feeling…	What is happening? What am I hearing, seeing…? What am I thinking, feeling, remembering, imagining…?	Be *attentive*—avoid turning a blind eye
Understanding	Intellectual	Inquiring, understanding, formulating what is being understood	How do I understand what is happening?	Be *intelligent*—avoid being uncritical or conformist
Judging	Rational	Marshaling evidence, testing, judging	Are there alternative explanations? How am I judging which insight fits? What am I filtering? Have I sufficient information to make a judgment? How sure, unsure am I? Do I need to inquire more?	Be *reasonable*—avoid suppressing consideration of opposites
Deciding/Acting	Responsible/Ethical	Deliberating, valuing, deciding, choosing, taking action, behaving…	What will I do? What is worthwhile, good…?	Be *responsible*—avoid lying cheating and injustice
Knowing	Collaboration with others	Listening Inquiring Sharing own views Collaborating	What is your experience? What are your questions? What are your insights? How have you formed this judgment? Do I appreciate your judgment and how you have reached it? What might we do?	Being authentic and open to co-inquiry, dialogue, and shared action

empirical method of being attentive, intelligent, reasonable, and responsible is a normative heuristic pattern of related and recurrent operations that yield ongoing and cumulative results. It envisages all data, both of sense and of consciousness. It doesn't treat objects without taking into consideration the operations of experience, understanding, and judgment. It enables us to appropriate our own conscious reality as existential subjects. It provides a key to the relationship between questioning and answering; it is a framework for collaborative creativity that deals with different kinds of questions, each with its own focus. So questions for understanding specific data (What is happening here?) have a different focus from questions for reflection (Does this fit?) or from questions of responsibility (What ought I to do?). As conscious subjects we can attend to what is going on, both inside and outside us, inquire intelligently, judge reasonably, decide freely, and act responsibly. As conscious existential subjects we can accept and confront the fact that it is up to us to decide that our actions will be responsible, our judgments reasonable, our investigations intelligent, and that we advert to data of both sense and consciousness. As Lonergan points out, human authenticity is not some pure quality or some serene freedom from all oversights, all misunderstandings, and all mistakes. Authenticity is ever precarious and we have a constant struggle to learn through uncovering still more oversights, acknowledging further failures to understand and correcting more errors.

Realms of meaning: practical knowing, theory, and interiority

Lonergan (1972) reflects on three realms of meaning: common-sense or practical knowing, theory, and interiority. These three realms of meaning are integrally linked to the process of human knowing.

The realm of practical knowing

Practical knowing focuses on the interest and concerns of human living and the successful performance of daily tasks (Lonergan, 1992 [1957]; Coghlan, 2016). It seeks to help us deal with situations as they arise and to discover immediate solutions that will work. Practical knowing is knowing that relates to us. In the realm of the practical we are interested in knowing, not just for its own sake, but for developing more intelligent and successful ways of living. It focuses on the concrete and the particular. For example, if we don't apply our intelligence when we are driving, then we may cause an accident.

The realm of theory

The realm of theory is not interested in things and people as they relate to us but rather as they relate to one another in a verifiable manner. Theoretically differentiated consciousness operates systematically, is governed by logic, and uses language in a technical and explanatory manner. Explanation has to be accurate, clear, and precise so the ambiguities of practical language are averted. Special methods are required to govern different types of investigation, as in botany, genetics, and statistical analysis, to take three examples.

The relationship between practical knowing and theory

The distinction between practical knowing and theory is not a distinction between practical and intellectual patterns of experience. Although they have different concerns and scope, they are not isolated from one another. Practical knowing may mistakenly claim general theoretical applicability. Practical knowing does develop general principles, but these generalizations are concerned with the concrete, practical affairs of a specific context, not with universal principles that scientific theory advances. In a similar vein, practical knowing may claim that theoretical investigation is pointless and that theory is irrelevant.

In the practical mind-set, deciding what to do, what is good/bad, right/wrong, what works or does not work, etc., is somewhat haphazard and uneven as the practical mind aims at the practical and short term and is difficult to objectify. In the realm of theory, clarity and rigor can be gained within the scope of logic and mathematics, but it cannot deal with the practical realm or critique its own limitations or provide criteria between conflicting theories. Hence there is a need for something that is beyond both the realm of practical knowing and of theory.

Interiority

The critical demand is a turn from the outer world of practical knowing and theory to the appropriation of one's own interiority, i.e., to oneself as a knower. This is a heightened intentional consciousness and is what Lonergan (1972) calls "interiority" (Coghlan, 2010b). The turn to interiority is not just cognition but is an appropriation of self and one's mind. Interiority marks a turn from the outer world of practical knowing and theory with the ability to recognize the competence of both forms of knowing and to meet the demands of both without confusing them. Interiority involves shifting from *what* we know to *how* we know, a process of intellectual self-awareness. Interiority analysis involves using one's knowledge of how the mind works to critique an intellectual search for truth in any area.

Interiority is characterized by awareness of the actual processes of human knowing and by reflection on the operations of knowing. It calls for self-knowledge not just of our feelings, dreams, and motivations but of how we see, think, judge, imagine, remember, criticize, evaluate, conclude, etc. Grasping the activity of human understanding is the main characteristic of interiority, how it happens in us. By using the general empirical method, we can attend to data, think a matter through, and ask the relevant questions. We can know when we have reached reasonable conclusions and can take responsibility for them. Interiority is being faithful to the deepest and the best inclinations of mind and heart. We do make mistakes and we can reflect and discover our mistakes. Then we investigate the source of our misunderstandings and false judgments, how we did not attend to all the data, or how we jumped to conclusions. We can learn about our own style of learning, of how, for instance, temperament plays a role. We can learn to recognize our biases, prejudices, fears, and anxieties. In collaborative research settings, both academics and practitioners can recognize and question each other's experience, understanding, judgments, and actions, and access the interiority from realms of practical knowing and theory. This is demanding work and a lifetime task. It may be worked on through methods of reflexivity and critical thinking where we learn to question insights and how we come to judgment (Coghlan, 2016).

Why is Lonergan important in this reflection? What is he contributing to a philosophy of social science and, in particular, to the subject of academic–practitioner engagement that this volume explores? Not only do the academics and practitioners aspire to be attentive, be intelligent, and be reasonable as much as possible but the actions and products of their shared engagement have to be explained as emerging from attention, intelligence, and reason, or lack thereof. Hence, exploring the common experience of how academics and practitioners endeavor to be attentive, intelligent, reasonable, and responsible as they engage together is set on a common ground. Lonergan's approach is empirical, not only because we can test the behavioral outcomes on ourselves and others but because each of us can experience within ourselves the same need to raise further questions about facts, values, intentions, and actions. He provides a ground for knowing how to know, for thinking about thinking, and learning about learning. He frames a method whereby we can, for example, work with the insight into paradox that Paula Jarzabkowski, Marianne Lewis, and Wendy Smith explore in Chapter 8 of this volume, Laura Empson's insight into liminality as a frame for her experience (Chapter 12), and Van de Ven's reflections (Chapter 7) on his course on developing capabilities for engaged scholarship. We can uncover the method in Ralph Hamann and Kristy Faccer's account of knowledge co-production across the research–practice boundary (Chapter 14) and MacLean and MacIntosh's insights into the lens of creative action in theoretical terms and the practices of creative actors in experiential terms (Chapter 9).

Action learning

The vignette at the outset of this chapter was located in a collaborative research project that was conducted through action learning research (Coghlan & Rigg, 2012). Action learning, as developed by Revans (1971, 2011), grew from a mid-twentieth-century disenchantment with positivism and the prevailing cultural beliefs in the dominance of expertise, which fostered the conviction that problems can be solved by purely technical solutions. As a counter position, Revans argued that there is more learning to be had through action being taken by those involved with an issue. His key idea was a synergy between learning and action: "there can be no learning without action and no (sober and deliberate) action without learning" (Revans, 2011: 71). In other words, praxis is fundamental to action learning in the sense that learning through activity or work is essential.

Revans (1971) proposed a theory of action in terms of a science of *praxeology*, comprising what he called systems alpha, beta, and gamma. In essence, *system alpha* focuses on the investigation of the problem, based on the managerial value system, the external environment, and available internal resources. *System beta* focuses on the problem resolution, through decisions, cycles of negotiation, and trial and error. *System gamma* focuses on the learning as experienced uniquely by each of the participants through their self-awareness and questioning. System *gamma* concerns the participants' cognitive framework, their assumptions and prior understanding. As Revans points out the engagement is both scientifically rigorous in confronting the issues and critically subjective through managers learning in action.

Underpinning Revans's praxeology is his theory of learning that is captured in his learning formula $L = P + Q$ introduced earlier. Q challenges both the usefulness of programmed knowledge (P) to the current situation and the ignorance of the participants. Questioning others both admits to lack of knowledge and increases the scope of understanding and for the search for solutions. It also carries the potential for new insight into the current state. A necessary reference point for the positioning of an insight is theory (or programmed knowledge). The insight arising from the questioning may challenge the fit with an extant theory. In that challenge, the usefulness or usability of the theory may be thrown into focus. So, as captured in the action learning formula, learning emerges as an outcome from the questioning in relation to the specific application of programmed knowledge. The verification of the learning informed by the insight takes place through theory-based reflection on the evidence emerging from the questioning.

For Revans, learning always begins with Q (thereby inverting the established Western educational and research system that typically begins with P). Experience in both the past and present is subjected to questioning with a view to gaining insights into what is going on regarding the problem at hand, why it is happening, and what might be done about it. Implementation of the praxeology of systems alpha, beta, and gamma provides a process through which the learner, in the company of peers in an action learning set, engages in critical inquiry into experience, gains insights, and takes risks in taking action on the problem, which sets up further experiences for reflection and so the process continues (Coghlan, 2012). Action learning creates an environment of inquiry and learning that enables academic scholars and practitioners to participate in a shared engagement.

While the practice of action learning is demonstrated through many different approaches, two core elements are consistently in evidence:

- participants work on real organizational problems that do not appear to have clear solutions; and
- participants meet on equal terms to report to one another and to discuss their problem and progress (O'Neil & Marsick, 2007).

These two elements provide a context for practitioner learning and for research-ers in intra- and inter-organizational settings (Coughlan & Coghlan, 2011). It also provides the basis for a collaborative research approach that is grounded in action-oriented inquiry aimed at generating actionable knowledge (Coghlan, 2013; Coghlan & Coughlan, 2010).

For practitioners and academics engaging in action learning research, knowing how we know and that insights are merely insights until affirmed by judgment are central to the process. Being attentive to data, intelligent in under-standing, reasonable in judging, and responsible in taking action provides both a solid foundation for inquiring-in-action and a benchmark by which to test how one is learning. It also provides a mechanism within an action learning group, whereby members may challenge one another as to how an insight emerges from questioning experience, and how an individual has weighed the evidence on which a particular judgment is based. It encourages members to attempt to articulate how their mind is working in, for example, how they weigh evidence and form judgments as to how an incident is good or bad from their perspective. Such a focus enables members of an action learning group to catch when they are making inferences, or attributions, or jumping to conclusions based on flimsy evidence. The peer relationship between participants facilitates this learning.

How, then, may academics and practitioner engage in shared inquiry that is explicit about the operations of knowing as they engage with the *Q* emerging from practical experience in dialogue with the *P* of science? To explore an answer I introduce the notion of metalogue.

Metalogue

Metalogue is an inquiry process, a "conversation about some problematic subject" in which the participants discuss not only the problem but the structure of the conversation as a whole, which is also relevant to the same subject (Bateson, 1972: 1). It is a relational form of inquiry (Zandee, 2013). Its under-lying assumptions are that knowing is embedded in and arises from distinctive patterns of relationships and conversation, and moves between intellect and emotion, subjectivity and inter-subjectivity, theoretical and practical knowing. In giving voice to the participants in a conversation or dialogue it allows individual and personal voices to be valued and heard, rather than some voices to dominate and other to be silenced. Tobin and Roth (2002) present a metalogue between the two authors as they explore critical issues and theory and practices associ-ated with peer review in the context of science education. Staller (2007) dis-cusses metalogue as a method of inquiry among authors, editors and referees as a way exploring the creation of scholarship. Allen and Marshall (2015) reflect that, in the context of metalogue, humility is an underlying disposition so that one voice does not dominate over others.

Metalogue is a term that has not yet appeared in mainstream organizational research literature and perhaps it is time that it does. It finds resonances with col-laborative management research (Shani, Mohrman, Pasmore, Stymne & Adler,

2008) and with dialogical organization development (Bushe & Marshak, 2015), which are grounded in the dialogical dynamics of meaning–making when there are multiple realities constructed by the variety of actors engaged in the development process. Metalogue involves an interaction among actors, each of which brings a wide variety of experience and ways of knowing to the endeavour. Where it resonates with the challenges underpinning this volume and this chapter is how it focuses on the operations of knowing as a foundation for conversation.

To explore how metalogue works within the frameworks of human knowing, authenticity and interiority let us look at what happens within participants and between participants in a metalogue. Participants reflect on their questioning and how they process their questions in conversation with one another and how they subject their knowing to self- and mutual critique. They address the subjectivity–objectivity issue through describing concrete experiences, sharing their emergent insights and articulating how they have to come to the judgment as to what understanding they have made that best fits the evidence and by demonstrating critical reflexivity in how they came to that judgment. Metalogue is grounded in efforts to be authentic and to demonstrate how participants can demonstrate how they are being attentive, intelligent, reasonable, and responsible.

In the metalogue conversations a spirit of inquiry and humility is needed. Schein's (2013) typology of questioning in a spirit of humble inquiry provides a useful framework for academic–practitioner engagement. Through *exploratory* questioning participants elicit the experience of others by asking questions about experience, such as what happened, who said and did what, to what outcome. Through *diagnostic* questioning they draw out understanding by exploring how the experiences are understood and asking what causal inferences or interpretations are being made. Through *confrontive* questioning the conversation may then move to a more explicit questioning of alternative insights.

Toward a framework for academic–practitioner engagement

To return to the vignette at the outset of this chapter, the aim of the action learning project was to deliver sustainable networks, which would benefit European traditional food producers by overcoming the vulnerability of their small-scale and limited resources through networking and learning within networks of like firms and researchers. A secondary aim was to generate insights into how a learning network is constructed and realized (Coughlan, Coghlan, O'Leary, Rigg & Barrett, 2016). As the project progressed, action learning facilitated the emergence of a learning network. The partners formed a learning network within which experience was shared, questions were asked, and, through reflection, insight and actionable knowledge were generated at individual and organizational levels. The involvement of both academics and practitioners in the action learning process in this network ensured commitment to both action and learning in a context where all participants were actors and inquirers. The cases written about the participants' experience were grounded in accounts of their commercial experiences and the challenges facing them as small traditional food producers. Their sharing these experiences and receiving relevant P opened up insights for their business development. Thus, network learning occurred in cycles of action learning as the actionable knowledge that was generated in response to an issue faced by one firm had application to issues faced by others. The firms in the network were able to exploit this knowledge to address their issues and to develop and grow simultaneously. The project matured from a network of disconnected firms to a learning network characterized by the co-direction, co-development and co-deployment of knowledge and learning.

The academics and technical experts could stand back from their theory-based knowledge to enter the practical world of the business knowing of the practitioners. The practitioners, to varying degrees, appreciated the lectures and science-focused language and knowing of the academics. Neither sought to dominate the other. While it is too soon to establish this as metalogue, it has its characteristics in-waiting. The practitioners described their experiences and understandings in their cases and, through the interaction with the researchers, these understandings were affirmed. Through enacting the learning formula, $L=P+Q$, the engagement enabled conversations and learning to take place.

Both action learning and metalogue focus on the process of reflective conversation, that is, where both content and process are afforded explicit attention and enabled by peer conversation based on questioning and insight. It is the assertion of this chapter that because they are explicit in giving central space to the operations of human knowing they provide something of a meta-approach to the subject of academic–practitioner collaboration.

Figure 3.1 illustrates a generic framework for academic–practitioner engagement. At the center are the operations of human knowing: experiencing,

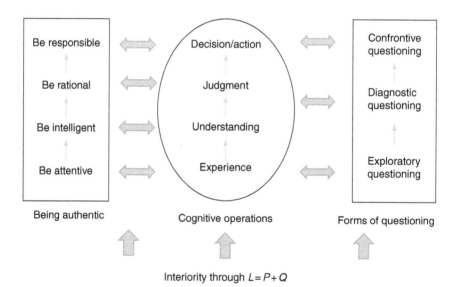

Figure 3.1 A framework for academic–practitioner engagement.

understanding, judging, and deciding/taking action. On the left side is the thrust to be authentic, that is, to be attentive to experience, be intelligent in understanding, be reasonable in judging, and be responsible in deciding and taking action. On the right side is the form of questioning that enables participants in a collaborative setting to inquire into the experiencing, understanding, judging, and deciding/taking action of the others. Exploratory questioning draws out experience. Diagnostic questioning draws out understanding, judging, and deciding while confrontive questioning draws out critical thinking by posing alternatives. The participants are practitioners and researchers. Each draws on their own perspective or community of practice to question and frame their understanding of what is taking place (experience), make judgment on that understanding, and then assess what needs to be done. The collaborative engagement brings these perspectives together and by means of exploratory, diagnostic and confrontive questioning in a spirit of humble inquiry enable the experience, understanding, judgments be explored. Holding the whole framework together and being attentive, intelligent, reasonable, and responsible in working with the process enables the experiences, understandings, judgments, and decision/actions of academic and practitioner participants be respectfully questioned as a process of interiority that accommodates the P and Q of both communities and lead to mutual learning.

Conclusions

This chapter is a philosophical reflection that has explored the common foundation in the operations of human knowing that both academics and practitioners share and how exploring insight and reflection are the foundations of collaboration between academics and practitioners. As Kane (2014) argues, the benefits of this approach are that it situates inquiry within ordinary human knowing. It situates participants non-hierarchically with other inquirers. It provides a touchstone from which inquiry can proceed collaboratively. As she notes, "a cognitional structure within which each inquirer operates differently makes collaborative inquiry possible" (Kane, 2014: 129). Accordingly, what becomes pivotal for the success of such collaboration is the creation and utilization of a space for dialogue among the members of a community of practice (the practitioner and researchers) to form a community of inquiry in order to improve a system's performance and to add to the broader body of knowledge in the field of management and organizations.

Acknowledgments

I acknowledge the most valuable support and critique in the development of this chapter from Jane McKenzie and from the members of the action research writing group in which I participate: Vivienne Brady, Ann Donohue, and Geralyn Hynes.

References

Allen, S. & Marshall, J. (2015). Metalogue: Trying to talk about (un)sustainability—a reflection on experience. *Tamara—Journal for Critical Organization Inquiry*, 13(1–2), 1–13.

Anderson, N., Herriot, P. & Hodgkinson, G. (2001). The practitioner–researcher divide in industrial, work and organizational (IWO) psychology: Where are we now and where do we go from here? *Journal of Occupational and Organizational Psychology*, 74(4), 391–411.

Bartunek, J. M. & Rynes S. L. (2014). Academics and practitioners are alike and unlike: The paradoxes of academic–practitioner relationships. *Journal of Management*, 40(5), 1181–201.

Bateson, G. (1972*). Steps to an Ecology of Mind*. New York: Balantine.

Bushe, G. R. & Marshak, R. J. (2015*). Dialogic Organization Development: The Theory and Practice of Transformational Change.* San Francisco CA: Berrett-Koehler.

Coghlan, D. (2008). Authenticity as first person practice: An exploration based on Bernard Lonergan. *Action Research*, 6(3), 351–66.

Coghlan, D. (2010a). Seeking common ground in the diversity and diffusion of action research and collaborative management research action modalities: Toward a general empirical method. In Pasmore, W.A., Shani, A. B. & Woodman, R. W. (Eds.) *Research in Organization Change and Development* (Vol. 18, pp. 149–81). Brinkley: Emerald.

Coghlan, D. (2010b). Interiority as the cutting edge between theory and practice: A first person perspective. *International Journal of Action Research*, 6(2–3), 288–307.

Coghlan, D. (2011). Action research: Exploring perspectives on a philosophy of practical knowing. *Academy of Management Annals*, 5(1), 53–87.

Coghlan, D. (2012). Understanding insight in the context of Q. *Action Learning: Research & Practice*, 9(3), 247–58.

Coghlan, D. (2013). Action learning research? Reflection from the colloquium at the Third International Action Learning conference. *Action Learning: Research and Practice*, 10(1), 54–7.

Coghlan, D. (2016). *Inside Organizations: Exploring Organizational Experiences*. London: Sage Publications.

Coghlan, D. & Brannick, T. (2014). *Doing Action Research in your Own Organization* (4th ed.). London: Sage Publications.

Coghlan, D. & Coughlan, P. (2010). Notes towards a philosophy of action learning research. *Action Learning: Research and Practice*, 7(2), 193–203.

Coghlan, D. & Rigg, C. (2012). Action learning as praxis in learning and changing. In Pasmore, W. A., Shani, A. B. & Woodman, R. (Eds.) *Research in Organization Change and Development* (Vol. 20, pp. 59–90). Brinkley, UK: Emerald.

Coghlan, D. & Shani A. B. (2013). Organizational developmental research interventions: Perspectives from action research and collaborative management research. In Loenard, S., Lewis, R., Freedman, A. & Passmore, J. (Eds.) *The Wiley–Blackwell Handbook of Psychology of Leadership, Change, and Organizational Development* (pp. 443–60). Chichester, UK: Wiley.

Coughlan, P. & Coghlan, D. (2011). *Collaborative Strategic Improvement through Network Action Learning: The Path to Sustainability*. Cheltenham: Edward Elgar.

Coughlan, P., Coghlan, D., O'Leary, D., Rigg, C. & Barrett, D. (2016). Supporting sustainability through developing a learning network among traditional food producers: Applications of action learning. In Cagliano, R., Caniato, F. & Worley, C. (Eds.) *Organizing*

Supply Chain Processes for Sustainable Innovation in the Agri-food Industry. Organizing for Sustainable Effectiveness (Vol. 5, pp. 59–81). Binkley, UK: Emerald.

Daly, P. R. (2009). A theory of health science and the healing arts based on the philosophy of Bernard Lonergan. *Theoretical Medicine and Bioethics*, 30(2), 147–60.

Empson, L. (2013). My affair with the "other": Identity journeys across the research–practice divide. *Journal of Management Inquiry*, 22(2), 229–48.

Kane, A. (2014). Lonergan's philosophy as grounding for cross-disciplinary research. *Nursing Philosophy*, 15(2) 125–37.

Flanagan, J. (1997). *Quest for Self-Knowledge: An Essay in Lonergan's Philosophy.* Toronto: University of Toronto Press.

Lonergan, B. L. (1972). *Method in Theology*. London: Longman Darton & Todd.

Lonergan, B. J. (1992 [1957]). *The Collected Works of Bernard Lonergan, Vol. 3. Insight: An Essay in Human Understanding.* F. Crowe & R. Doran (Eds.) Toronto: University of Toronto Press.

McCarthy, M. H. (1990). *The Crisis of Philosophy*. Albany, NY: SUNY Press.

McNelis, S. (2014). *Making Progress in Housing: A Framework for Collaborative Research*. Abingdon UK: Routledge.

Marroum, R. M. (2004). The role of insight in science education: An introduction to the cognitional theory of Bernard Lonergan. *Science & Education*, 13(6), 519–40.

Melchin, K. R. & Picard, C. A. (2008). *Transforming Conflict through Insight*. Toronto: University of Toronto Press.

Meynell, H. A. (1998). *Redirecting Philosophy: The Nature of Knowledge from Plato to Lonergan.* Toronto: University of Toronto Press.

O'Neil, J. & Marsick, V. J. (2007). *Understanding Action Learning*. New York: AMACOM.

Perry, D. J. (2004). Self-transcendence: Lonergan's key to integration of nursing theory, research and practice. *Nursing Philosophy*, 5(1), 67–74.

Revans, R. W. (1971). *Developing Effective Managers*. New York: Praeger.

Revans, R. W. (2011). *ABC of Action Learning*. Farnham, UK: Gower.

Roscoe, K. (2004). Lonergan's theory of cognition, constructivism and science education. *Science & Education*, 13(6), 541–51.

Sawa, R. J. (2005). Foundations of interdisciplinarity: A Lonergan perspective. *Medicine, Health Care and Philosophy*, 8(1), 53–61.

Schein, E. H. (2013). *Humble Inquiry: The Gentle Art of Asking before Telling*. San Francisco, CA: Berrett-Koehler.

Scolari, L., Coghlan, D. & Shani, A. B. (2015). Sense-making in collaborative management research: Insights from an Italian social cooperative. In Shani, A. B. & Noumair, D. (Eds.) *Research in Organizational Change and Development* (Vol. 23, pp. 167–94). Bingley, UK: Emerald.

Shani, A. B., Mohrman, S. A., Pasmore, W. A., Stymne, B. & Adler, N. (Eds.). (2008). *Handbook of Collaborative Management Research*. Thousand Oaks, CA: Sage.

Staller, K. (2007). Metalogue as methodology: Inquiries into conversations among authors, editors and referees. *Qualitative Social Work*, 6(2), 137–57.

Tobin, K. & Roth, W. M. (2002). The contradictions in science education peer review and possibilities for change. *Research in Science Education*, 32(2), 269–80.

Zandee, D. (2013). The process of generative inquiry. In Cooperrider, D., Zandee, D., Godwin, L. N. & Avital, M. (Eds.) *Organizational Generativity: The Appreciative Inquiry Summit and a Scholarship of Transformation, Advances in Appreciative Inquiry* (Vol. 4, pp. 69–88). Bingley, UK: Emerald.

4 Who do we identify with?

Ontological and epistemological challenges of spanning different domains of academic–practitioner praxis

Richard P. Nielsen

Who are we primarily trying to serve, a community of academics or a community of practitioners; or, can service to a community of practitioners and a community of academics be moments and dimensions of a single, dialectic process? This chapter:

- explores, with an Aristotelian interpretation, an ontology of academic–practitioner praxis as action that developmentally and ethically changes the actor and the external world (Bernstein, 1971; Eikeland, 2008; Reeve, 2012; Nielsen, 2016).
- considers, again with an Aristotelian interpretation, three epistemological, developmental, and dialectic process moments of praxis:
  - inductive attention to experience based empirical data;
  - interpretative theory based reflective, ethical action; and
  - developmental, ethical practice and theory building.
- offers examples of academics who have worked in this way.
- considers particular challenges of working in this way.

Aristotle's ontology of "praxis"

A frequently quoted summary interpretation of Aristotle's ontology of praxis is Durant's (1926: 87) interpretation of the Aristotelian perspective as "We are what we regularly do." What do we regularly do as professors in our relationships with practitioners and practice?

Bernstein (1971), Eikeland (2008), and Reeve (2012), three of the leading intellectual historians of the idea of "praxis," interpret Aristotelian praxis as intentional and reflective action that developmentally changes both the actor and the external world (Nielsen, 2016). That is, praxis is reflective action that intentionally tries to make the actor a better person and the world a better place. Praxis is ethical intention joined with practical, reflective action and theory building. If there is no ethical intention, then, and according to Bernstein's (1971), Eikeland's (2008), and Reeve's (2012) interpretations of Aristotle, in that moment the action is a lesser *techne*, an application of technical skill, and the actor is acting in that moment as a technician, not as a professional or a "citizen" of a community of academics or of a community of practitioners. In an extended reflective action process, there can be moments of both *techne* and praxis.

This interpretation of the ontology of praxis is very similar to the one expressed by the political philosopher Hannah Arendt in her 1958 book *The Human Condition* and her 1963 book *Eichmann in Jerusalem: A Report on the Banality of Evil* (Nielsen, 2014). In addition, this interpretation of praxis is very similar to and was influential in the praxis work of the organizational learning scholar, Donald Schön, particularly as explained in his 1983 book, *The Reflective Practitioner*.

For Aristotelian praxis, ethical ends do not justify unethical means. This is a key difference between the Aristotelian approach and that of many authoritarian "ends justify the means" political officials, military commanders, organizational managers, academics, and even sports figures whose behavior might be captured by the popularly cited quotation and perhaps exaggerated sentiment of the late football coach Vince Lombardi, who observed that "Winning [effectiveness] is not the most important thing, it is the only thing" (Maraniss, 1999: 184).

From an Aristotelian perspective, there is also an important critical dimension. That is, developmental change requires a qualitatively, critical view of a former status quo relative to a potential better state that is also normatively critical of the previous condition and actions of the actor and the external world.

Eikeland (2008) also interprets Aristotle as recognizing the existence and possibility of collective and even organizational praxis (Nielsen, 2016). That is, there can be internal development within employees or members of an organizational community or a decentralized community of practitioners, where, according to Eikeland's (2008: 87) interpretation, "Praxis is not only individual.... Collective praxis is possible."

Aristotle's developmental, reflective, ethical perspective is different from what might be considered a characteristic modernist and positivist Machiavelli's *Prince*, where Machiavelli analyses the macro effectiveness of different micro means for achieving different ends without considering the ethics or normative values of the ends or the means. Machiavelli is often considered one of the first modernists (Berlin, 1979). In critical contrast, for Aristotle, Durant (1926), Arendt (1958, 1963), Bernstein (1971), Argyris et al. (1985), MacIntyre (1981), Schön (1983), Nielsen (1996, 2014, 2016), Eikeland (2008), Reeve (2012) and many other academic–practitioner praxis scholars and practitioners, ethics, values, ends and means can and should be lived and practiced in developmental relationships.

Aristotle's epistemology of praxis and developmental learning as a three-moment dialectic process

This section considers, again with an Aristotelian interpretation, three moments in a dialectic, developmental process:

- inductive attention to experience-based empirical data and context;
- interpretative theory and situation-based reflective, ethical action; and,
- developmental, ethical practice and theory building.

A moment here is a sequential and developmental part of whole process. It is metaphorically similar to how a whole play or a whole piece of music emerges and is developed where there are three sequential movements that transform in the final act or movement to a successful and qualitatively different third act or third movement and whole play or symphony. The transformed third moment is composed of parts of the previous movements and acts, but is nonetheless qualitatively different and better relative to the circumstances of the first two moments than the sum of the first two parts. Dialectic processes can be at least temporarily unsuccessful in the sense that various combinations need to be experimented with, fail, and be learned from before there can emerge the better transformed play or symphony.

In a successful Aristotelian type of dialectic:

- First, there is an inductive moment of attention by the actor to experience-based empirical data, circumstances and context.
- Second, based on the experience of the data, circumstances, and context in the first movement and then theoretical interpretation of the data in context, the actor takes what the actor hopes is appropriate reflective action in the second moment.
- Third, out of the experience of reflective action in context can emerge creative learning, improved practice, and improved theory building, in the third moment. In the metaphor of the play or symphony, a good final act or movement, a good play or symphony is one that in the final act or movement appropriately resolves the disparate elements in the first two acts and movements.

Not all dialectic processes are successful in the sense of having better practice and theory building emerge, but with continued practice and experimentation, better practice, and theory building can emerge from Aristotelian dialectic processes.

Moment 1: inductive attention to experience based empirical data

For Aristotle, induction is a foundational process. In the *Nicomachean Ethics* (Books 1 and 6) Aristotle observes that:

> For these variable facts are the starting-points for the apprehension of the end, since the universals are reached from the particulars ... Practical wisdom ... involves knowledge of particular facts, which become know from experience; and a young man is not experienced, because experience takes some time to acquire.

As Monan (1968: 71) concludes, for Aristotle, "universal moral knowledge both originates in the singular variety and also is orientated toward evaluations of singular cases of conduct."

Similarly for Argyris et al. (1985), their action learning approach begins with induction. It begins with inductive, experiential data that the actor is very close to. It begins by paying attention to actions/behaviors, the effects of actions, changed actions, and the driving values, interests, and paradigms that guided the initial actions. It does not begin with an academic literature review and search for "gaps in the literature." It is not theory that comes first and is then applied to action. The process begins with experience of actors with actions, effects of actions, changed actions, and the driving variables.

Moment 2: interpretative theory-based reflective, ethical action

With respect to the reflective action moment in Aristotelian praxis, according to Bernstein (1971: 34):

> Theoria … is the articulation of the rationality ingredient in praxis. There is then an ultimate harmony of theory and practice—theoria and praxis—not in the sense that philosophy guides action, but rather in the sense that philosophy is the comprehension of what is; it is the comprehension of the logos ingredient in praxis…. There is an ultimate unity of theory and practice … in its self-reflective form, theoria.

Aristotle offers the following example of the reflective practice moment: "For example, suppose that someone knows [from theory] that light flesh foods are digestible and wholesome, but does not know what kinds are light." The theoretical knowledge is that "light flesh foods are digestible and wholesome." For praxis to be complete, it needs an additional dimension of interpretative, actionable theoretical knowledge, that the chicken Aristotle refers to is a type of light, flesh food. Through induction and theoretical reflection on experience, it is learned that chicken is digestible and wholesome. *Theoria*, theoretical understanding, helps frame the situation with respect to the issue being about choices that have to do with health and the relevance of light, flesh foods, and the particular choices of light fish, chicken vs., for example, heavy pork. Insofar as we frame a situation in a particular way, we can reframe it. Through *theoria* we can inquire about our actions and assumptions and attempt to see things more clearly than before.

Moment 3: developmental, ethical practice, and theory building

Continuing with the Aristotelian example about "light, fresh foods," through further induction and theory-based reflective action with other types of foods such as light fish, a broader theory is developed about light, flesh foods. That is, there is also a theory-building, theory-development moment and dimension in the dialectic, praxis process.

For Aristotle, praxis is foundationally critical and normative. The critical dimension and moment is central to the Aristotelian concept of praxis. Aristotle discussed the ideas of praxis, moral knowledge, and its methodology in the *Protrepticus*, the *Eudemian Ethics*, and the *Nicomachean Ethics*. As referred to above, Aristotle considers praxis as action that developmentally changes both the actor and the external world. That is, praxis is action that makes the actor a better person and the world a better place. This is a foundationally critical concept. Development requires a qualitatively critical understanding of a former status quo relative to a potential better state that is essentially and normatively critical of the previous condition. This developmental next step is critical theory building.

Similarly, Argyris et al. (1985) join their action-learning method with critical theory building. For Argyris, there are two broad types of action-learning, single-loop action learning and double-loop action learning. Single-loop action learning accepts consciously or unconsciously received driving values and theories, and then tries to learn and practice more efficient techniques for achieving and implementing those received driving values and theories. Double-loop action learning critically examines those driving values and theories, holds them open for criticism and change, and tries to learn and practice more effective methods and develop improved and changed theories (Nielsen, 2016).

In contrast, the traditional view of actionable knowledge has taken the form of a narrower, uncritical, instrumental knowledge: the latter is thought to be an instrument to be used at will. Mainstream, modernist, social scientific knowledge is first produced by scholars and, after being proved valid, is then used by practitioners to accomplish ends that might not be critically examined. The context of critical discovery is clearly demarcated from the context of instrumental application. The problem with such a view, however, is that it reduces knowledge to technique. While techniques may be useful, they nonetheless:

a   incorporate ethical and normative values, issues, and assumptions, which may not always be transparent to their user;
b   they deal with specific problems at the expense of aiding their user form a broader understanding of the problem at hand; and
c   the technique is directed at the world, leaving the user intact, unchanged with little or no development (Nielsen, 2016).

An example of an academic who worked in this way

This section of the chapter offers one example of the many academics who more or less work in this way: Adam Curle (1973, 1981, 1986, 1990), an academic who did both transformative practice and transformative theory-building in the area of conflict resolution, psychology, education, and socioeconomic development. His background and work is briefly described. Then, his work is discussed with respect to the three Aristotelian epistemological moments and dimensions of praxis.

Adam Curle was a British academic and social psychologist who worked in the areas of education, socioeconomic development, and later mediation and peace-making, and was one of the key founders of the academic area of peace studies. He served for many years as a professor and researcher at the University of Oxford, the Tavistock Institute of Human Relations, Harvard University, and the University of Ghana. He founded the Harvard University Center for Studies in Education and Development. He worked with practitioners in Pakistan, India, Nigeria, Tunisia, Central America, Barbados, Zimbabwe, South Africa, the United States, Northern Ireland, Sri Lanka, and several Balkan countries. He served as a key mediator in the Pakistan–Indian war and the Nigerian Civil War. Among his many awards was the Gandhi Foundation International Peace Award. He was also nominated for the Nobel Peace Prize.

Inductive attention to experience-based empirical data

In Curle's (1990) autographical and methodological book, *Tools for Transformation: A Personal Study*, he describes his career, his experiences with practitioners, his own practices, and his personal and theory-building transformations. In his early career he was a very successful academic doing more or less traditional academic social science work in the areas of social psychology, education, and socioeconomic development. His research work was structured according to the more or less typical social science research stages of literature review, identification of gaps in the literature, development of literature-based hypotheses, selection of convenient research sites, testing of hypotheses, and discussion of practice implications of his social science theory development.

His traditional and successful academic work gave him the opportunity to work internationally with and learn from education and socioeconomic development practitioners in the field. Because of his excellent academic and personal reputation for getting along with and helping many different types of people solve different types of problems, he was asked to help mediate several socioeconomic development and educational planning conflicts and later very violent war and civil war disputes. He paid great attention to and was even shocked at how much and how intensely the empirical data in the socioeconomic development, education, war situations were so greatly different than what he had previously experienced and what was represented in the socioeconomic development, education, and conflict resolution literature of the time.

Interpretative theory-based, ethical reflective action

Curle found that some of the analytic literature he was familiar with from socioeconomic development, education, and conflict resolution helped him frame what was happening in the conflicts and understand some of the very dysfunctional and viciously destructive behaviors. For example, Curle was very familiar with and appreciated both the insights and power of some of the top-down, macro, central planning literature in the area of socioeconomic development in very poor countries such as Tinbergen and Bos's (1965) *A Planning Model For The Educational Requirements of Economic Development* and Eckaus and Parikh's (1968) *Planning For Growth.*

However, he also found through his experiences with practitioners in the field that this type of analytic, impersonal, top-down, centralized planning literature, which often concentrated on development of large-scale infrastructure projects and natural resources development projects, did not offer much attention to the narrow control of those large-scale resources and projects by centralized ethnic and class elites that often resulted in conflicts and even civil wars and coups over who would receive the large corruption benefits associated with these large-scale projects.

His experiences with field development workers also revealed that these large-scale, centralized planning development literatures were very inadequate for understanding the local conditions and bottom-up participative decision-making that was very important for developing locally appropriate types of change and peaceful change.

Instead, Curle (1973) found that his mediation, education, and socioeconomic development work fit much more appropriately with the personalist, dialogic, and bottom-up perspectives he found in such work as Paulo Friere's (1970) *Pedagogy of the Oppressed*, Albert Hirschman's (1970) *Exit, Voice, and Loyalty: Responses to Decline in Firms, Organizations, and States*, and Mike Yarrow's (1978) *Quaker Experiences in International Conciliation.*

Further, Curle in his private life was familiar with philosophical and spiritual literatures from Quakerism and Buddhism. He reflected on these in conjunction with his reflections on the inadequacies of the central planning-oriented social science development literature amidst the very destructive, vicious, and passionate experiences he witnessed with other practitioners in conflict and war situations. In a sense, he was surprised about how he could still see and feel the humanity and good in many of the leaders and soldiers who were doing very terrible things.

Through reflective practice he was able to partly reframe the top-down, central planning, analytic theoretical interpretations to include compassion and sympathy for not only the victims of terrible violence, but also compassion and sympathy for the perpetrators of the violence who he and other practitioners he was working with could see were being negatively transformed into their worst and like the images of their enemies that they were doing the violence to.

Curle made reflective decisions and took actions to partly step out of his professional, analytic academic behaviors and consciously reveal his sympathy, compassion, and even friendship to both the victims and their adversaries. For example, in his Nigerian Civil War mediation work he would listen very carefully and quietly to the leaders of both sides as they talked about their personal situations, families, friends, and pressures, and then he would discuss these personal examples with the opposing leaders in order to humanize rather than demonize the opposing leaders as well as illustrate each others' struggles, and sometimes similar struggles, to find room for peaceful solutions. Apparently, this genuine and changed personal and theoretical interpretation led to changed reflective action that was noticed and appreciated by adversaries, victims, and perpetrators.

Developmental, ethical practice, and theory-building

Curle considered the types of change that he and many of the practitioners experienced to be not only developmental but even transformational. For example, he transformed his professional, theory-building and practice from sep-arated, discipline-based analysis, to a synthesis approach to theory-building by synthesising: social psychology, education, development, and peace-making; and, more broadly, social science theory with philosophical and even spiritual theory. Curle (1990: 175) explains:

> I choose as examples, the three types of [separate] activity in which I had been engaged throughout my adult life, education, development, peace-making, mostly in the form of mediation. The things that went wrong and those that went more or less right seemed to illustrate some of the chief issues.... In a more generalized sense, however, they all flow together. The specific of one may be the politics and strategy of the battlefield; of another, futurology, the planning office and the economics of poverty; of a third, the classroom or lecture hall. Essentially, however, they are all concerned with human beings, their enslavement to a false reality which may also be a very sick one, and their liberation from it. To the extent that we are liberated we are free from ignorance and the fearful pressures of craving and dislike. Thus we are also more free to make wise decisions, to act with compassion rather than with compulsion, and to establish peaceful relations with others, whether they be "enemies," or students, or indeed anyone we encounter in everyday life.

With respect to his transformation as a person as a result of this type of three-moment Aristotelian dialectic process, Curle transformed from a separated, ana-lytic, academic actor–adviser into a changed self where he thought and felt to be a real part of the communities that he was working within. Curle explains:

> The more we recognize our basic unity with others, the truth that we share, the same ground of being, the more we feel for them as ourselves ... the growth of awareness is inseparable from the growth of compassion for the pain of others [both victims and perpetrators], while compassion for their anguish also serves as a spur to develop the awareness that enables us better to serve them.... This constitutes a sort of prism refracting differently in every case the limitless and unquenchable light of what is universal and eternal, a miracle of diversity within unity.... It is this everlasting essence, non-personal and ego-free yet unique and distinctive, that is the true nature of our being, the ultimate reality of our lives.
>
> (Curle, 1990: 184)

The sociologist Elise Boulding, who along with her husband and economist Kenneth Boulding were also nominated for a Nobel Peace Prize, observed about Curle that:

> Adam knows all the best of textbook mediation, and he has a sound theoretical understanding of the social systems and political, economic and cultural structures within which he must work.... He also has credentials as a professor of education and psychology at prestigious universities on both sides of the Atlantic. As both a practitioner and one of the founders of the academic field of peace studies, he cannot be accused of fuzzy-mindedness or of preferring abstraction to reality. Yet his very sensitivity to the ugliest aspects of human behavior has led him to look past the self-constructed misery of the human race to the underlying problem of undeveloped humanity.... For Adam, the role of mediator is a transforming role both for himself and for those with whom he works. The stilling of the self so as not to impose personal reactions or carry loaded messages as he moves back and forth between two warring camps ... the listening to the other in ways that open channels from mind to mind and heart to heart so new words can get through, this is a mediation that goes beyond what the books tell us.
>
> (Boulding, 1989: 1–2)

Challenges of praxis-based learning and theory-building

There appear to be many very distinguished academics who use various versions of this type of three-moment Aristotelian praxis-based learning and theory-building process who have written about their methods with autobiographical dimensions and who appear to conclude that the benefits far outweigh the difficulties and any challenges or negative factors associated with this approach. Examples of such distinguished academics and their publications with autobiographical, methodological, ontological, and epistemological dimensions include: Donald Schön (1983) and Chris Argyris (2003) in the area or organizational and learning and transformation; Scott Nearing (1972), John Gardner (1981), and William Foote Whyte (1994) in the area of participatory political–economic change; Gene Sharp (1973) and Kenneth Boulding (1989) in the area of developmental peace-making; Robert Greenleaf (1977), Albert Hirschman (1995), and Howard Zinn (1994) in the area of leadership and developmental social change; Michael Walzer (1988) and Edward Said (2003) in the area of social criticism; and Clodovis Boff (1987), Gerard Fourez (1982), Daniel Berrigan (1987), Parker Palmer (1990), Robert Coles (1999), and Douglas Steere (1957) in the area of spiritual philosophy and social change. Perhaps by coincidence, all of the above people also have or had a strong interest in ethical and spiritual philosophy.

While I agree that the benefits far outweigh the challenges, nonetheless, there are challenges and difficulties that need to be overcome and/or navigated. Among the challenges considered are:

- ethical protection of practitioners;
- career issues associated with the artificial separation of ethics and social science, and the devaluation of praxis-based practice and theory-building;
- balancing of service responsibilities to a community of scholars and a community of practitioners; and,
- communicative problems with expressing the ethical idea and practice of service as acts of friendship and even love in separated ethics and social science environments.

Ethical protection of practitioners

There are academic–practitioner, research–practice areas where practitioners can be very vulnerable to severe retaliations and their anonymity and/or identities need to be protected. For example, this is particularly the case in such areas as corruption reform, conflict resolution in war situations, and even in more or less "normal" wrongdoing cases as are frequent in such industries as the military–intelligence–industrial complex, natural resources industries, pharmaceutical industries, and financial institutions (Palmer, 2012; Palys & Lowman, 2012; Nielsen, Balachandra & Nielsen, 2013).

For example, practitioners can sometimes be simultaneously reformers and participants in unethical, illegal, and even war crimes activities. Among the reasons practitioners can be working with academics in such areas are combinations of an opportunity to think through a problem and potential solutions with an academic outsider to the organization or sector or country the practitioner is working within, seeking help with whistle-blowing through the academic, and a sincere belief that one cannot survive in the practitioner's area of practice without sometimes cooperating with the unethical, illegal, and even war crimes being committed by their organizations with their knowledge and sometimes even help in implementation.

The situation can be further complicated in situations and sectors and countries where the unethical and illegal activities are normal and a condition of employment and can then be used selectively in prosecutions against reformers and political opponents. That is, ethics is used as an excuse to eliminate reformers rather than a real concern for ethics. This is where academics need to be very careful in not exposing reformers.

The situation can be even further complicated when researchers and academic institutions make incorrect promises to practitioners about the ability and willingness of the researcher and/or the institution to legally and politically withstand selective prosecution and retaliation against participant practitioners who have both cooperated with the illegal activities and are cooperating with the researchers and academic institutions (Palys & Lowman, 2012). Ethics and law can conflict. Laws can be unethical. Administration and enforcement of ethics and law can be selective, political, and corrupt.

Career issues associated with artificial separation of ethics and social science, and the devaluation of praxis-based practice and theory-building

As referred to above, from an Aristotelian perspective, there can be no praxis without an ethical moment or dimension. That is, praxis without an ethical moment is *techne*, not praxis. Nonetheless, many social scientists appear to believe that, in their professional, academic lives, one can and should separate science from normative ethics. In a related problem, many social scientists, even in professional schools, appear to believe that the highest order of academic work is theory for theory's sake or academic literature-based theory–practice research and devalue practice–based theory–building. This can discourage both PhD students and pre-tenure junior faculty from pursuing academic praxis-type work.

George Elliot's observation that "It is never too late for what might have been," is often true, but it is not always the case. That is, for academic career advancement reasons, one can delay and delay the development of praxis-type work long enough, that one in a sense forgets about and/or gives up on the transformation to praxis. On the other hand, and as George Elliot observed, it is never too late. For example, some academics, such as Adam Curle, did most of their praxis-type work after their theory-for-theory's-sake career had been well established.

With respect to the science–ethics separation issue, a complete separation of ethics from praxis is also inconsistent with the foundations of social science theory–building (Nielsen & Massa, 2013). For example, Weber (1949) articulates and explains clearly in his *The Methodology of the Social Sciences* that value-free social science is both impossible and undesirable. Similarly, Veblen (1919) argued that a total separation was not appropriate and suggested that social scientists who claimed that they were separating ethics and science were instead obscuring their own normative biases.

The key here is whether there is total separation or there is a moment of "science" and a moment or dimension of "ethics" in a larger process. A holistic process might include different moments performed by the same person and/or even different people in a collective, cooperative academic–practitioner praxis community where some do only the science part, some do only the ethics part, and others combine the ethics and science moments. In this sense, there may even be collective praxis as well as individual praxis (Eikeland, 2008).

Balancing service responsibilities to communities of scholars and practitioners

Both university life and praxis work in the field can be so intrinsically satisfying and/or urgent that academics who do praxis work can fail to adequately balance their responsibilities to their academic community and/or their practitioner community. For example, sometimes when the academic becomes genuine friends with academic colleagues and practitioners and either the practitioners or the academics are in need and/or the timing of the work is so interesting or opportunity/problem so important, it can be very hard to temporarily withdraw from one in order to fulfill one's responsibilities to the other.

This issue is somewhat similar to the issue of work–family balance where one needs to but sometimes fails to balance one's responsibilities to family and work colleagues. In such situations, good communication with colleagues and friends, self-discipline, and make-up behaviors can be very important. It is also possible to get so involved with one or the other communities that one loses one's way. That is, one can get so busy with the practice side that one neglects to do the theory-building side and the reverse. Sometimes, it is also possible to become so burned out and exhausted that one is unable to fulfill one's responsibilities and desires to serve both communities and, derivatively, oneself.

Communicative problems with expressing the ethical idea and practice of service as acts of friendship and even love in separated ethics and social science environments

One of the key motivations and/or results of praxis-type service to communities of scholars and practitioners is the idea and practice of friendship and love in the sense of trying to help others, to be of service to others, to give of oneself to others because of friendship and love. This is key to the ethics dimension of praxis. If it is hard to adequately communicate the idea that ethics and science can and often should be synthesized, it can be even harder to adequately communicate to one's colleagues and friends in academic and practitioner communities that one is receiving and giving friendship and love and that it is a foundational aspect of the idea and practice of service.

In the ancient Greek language, a distinction was made between the ideas and words of sympathy and empathy that can be interpreted in reverse in modern English. In ancient Greek, the idea and word of empathy referred to more or less pure emotion, which was considered problematical. The idea and word of sympathy referred to combined reason with feeling, particularly the feeling of friendship and love, which was considered very important for genuine praxis (Reeve, 2012; Nielsen, 2016).

One could feel both friendship and love in service to both communities of academics and communities of practitioners, but either be unable to adequately express those feelings and/or be worried about appearing too sentimental and inadequately professional by so expressing those sentiments and sympathies. That is, since some social scientists believe that normative and feelings issues should be separated from scientific pursuits, academics who do reveal motivations of friendship and love might be reluctant to reveal such motivations because the more or less pure scientists might consider them too sentimental or unprofessional. However, since friendship and love are key foundations for both one's motivation and one's effectiveness and development, then it needs to be well expressed and communicated.

Conclusion

A frequently quoted and common interpretation of Aristotelian ontology is that "We are what we normally do" (Durant, 1926: 87). Who are we primarily trying to serve, a community of academics or a community of practitioners? From an Aristotelian ontological and epistemological perspective, can service to both a community of practitioners and a community of academics be moments and dimensions of a single, dialectic process? Bernstein (1971), Eikeland (2008), and Reeve (2012), three of the leading intellectual historians of the idea of "praxis," interpret Aristotelian praxis as intentional and reflective action that developmentally changes both the actor and the external world. That is, praxis is reflective action that intentionally tries to make the actor a better person and the world a better place. Praxis is ethical intention joined with practical, reflective action and theory-building. If there is no ethical intention, then, and according to Bernstein's (1971), Eikeland's (2008), and Reeve's (2012) interpretation of Aristotle, in that moment the action is a lesser *techne*, an application of technical skill, and the actor is acting in that moment as a technician, not as a professional or a "citizen" of a community of academics or of a community of practitioners. In an extended reflective action process, there can be moments of both *techne* and praxis.

Further, Aristotle's epistemology of praxis and developmental learning contains three moments or dimensions in a dialectic, developmental process:

- inductive attention to experience-based empirical data;
- interpretative theory-based reflective, ethical action; and
- developmental, ethical practice and theory-building.

A holistic process might include different moments performed by the same person over time and/or even different people in a collective, cooperative academic–practitioner praxis community where:

- some do only the inductive, empirical attention part;
- some do only the reflective ethical practice part;
- some do only the transformational practice and theory-building parts; and
- others combine all three moments.

In this sense, there may even be collective praxis as well as individual praxis. However, this type of collective praxis community appears to be relatively rare (Eikeland, 2008). Individual academic–practitioner praxis appears to be more common. In the example of Curle's individual and collective practice and theory-building transformational work, he appears to have done and experienced both individual and collective academic–practitioner praxis.

There are several challenges to working in this way including:

- ethical protection of practitioners;
- career issues associated with the artificial separation of ethics and social science, and devaluation of praxis-based practice and theory-building;

- balancing difficulties of service responsibilities to a community of scholars and a community of practitioners; and
- communicative problems with expressing the ethical idea and practice of service as acts of friendship and even love in separated ethics and social science environments.

There appear to be many very distinguished academics who use various versions of this type of three-moment Aristotelian academic–practitioner praxis-based learning and theory-building process in many different fields who appear to conclude that the benefits far outweigh the difficulties and any challenges or negative factors associated with this approach.

References

Arendt, H. (1958). *The Human Condition*. New York: Viking Press.

Arendt, H. (1963). *Eichmann in Jerusalem: A Report on the Banality of Evil*. New York: Viking Press.

Argyris, C. (2003). A life full of learning. *Organization Studies*, 24(7), 1178–92.

Argyris, C., Putnam, R. & Smith, D. L. (1985). *Action Science: Concepts, Methods, and Skills for Research and Intervention*. San Francisco, CA: Jossey-Bass.

Berlin, I. (1979). *Against the Current: Essays in the History of Ideas*. New York: Penguin Press.

Bernstein, R. J. (1971). *Praxis and Action: Contemporary Philosophies of Human Activity*. Philadelphia, PA: University of Pennsylvania Press.

Berrigan, D. (1987). *To Dwell in Peace: An Autobiography*. San Francisco, CA: Harper and Row.

Boff, C. (1987). *Theology and Praxis: Epistemological Foundations*. New York: Orbis Books.

Boulding, K. (1989). *Three Faces of Power*. New Bury Park, CA: Sage Publications.

Coles, R. (1999). *The Secular Mind: Now and Ahead*. Princeton, NJ: Princeton University Press.

Curle, A. (1973). *Education for Liberation*. London: Tavistock Publications.

Curle, A. (1981). *True Justice: Quaker Peace Makers and Peace Making* (Vol. 1981). Quaker Home Service.

Curle, A. (1986). *In the Middle: Nonofficial Mediation in Violent Situations*. Leamington Spa, UK: Berg Publishing Ltd.

Curle, A. (1990). *Tools for Transformation: A Personal Study*. Stroud, UK: Hawthorn Press.

Durant, W. (1926). *The Story of Philosophy: The Life and Opinions of the Greater Philosophers*. New York: Simon & Schuster.

Eckaus, R. S. & Parikh, K. S. (1968). *Planning for Growth: Multi-sectoral, Intertemporal Models Applied to India*. Cambridge, MA: MIT Press.

Eikeland, O. (2008). *The Ways of Aristotle: Aristotelian Phronesis, Aristotelian Philosophy of Dialogue and Action Research*. Bern: Peter Lang.

Fourez, G. (1982). *Liberation Ethics*. Philadelphia, PA: Temple University Press.

Friere, P. (1970). *Pedagogy of the Oppressed*. New York: Herder and Herder.

Hirschman, A. O. (1970). *Exit, Voice, and Loyalty: Responses to Decline in Firms, Organizations, and States*. Boston, MA: Harvard University Press.

Hirschman, A. O. (1995). *A Propensity to Self-Subversion*. Boston, MA: Harvard University Press.

Gardner, J. (1981). *Self-Renewal*. New York: Norton.

Greenleaf, R. K. (1977). *Servant Leadership*. New York: Paulist Press.

MacIntyre, A. (1981). *After Virtue*. London: Gerald Duckworth & Co.

Maraniss, D. (1999). *When Pride Still Mattered: A Life of Vincent Lombardi*. New York: Simon & Schuster.

Monan, J. D. (1968). *Moral Knowledge and its Methodology in Aristotle*. Oxford: Oxford University Press.

Nearing, Scott (1972). *The Making of a Radical*. New York: Harper and Row.

Nielsen, R. P. (1996). *The Politics of Ethics*. Oxford: Oxford University Press.

Nielsen, R. P. (2014). Hannah Arendt. In Helin, J., Hernes, T., Hjorth, D. & Holt, R. (Eds.) *The Oxford Handbook of Process Philosophy and Organization Studies*. Oxford: Oxford University Press.

Nielsen, R. P. (2016). Action-research as ethics praxis method. *Journal of Business Ethics*, 135(3), 419–28.

Nielsen, R. P. & Massa, F. G. (2013). Reintegrating ethics and institutional theory. *Journal of Business Ethics*, 115(1), 135–47.

Nielsen, R. P., Balachandra, L. & Nielsen, A. (2013). Whistle-blowing methods for navigating within and helping reform regulatory institutions. *Journal of Business Ethics*, 112(3), 385–95.

Palmer, P. J. (1990). *The Active Life: A Spirituality of Work, Creativity, and Caring*. New York: Harper and Row.

Palmer, D. (2012). *Normal Organizational Wrongdoing: A Critical Analysis of Theories of Misconduct in and by Organizations*. Oxford: Oxford University Press.

Palys, T. & Lowman, J. (2012). Defending research confidentiality to the extent the law allows: Lessons from the Boston College subpoenas. *Journal of Academic Ethics*, 10(4), 271–97.

Reeve, C. D. C. (2012). *Action, Contemplation, and Happiness: An Essay on Aristotle*. Cambridge, MA: Harvard University Press.

Said, E. W. (2003). *Humanism and Democratic Criticism*. New York: Columbia University Press.

Schön, D. (1983). *The Reflective Practitioner: How Professionals Think in Action*. New York: Basic Books.

Sharp, G. (1973). *The Politics of Nonviolent Action*. Boston, MA: P. Sargent.

Steere, D. V. (1957). *Work and Contemplation*. New York: Harper and Brothers.

Tinbergen, J. & Bos, H. C. (1965). A planning model for the educational requirements of economic development. *Organisation for Economic Co-operation and Development*.

Veblen, T. (1919). *Place of Science in Modern Civilization*. New York: Huebsch.

Walzer, M. (1988). *The Company of Critics*. New York: Basic Books.

Weber, M. (1949). *On the Methodology of the Social Sciences*. New York: Free Press.

Whyte, W. F. (1994). *Participant Observer: An Autobiography*. New York: ILR Press.

Yarrow, C. H. M. (1978). *Quaker Experiences in International Conciliation*. New Haven, CT: Yale University Press.

Zinn, H. (1994). *You Can't Be Neutral on a Moving Train*. Boston, MA: Beacon Press.

5 Connecting—making social science matter

The collaborative and boundary-spanning work of intellectual shamans

Sandra Waddock

This chapter focuses on three ways scholars called "intellectual shamans" (Waddock, 2015) connect across boundaries to inform, learn from, or engage with practice, in the context of research settings and with other researchers and students. Their approaches suggest the range of possibilities available for such collaborative interactions, as well as highlighting issues and obstacles along the way. Below I use interviews conducted with these scholars and, sometimes, their written work, to observe the ways in which these intellectual shamans work in the context of boundary-spanning efforts.

Shaman and intellectual shaman

The shaman is the healer in traditional cultures, often known as medicine man or woman. In interviewing 28 leading management scholars across a variety of sub-disciplines, I concluded that there are scholars who are what I termed *intellectual* shamans. Intellectual shamans are healers, connectors, and sense-makers who use their scholarship in the service of a better world (Waddock, 2015; cf. Egri & Frost 1991; Frost & Egri, 1994). They also "become fully who they must be" by following their passion for work that matters. As *intellectual* shamans, they perform these functions through intellectual work of research, teaching, consulting, and writing. Further, through their work and lives, these individuals move towards wisdom, defined as the integration of moral imagination, systems understanding, and aesthetic sensibility in the service of the greater good or a better world (Waddock, 2010, 2014). This chapter focuses particularly on "connecting" across research, teaching, and practice boundaries, although linkages to healing and sense-making roles of the shaman are also made.

The three roles of the shaman—healing, connecting, and sense-making—need further explication, as does the idea of the shaman. Shamans can be found in virtually all cultures and geographies. Indeed, shamanism is often said to be the world's oldest spiritual tradition (Eliade, 1964). Shamanism is not a religion, but rather a set of traditions that typically involve "knowing" or insight that derives from realms beyond everyday experience. Shamanism does have spiritual overtones in that the "connecting" which traditional shamans do involves traveling spiritually (journeying) to spiritual realms to gather information, I would suggest, from what Jung called the collective unconscious. Shamans then bring the information back for healing and sense-making purposes in their communities and with individual patients.

More positivist approaches to management research are associated with a scientific orientation. Typically, "knowing" in the positivist sense is found within singular disciplinary and even relatively narrow sub-disciplinary streams. Most such knowing is conceptual, theoretical, and empirical. In journal articles management scholars are increasingly asked to engage with specific "conversations" that limit the boundaries of their thinking and empirical work. Yet there are some scholars who bring into their work insights that transcend narrowly focused sets of ideas, research, or impacts, in effect crossing boundaries as shamans do. For intellectual shamans, these boundaries tend to be inter-, multi-, or trans-disciplinary, between theory and practice, or teaching–research. Sometimes such boundary-spanning scholars as sense-makers "translate" their work for the general public to understand.

Many of us recognize the value that individuals who draw from a variety of sources and resources, tapping across disciplinary and functional lines, working directly with practitioners, or in other ways connecting across multiple boundaries can bring to understanding and insight about organizational scholarship. Such individuals often have what former Academy of Management president Jim Walsh describes as an inner "light." This light draws us to these individuals and opens us to what they know, however they have come to know it. These scholars often develop interesting insights by connecting ideas across disciplinary boundaries, creating new approaches, theories, and practices that link across organizational, sector, and functional lines. Sometimes they bridge between scholarship and practice in unusually deep ways, or find creative new ways to engage, learn, and produce scholarship.

There are many such scholars—intellectual shamans are certainly not limited to the 28 management scholars I happened to interview (see, e.g., Nielsen, Chapter 4, for other examples, and MacLean and MacIntosh, Chapter 9, for a story that illustrates how intellectual shamans function in practice). Many scholars work across a range of boundaries attempting to gain new insights and understanding, shed light on practice, forward their ideas as public intellectuals, consultants, or writers, or in a variety of others ways. These people tend to ask big questions, think holistically, and attempt work that has some inherent element of healing—or making the world, sometimes of ideas, sometimes of practice, and sometimes in other ways, a better place.

Healer

The shaman is fundamentally a healer. According to Kahili King (2009), and relevant to the idea of collaboration across academic–practice boundaries at the core of this book, the shaman is a healer of relationships of all sorts—to self, other, community, the world. Often traditional shamans do their healing work on individual patients working with the community's mythology. Shamans believe that healing a broken or problematic cultural mythology will help to heal the patient (Dow, 1986). Similarly, intellectual shamans work on broken mythologies (theories, ideas, practices, memes) that guide our world, finding new ways to make sense of them, often connecting new insights to those mythologies and reshaping them. For example, intellectual shamans might try to heal the theories that guide many businesses, as Sumantra Ghoshal (2005) did, in arguing that "bad management theories are destroying good management practices."

Connector

The second function of the shaman and primary focus of this chapter is connecting. Connecting means crossing boundaries to bring back relevant ideas, insights, and information to be used in the healing process. Egri and Frost (Egri & Frost, 1991; Frost & Egri, 1994) call this function "mediating realities." For traditional shamans these boundaries go from ordinary reality to spiritual realms. Today's shaman, particularly the intellectual shaman doing collaborative work, crosses boundaries that include disciplinary, research–practice, teaching–research, artistic–intellectual, and researcher–leader/community member boundaries, among others. Connecting helps the intellectual shaman "see" in new ways, because in connecting across boundaries, different perspectives can be brought to bear on an issue, situation, theory, or idea that can foster new insights, ideas, theories, and ways of seeing the world.

Sense-maker

The third function of the intellectual shaman is what Weick (Weick, 1995; Weick, Sutcliffe & Obstfeld, 2005) terms sense-making, and what Frost and Egri (Egri & Frost, 1991; Frost & Egri, 1994), who also use the sense-making term, note is a form of spiritual leadership. As Krippner (2002) notes, shamans deconstruct reality as it has been known and reconstruct it in new ways through the sense-making role, helping others make sense of their world, i.e., create meaning. In this sense, shamans are often seen as prophets (Egri & Frost, 1991), because they sense or see things, i.e., make new connections, before others do. Further, in their sense-making capacity and as storytellers, intellectual shamans share what they have learned, in that same process cultivating wisdom (see Walsh, 1989). Of course, not all prophets and sense-makers are accurate and many like the mythical Cassandra have trouble being heard. Nonetheless, the sense-making role is vitally important to the intellectual shaman, whose responsibility is to heal whatever broken cultural mythology she or he observes and researches, and that needs to be done via a sense-making—or meaning-making—process.

Shaman as intellectual

I would like to put forward the proposition that there is a role for the shaman as intellectual in the management academy which has not previously been recognized. In a context of academic–practitioner research partnerships, exploring the connecting role in more depth seems particularly a propos. I would also argue that many more of us can and should step into this role, because the world is troubled and much healing is needed. Obviously, the traditional idea of the shaman as medicine man or woman is less relevant in the modern context than in indigenous settings, so translation is needed. The idea of the shaman as healer, connector, and sense-maker in the service of a better world, however, is vitally important to making our world a better place. The notion of an intellectual shaman in the context of today's problems suggests a role for scholars to engage with practice, theories, ideas, and insights in ways that go beyond narrow empiricism and disciplinary focus, connecting across realms that are typically not bridged. Shamans in this sense are both connectors and meaning- or sense-makers.

Connecting and collaboration

Below I focus on three particular ways of connecting:

- linking theory and practice across boundaries;
- developing new memes, insights, and ideas that transcend traditional academic–practitioner boundaries; and
- explicitly researching and collaborating across boundaries.

To illustrate these different ways of "connecting," I use the work of some of the intellectual shamans interviewed. (Note: where quotes are not cited, they come from personal interviews conducted for intellectual shamans though not used in the book).

Linking theory and practice

Creating networks that engage both academics and practitioners (Tima Bansal), and developing methodologies that bring a wide range of stakeholders together (David Cooperrider and Otto Scharmer) are two approaches to connecting.

Networks

Fostering greater interaction between academics and practitioners by creating networks that bring these groups together can play a crucial "translation" role in making academic work accessible, as well as providing practitioner insights to scholarship. A notable initiative is the Network for Business Sustainability (NBS), where Western University's Tima Bansal is Executive Director. Bansal is also J. Allyn Taylor/Arthur H. Mingay Chair in Business Administration, and Canada Research Chair in Business Sustainability at the Ivey Business School, Canada. Bansal notes in reflecting on the work of the NBS:

> It is an article of faith that management research intends to inform practice. In reality, however, it is an open secret that most of what most management researchers do utterly fails to resonate with management practice (Bansal, Bertels, Ewart, MacConnachie & O'Brien, 2012: 73). NBS is an academic–practitioner network that focuses on fostering greater sustainability in businesses through research and synthesis of ideas. Bansal argues that three connecting roles enhance the potential of such a network for creating important linkages: convening, facilitating, and supporting (or translating the research).
>
> (Bansal et al., 2012: 89)

Bansal draws important lessons from these interactions, noting that neat research and engagement protocols often do not reflect the messy reality of on-the-ground interactions among scholars and practitioners notes (Bansal et al., 2012: 79). Practitioners tend to be interested in the "authority" of researchers more than their ideas or what they are finding, preferring the experiences of other practitioners to the more arid treatises of scholars. Models and frameworks need to be tractable and easily understood for busy practitioners to engage with them. Nor do practitioners necessarily care about academic rigor, though it is only within the context of rigorous analyses that Bansal believes research "challenges what might be taken for granted" (Bansal et al., 2012: 79).

Bansal states unequivocally that the linkage to practitioners is crucial to getting academic ideas into practice. She forwards this idea by "inviting people into our own constellation as a friendly face, as opposed to an angry or whatever, an outsider. I think we have to be insiders." Deliberately positioning NBS as "intended to break down the silos that have been erected," Bansal recognizes that everyone cares about the state of the world and, for NBS, the issue of sustainability. Thus, NBS is in part about creating a safe space where everyone's voice can be heard, academic and practitioner alike, becoming what she characterizes as a "space to collaborate."

The main idea, according to Bansal, is "to put the language of research into the language of practice, so that we can inform practice. It's about time to have the barriers that have built up across industries, functions, across sectors, broken down." NBS deliberately uses research translations as a medium for facilitating the breaking down of those silos. The key, of course, is that the research has the "authority" that is needed for it to maintain its credibility with other scholars, i.e., that its status as objective, valid, and reliable is not questioned, while having the tractability (and translation) to be accessible to practicing managers.

Interactive multi-stakeholder engagement strategies

Another approach to connecting is developing methodologies that bring a variety of stakeholders together in interactive forums, where they can share ideas and learn from each other. Two notable examples of such multi-stakeholder engagement strategies are Appreciative Inquiry (AI), developed by Case Western Reserve's David Cooperrider (Cooperrider & Srivastava, 1987; Cooperrider & Whitney, 2005), and Theory U, developed by MIT's Otto Scharmer (Scharmer, 2009, 2013).

Both AI and Theory U bring wide ranges of stakeholders into forums where they can engage on issues that are important to them; both take a positive approach that builds on what is already good in a system, i.e., taking into account where positive deviants are (Cameron & Dutton, 2003; Spreitzer & Sonenschein, 2004; also, Sternin & Choo, 2000), and building on them rather than where the problems are. Cooperrider and Whitney (2005) assert that AI is a co-evolutionary process of engagement that seeks out what is best in people, enterprises, or situations, i.e., as Cooperrider terms it "what gives 'life' to a living system."

Arising out of a belief that there are "no limits to human cooperation," AI processes deliberately builds on interactions among a variety of people who bring very different perspectives to a situation. Cooperrider comments explicitly on this approach, stating:

> For example, one of the applications of appreciative inquiry is to say it's not just us, as a theorist, who should be doing the theorizing. That in a participatory theory building, we should be lifting up new theory with the groups that we're working with. That they are building theory alongside of us or vice versa.... It's taking it a step further and asking the people of the system to not just be using new behavioral sciences to improve their system but to help build theory together. I call it corporate theory, corporate meaning the whole body corporate or cooperative theory building.

Toward these ends, Cooperrider uses a large-scale AI Summit, which brings from 500 to as many as 8,000 people together in a:

> grounded theory building process, where we're lifting up the DNA of what gives life to that living system, and using that to dream and design and imagine propositions and prototypes for the future. So it's really a form of cooperative theory building, collaborative theory building.
>
> (Ludema, Whitney, Mohr & Griffin, 2003)

Cooperrider evolved his thinking on AI into a global initiative called Business as an Agent of World Benefit, which uses both AI and positive approaches to position businesses as:

> a force for peace in high conflict zones, ... as a force for eradicating extreme poverty, ... as a force for eco-innovation. Where is it happening? What does

it look like? What are the enablers? And what are the ecosystems that help unleash the strengths of business and the service of a global agenda?

Similarly, Otto Scharmer's Theory U (following Friedrich Glasl and Dirk Lemson's initial framing in 1968 in the Netherlands) integrates a variety of earlier approaches to change, synthesizing innovation and change leadership around systems thinking, by adding the perspective of consciousness. As Scharmer noted:

> [Theory U] integrates earlier approaches, but also adds something. In particular, [Theory U] gives permission to some academics, but particularly also practitioners, to bring in the deeper dimension or the most subtle dimension of our experience into the conversation. Make it a legitimate part. So that's sometimes referred to as consciousness. It's sometimes referred to as awareness. It's sometimes referred to as spirituality. What I mean with spirituality is really our sources of creativity. It's kind of the source dimension. It's kind of where we are drawing from when we do our best work. So that's a dimension that's always there, but usually not intended. So what the framework of Theory-U and Presencing does is gives us a framework and a language that helps us to become more aware of that and to make it more part of our regular conversation.

For Scharmer, that conversation takes place between academics and people acting in the "real" world.

The Presencing Institute, which Scharmer founded, connects "a community of practitioners, social technologies, and capacity-building programs, as well as learning from what happens within the Institute." The goal, for Scharmer, as for many of the intellectual shamans interviewed, is to effect positive changes in the world. He explicitly states:

> To my surprise over the years, what has happened is that this type of work connected with other communities, has been seeing a global ecology of innovation platforms and initiatives that I find absolutely amazing. I'm not interested, really, in a new academic framework. I'm not interested in just another article or book. I'm really interested, at the end of the day, in impact. And impact means you're part of a movement. I always felt part of a movement, where as a generation of change makers in this century, we actually rise to the occasion and help transform our institutions of business, government, civil society, and education to a new and better way of operating that connects with a deeper level of humanity and awareness that we all can operate from.

Like Bansal's NBS, the Presencing Institute is organized as a network. Indeed, there are no employees, but rather a network that brings together practitioners with academics around specific projects and collaborations. Its presence is global, with the end goal of creating what Scharmer calls a U-School, to:

apply a consciousness-based framework onto the transformation of society, business, and self. [This] results in participation in real world prototypes, where you explore the future by activating and realizing your entrepreneurial potential, and where you collaborate and help some of these seed initiatives of how business or how collaboration across boundaries can look, … and allow them to come into being.

Notice, however, that Scharmer is "connecting" not only across sector boundaries and between theory and practice, but also, as Cooperrider is doing as well, with deeper levels of consciousness. This type of connecting is in a sense deeply aligned with the spiritual work of traditional shamans, who connect across spiritual realms (realms of meaning and insight) to gather information and bring it back to the day-to-day realm for healing purposes.

Thinking across boundaries: memes that resonate and shift thinking

Another way that academics transcend the theory–practice boundary and "connect" with others, particularly in their roles as public intellectuals, is create new memes that resonate broadly across academic boundaries as well as with others who are not academics. Memes are basic units of culture, cultural equivalents to genes (Dawkins, 1976). Memes, that is, are the ideas, concepts, phrases, images, and symbols that allow us to identify something (Blackmore, 2000). Memes shape how we see the world and, hence, our theories, research frameworks, values, belief systems, ideologies, and perspectives, not to mention actions, because they are what we pay attention to. Memes both enhance the breadth of our perspectives and, sometimes, limit those perspectives. Theories are constructed of what Blackmore (2000) calls "memeplexes," sets of memes that cohere into some sort of sensible narrative or "story."

The idea of the meme comes from evolutionary biologist Richard Dawkins (1976), who was searching for a cultural equivalent to the construct of the gene. Genes transmit biological information from one generation to the next, usually reasonably accurately, albeit with some modifications as time and life go on. Memes, as core cultural artifacts, do much the same in cultures, when they resonate broadly within a given context. Indeed, the word meme, truncated from "mimeme," is meant to suggest this replication process. Successful memes cross a number of boundaries and enable new conversations to emerge that shed light on what is going on.

Consider, for example, the current economic paradigm, with its oft-stated meme that "the purpose of business is to maximize shareholder wealth." The ideas of shareholder primacy embedded in this meme, as well as the narrowing of purpose in business to maximization of profits, are analogous to religious beliefs among many economists and business people of believers in what Richard Norgaard has called the "church of economism" (Norgaard, 2015). Alternative memes that resonate—and pass from one individual or group to the others—are needed to effect significant change (Waddock, 2015) that might head the planetary (and local) economic system towards sustainability.

Scholars who can create successful memes are implicitly and sometimes explicitly reaching across traditional boundaries and collaborating with others to generate new ideas and replicate them across a variety of contexts. R. Edward Freeman, of the University of Virginia, often noted as the "father of stakeholder theory," has frequently stated that business needs to shift away from the "economistic" paradigm promulgated by neoclassical economics (Pirson & Lawrence, 2010; Norgaard, 2015) towards a new narrative based in pragmatism by focusing on stakeholders instead of just shareholders (Freeman, Harrison, Wicks Parmar & De Colle, 2010). Freeman offers a different narrative for businesses, premised on shifting to stakeholders from shareholders as businesses' primary constituency, and in doing so has promulgated a successful new meme. By articulating the idea that businesses have responsibilities to a wide variety of stakeholders, who actually constitute and ensure the success of the business in a mutually engaged and interactive way, Freeman uses this new meme to recast an important economic narrative (Freeman, 1984; Freeman, Martin & Parmar, 2007). At this writing, Google shows more than 41 million "hits" for the term stakeholder compared to nearly 53 million for "shareholder," a much older meme deeply embedded in the dominant economistic narrative. Successful memes, like the notion of stakeholders, replicate across a wide range of settings and contexts with similar, albeit probably not exactly the same, meanings and understanding among different, ahem..., stakeholders.

Another relatively new meme is that of sustainability, a term that was coined as "sustainable development" in 1987 by the Brundtland Commission (Brundtland, 1987). Although sustainability is a term that has numerous different meanings to different stakeholders (Steckler, 2014), there is little doubt that the term has gained widespread visibility and acceptance globally (Google delivers more than 114 million "hits" on the term at this writing). In the business school context, scholars like Stuart Hart (now at the University of Vermont, previously Michigan and Cornell), Andrew Hoffman (Michigan), Paul Shrivastava (previously Concordia, now CEO of Future Earth), and Tima Bansal, among others, have worked tirelessly to promote the idea of sustainability. All initially encountered skepticism from colleagues around their sustainability orientation, and a sense that to speak about sustainability in its core meaning as ecological sustainability in a business context was nothing less than career suicide.

These intellectual shamans early on recognized the importance of putting forward the relatively new meme of sustainability in ways that businesses could understand. Successful memes like sustainability transcend numerous boundaries, particularly between theory and practice. Stuart Hart, for example, wrote a piece for the *Harvard Business Review* called "Beyond Greening: Strategies for a Sustainable World" (Hart, 1997) that served as a bridge for his sustainability work to the world of practice. As Hart recalls:

> I had written several other things that were more academic, but that one piece ... had more impact than everything else I had done in my entire

career up to that point by a factor of ten.... Suddenly, companies were interested.... That really convinced me that [writing that transcends the theory–practice boundary] was a really important piece of this puzzle, and just doing academic publishing is ridiculous, ... especially if our role is to have some impact.

Note that what Hart had done with this piece, and with his 2002 co-authored paper with the late C. K. Prahalad (Michigan), "The Fortune at the Bottom of the Pyramid" (Hart & Prahalad, 2002) is to help popularize two new memes, "sustainability" and "bottom of the pyramid," a meme that took off with publication of the article and Prahalad's 2006 book by that title (26 million Google hits). Similar meme development has happened with Andrew Hoffman's work with MIT's John Ehrenfeld on Flourishing and the work of Jane Dutton, Robert Quinn, and Kim Cameron (among others now) on positive organizational scholarship, following Martin Seligman's construct and new meme of positive psychology (e.g., Seligman & Csikszentmihalyi, 2000) (more than 25 million Google hits).

Part of the problem for scholar–practitioner collaborations and interactions is the so-called jingle and jangle problem (Block, 1995, citing Thorndike, 1904, and Kelly, 1927; see also Stephanie Bertel's reflections in Bansal et al., 2012: 80–82). The [jingle] problem is that of using the same word in different ways—a problem that the term sustainability suffers from. The [jangle] problem means that different words are used to mean the same thing. Even successful memes like sustainability sometimes suffer from the jingle/jangle problem (Bansal et al., 2012; also Steckler, 2014). Since the role of the new memes is to transcend old boundaries, however, sometimes a bit of confusion about meaning is needed before people with varying perspectives can come to agreement. In this regard, intellectual shamans play vital parts in fostering new language that has the potential to reshape ideas, thinking, theories, insights, and, ultimately, practices and actions.

Researching and collaborating across boundaries

The third way that intellectual shamans connect is by explicitly collaborating and researching across boundaries. One approach is through what Van de Ven and Johnson (2006) called engaged scholarship, which has been going on for years under other rubrics (or memes). Another is engaging people in a co-evolutionary process of idea and action development.

Engaged scholarship as collaborative practice

Van de Ven and Johnson (2006) encouraged scholars to undertake what they termed "engaged scholarship." They defined it as a "collaborative form of inquiry in which academics and practitioners leverage their different perspectives and competencies to coproduce knowledge about a complex problem or phenomenon that exists under conditions of uncertainty found in the world" (Van de Ven & Johnson, 2006: 803). Such scholarship focuses on the interaction between scholars and practicing managers, leaders, or organizational participants rather than simply among a group of researchers, a more common form of collaborative research. L. Dave Brown of Harvard's Kennedy School and formerly Boston University (now retired), epitomizes how this type of collaborative work is done.

Much of Brown's career was spent in directly engaging with community members to foster system change at the whole community level, through organizational development and different forms of action research. While he was a professor at Boston University, Brown's research ran through an enterprise he co-ran with his wife, Jane Covey, the Institute for Development Research (IDR). Through IDR, Brown and Covey came to connect with communities as partners, rather than subjects, for both organizational/community change and research purposes. Rather than simply "impose" what IDR saw as the proper way to change the system, Brown and Covey sought the input, advice, and participation of community members directly in the change and research processes. As he recalls, eventually, "We began to develop a set of ideas about how you work with NGOs, development NGOs, to build their capacity."

For example, IDR brought leaders from key NGOs in six Asian countries to Boston to talk about leadership, personal leadership development, and the evolution of civil society in their countries. He recalls:

> That had a number of impacts. One is we learned a lot about the challenges facing NGOs. We also built relations [connections] with key players that continue today.... And we began to amass this sense of what it takes to do strategy in these contexts.

Working directly with leaders and learning from them meant that IDR, hence Brown and Covey, were connected with large international aid organizations, funders, and NGOs. They focused on trying to figure out what it takes for a strong civil society to evolve, for example what types of institutions were needed? The next step was to strengthen connections among the entities being studied. So IDR began building networks of support organizations around the world, exploring the "possibility of grassroots civil society organizations, NGOs, and governments cooperating to solve problems that none of them could solve by themselves."

Such collaborative efforts are needed to resolve complex problems or what Russell Ackoff called "messes," the type of bigger picture problems that cannot be solved by one institution acting alone (Ackoff, 1975). A series of case studies of collaborations among grassroots organizations, NGOs, and governments began, in Brown's words, "to elaborate into inter-sectoral cooperation and inter-organizational relations and sector development." Brown views himself as a bit of a "hybrid," stating, "I'm partly academic and partly activist, and if I have to choose where I put the emphasis, I'd rather make a difference than make a publication."

The evolving and co-creative nature of collaborative work means, as Brown put it:

> We were making it up as we went along, all the way. We were almost always out on the edge of our competence, and frequently way over the edge.... I think IDR was partly ideas, but it was also very much relation-ships and engagement, and part of a process, I guess. I think one of the things that we found ways to do was to co-invent a lot of ideas.

Brown describes a conference where IDR brought together the NGOs from their case studies which was built on work that had been done at Brown University, but "also built on the work of all those people to take a new look at these issues and identify a new paradigm for understanding what was going on out there."

Summarizing, Brown notes:

> This was taking practice and turning it into ideas that then go back to affect the practice. There was this kind of interchange that nobody knew where it was going to come out. It was a long way from controlled experiments. But I think it ended up influencing the participants in the process, some of whom were predominantly practitioners, who then went out and practiced in a different way. Some were predominantly academics, who went out and academized in a different way.

Engaging learners with paradox and ambiguity

The skill of transcending paradox and ambiguity, of essentially holding opposites in tension, can be considered part of the connecting role. It is evident in the way that Karl Weick handled the interview itself. Weick, Rensis Likert Distinguished University Professor Emeritus of Organizational Behavior and Psychology, University of Michigan, is well known for many things, particularly developing the idea of sense-making (Weick, 1988, 1993; Weick, Sutcliff & Obstfeld, 2005).

Weick's way of inquiring "called out significant insight and analysis in me" (from a research memo). He has a way of letting others find their voice and make new connections, intellectual, spiritual, theoretical, or practical, while simultaneously holding a space in which that voice can emerge. Weick states:

> I'm not sure we make enough use of people's own experience or use that as a platform for them to think their way out from those experiences to what they have learned from them, how they could interpret them differently and so forth.

In Weick's interview I was struck by how his apparent "uncertainty" forced me to make connections among the ideas we were discussing that might not otherwise have been made. Notably, this is exactly the technique that he talks about in discussing management education, letting others find their voice, and is similar to what IDR did with community groups. It strikes me as distinctly shamanic in nature, and an incredible gift to his students.

Via inquiry, asking questions, reframing, trying out new languages, Weick probes deeply, presumably with his students and practitioners as well as with his interviewer. Here is an example in the context of the interview. Weick states about teaching:

> I think there's an awful lot of hubris on the faculty side in areas like, oh, let's say neuroscience and maybe economics also. I think that works against people being attentive to detail, to nuance, to alternatives, to reshuffling things, to trying out different kinds of languages. I'm really torn on that, because for me the important thing is some humility in the face of just the world that we face. On the other hand, given its complexity, maybe you want to really reinforce boldness so that you make a dent in things. You make an impression. You have an impact. If you're going to do that, maybe you have to scuttle humility or make it a distant second. I can really make the argument that that's exactly the opposite of what you need when you need to assert yourself, when you need to enact something.

Weick's comment triggered a new connection on my part, the idea of being "Boldly humble," which means that the researcher/scholar does not have all the insights, but allows practitioners and students alike to engage with the idea and come up with their own, in a sense, co-created insights. In much the tradition of the shaman who understands that healing comes from within the patient or the community, Weick is not providing a prescription or a solution; instead, he is providing an opportunity for the learner and practitioner to engage with whatever idea is at hand, and ultimately give voice to his or her own version of that idea, creating new mythologies that work better than the old ones.

Concluding thoughts

"The essence of management research is the mission to understand and explicate (as far as possible) management practice" (Tranfield & Starkey, 1998: 352). Too often that goal is overlooked. For intellectual shamans and all of us who aspire to making a difference through our scholarly work, the idea of connecting is particularly powerful. Through linking theory and practice across boundaries, creating memes that shape narratives, theories, ideas, and insights that transcend boundaries, and explicitly researching and collaborating co-creatively with "subjects" across boundaries, scholars "connect."

Intellectual shamans seek out and focus on big ideas, big picture thinking, and making a difference in their work. Necessarily big picture ideas transcend boundaries. The intellectual shamans interviewed did not shy away from that connecting activity. None of the intellectual shamans interviewed would have been content to simply build on the work of others or focus on narrowly defined ideas and research topics. Instead, they were intrigued by big questions that by their nature transcend boundaries, demanding new connections if they are to be made sense of.

Intellectual shamans as connectors want their work to matter, to make a difference. Given the state of our world today and its many problems, it seems that there is a significant need for many more of us as scholars linking with practice to explicitly assume the mantle of the shaman. Making a difference can be in practice, organizations, classrooms, communities, and, most optimistically, the world, crossing multiple boundaries. Intellectual shamans recognize the co-evolutionary and mutuality of relationships between practice and theory and among scholars and practitioners. Theirs is not a one-sided relationship, but rather one from which they themselves are constantly learning from "subjects" and their contexts, viewed as collaborators and co-creators of insights, ideas, frameworks, and scholarship.

Further, when they are creating new memes and associated narratives, intellectual shamans recognize that memes always cross into unexpected realms, especially as they replicate in the minds of others. The more a meme gains traction, the more boundaries it crosses (otherwise millions of Google "hits" would not occur). The idea of "stakeholder," for example, can now be found throughout companies' websites and in the everyday language of business, as well as in more theoretical and academic treatises; and similarly for "sustainability" and other successful memes.

Indeed, "the ability to develop ideas and relate them to practice should be the distinguishing competence of the skilled management researcher" (Tranfield & Starkey, 1998: 352). Mode 2 research, according to Tranfield and Starkey, demands trans-disciplinarity, is characterized by "a constant flow back and forth between the fundamental and the applied, between the theoretical and the practical," and is "socially distributed" beyond the boundaries of academia (Tranfield & Starkey, 1998: 347–8). Such research inherently recognizes the role of context—connecting elements into a systemic or holistic framework rather than isolating them, focusing on informing—and, importantly, being informed by—the work of practice, and recognizing the integral complexity of human and natural systems of which the management of enterprises of all sorts is inherently a part.

Approaches based on the three core functions of the intellectual shaman—healing, connecting, and sense-making, illustrated above primarily through the connecting function—seem to meet the quest articulated by Bartunek and Rynes (2014: 2) for research that doesn't try to "bridge the academic–practitioner gap" but rather "treats it as fundamentally important in itself for scholarly research and theorizing." Fundamentally, that is the work of the intellectual shaman.

References

Ackoff, R. (1975). *Redesigning the Future*. New York: Wiley.

Bansal, P., Bertels, S., Ewart, T., MacConnachie, P. & O'Brien, J. (2012). Bridging the research–practice gap. *Academy of Management Perspectives*, 26(1), 73–92.

Bartunek, J. M. & Rynes, S. L. (2014). Academics and practitioners are alike and unlike: The paradoxes of academic–practitioner relationships. *Journal of Management*, 40(5), 1181–201.

Blackmore, S. (2000). *The Meme Machine*. Oxford: Oxford University Press.

Block, J. (1995). A contrarian view of the five-factor approach to personality description. *Psychological Bulletin*, 117(2), 187.

Brundtland, G. H. (1987). *Our Common Future: World Commission on Environmental Development*. (The Brundtland Report). Oxford: Oxford University Press.

Cameron, K. & Dutton, J. (Eds.). (2003). *Positive Organizational Scholarship: Foundations of a New Discipline*. San Francisco, CA: Berrett-Koehler Publishers.

Cooperrider, D. L. & Srivastava, S. (1987). Appreciative inquiry in organizational life. *Research in Organizational Change and Development*, 1(1), 129–69.

Cooperrider, D. & Whitney, D. D. (2005). *Appreciative Inquiry: A Positive Revolution in Change*. San Francisco, CA: Berrett-Koehler Publishers.

Dawkins, R. (1976). *The Selfish Gene*. New York: Oxford University Press.

Dow, J. (1986). Universal aspects of symbolic healing: A theoretical synthesis. *American Anthropologist*, 88(1), 56–69.

Egri, C. P. & Frost, P. J. (1991). Shamanism and change: Bringing back the magic in organizational transformation. *Research in Organizational Change and Development*, 5, 175–221.

Eliade, M. (1964). *Shamanism: Archaic Techniques of Ecstasy* (Willard R. Trask, Trans.). New York: Bollingen Foundation.

Freeman, R.E. (1984). *Strategic Management: A Stakeholder Approach*. Boston: Pitman

Freeman, R. E., Martin, K. & Parmar, B. (2007). Stakeholder capitalism. *Journal of Business Ethics*, 74(4), 303–14.

Freeman, R. E., Harrison, J. S., Wicks, A. C., Parmar, B. L. & De Colle, S. (2010). *Stakeholder Theory: The State of the Art*. Cambridge, UK: Cambridge University Press.

Frost, P. J. & Egri, C. P. (1994). The shamanic perspective on organizational change and development. *Journal of Organizational Change Management*, 7(1), 7–23.

Ghoshal, S. (2005). Bad management theories are destroying good management practices. *Academy of Management Learning & Education*, 4(1), 75–91.

Hart, S. L. (1997). Beyond greening: Strategies for a sustainable world. *Harvard Business Review*, 75(1), 66–77.

Hart, S. & Prahalad, C. K. (2002). The fortune at the bottom of the pyramid. *Strategy and Business*, 26(1), 54–67.

Kahili King, S. (2009). *Urban Shaman*. New York: Simon and Schuster.

Krippner, S. C. (2002). Conflicting perspectives on shamans and shamanism: Points and counterpoints. *American Psychologist*, 57(11), 962–77.

Ludema, J. D., Whitney, D., Mohr, B. J. & Griffin, T. J. (2003). *The Appreciative Inquiry Summit*. San Francisco, CA: Berret Koehler.

Norgaard, R. (2015). The Church of Economism and Its Discontents: Great Transition Initiative, Boston: Tellus Institute. Retrieved April 3, 2017 from www.greattransition. org/images/pdf/Norgaard-The-Church-of-Economism-and-Its-Discontents.pdf.

Pirson, M. A. & Lawrence, P. R. (2010). Humanism in business: Towards a paradigm shift? *Journal of Business Ethics*, 93(4), 553–65.

Prahalad, C. K. (2006). *The Fortune at the Bottom of the Pyramid*. Philadelphia, PA: Wharton School Publishing.

Scharmer, C. O. (2009). *Theory U: Learning from the Future as it Emerges*. San Francisco, CA: Berrett-Koehler.

Scharmer, C. O. (2013). *Leading from the Emerging Future: From Ego-System to Eco-System Economies*. San Francisco, CA: Berrett-Koehler.

Seligman, M. E. & Csikszentmihalyi, M. (2000). Positive psychology: An introduction. *American Psychologist*, 55(1), 5–14.

Spreitzer, G. M. & Sonenschein, S. (2004). Toward the construct definition of positive deviance. *American Behavioral Scientist*, 47(6), 828–47.

Steckler, Erica (2014). The social construction of authenticity by stakeholders. Doctoral Dissertation. Boston, MA: Boston College.

Sternin, J. & Choo, R. (2000). The power of positive deviance. *Harvard Business Review*, 78(1), 14–15.

Tranfield, D. & Starkey K. (1998). The nature, social organization and promotion of management research: Towards policy. *British Journal of Management*, 9(4), 341–53.

Van De Ven, A. H. & Johnson, P. E. (2006). Knowledge for theory and practice. *Academy of Management Review*, 31(4), 802–21.

Waddock, S. (2010). Finding wisdom within: The role of seeing and reflective practice in developing moral imagination, aesthetic sensibility, and systems understanding. *Journal of Business Ethics Education*, 7, 177–96.

Waddock, S. (2014). Wisdom and responsible leadership: Aesthetic sensibility, moral imagination, and systems thinking. In Koehn, D. & Elm, D. (Eds.) *Aesthetics and Business Ethics, Issues in Business Ethics* (Vol. 41, pp. 129–47). Netherlands: Springer.

Waddock, S. (2015). *Intellectual Shamans: Management Academics Making a Difference*. Cambridge, UK: Cambridge.

Walsh, R. (1989). What is a shaman? Definition, origin and distribution. *Journal of Transpersonal Psychology*, 21(1), 1–11.

Weick, K. E. (1988). Enacted sense-making in crisis situations. *Journal of Management Studies*, 25(4), 305–17.

Weick, K. E. (1993). The collapse of sense-making in organizations: The Mann Gulch disaster. *Administrative Science Quarterly*, 38(4), 628–52.

Weick, Karl E. (1995). *Sense-making in Organizations* (Vol. 3). Thousand Oaks, CA: Sage Publications.

Weick, K. E., Sutcliffe, K. M. & Obstfeld, D. (2005). Organizing and the process of sense-making. *Organization Science*, 16(4), 409–21.

6 Narrative foundations for theorizing about academic–practitioner relationships

Jean M. Bartunek and Sara L. Rynes

There is a considerable literature on the "academic–practitioner gap" in multiple social science disciplines (e.g., Orr & Bennett, 2012; Chan, Chan & Liu, 2012). The gap in management (e.g., Rynes, Bartunek & Daft, 2001) is of particular significance, since practitioner absorption of scholarly knowledge may improve organizational practice and performance, and academic adoption of practitioner innovations may further scholarship. It is this gap that we address. Our hope is to develop a way to bring to the surface the mostly implicit theorizing that underlies empirical literature in this area, and thus suggest new ways of considering what is going on in academic–practitioner relationships.

A number of articles address the academic–practitioner gap and academic–practitioner relationships in management. Bartunek and Rynes (2014) reported that a search of databases using terms such as research and theory, theory and practice, science and practice, and rigor and relevance turned up 265 articles, with a dramatic increase in the number of articles published since 2000. Kieser, Nicolai and Seidel (2015) identified an even larger literature on this topic, and it continues to grow.

Despite the dramatic increase in scholarly attention to the gap, very few of the articles have been empirical, and this includes most articles published since 2000. Rather, the great majority of published articles addressing the academic–practitioner gap and academic–practice relationships more generally are opinion pieces that neither build theory nor produce new data. This is due partly to the fact that, while the number of journal special issues on the topic has substantially increased since 2000, only a small number of these special issues (*Academy of Management Journal*, 2001; *Organization Studies*, 2010) have explicitly encouraged and incorporated empirical and conceptual papers.

Thus, very little contemporary theorizing directly addresses academic–practitioner relationships. In this volume, for example, the conceptual foundations presented for academic–practitioner relationships come largely from Aristotle (see Chapters 2 and 4 by Shani et al. and Nielsen respectively), Hume, Kant, Comte, and Popper (as Shani et al. identify in Chapter 2) and Bernard Lonergan, a twentieth-century philosopher (whom Coghlan discusses in Chapter 3). Shamanism, an ancient spiritual tradition considered by Waddock in Chapter 5, also provides a foundation for thinking about academic–practitioner relationships.

These sources are all very valuable, but they were established entirely outside of, and, generally speaking, long before the practice and academic discipline of management were formally developed. Can empirical scholarship on academic–practitioner relationships provide a source of theorizing itself?

Recently, with the rise of qualitative research in management and other social science disciplines (Elsbach & Kramer, 2015), there has come an enhanced interest in inductive theorizing. That is, rather than starting with theories established outside a particular context and testing relationships that should occur if these theories are correct, scholars attempt to induce theory from the words and actions of those within the context itself. Generally following a type of grounded theory approach (e.g., Glaser & Strauss, 1967, Strauss & Corbin, 1998), many qualitative studies collect a good deal of data from sources such as semi-structured interviews, observations, and archival texts. They cull through these data to induce conceptual categories, and from these develop new theoretical understandings.

For example, Corley and Gioia (2004) used an inductive approach to develop an emergent conceptual model of identity change during a corporate spin-off. Pratt, Rockmann and Kaufman (2006) used an inductive approach to build theory about how medical residents construct their professional identities. Walsh and Bartunek (2011) used this method to develop a conceptual model of the processes through which new organizations are formed in the wake of older ones that cease operations.

In an example particularly pertinent for our chapter, Sonenshein (2010) built on the narratives managers and employees told during a major organizational change initiative to develop a model of meanings of strategic change implementation. We also build on narratives to carry out inductive theorizing, though the narratives we consider are quite different from the ones Sonenshein's respondents told. We make use of the stories that are implicit, if not explicit, in recent *empirical papers* published about academic–practitioner relationships in management.

This may seem strange. However, scholarly articles typically include the basic anatomy of stories (Bruner, 1986; Carter, 1993; Dailey & Browning, 2014; Gersick, Dutton & Bartunek, 2000). Empirical articles, like other stories, "have an Aristotelian beginning, middle, and end—that is, 'events and happenings are configured into a temporal unity by means of a plot'" (Polkinghorne, 1995: 5, cited in Dailey & Browning, 2014: 23). Or, to put it another way, empirical academic articles include a predicament or concern (an issue that hasn't been settled by prior research), action taken to resolve the predicament (the study that is carried out), and an outcome (the findings of the study) in which the predicament is resolved in some way. Further, even if the narratives underlying empirical studies are not about the self (as were those in Sonenshein, 2010), they are narratives constructed by scholars about their explorations of important topics using empirical data.

Thus, for example, when Sonenshein (2010) starts his study by stating that not enough is known about the meanings managers and employees construct during strategic change, he is describing a research *predicament*. When he describes how he carried out his study to determine the managers' and employees' meanings and their impacts, he is describing *action* taken to address the predicament. The *outcome* presented in the findings is about the pathways through which managers' and employees' meanings affect implementation of strategic change. In this chapter we are using these basic components of empirical academic studies as the basis for our theorizing.

We make use of another characteristic of stories as well: the fact that they often include tensions in the form of dualities, in which two essential elements that would typically be seen as in conflict with each other are instead viewed as interdependent, as "mutually enabling and a constituent of one another" (Farjoun, 2010: 203). For example, Dailey and Browning (2014: 22) distinguished three dualities in a set of organizational stories, all of which were situated within cultural issues of sameness and difference. These were control/resistance, differentiation/integration, and stability/change. Their dualistic approach treated these tensions as enabling as opposed to interfering with each other. In another illustration, in her exploration of the relationship between identity work and courage, Koerner (2014) distinguished several types of dualistic tensions. Again, she interpreted these dualities as mutually enhancing.

Bartunek and Rynes (2014) identified multiple tensions and dualities of academic–practitioner relationships in management, such as apparently conflicting logics, time dimensions, communication styles, rigor and relevance, and interests and incentives. Summarizing and analyzing the stories told in empirical scholarship about academic–practitioner relationships enables us to build on this work and explore potential dualities in more depth.

Method

Sample. In the reference section we have placed asterisks before each reference that stands for an *empirical* paper published between 1999 and 2015 that addresses academic–practitioner relationships in management. All of them included at least one academic co-author, and most were authored entirely by academics. Thus, these are stories academics were telling.

We located these papers through searches of Business Source Complete, PsycINFO, Scopus, and similar databases. In total, we found 44 empirical articles. We began with 1999 because it was a paper by Rynes, McNatt and Bretz (1999) that sparked the special research forum published in the *Academy of Management Journal* in 2001 edited by Rynes et al., and because there were almost no other empirical papers on this topic published during the 1990s. We excluded papers that addressed course materials for teaching (e.g., Pearce & Huang, 2012), because those focus comparatively little on actual relationships between academics and practitioners. There may be more papers that are not accessible through the means we used, but we believe we have constructed a fairly comprehensive sample.

Following procedures used by Gersick et al. (2000) and Koerner (2014: 70), we took several steps to determine common storylines. First, following Gersick et al., we sketched out the skeletal stories containing the core components for each empirical paper. Then, again following Gersick et al. together with Koerner, we engaged in a basic form of coding in which we determined the fundamental components of the "plot" of each story. These included the predicament, or concern (usually described in the purpose of the study), the action(s) taken by the researcher to address the concern, most often in the form of exploring why it exists and/or what may be done to remedy it, and, finally, the outcomes of the studies, including (hoped for) resolution of the predicament.

Following this we explored which types of concern, action and outcome occurred in tandem with each other in our dataset and how often these appeared. We labeled these as storylines, and there were five storylines that appeared in at least three studies. Table 6.1 summarizes labels for these, the storylines that most frequently occurred and the studies in which we found them.

Findings and analysis

As a shorthand, we labeled the five storylines that most frequently occurred as contact stories, discrepancies stories, culture stories, impact stories, and similarities stories. We summarize each one below, with illustrations from the articles.

Labels and storylines

Contact stories

The contact storyline is that academic–practitioner contact enhances both practitioner implementation of academic findings and citations of academic articles. These stories start with a question about whether contact between academics and practitioners can be fruitful for either group or both. The exploration largely focuses on various types of contact between individual academics and organizations (e.g., academic presence in organizations for some period of time) and determines whether this has had any impact for better or worse. In contact stories, the outcome of the contact is positive for both groups.

For example, Rynes et al. (1999) and Rynes and McNatt (2001) found that researcher time spent on-site at companies was associated with an increased likelihood of implementation of research findings and higher citation rates of academic articles. Knights and Scarborough (2010) found that the production by academics of relevant knowledge depended at least in part on an evolving network that could sustain translation between academics and practitioners.

Discrepancies stories

The discrepancies storyline is that differences in interests and the value placed on research lead to discrepancies between academics and practitioners in beliefs and values. This has been most fully studied in Human Resources (HR). The discrepancies storyline typically starts with a question about whether (human

Table 6.1 Storylines in empirical academic papers about academic–practitioner relationships

Story label	Frequency	Storyline	Studies in which storyline appears
Contact stories	11%	Academic–practitioner contact enhances both practitioner implementation of academic findings and citations of academic articles.	Rynes et al., 1999, 2002; Mohrman et al., 2001; Knights & Scarbrough, 2010; Chen et al., 2013
Discrepancies stories	14%	Differences in interests and values placed on research lead to discrepancies between academics and practitioners. This has often been found in HR.	Rynes et al., 2002, 2007; Deadrick & Gibson, 2007, 2009; Tenhiälä et al., 2014; Sanders et al., 2008
Culture stories	11%	Fundamental differences in the underlying cultures of academics and practitioners foster tensions.	Beech et al., 2010; Empson, 2013; Moisander & Stenfors, 2009; Wasserman & Kram, 2009; Kram et al. 2012
Impact stories	7%	Practitioner journals have more impact on academia than academic journals have on practice.	Spencer, 2001; McWilliams et al., 2009; Schulz & Nicolai 2015
Similarities stories	11%	Exploration of interests and concerns shows that academics and practitioners are often similar to each other.	Baldridge et al., 2004: 13; Shapiro et al., 2007; Salter & Varney, 2008; Gibson & Deadrick, 2010; Newman et al., 2015

resources) academics and practitioners share the same primary interests. The exploration largely focuses on the relationship between topics considered very important in HR academic research and the topics emphasized in more practitioner-focused HR outlets. In these stories the outcome is that there are discrepancies between the two groups.

For example, Rynes et al. (2002) found that there was widespread disbelief among practitioners about particular common research findings, such as the importance of intelligence in job performance. Deadrick and Gibson (2007) found that practitioner journals in Human Resources have had a consistently greater interest than academic HR journals in compensation and rewards, while academic HR journals have had a consistently greater interest than practitioner journals in motivation and organizational behavior. Moreover, Deadrick and Gibson (2009) found that differences between academic and practitioner interests have widened over time.

Culture stories

The culture storyline is that fundamental differences in the underlying cultures of academics and practitioners foster tensions between them. These stories start with a question about how similar and/or different are the fundamental assumptions and cultures of academia and practice, and the exploration largely focuses on attempts to understand the two cultures. The outcome is that cultural differences between academia and practice are much more fundamental than a simple lack of interest in similar topics.

For example, Moisander and Stenfors (2009: 227) argued that differences between academics' and practitioners' epistemic cultures "may complicate communication and co-operation ... and may also result in management scholars producing knowledge and strategy tools that lack practical pertinence for corporate actors." In addition, Beech et al., addressing assumptions, a fundamental component of culture, argued that:

> at the end of (a process of academics and practitioners engaging with each other), the social roles remain as they were at the beginning.... There is little sense of (academics and practitioners) stepping out of their roles or outside their area of expertise.
>
> (Beech et al., 2010: 1352)

Impact stories

The impact storyline is that practitioner journals have more impact on academia than academic journals have on practice. This storyline starts with a question about how academic and practitioner writings affect each other. The exploration focuses on comparing how much academic journals and practitioner journals cite each other's work. The outcome of the exploration is that practitioner journals tend to have more impact on academic writing than vice versa.

For example, McWilliams et al. (2009: 75) found that practitioner journals "hold high levels of influence with the Core ... Anglo-European (academic) clusters ... (but) practitioner journals import very little from Core (academic) journals." Spencer (2001: 438) found that in Japan university research has less influence on practitioners than corporate research on academics, and even in the US commercial journals and industry conferences may be important for academic research to become more commercially practical.

Similarities stories

The similarities storyline is that exploration of interests and concerns shows that academics and practitioners are often similar to each other. These studies start with a very similar concern as discrepancy stories, but reach the opposite conclusion. This storyline starts with a question about how similar to or different academics' and practitioners' perspectives are from each other. It explores the extent to which they express shared concerns and approaches, even if these shared concerns might be about their differences. The outcome of these investigations is that there was considerable similarity between academics and practitioners, with some differences.

Shapiro et al. (2007) showed that both academic and practitioner members of the Academy of Management perceive a gap between management research and practice. Gibson and Deadrick (2010) found that academics and practitioners shared some, but not all, interests and disinterests. Baldridge et al. (2004: 1072) found "a positive correlation between an expert panel's assessment of practical relevance and an objective measure of academic quality" of articles in a particular journal, as well as "a positive correlation between the expert panel's a posteriori assessments of interestingness and a priori judgments of global relevance." (On the other hand, Nicolai, Schulz & Göbel, 2011, found complete differences in ratings of the quality of journal articles between academics and practitioners).

Discussion: the stories as a foundation for theorizing

For the most part, the individual storylines do not contain dualities. They tell straightforward tales of similarities *or* differences between academics and practitioners, including which is more influential than the other. Taken together, on the other hand, these storylines comprise contradictory sets of messages that do reflect dualities. Academic–practitioner contact is productive. But academics and practitioners (at least those in HR) have very different sets of priorities and interests. Further, academics and practitioners operate out of very different cultural norms and assumptions, and practitioner journals have more impact on academic journals than vice versa. On the other hand, academics and practitioners often have similar concerns.

What kind of theorizing comes out of a set of empirical stories like this? The answer, we suggest, is theorizing centered on tensions and dualities associated with sameness and difference. As we will show, the emphasis on dualities and tensions linked with sameness and difference ultimately leads to the recognition of the crucial importance of *identity* and *identity work* (Brown, 2015) that underlies empirical studies regarding academic–practitioner relationships.

Underlying tensions and dualities

The philosopher Paul Ricoeur (1984, 1991) originally developed the notion of sameness/difference to refer to identity as it was expressed in individuals' self-narratives. This distinction did not refer to the individual as the same or different from other people so much as an individual identity that includes dimensions of both sameness and otherness. Crowley (2003: 1–2) described this distinction as: Ricoeur "begins by dividing identity into two categories, idem and ipse. Idem refers to a notion of identity based on sameness, whereas ipse, described as Self-hood, can incorporate change within a recognizable entity." In other words, for Ricoeur, sameness and difference and the tension between them are *both* integral to an individual's identity. They enable it to remain a "recognizable entity" over time while also incorporating change and growth. Thus, tensions of sameness and difference, (which Ricoeur sometimes also called otherness), point to deep dimensions of identity over time. Thus, also, when stories are told of relationships between academics and practitioners that emphasize sameness and/or difference (as is the case with the empirical studies we explored), they are likely also referring to identity, whether this is explicit or not.

In fact, organizational scholars have emphasized how dialectics of sameness and difference characterize identity within organizational groupings. Durand and Calori (2006: 93) described the organizational sameness principle as "that despite successive changes, significant and enduring organizational traits and characteristics continue to persist." Langley, Golden-Biddle, Reay, Denis, Hébert, Lamothe and Gervais (2012: 136) described mergers as "inevitably disturb[ing] peoples' understandings of sameness and difference with respect to others, a fundamental dialectic tension that is inherent to the very concepts of identity and identification." Ghorashi and Sabelis (2013: 81), discussing complexities of diversity in organizations, ask, "How can conditions for engagement and inclusion of cultural others be created without essentializing cultural differences, and thereby running the risk of fixing people's (identity) position?" Kreiner, Hollensbe and Sheep (2006: 985) explored the identity tensions experienced by Episcopal priests and the strategies of differentiation (difference) and integration (sameness) they used to ameliorate these tensions (see also Chapter 8, by Jarzabkowski, Lewis, and Smith, in this volume). Kreiner, Hollensbe, Sheep, Smith and Kataria (2015: 985) built on this to explore how "members in the (Episcopal) Church were struggling both with how to stay the same (e.g., maintain organizational tradition and history) and how to change (e.g., adopt or interpret new aspects of identity)" during a major change in the church.

Jenkins (2008: 18) commented, "Taken—as they can only be—together, similarity and difference are the dynamic principles of identification, and are at the heart of the human world." In other words, from the perspective of academics studying academic–practitioner relationships, sameness and difference are not (just) about academics who are similar and practitioners who are different (or vice versa). Rather, they are tensions regarding how to enable fundamental identities of academics and practitioners to both remain the same and change in coherent and meaningful ways (Ricoeur, 1991).

The tensions in these storylines not only reflect the overarching sameness/difference dialectic, but also the dualities Dailey and Browning (2014) described that flesh it out: control/resistance, differentiation/integration, and stability/change. For example, it is likely that *control/resistance* dualities underlie interest in the comparative *impact* of academic and practitioner journals on each other. It is likely that *differentiation/integration* (Kreiner et al., 2006) which often reflects desires for a proper degree of uniqueness (Dailey & Browning, 2014), underlie the stories about both *similarities* and *discrepancies* between academics and practitioners. Finally, it is likely that *stability/change*, which reflects desires both to maintain consistency and to enable change (Ricoeur, 1991), underlies the stories about both deep *cultural* differences and the positive outcomes of *contact* between academics and practitioners. These are all reflections of identity dynamics at work on the part of the scholars conducting and authoring the studies.

The crucial importance of identity and identity work

Identity has been described by some scholars (e.g., Bartunek & Rynes, 2014; Empson, 2013; Gulati, 2007) as central to academic–practitioner relationships. However, it has not been fleshed out very much, and the tensions surrounding it have not been generally recognized as salient. The empirical studies that come closest to recognizing identity tensions associated with academia and practice are those by Empson (2013), Wasserman and Kram (2009) and Kram, Wasserman and Yip (2012) that focus on the experiences of those playing dual academic–practitioner roles. Our work suggests, however, that identity issues evoked by academic–practitioner relationships are much broader than has been recognized. Further, at least one of the ways these identity issues are expressed is in the studies scholars conduct and the findings of these studies.

Brown and Coupland (2015: 1316) describe identity as "the meanings that people attach reflexively to themselves in response to questions such as "who am I?" and "who do I want to be in the future?" These meanings are dynamic as well as stable (Ricoeur, 1991), and often threatened, especially during times of significant change (Brown & Coupland, 2015; Kreiner et al., 2015; Mallett & Wapshott, 2012). Threats to identity require significant identity work (Brown, 2015), which Sveningsson and Alvesson (2003: 1165) describe as "people being engaged in forming, repairing, maintaining, strengthening, or revising the constructions that are productive of a sense of coherence and distinctiveness." Such identity work is often carried out by means of the narratives (Brown, 2015;

Mallett & Wapshott, 2012) people tell about themselves and, if academics, the stories underlying the studies they conduct about academic–practitioner relationships.

Implications for theorizing about academic–practitioner relationships

The combined storylines of the studies described here heighten awareness of how much identity and its associated dualities of sameness and difference play crucial roles in understandings of academic–practitioner relationships, whether this is recognized or not. Our work, which focuses on stories that are more or less explicit in the empirical studies of such relationships, provides an overall narrative that is consistent with and extends the contributions of Ricoeur (1984, 1991), Kreiner et al. (2006, 2015) and others focusing on the importance of dualities in identity.

Yet, we have focused on the combination of stories, not the individual stories. As we have noted, the primary storyline of each study tended be about *either* sameness or difference, one side versus the other. Thus, the individual studies tend not to consider the possibilities of dualities concerning sameness and difference. Addressing issues in ways that reflect only one pole of academic–practitioner dualities is limiting in terms of the adequacy of the portrayal it can enable. Our chapter suggests instead the importance of designing empirical studies that—like the qualitative studies carried out by Empson (2013) and Kreiner et al. (2006, 2015)— provide room to surface dualities.

Recent work by Vaaro, Sonenshein and Boje (2016) summarizes the central role of narratives in the understanding of stability and change of identity in organizational settings. Thus, the narrative approach we took may have been particularly likely to highlight the identity issues present in academic–practitioner relationships. Scholars have not previously sought for the narrative storylines embedded in academic articles. However, our chapter suggests the possibilities of this type of exploration; there is much more to empirical studies than is apparent on the surface.

In conclusion, consistent with our aims, our work has induced a conceptual foundation—in identity and identity work—for deeper understanding of academic–practitioner relationships. The foundation it has induced is built on dualities of sameness and difference, a somewhat different topic than has characterized theorizing about academic–practitioner relationships before. We encourage attention to these foundations, and hope they will be both practically useful and academically productive.

Acknowledgments

We thank Jane McKenzie and Violetta Splitter for their helpful suggestions.

References

References preceded by an asterisk indicate empirical papers that address academic–practitioner relationships in management.

*Amabile, T. M., Patterson, C., Mueller, J., Wojcik, T., Kramer, S. J., Odomirok, P. W. & Marsh, M. (2001). Academic–practitioner collaboration in management research: A case of cross-profession collaboration. *Academy of Management Journal*, 44(2), 418–31.

*Baldridge, D. C., Floyd, S. W. & Markóczy, L. (2004). Are managers from Mars and academicians from Venus? Toward an understanding of the relationship between academic quality and practical relevance. *Strategic Management Journal*, 25(11), 1063–74.

*Bansal, P., Bertels, S., Ewart, T., MacConnachie, P. & O'Brien, J. (2012). Bridging the research–practice gap. *Academy of Management Perspectives*, 26(1), 73–92.

*Bartunek, J. M. & Rynes, S. L. (2010). The construction and contributions of "implications for practice": What's in them and what might they offer? *Academy of Management Learning & Education*, 9(1), 100–117.

Bartunek, J. M. & Rynes, S. L. (2014). Academics and practitioners are alike and unlike: The paradoxes of academic–practitioner relationships. *Journal of Management*, 40(5), 1181–201.

*Beech, N., MacIntosh, R. & MacLean, D. 2010. Dialogues between academics and practitioners: The role of generative dialogic encounters. *Organization Studies*, 31(9), 1341–67.

*Boland Jr., R. J., Singh, J., Salipante, P., Aram, J. D., Fay, S. Y. & Kanawattanachai, P. (2001). Knowledge representations and knowledge transfer. *Academy of Management Journal*, 44(2), 393–417.

*Booker, L. D., Bontis, N. & Serenko, A. (2012). Evidence-based management and academic research relevance. *Knowledge and Process Management*, 19(3), 121–30.

Brown, A. D. (2015). Identities and identity work in organizations. *International Journal of Management Reviews*, 17(1), 20–40.

Brown, A. D. & Coupland, C. (2015). Identity threats, identity work and elite professionals. *Organization Studies*, 36(10), 1315–36.

Bruner, J. (1986). *Actual Minds, Possible Worlds*. Cambridge, MA: Harvard University Press.

*Bullinger, B., Kieser, A. & Schiller-Merkens, S. (2015). Coping with institutional complexity: Responses of management scholars to competing logics in the field of management studies. *Scandinavian Journal of Management*, 31(3), 437–50.

*Butler, N., Delaney, H. & Spoelstra, S. (2015). Problematizing "relevance" in the business school: The case of leadership studies. *British Journal of Management*, 26(4), 731–44.

Carter, K. (1993). The place of story in the study of teaching and teacher education. *Educational Researcher*, 22(1): 5–12, 18.

*Cascio, W. F. & Aguinis, H. (2008). Research in industrial and organizational psychology from 1963 to 2007: Changes, choices, and trends. *Journal of Applied Psychology*, 93(5), 1062–81.

Chan, E. A., Chan, K. & Liu, Y. W. J. (2012). A triadic interplay between academics, practitioners and students in the nursing theory and practice dialectic. *Journal of Advanced Nursing*, 68(5), 1038–49.

*Chen, C. Y., Jim Wu, Y. C. & Wu, W. H. (2013). A sustainable collaborative research dialogue between practitioners and academics. *Management Decision*, 51(3), 566–93.

*Colbert, A. E., Rynes, S. L. & Brown, K. G. (2005). Who believes us? Understanding managers' agreement with human resource research findings. *The Journal of Applied Behavioral Science*, 41(3), 304–25.

Corley, K. G. & Gioia, D. A. (2004). Identity ambiguity and change in the wake of a corporate spin-off. *Administrative Science Quarterly*, 49(2), 173–208.

Crowley, P. (2003). Paul Ricoeur: The concept of narrative identity, the trace of autobiography. *Paragraph*, 26(3), 1–12.

Dailey, S. L. & Browning, L. (2014). Retelling stories in organizations: Understanding the functions of narrative repetition. *Academy of Management Review*, 39(1), 22–43.

*Deadrick, D. L. & Gibson, P. A. (2007). An examination of the research–practice gap in HR: Comparing topics of interest to HR academics and HR practitioners. *Human Resource Management Review*, 17(2), 131–9.

*Deadrick, D. L. & Gibson, P. A. (2009). Revisiting the research–practice gap in HR: A longitudinal analysis. *Human Resource Management Review*, 19(2), 144–53.

Durand, R. & Calori, R. (2006). Sameness, otherness? Enriching organisational change theories with philosophical considerations of the same and the other. *Academy of Management Review*, 31(1), 93–114.

Elsbach, K. D. & Kramer, R. M. (Eds.) (2015). *Handbook of Qualitative Organizational Research: Innovative Pathways and Methods*. New York: Routledge.

*Empson, L. (2013). My affair with the "other": Identity journeys across the research–practice divide. *Journal of Management Inquiry*, 22(2), 229–48.

Farjoun, M. (2010). Beyond dualism: Stability and change as a duality. *Academy of Management Review*, 35(2), 202–25.

*Flickinger, M., Tuschke, A., Gruber-Muecke, T. & Fiedler, M. (2014). In search of rigor, relevance, and legitimacy: What drives the impact of publications? *Journal of Business Economics*, 84(1), 99–128.

Gersick, C. J., Dutton, J. E. & Bartunek, J. M. (2000). Learning from academia: The importance of relationships in professional life. *Academy of Management Journal*, 43(6), 1026–44.

*Gibson, P. A. & Deadrick, D. 2010. Public administration research and practice: Are academician and practitioner interests different? *Public Administration Quarterly*, 34(2), 145–68.

Ghorashi, H. & Sabelis, I. (2013). Juggling difference and sameness: Rethinking strategies for diversity in organizations. *Scandinavian Journal of Management*, 29(1), 78–86.

Glaser, B. G. & Strauss, A. L. (1967): *The Discovery of Grounded Theory: Strategies for Qualitative Research*. London: Weidenfeld & Nicolson.

Gulati, R. (2007). Tent poles, tribalism, and boundary spanning: The rigor–relevance debate in management research. *Academy of Management Journal*, 50(4), 775–82.

*Halfhill, T. & Huff, J. (2003). The scientist–practitioner gap: Present status and potential utility of alternative article formats. *The Industrial–Organizational Psychologist*, 40(4), 25–37.

*Hughes, T., O'Regan, N. & Wornham, D. (2008). The credibility issue: Closing the academic/practitioner gap. *Strategic Change*, 17(7–8), 215–33.

Jenkins, R. (2008). *Social Identity*. Abingdon, UK: Routledge.

*Kelemen, M. & Bansal, P. (2002). The conventions of management research and their relevance to practice. *British Journal of Management*, 13(2), 97–108.

Kieser, A., Nicolai, A. & Seidl, D. (2015). The practical relevance of management research: Turning the debate on relevance into a rigorous scientific research program. *The Academy of Management Annals*, 9(1), 143–233.

*Knights, D. & Scarborough, H. (2010). In search of relevance: Perspectives on the contribution of academic–practitioner networks. *Organization Studies*, 31(9–10), 1287–309.

Koerner, M. M. (2014). Courage as identity work: Accounts of workplace courage. *Academy of Management Journal*, 57(1), 63–93.

*Kram, K. E., Wasserman, I. C. & Yip, J. (2012). Metaphors of identity and professional practice: Learning from the scholar–practitioner. *Journal of Applied Behavioral Science*, 48(3), 304–41.

Kreiner, G. E., Hollensbe, E. C. & Sheep, M. L. (2006). Where is the "me" among the "we"? Identity work and the search for optimal balance. *Academy of Management Journal*, 49(5), 1031–57.

Kreiner, G. E., Hollensbe, E., Sheep, M. L., Smith, B. R. & Kataria, N. (2015). Elasticity and the dialectic tensions of organizational identity: How can we hold together while we are pulling apart? *Academy of Management Journal*, 58(4), 981–1011.

Langley, A., Golden-Biddle, K., Reay, T., Denis, J. L., Hébert, Y., Lamothe, L. & Gervais, J. (2012). Identity struggles in merging organizations renegotiating the sameness–difference dialectic. *The Journal of Applied Behavioral Science*, 48(2), 135–67.

Mallett, O. & Wapshott, R. (2012). Mediating ambiguity: Narrative identity and knowledge workers. *Scandinavian Journal of Management*, 28(1), 16–26.

*McWilliams, A., Lockett, A., Katz, J. & Van Fleet, D. D. (2009). Who is talking to whom? The network of intellectual influence in management research. *Journal of Applied Management and Entrepreneurship*, 14(2), 61–81.

*Mohrman, S. A., Gibson, C. B. & Mohrman, A. M., Jr. (2001). Doing research that is useful to practice: A model and empirical exploration. *Academy of Management Journal*, 44(2), 357–75.

*Moisander, J. & Stenfors, S. (2009). Exploring the edges of theory–practice gap: Epistemic cultures in strategy-tool development and use. *Organization*, 16(2), 227–47.

*Newman, J., Cherney, A. & Head, B. W. (2016). Do policy makers use academic research? Reexamining the "two communities" theory of research utilization. *Public Administration Review*, 76(1), 24–32.

*Nicolai, A. & Seidl, D. (2010). That's relevant! Different forms of practical relevance in management science. *Organization Studies*, 31(9), 1257–85.

*Nicolai, A. T., Schulz, A. C. & Thomas, T. W. (2010). What Wall Street wants: Exploring the role of security analysts in the evolution and spread of management concepts. *Journal of Management Studies*, 47(1), 162–89.

*Nicolai, A. T., Schulz, A. & Göbel, M. (2011). Between sweet harmony and a clash of cultures: Does a joint academic–practitioner review reconcile rigor and relevance? *Journal of Applied Behavioral Science*, 47(1), 53–75.

*Offermann, L. R. & Spiros, R. K. (2001). The science and practice of team development: Improving the link. *Academy of Management Journal*, 44(2), 376–92.

Orr, K. & Bennett, M. (2012), Public administration scholarship and the politics of coproducing academic–practitioner research. *Public Administration Review*, 72(4), 487–95.

*Palmer, D., Dick, B. & Freiburger, N. (2009). Rigor and relevance in organization studies. *Journal of Management Inquiry*, 18(4), 265–72.

Pearce, J. L. & Huang, L. (2012). The decreasing value of our research to management education. *Academy of Management Learning & Education*, 11(2), 247–62.

Polkinghorne, D. (1995). Narrative configuration in qualitative analysis. *International Journal of Qualitative Studies in Education*, 8(1): 5–23.

Pratt, M. G., Rockmann, K. W. & Kaufman, J. B. (2006). Constructing professional identity: The role of work and identity learning cycles in the customization of identity among medical residents. *Academy of Management Journal*, 49(2), 235–62.

*Radaelli, G., Guerci, M., Cirella, S. & Shani, A. B. R. (2014). Intervention research as management research in practice: Learning from a case in the fashion design industry. *British Journal of Management*, 25(2), 335–51.

Ricoeur, P. (1984). *Time and Narrative*, Vol. 1. (K. McLaughlin & D. Pellauer, Trans.) Chicago, IL: University of Chicago Press.

Ricoeur, P. (1991). Narrative Identity. *Philosophy Today*, 35(1), 73–81.

*Rynes, S. L. & McNatt, D. B. (2001). Bringing the organization into organizational research: An examination of academic research inside organizations. *Journal of Business & Psychology*, 16(1), 3–19.

*Rynes, S. L., McNatt, D. B. & Bretz, R. D. (1999). Academic research inside organizations: Inputs, processes and outcomes. *Personnel Psychology*, 52(4), 869–98.

Rynes, S. L., Bartunek, J. M. & Daft, R. L. (2001). Across the great divide: Knowledge creation and transfer between practitioners and academics. *Academy of Management Journal*, 44(2), 340–55.

*Rynes, S. L., Colbert, A. E. & Brown, K. G. (2002). HR professionals' beliefs about effective human resource practices: Correspondence between research and practice. *Human Resource Management*, 41(2), 149–74.

*Rynes, S. L., Giluk, T. L. & Brown, K. G. (2007). The very separate worlds of academic and practitioner periodicals in human resource management: Implications for evidence-based management. *Academy of Management Journal*, 50(5), 987–1008.

*Salter, N. P. & Varney, G. H. (2008). A comparative analysis of program content for the 2007 OD network and the AOM-ODC division conferences. *Organization Development Journal*, 26(4), 33–42.

*Sanders, K., van Riemsdijk, M. & Groen, B. (2008). The gap between research and practice: A replication study on the HR professionals' beliefs about effective human resource practices. *The International Journal of Human Resource Management*, 19(10), 1976–88.

*Schulz, A. C. & Nicolai, A. T. (2015). The intellectual link between management research and popularization media: A bibliometric analysis of the Harvard Business Review. *Academy of Management Learning & Education*, 14(1), 31–49.

*Shapiro, D. L., Kirkman, B. L. & Courtney, H. G. (2007). Perceived causes and solutions of the translation problem in management research. *Academy of Management Journal*, 50(2), 249–66.

Sonenshein, S. (2010). We're changing—or are we? Untangling the role of progressive, regressive, and stability narratives during strategic change implementation. *Academy of Management Journal*, 53(3), 477–512.

*Spencer, J. W. (2001). How relevant is university-based scientific research to private high-technology firms? A United States–Japan comparison. *Academy of Management Journal*, 44(2), 432–40.

Strauss, A. L. & Corbin, J. (1998). *Basics of Qualitative Research: Techniques and Procedures for Developing Grounded Theory*. Thousand Oaks, CA: Sage Publications.

Sveningsson, S. & Alvesson, M. (2003). Managing managerial identities: Organizational fragmentation, discourse and identity struggle. *Human Relations*, 56(10), 1163—93.

*Swan, J., Bresnen, M., Robertson, M., Newell, S. & Dopson, S. (2010). When policy meets practice: Colliding logics and the challenges of "Mode 2" initiatives in the translation of academic knowledge. *Organization Studies*, 31(9), 1311–40.

*Tenhiälä, A., Giluk, T. L., Kepes, S., Simón, C., Oh, I. S. & Kim, S. (2014). The research–practice gap in human resource management: A cross-cultural study. *Human Resource Management*, 55(2), 179–200.

Vaaro, E., Sonenshein, S. & Boje, D. (2016). Narratives as sources of stability and change in organizations: Approaches and directions for future research. *Academy of Management Annals*, 10(1), 495–560.

Walsh, I. J. & Bartunek, J. M. (2011). Cheating the fates: Organizational foundings in the wake of demise. *Academy of Management Journal*, 54(5), 1017–44.

*Wasserman, I. C. & Kram, K. E. (2009). Enacting the scholar–practitioner role: An exploration of narratives. *Journal of Applied Behavioral Science*, 45(1), 12–38.

Part II
Developing capabilities

Introduction to Part II

Part I of this book offered a review of the conceptual boundaries of the space in which academic–practitioner relationships can be productive. Part II considers what capabilities are helpful for navigating the terrain, and what we know about the experience of developing them. Two chapters examine how capabilities are developed through a doctoral education. Three reflect on the experience of developing capabilities through subsequent practice. In this introduction, we offer an overview of some themes that repeatedly emerge across the chapters.

The question at the heart of this section is, what does it mean to be a "professional" researching at the interface between academia and practice? The answer to the question has identity implications as well as providing insights about the capabilities supporting effective performance. Critically, the capabilities, which emerge from the section authors' experiences of working at the interface are not the sole preserve of academics. As Van de Ven notes in the opening chapter (Chapter 7) "engaged scholarship involves a relationship between academics and practitioners, and BOTH parties need to build their skills to perform these tasks well." The chapters in this section are less about the technical requirements of rigorous research and more about the human qualities that help both constituencies relate effectively in the service of something more than just the institution they work for. They build on the human qualities introduced in Part I.

Professional researchers aspire to serve societal needs

As we noted in our general introduction, in Chapter 1, the purpose of academic professionalism is to generate and disseminate knowledge that enhances the economic and social well-being of society as a whole. Fundamentally, this aim underpins growing concern that universities demonstrate research impact to justify the funding they receive. Adler, Kwon and Hecksher (2008) even suggest that the welfare of modern society depends on effective organization of professional practice: addressing the complex questions and problems of a modern society can only be achieved through multidisciplinary collaborations. Traditional mechanisms of market and hierarchy[1] place unhelpful limitations on knowledge generation and use, so professional knowledge workers such as doctors, architects, lawyers, consultants, and engineers pool their knowledge in search of answers. Van dc Vcn echoes this call with respect to engaged scholarship in Chapter 7, when he suggests that although academics have responsibility for defining the BIG questions, "complex social problems ... often exceed our limited capabilities to study on our own" and "the more ambiguous and complex the problem, the greater the need for engaging others who can provide different perspectives for revealing critical dimensions of the nature, context, and implications of the study." As Waddock suggested in Chapter 5, successful engaged scholarship may require the work of intellectual shamans.

In Chapter 9 MacLean and MacIntosh challenge us to reconsider "what it means to be a 'professional researcher'" concluding "that many of what might be considered the symptoms of 'unprofessional research' are in fact the unacknowledged hallmarks of good research when creative partnership working is a key feature. These "symptoms" are the more aesthetic, intuitive, and emotionally intelligent capabilities, which are an undeniable part of human creative action in the social setting we are committed to studying. Usually these are undervalued as research skills. They also show how they have developed these skills over their careers in ways consistent with Coghlan's description of skills to learn over time (see Chapter 3).

Antonacopoulou extends this line of thought in her examination of the foundations of *impactful* research She argues that IMProving ACTion requires characteristics such as curiosity and conscience, which, when deployed alongside the exercise of a set of positive virtues (see Chapter 11, Figure 11.2), build confidence and trust that the professional is concerned for the consequences of their work. Combining 15 years personal experience running an academic–practitioner research network with the findings of her recent research for the think tank Res Publica, on ways to foster virtue in the medical, legal, and teaching professions, she elaborates the professional qualities that produce *phronesis*, or practical judgment in these complex settings. Her work is consistent with the work of Part I authors such as Shani et al. and Nielsen, who develop notions of *phronesis* more conceptually.

Both MacLean and MacIntosh and Antonacopoulou emphasize the importance of "re-humanizing" scholarship as a professional practice. Rational, detached objectivity has been overplayed as a distinguishing feature of academic professionalism. Intuition, artistic expression, emotionality, surprise can be complementary to rationality, scientific thinking, habit, and sound methodological implementation. They have been the source of great breakthroughs in science and provide the necessary sensitivity to more precisely identify what bounds a problem and its context.

Skill in arbitrage: developing the capability to differentiate and integrate

Arbitrage is an essential element of scholarship that involves academics and practitioners jointly engaging in knowledge co-creation. Van de Ven (2007: 15) defined arbitrage as "a strategy of explaining differences by seeing the interdependencies and webs of entanglement between different and divergent dimensions of a problem, its boundaries and context." Differences, rooted in deeply held professional beliefs, values, preferences, and experiences of academics and practitioners, or even academics from different disciplines, can be divisive and create conflict and tension in collaborative relationships. Recognizing and managing the implications of their entanglement in any academic–practitioner relationship is a skill that is vital to the process of knowledge co-creation.

When academics and practitioners seek to co-create worthwhile knowledge they enter a "space between" two different professional worlds (Bradbury & Lichtenstein, 2000). The space is riddled with tensions that arise from differences in logics, communication styles, time horizons, incentives, and interests between the world of academia and organizations (Bartunek & Rynes, 2014). Priorities on each of these dimensions are often norms, which are fundamental to what it means to be a professional in each world. They are socially constructed in local professional practice and may be more skillfully constructed by the intellectual shamans which Waddock discussed in Chapter 5.

To fulfil the goal of knowledge generation serving wider society whilst, simultaneously, satisfying local institutional stakeholder interests and remaining true to one's professional norms and values, it is necessary to distinguish the driving forces behind multiple agendas and to work through the many apparently contradictory priorities and requirements. Making either/or choices between them can neglect important evidence, devalue expertise, and marginalize vital interests, reducing the value and impact of the output. Framing those contradictions as dualities that merit a "both/and" response to take advantage of complementarities between them is an important capability for anyone aspiring to work at the interface between the worlds of practice and academia. Jarzabkowski, Lewis, and Smith explain what this means both in theory and with examples from their own practice in Chapter 8. They offer some fine practical examples of how, in various modes of interaction with practice, the capacity to both differentiate and integrate (the very essence of a paradoxical mind-set: Lewis & Smith, 2014; Smith, 2015) is a valuable academic capability. In Chapter 8 we learn that,

> Differentiating practices include, for example, segmenting time and space for each agenda, surfacing distinct goals, missions and rewards, and linking with unique stakeholder groups. Integrating practices involve generating an overarching identity, highlighting linkages between alternative demands, and managing a portfolio of activities. Integrating practices encourage us to realize how the differences can come together toward an overarching pursuit and application of knowledge, and the value of improving our world. Integrating practices further emphasize deeper linkages; practitioners generate real world questions and access to data to answer these questions; academics offer methods and tools to effectively address those questions by collecting, analyzing and interpreting the data.

The subsequent chapters in this section illustrate how this capability to differentiate and integrate is developed from experiences in different contexts.

In Chapter 9, MacLean and MacIntosh offer a fascinating story of how this has played out over various phases of action research and how complexity theory became a useful paradigm for integrating the paradoxical differentiations. Their account of going back and forth between spending time in the field and time apart reflecting shows how acceptance of "emerging intention" and sensitivity to "embodied expression" of knowledge (Blackler, 1995) are critical in the process of developing creative insights.

Collins and McBain in Chapter 10 illustrate the experience of working with the personal challenges of differentiation and integration as an apprentice researcher on a practice-based doctoral programme (DBA) in the UK. The personal development experienced by the individual is one of understanding the different language, norms, and values of each world and then integrating them into a capability to deliver results in both effectively.

In Chapter 11, Antonacopoulou offers some helpful guidance for designing a space conducive to managing the tensions and paradoxes arising from differences at boundaries between national and institutional contexts, scientific disciplines, and fields of action and facilitating integration, and knowledge co-creation.

Together the paradoxical mind-set combined with a capacity to relate to others with empathy and without preconception about the complex reality of the other's world seem to offer some insight into what arbitrage actually entails. But to move the insights and knowledge generated beyond the research group that generated it also requires development of effective communication capabilities and the ability to build trust in the value of the research output.

Communicating meaningfully: adapting to the audience

Communicating research so it seems meaningful and useful depends on the extent of emotional and cognitive connection potential users make with the narrative and the perceived value of the new knowledge in relation to their particular practice (Todorova & Durisin, 2007). A user's capacity to connect and what the user will connect with will depend on where they come from and what they already know. In Action Research, as MacLean and MacIntosh illustrate, being capable of facilitating generative dialogue is part of translating and transforming relevant input into something meaningful output (Carlile, 2004). In the other types of engaged scholarship, which Van de Ven identifies in his framework (Chapter 7, Fig. 7.4), the knowledge generation process may be separated from testing through immediate application to a greater degree. To communicate the relevance of knowledge from types of research where dialogue is divorced from the generation process requires language that has meaning and resonance in the user's context. As Collins and McBain note in Chapter 10, practitioners entering a DBA programme as apprentice scholars initially find academic language difficult, yet, once they master it, they find it equally challenging to revert to the language of practice back in the work place.

Unless research is communicated through the medium which a particular audience recognizes and appreciates, its value can be overlooked. Versatility in communicative capability develops in many ways. In Chapter 8 Smith illustrates how teaching on executive education enhances both her communication capabilities and her access to research data. In Chapter 10, Collins and McBain suggest that practice in explaining the same thing to different audiences both refines doctoral research thinking and communication skills. Antonacopolou (Chapter 11) promotes careful choice of creative modes of communication which feel unfamiliar to *both* academics and practitioners. Shared unfamiliarity creates a level playing field which seems to allow people from different epistemic cultures to start their sense-making on an equal footing, without the prejudice of pre-determined identity perceptions (Knorr Cetina, 1999). They can make better connections back to their own world, which is particularly useful for the inter-disciplinary translation process.

Careful development of a shared terminology for complex concepts whilst choosing words that are commonly understood wherever possible is important in all interactions. Both Van de Ven (Chapter 7) and MacLean and MacIntosh (Chapter 9) suggest that iteration towards understanding is an essential part of that process.

What all these chapters have in common is a view that, whatever knowledge research produces, it is only ever partial. However rigorous the process, research findings can only ever be imperfect and incomplete abstract guides to the complex reality or organizations and social systems. "The map is not the territory" as the philosopher Alfred Korzybski famously said. Producing any map of the ever-changing territory of social science involves journeying with people from different paradigms, domains of theory, and experiences. Integrating their findings requires a higher level of abstraction (Bateson, 1972), which both compounds communication problems, because it strips out detail and nuances in the service of simplicity, and opens up opportunities for interpretation that prompt new questions and avenues of exploration. Sophisticated communication capabilities become vital for moving research knowledge appropriately across semantic and pragmatic boundaries (Carlile, 2004) without compromising the rigour that bounds valid application.

Evolving the identity of the professional scholar

Several authors suggest that working at this interface requires a willingness to engage in unsettling and interactive identity work in a way somewhat consistent with Bartunek and Rynes in Part I, Chapter 6.

In Chapter 10, Collins and McBain explore international doctoral students' transition from a singular identity as an expert practitioner to that of an integrated scholar practitioner during a UK-based DBA programme. They explain how identity development is supported and explore the experience of apprentice researchers as they move from the feelings of ignorance and insecurity when they enter the academic world, through liminal (Beech, 2011) spaces full of tension and paradox to become more comfortable working across both worlds of academia and practice. Interaction and interdependence in relationships with peers, mentors and supervisors are vital in supporting their transition.

MacLean and MacIntosh (Chapter 9) share their own developmental journey, describing a process of interactive identity formation emerging over progressive phases of action research. The experience of trying to remain professional without controlling the research process offers an inspiring story that illustrates what happens when academics acknowledge the limits of rational science and logic and embrace the richness of human capacities for art, poetry, and aesthetics in the action research process. To let go, so as to truly inquire into the dynamics of a human system *with* the people who constitute it, allows the embodied experience of all the parties to generate insight that is meaningful for everyone. Periods of interaction punctuated by periods of reflection and sense-making on both sides allows the theory and action to become entangled to produce creative insight. In this way our different experiences, understandings, intuitions, feelings, and imaginations become complementary perspectives on a complex system. However, to fully use the plurality of knowledge in a community of academics and practitioners requires values simultaneously high in collectivism and individualism together with a mental orientation simultaneously high in particularism and universalism, and a view of self or at least one's professional identity as being one of INTER-dependent self-construal (Adler et al., 2008).

The tension between "me" and "we" (Kreiner, Hollensbe & Sheep, 2006) as professionals move into the space between worlds constitutes a paradox of belonging (Smith & Lewis, 2011), which several authors suggest will create insecurity and defensive routines. As Jarzabkowski et al. (Chapter 8) point out, "changing our hearts and minds is difficult, time-consuming work."

Developing professional capabilities

In this Part, the experiences of the five authors paint a rich picture of the capabilities an engaged scholar needs to develop. A paradoxical mind-set that accepts and works with the tensions pervading the relationship and uses them generatively to challenge one's world view seems fundamental. The capability to flexibly bring to bear appropriate educational and research approaches and work confidently across multiple paradigms and disciplines with concern for the consequences is required to big theoretical questions that challenge society and develop policy. Engaged scholars know how to work through arbitrage and negotiate sufficiently trusting and mutually valuable relationships. They can create a safe space in which the relationships between academics and practitioners can transcend the boundaries that define their separate professional identities, facilitate generative dialogue, and communicate with empathy and understanding of the other's worlds.

Such sophisticated skills are surprisingly underrated and undervalued in a university setting that traditionally rewards faculty on the production of more insular and inward-looking values of objective rigour evaluated by peers in single academic disciplines. This Part offers evidence from some distinguished scholars who have worked successfully within that more esoteric and narrow regime, *and* have learned how to break out, developing the capabilities to work through the tensions in a more relational way across boundaries, and with a purpose beyond simply meeting targets.

Note

1 Hierarchy constrains knowledge generation because it tends to ignore the contribution of tacit knowledge, market forces provide strong incentives for knowledge generation, but limit appropriability, which "impede(s) the socially optimal dissemination of knowledge" (Adler et al., 2008: 360).

References

Adler, P. S. & Kwon, S.-W. (2002). Social capital: Prospects for a new concept. *Academy of Management Review*, 27(1), 17–40.

Adler, P. S., Kwon, S.-W. & Heckscher, C. (2008). Professional work: The emergence of collaborative community. *Organization Science*, 19(2), 359–76.

Bartunek, J. M. & Rynes, S. L. (2014). Academics and practitioners are alike and unlike: The paradoxes of academic–practitioner relationships. *Journal of Management*, 40(5), 1181–201.

Bateson, G. (1972). *Steps to an Ecology of Mind: A Revolutionary Approach to Man's Understanding of Himself.* New York: Chandler Publishing Co.

Beech, N. (2011). Liminality and the practices of identity reconstruction. *Human Relations*, 64(2), 285–302.

Blackler, F. (1995). Knowledge, knowledge work and organizations: An overview and interpretation. *Organization Studies*, 16(6), 1021–46.

Bradbury, H. & Lichtenstein, B. M. B. (2000). Relationality in organizational research: Exploring the space between. *Organization Science*, 11(5), 551–64.

Carlile, P. R. (2004). Transferring, translating and transforming: An integrative framework for managing knowledge across boundaries. *Organization Science*, 15(5), 555–68.

Gulati, R. (2007). Tent poles, tribalism, and boundary spanning: The rigor–relevance debate in management research. *Academy of Management Journal*, 50(4), 775–82.

Gustavsen, B. (2001). Theory and practice: The mediating discourse. In Reason, P. & Bradbury, H. (Eds.) *Handbook of Action Research* (pp. 17–26). London: Sage Publications.

Knorr Cetina, K. (1999). *Epistemic Cultures: How Sciences Made Knowledge*. Cambridge, MA: Harvard University Press.

Kreiner, G. E., Hollensbe, E. C. & Sheep, M. L. (2006). Where is the "me" among the "we"? Identity work and the search for the optimal balance. *Academy of Management Journal*, 49(5), 1031–57.

Lewis, M. W. & Smith, W. K. (2014). Paradox as a meta-theoretical perspective: Sharpening the focus and widening the scope. *The Journal of Applied Behavioral Science*, 50(2), 127–49.

Smith, W. K. (2015). Dynamic decision-making: A model of senior leaders managing strategic paradoxes. *Academy of Management Journal*, 57(6), 1592–623.

Smith, W. K. & Lewis, M. W. (2011). Towards a theory of paradox: A dynamic equilibrium model of organizing. *Academy of Management Review*, 36(2), 381–403.

Todorova, G. & Durisin, B. (2007). Absorptive capacity: Valuing a reconceptualization. *Academy of Management Review*, 32(3), 774–86.

Van de Ven, A. H. (2007). *Engaged Scholarship: A Guide for Organizational and Social Research.* Oxford: Oxford University Press.

Wenger, E. (1998). *Communities of Practice: Learning, Meaning and Identity.* Cambridge, UK: Cambridge University Press.

7 Developing capabilities of engaged scholarship

Andrew H. Van de Ven

Introduction

Motivations and capabilities of engaged scholarship are necessary requirements for academic–practitioner research partnerships. Typically, the lightning rod that motivates academics and practitioners to work together is addressing a big research question or problem that requires multiple perspectives. In addition to motivation, sharing knowledge across academic–practitioner boundaries requires developing interactive expertise. As Collins (2004) discusses, one cannot study or engage meaningfully across different communities of practice without under-standing the language, norms, and procedures used in the specialized domain of work being carried out at the boundary. Given the tensions and paradoxes in academic–practitioner research discussed by Bartunek and McKenzie in Chapter 1 and by Jarzabkowski, Lewis, and Smith in Chapter 8, such research partner-ships represent a highly challenging form of cross-boundary work. If academics and practitioners are to meaningfully engage in research partnerships (which is the central focus of this book), then all parties involved need to develop inter-active expertise. Specifically, in this chapter I argue that participating in research partnerships requires both academics and practitioners to develop capabilities in formulating research problems, developing theories, designing and conducting research, and communicating and using research findings. While different parties in a research partnership may negotiate who takes the lead in performing these four tasks, all partners need sufficient interactive expertise in order to under-stand, appreciate, and negotiate what each other is doing and why they are doing it.

This chapter focuses on the development of these capabilities for both aca-demics and practitioners. It introduces an educational course on engaged scholar-ship that can be accessed at z.umn.edu/mgmt8101. This free and publicly available website contains 14 sessions, shown in Figure 7.1, of a semester-long graduate course on engaged scholarship. As exemplified in Figure 7.2 for the problem formulation class, each session contains a web page that provides access to all the topics, readings, exercises, and video lectures for each class. In addi-tion, the course website provides links to a library course page that was created with the help of the University of Minnesota Libraries. It provides a virtual

Session	Topics
1	Introduction and overview
2	Developing a research proposal (submit research proposal worksheet)
3	Philosophy of science underlying engaged scholarship
4	Formulating the research problem or question
5	Grounded methods of problem formulation (submit research problem report)
6	Building a theory
7	Justifying a theory (share theory reports with peers)
	University spring break – no class
8	Two modes of thought: variance and process models
9	Variance research designs
10	Process research designs
11	Constructing measurement instruments (submit research design)
12	Communicating research and problem solving
13	Writing and reviewing crafts
14	Practicing engaged scholarship (student final research proposal)

Figure 7.1 Engaged scholarship website course sessions.

Session 04: Formulating the Research Problem

Topics
What problem and question do you want to study?

1. Situating the problem
2. Grounding the problem in reality
3. Diagnosing the problem
4. Problem solving by formulating the crucial question

Video Clips

- Problem Formulation
- Diagnosing a Problem Space

Reading

- *Engaged Scholarship*, Chapter 3
- Edmondson, Crossing Boundaries to Investigate Problems in the Field. 2011
- Supplementary Readings:
    - Davis, "That's Interesting." (1971) and "That's Classic!" (1986).
    - Eden & Jones (1983) "Messing About in Problems," pp. 39–59.

Notes

- Class Slides on Problem Formulation

Exercise

- Complete this Problem Formulation Exercise, and bring to class for discussion.

Figure 7.2 Example of session web page.

treasury of resources and information that, as best as I know, represents the richest knowledge infrastructure available for engaged scholarship. The course web pages are revised annually each time I teach the engaged scholarship course.

While teaching this course each year with about 15 doctoral students, the course website attracts about 30,000 hits from more than 40 different countries. Faculty teaching research methods courses in many other schools and countries refer their academic and practitioner doctoral students and colleagues to the website. While this website provides the curriculum for a distance learning course, it is not intended to replace the need for face-to-face class meetings.

Just as I do in my weekly face-to-face classes with students, I encourage faculty who refer their students to this website to meet weekly with them to do three things in class:

- discuss student questions about assigned video lectures and readings;
- mentor students in completing assigned learning exercises; and
- have students make class presentations and receive feedback on the application of the class topic to their research proposal.

Although I have unfortunately not conducted a systematic before-and-after flipped course study, I have noticed that most students have developed higher quality research proposals in courses after the two years since flipping the course on the web than before. I think this higher performance is due to students having more "air time" in class and getting more feedback on their research proposals because I no longer lecture in class. In addition, foreign students tell me they greatly appreciate being able to view the video lectures on class web pages several times before or after class.

I receive and respond weekly to email inquiries from individuals who follow the course website from anywhere in the world. In addition, I am periodically invited by schools as a guest faculty in person and via Skype to conduct workshops or seminars on engaged scholarship. However, to date, the course website has not been designed or conducted as a MOOC (massive open online course).

The outcome-based education objective of this course is that students develop a good research proposal, as is necessary to undertake a research project or a dissertation. A good research proposal is defined as one that covers all the bases of the "Diamond Model" shown in Figure 7.3, and measured in terms of the criteria presented in Table 7.1. As I discuss in this chapter, this model serves as the organizing framework for the course, and focuses on the four key activities in any research project:

- problem formulation;
- theory building;
- research design; and
- problem solving.

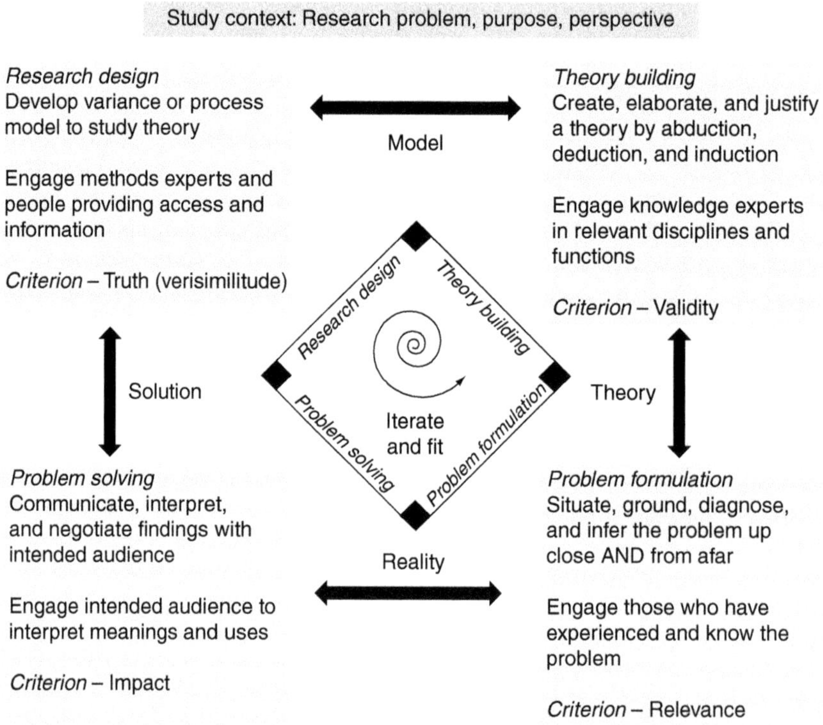

Study context: Research problem, purpose, perspective

Research design
Develop variance or process
model to study theory

Theory building
Create, elaborate, and justify
a theory by abduction,
deduction, and induction

Model

Engage methods experts and
people providing access and
information

Engage knowledge experts
in relevant disciplines and
functions

Criterion – Truth (verisimilitude)

Research design

Theory building

Criterion – Validity

Solution

Iterate
and fit

Theory

Problem solving

Problem formulation

Problem solving
Communicate, interpret,
and negotiate findings with
intended audience

Problem formulation
Situate, ground, diagnose,
and infer the problem up
close AND from afar

Reality

Engage intended audience to
interpret meanings and uses

Engage those who have
experienced and know the
problem

Criterion – Impact

Criterion – Relevance

Figure 7.3 Engaged scholarship diamond model.

Each class session examines one of these four activities in the diamond model. Before each session, students are asked to review the video clips, readings, notes, and assignments on the course website. In each class session, having asked students to come prepared, I begin by asking them to lead discussions with their questions and comments about the website materials. Then, I engage students in various individual and group exercises on the substantive and methodological issues involved in performing each research activity.

Working knowledge of the subject matter is also gained by students developing a research proposal on a topic of their choosing. As the course advances through the topics, students write reports on four consecutive sections of their research proposal (problem formulation, theory building, research design, and problem solving), culminating in their overall research proposal. Student peers and I review and provide feedback on ways to improve reports. Based on this feedback, students are asked to revise their proposals several times until it is judged to be of sound conceptual quality and operational clarity. After the outcome-based learning objective is achieved in this course, I expect students to actually implement their research proposals either as a research project or as an initial draft of their dissertation proposal. Most students who have taken the course have done so.

Table 7.1 Criteria for evaluating a research proposal

Please evaluate this report using this five-point scale
1 Not addressed or evident in the report
2 Attempt made but some errors occurred in the analysis/answer
3 Attempt made but he result needs more work, elaboration or refinement
4 Attempt made with good result; issue accomplished; no further work needed.
5 Attempt made with excellent result; issue accomplished with distinction.

1 Statement of the research problem: _____
   • is situated in terms of perspective, focus, level and scope
   • is grounded in reality by addressing journalist's question up close and from afar
   • data are diagnosed/analyzed properly to infer the problem
   • the research question focuses on an important researchable aspect of problem
   • the research question permits more than one plausible answer

2 The research proposition (theory) _____
   • clearly states an expected relationship among concepts or events
   • is supported with an argument (i.e. claim, reasons, evidence, assumptions and reservations)
   • directly addresses the research question and problem
   • is compared with a plausible alternative theory or the status quo answer
   • travels across levels of abstraction

3 The research design clearly spells out: _____
   • theoretical unit of analysis and unit of observation
   • key design elements of a variance or process model
   • sample or replication logic and sample selection
   • definitions and measurement procedures for variables or events
   • threats to internal, statistical, external and construct validities

4 Research implementation and problem solving for theory and practice : _____
   • research contributions/implications for science AND practice are clearly stated
   • steps for developing and sharing findings with target audiences/users are discussed
   • statement of how research findings will be used/applied is prudent
   • relevant stakeholders are engaged in each of the above steps

   • Total Score _____

This chapter now summarizes the engaged scholarship model and the proposed four key capabilities that academics and practitioners need to know in order to engage meaningfully in research partnerships undertaken for the purpose of advancing knowledge for both theory and practice. Throughout the course, I emphasize that there is far more to learn about problem formulation, theory building, research design, and problem solving than commonplace meanings of these terms imply.

The engaged scholarship model

My book (Van de Ven, 2007), on which the course is based, proposes a method of *engaged scholarship* for studying complex social problems that often exceed our limited capabilities to study on our own. *Engaged scholarship* is a participative form of research for obtaining the advice and perspectives of key stakeholders (researchers, users, clients, sponsors and practitioners) to understand a complex problem or phenomenon. Using the diamond model illustrated in Figure 7.3, I argue (Van de Ven, 2007) that researchers can significantly increase the likelihood of producing knowledge that advances theory and practice by engaging others whose perspectives are relevant in each of the four study activities:

- *Problem formulation*—situate, ground, and diagnose the research problem by determining who, what, where, when, why, and how the problem exists up close and from afar. Answering these journalist's questions requires meeting and talking with people who experience and know the problem, as well as reviewing the literature on the prevalence and boundary conditions of the problem.
- *Theory building*—develop plausible alternative theories (or propositions) that address the problem as it exists in its particular context. Developing these alternative theories requires conversations with knowledge experts from the relevant disciplines and functions that have addressed the problem, as well as a review of relevant literature.
- *Research design*—gather empirical evidence to compare the plausible alternative models that address the research problem. Doing this well typically requires getting advice from technical experts in research methodology and the people who can provide access to data, and, of course, the respondents or informants of information.
- *Problem solving*—communicate, interpret, and apply the empirical findings on which models better answer the research question about the problem. The greater the difference in content-specific knowledge between researchers and stakeholders, the more they need to communicate in order to understand and use the research findings. Communications might begin with written reports and presentations for knowledge transfer, then conversations to interpret different meanings of the report, and then pragmatic and political negotiations to reconcile conflicting interests.

Engaged scholarship can be practiced in many different ways, including the four approaches outlined in Figure 7.4. These different approaches depend on:

- whether the purpose of a research study is to examine basic questions of description, explanation, and prediction, or applied questions of design, evaluation, or action intervention; and
- the degree to which researchers examine the problem domain as external observers or internal participants.

1 *Informed basic research* is undertaken to describe, explain, or predict a social phenomenon. It resembles a traditional form of basic social science where the researcher is a detached outsider of the social system being

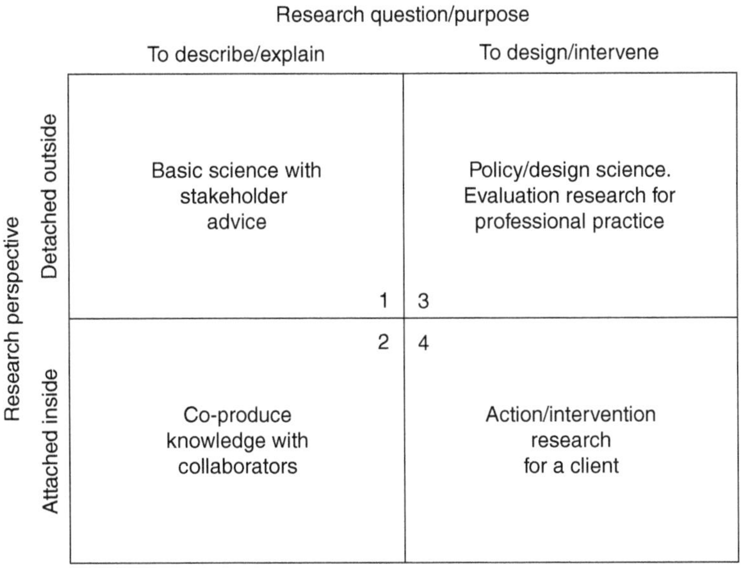

Research question/purpose

	To describe/explain	To design/intervene
Detached outside	Basic science with stakeholder advice	Policy/design science. Evaluation research for professional practice
	1	3
	2	4
Attached inside	Co-produce knowledge with collaborators	Action/intervention research for a client

Research perspective

Figure 7.4 Alternative forms of engaged scholarship.
Source: Van de Ven, 2007: 27.

examined, but it also solicits advice and feedback from key stakeholders and inside informants on each of the research activities as listed in Figure 7.3. These inside informants and stakeholders play an advisory role, and the researcher directs and controls all research activities.

2   ***Collaborative basic research*** entails a greater sharing of power and activities among researchers and stakeholders than informed research. As Bartunek and McKenzie discuss in Chapter 1, collaborative research teams are often composed of insiders and outsiders who jointly share the activities listed in Figure 7.3 in order to co-produce basic knowledge about a complex problem or phenomenon. The division of labor is typically negotiated to take advantage of the complementary skills of different research team members, and the balance of power or responsibility shifts back and forth as the tasks demand. Because this collaborative form of research tends to focus on basic questions of mutual interest to the partners, it has much less of an applied orientation than the following two forms of engaged scholarship.

3   ***Design and evaluation research*** is undertaken to examine normative questions dealing with the design and evaluation of policies, programs, or models for solving the practical problems of a profession in question. Variously called "design or policy science" or "evaluation research," this form of research goes beyond describing or explaining a social problem by also seeking to obtain evidence-based knowledge of the efficacy or relative success of alternative solutions to applied problems. Evaluation researchers

typically take a distanced and outside perspective of the designs or policies being evaluated. Inquiry from the outside is necessary because evidence-based evaluations require comparisons of numerous cases, and because distance from any one case is required for evaluation findings to be viewed as impartial and legitimate. But the engagement of stakeholders is important so that they have opportunities to influence and provide consent to those evaluation study decisions that may affect them. These decisions include the purposes of the evaluation study (problem formulation), the criteria and models used to evaluate the program in question (research design), and the ways the study findings will be analyzed, interpreted, and used (problem solving).

4   *Action/intervention research* takes a clinical intervention approach to diagnose and treat a problem of a specific client. Kurt Lewin (1951), a pioneer of action research, suggested a learning strategy of both engaging with and intervening in the client's social setting. The foundation of this learning process was client participation in problem solving using systematic methods of data collection, feedback, reflection, and action. Since Lewin's time, action research has evolved into a diverse family of clinical research strategies in many professional fields. For example, in Chapter 9 of this volume, MacLean and MacIntosh discuss a creative action perspective that incorporates the power of intentions, emotion, intuition, and imagination in academic–practitioner engagements. Action research projects tend to begin by diagnosing the particular problem or needs of an individual client. To the extent possible, a researcher utilizes whatever knowledge is available from basic or design science to understand the client's problem. However, this knowledge may require substantial adaptation to fit the ill-structured or context-specific nature of the client's problem. Action research projects often consist of N-of-1 studies, where systematic comparative evidence can only be gained through trial-and-error experiments over time. In this situation, action researchers have argued that the only way to understand a social system is to change it through deliberate intervention and diagnosis of responses to the intervention. This interventionist approach typically requires intensive interaction, training, and consulting by the researcher with people in the client's setting.

Sometimes advocates of a particular research approach make disparaging remarks about other forms. This is unfortunate, because all four forms of engaged scholarship are legitimate, important, and necessary for addressing different research questions posed by science and practice (description, explanation, design, or control of a problematic situation). Which approach is most appropriate depends on the research question and the perspective taken to examine the question. Pragmatically, the effectiveness of a research approach should be judged in terms of how well it addresses the research question for which it was intended (Dewey, 1938).

Although the four forms of engaged scholarship entail different kinds of relationship between the researcher and stakeholder in a study, engagement is the common denominator. The more ambiguous and complex the problem, the greater the need for engaging others who can provide different perspectives for revealing critical dimensions of the nature, context, and implications of the study.

Skills for academic–practitioner engagement

Whether the objectives are basic research or applied problem solving, engaged scholarship represents a strategy for surpassing the dual hurdles of relevance and rigor in advancing evidence-based knowledge of complex problems in the world. By exploiting differences in the kinds of knowledge that academics and practitioners from diverse backgrounds can bring forth on a problem, I claim that engaged scholarship produces knowledge that is more penetrating and insightful than when scholars or practitioners work on the problem alone. As the course website shows, each session focuses on developing ideas, skills, and methods that researchers can use to accomplish this claim.

The remainder of this chapter examines only a few key issues that pertain to this book's theme of developing academic–practitioner research partnerships. They include:

* negotiating the research relationship;
* formulating the research problem and question;
* comparing alterative models or propositions that address the research question;
* communicating and using the research findings in ways that change how academics and practitioners think about the research question and problem; and
* designing the research as a collaborative learning community of scholars and practitioners with diverse perspectives.

As discussed here, engaged scholarship involves a relationship between academics and practitioners, and *both* parties need to build their skills to perform these tasks well.

Negotiating the research relationship

Negotiating a relationship with academic and practitioner stakeholders and obtaining access to data sources are formidable challenges in launching any form of social research. As discussed in the next task, most research questions and problems represent novel and ambiguous ideas that are difficult to understand and are open to many interpretations and interests. As a result, negotiating a research relationship is not a one-time event: it requires many discussions to convey (transfer) the research message, interpret (translate) its many possible meanings, and negotiate (transform) differing interests into pragmatic uses that the parties find acceptable (Carlile, 2004). Rarely does a single meeting (particularly if it is a "cold call" among strangers) achieve sufficient common understandings and interests among parties to motivate their commitment to a research project. In discussing their lessons in developing collaborative relationships in Chapter 16, Landman, Glowinkowski and Demes emphasize that it takes time to develop, explore, and change ideas as opportunities come and go, and this is facilitated when partners:

- are in close proximity;
- are intellectually and methodologically interested in studying the research question;
- are recruited with the training and skills to develop and operationalize project objectives; and
- involve key stakeholders on an advisory group for the project.

These negotiations should recognize that not all research relationships are alike, and that practitioners (like academics) are not homogeneous (as discussed by McKenzie and Van Winkelen in Chapter 17).

The different research questions examined with the four forms of engaged scholarship can be studied *with* and/or *for* practitioners and other stakeholders. Although this distinction is seldom made, it importantly influences the research relationship and the form of engagement. Research done *for* others (as in design/ evaluation, and action research) typically implies an *exchange* relationship where research is undertaken in the service of solving a problem of a client or a user group. In an exchange relationship, the purpose of engagement is to ensure that the interests and values of the client are reflected in the study. In contrast, research undertaken *with* others implies a *collaborative* relationship, as in the informed and collaborative forms of research. In a collaborative relationship, the purpose of engagement is to obtain the different but complementary perspectives of collaborators for understanding the problem domain. Being clear about the nature of the relationship between researchers and practitioners is obviously important for clarifying the expectations and roles of all parties to a research partnership. However, sometimes researchers unwittingly negotiate studies both for and with other stakeholders without understanding their mixed and unintended consequences.

The interests of the researcher and consumer or client are often not the same and thus difficult to align. In an exchange relationship, the client or consumer typically views the researcher as a consultant who is expected to solve his or her particular problem. Companies often institutionalize this kind of exchange relationship by asking the academic researcher to sign a confidential consulting contract. But engaged research should not be confused with consulting. Researchers are often less interested in the client's particular problem, but more interested in the general class of phenomena of which the particular problem is a part. In these cases, the researcher may be willing to serve as a research consultant for the client in exchange for obtaining resources and data needed to pursue his or her own basic research agenda. The researcher is viewed in these situations as having the power of expert knowledge over the less powerful and dependent client, patient, user, or subject, but the latter's consent, access, and resources are needed to conduct the social research.

Research relationships often have false starts with mixed motives—tit-for-tat game situations that may result in win–lose or lose–lose situations for the researcher or the client. Clarifying whether research is undertaken *with* or *for* academics and practitioners is important to negotiate carefully and openly. In exchange relationships, engagement often represents an instrumental way to increase the likelihood that the research addresses the questions, problems, and interests of the client. Given divergent interests, it is not surprising that researchers fear involving clients in designing the research, for it may "misdirect" or "hijack" achievement of the researcher's objectives. For example, Brief and Dukerich (1991) and Kilduff and Kelemen (2001) argued that practitioner involvement in formulating research questions may steer the research in narrow, short-term, or particularistic directions. Such criticisms are premised on the researcher having an exchange relationship, rather than a collaborative relationship with stakeholders. The divergent objectives, conflicting interests, and power asymmetries that Jarzabkowski et al. discuss in Chapter 8 often produce instrumental and calculative consequences between researchers and clients that inhibit learning.

Research undertaken *with* practitioners implies a collaborative relationship among equals whose differences are complementary in reaching a goal. The goal is to understand a problem or issue that is too complex for any party to study alone. Appreciating these individual limitations motivates some (but certainly not all) researchers and practitioners to collaborate and learn with each other. In order to do this, the parties must come to know each other and negotiate their advisory or collaborative relationship, including how they will accommodate, adapt, and integrate their different perspectives on a problem or question being examined. Such a collaborative relationship is premised on a common desire to learn and to understand a complex problem or question that drives the engagement.

Engaging advisers and collaborators in a study does not necessarily imply that a researcher loses control of his or her study, but it does entail greater accountability to the stakeholders involved in a study. Engagement often raises false expectations that the suggestions and concerns expressed will be addressed. Engagement does not require consensus among stakeholders: much learning occurs through arbitrage by leveraging differences among stakeholders. Negotiating different and sometimes conflicting interests implies that creative conflict management skills are critical for engaged scholars. Without these skills, engagement may produce the ancient Tower of Babel, where intentions to build a tower to reach heaven were thwarted by the noisy and confusing language of the people.

Formulating the research problem and question

The lightning rod that attracts academics and practitioners to jointly engage in research is the research problem or question (Bartunek, Rynes & Ireland, 2006). Hence, I suggest that researchers start with problems, go into the field and the literature, and reach across boundaries to gain a clear and holistic appreciation of the problem or phenomenon being examined. As Edmondson (2011: 39) states:

> Problems provide a natural connection with practice. Studying a compelling problem, researchers are motivated to care about action. Problems matter! ... Unless you have an unusual office location, sitting at your desk is unlikely to be the most conducive situation for gaining insight into organizational phenomena. Although one can learn about an industry or company from written materials, fuller understanding and new ideas are more likely when meeting and observing people who work in that setting.

Learning the nature of a question or phenomenon in ambiguous settings often entails numerous false starts and dead ends. Learning involves waste. We tend to forget how much paper was thrown away in order to learn how to write. Maclean and MacIntosh (Chapter 9) discuss how formulating an initial research question may begin with a rational design or plan, but as the research begins it gives way to an emergent phenomenon of reflective sense-making and (re)planning conversations. This is learning by engaging others when confronting the research phenomenon in the field. Heedful accommodation to the diverse viewpoints of advisers and collaborators in a research project may be challenging, but when we develop the skills of appreciating diverse viewpoints we can gain a richer gestalt of the question being investigated than by relying on the sense-making of a single stakeholder (Weick, 1995).

As noted before, time is critical for building relationships of trust, candor, and learning among researchers and practitioners. Time is also critical to develop an understanding of the phenomenon being investigated, to facilitate implementation of research findings, and to increase the likelihood of making significant advances to a scholarly discipline. Cross-sectional studies seldom provide researchers sufficient time and trials to become knowledgeable about their research topic.[1] Longitudinal research promotes deeper learning because it provides repeated trials for approximating and understanding a research question or topic. Becoming "world class" is a path-dependent process of pursuing a coherent theme of research questions from project to project over an extended period of time.

A basic but often overlooked fact of most academic research is that researchers are exposed to only the information that people in research sites are willing to share. Interviews in cross-sectional studies or initial interviews in longitudinal studies with research sites tend to be formal and shallow. Greater candor and penetration into the subject matter seldom occur until a sufficient number of interactions over time have have happened for participants to come to know and trust one another. Perhaps the "one-minute manager" is an unfortunate social construction of the one-minute researcher.

Rynes, McNatt and Bretz (1999) found a significant positive relationship between the hours spent by academic researchers at organizational sites and the implementation of research findings as well as the scholarly contribution of the research (based on paper citation rates). Their explanation for this finding was that increased "face time" increases affective trust of organizational members toward the researcher (e.g., Osborn & Hagedoorn, 1997), and keeps the research project salient in their minds. In addition, time spent on site is likely to bring the researcher closer to the phenomenon being studied, as well as to increase the researcher's awareness of the ways in which organizational members are framing the topic or problem under investigation (Beyer, 1997). Both of these types of insight are likely to increase the chances that the research findings make significant contributions and are implemented (Rynes et al., 1999: 873).

In addition to engaging with people, another critical source of knowledge is to engage the relevant literature for each step in the diamond model in Figure 7.3: problem formulation, theory building, research design, and problem solving. The literature provides access to prior research and models that inform and shape the research question and conceptual answers. Familiarity with what has come before provides the status quo baseline for understanding a research question and how prior findings might be integrated, elaborated, or refuted in the current work. Finding out what others have done to understand a problem lowers the risk of reinventing the wheel. Prior research is also useful for understanding the context and pervasiveness of the particular problem or issue observed in the field. As a consequence, we rely on the relevant literature to know what parts of a problem have already been studied, what questions deserve to be studied, and which questions might be deferred to future research.

The need for alternative models to examine big questions

Given all of the challenges chapter authors discuss in making academic–practitioner research collaborations work, we should ask: Why do it? What kinds of research problems require academic–practitioner engagement? I argue that the more complex the problem or the bigger the research question, the greater the need to engage researchers from different disciplines and practitioners with different functional experiences. Engagement of others is necessary because most real-world problems are too complex to be captured by any one investigator or perspective. There are many big questions and problems that are very difficult to study in a productive way without engagement and close interaction among scholars and practitioners.

Big questions have no easy answers, and they seldom provide an immediate payoff to practitioners or academics (Pettigrew, 2001). By definition, big questions often do not have clear solutions until after the research has been conducted and policy questions have been addressed. They also require a process of arbitrage in which researchers and practitioners engage each other to co-produce solutions whose demands exceed the capabilities of researchers or practitioners alone. Thus, at the time of designing a research project, prospective solutions to research questions are secondary in comparison with the importance of the research question that is being addressed. A good indicator of a big question is its self-evident capability to ignite the attention and enthusiasm of scholars and practitioners alike.

The study of big questions requires developing and comparing plausible alternative theories or models. Multiple models and frames of reference are needed to understand complex reality. Any given theory is an incomplete abstraction that cannot describe all aspects of a phenomenon. Theories are fallible human constructions that model a partial aspect of reality from a particular point of view with particular interests in mind. Comparing and contrasting plausible alternative models that reflect different perspectives is essential for discriminating between credible, erroneous, and noisy information. The choice of models and methods varies, of course, with the particular problem and purpose of a study. The more complex the problem or question, the greater the need to map this complexity by employing multiple and divergent models. Triangulation of methods and models increases reliability and validity. It also maximizes learning among members of an engaged scholarship team. Presumably, different models reflect the unique hunches and interests of different participants in the research project. Sharing approaches and findings enhances learning among co-investigators. Each strategy represents a different thought trial to frame and map the subject matter. As Weick (1989) argues, undertaking multiple independent thought trials facilitates good theory building.

Communicating and using research findings

A pervasive problem of social science research is that research findings are not used, neither to advance scientific knowledge (as measured by few citations of journal papers that advance subsequent science: Starbuck, 2005) nor to advance management practice (as indicated by the general lack of implementation of evidence-based management research: Rousseau & Boudreau, 2011). A deeper understanding of communicating knowledge across boundaries and a more engaged relationship between the researcher and their audience are needed if research findings are to have an impact in advancing science and practice.

Carlile's (2004) framework of knowledge transfer, translation, and transformation is useful for learning how to communicate study findings with different audiences. The framework emphasizes that communication requires a common knowledge of syntax, semantics, and pragmatics of language among people to understand each other's domain-specific knowledge. When the novelty of domain-specific knowledge between people increases, then progressively more complex processes of knowledge transfer, translation, and transformation are needed to communicate the meanings and potential uses of that knowledge.

When the people at a knowledge boundary share the same common syntax for understanding their different and interdependent domain-specific knowledge, then it can be communicated using a conventional information processing view of knowledge transfer from a speaker to listeners through written and verbal reports. The major challenge of knowledge transfer is to craft a sufficiently rich message and medium to convey the novelty of the information from the speaker to the audience. For example, written reports, verbal presentations, and face-to-face interactions between the speaker and listeners represent three increasingly rich media for knowledge transfer.

In addition, extensive research on innovation adoption and diffusion (reviewed by Rogers, 2003) suggest that research findings are more likely to be adopted and diffused when:

1   The audience perceives the findings as having a relative advantage over the status quo, are compatible with current understandings of things, are simple to understand, and are explicit, observable, and can be tried out.
2   They engage and reflect the views of leading members of the adopting community.
3   They are presented in a rhetorically persuasive argument with pathos, logos, and ethos justifications of research findings.

Knowledge transfer, however, typically remains a one-way transmission of information from a sender to a receiver. The listener in knowledge transfer remains relatively silent, but is never inactive. Authors of research reports will not know this unless they engage in conversations with readers or listeners of a report where it will become clear that listeners often have different interpretations and meanings of the novel information than the speaker intended. A research report is not treated as a social fact or as having a "fixed" meaning. Rather, it is open to multiple and unlimited meanings, interpretations, and actions among participants engaged in the text. Hence, when communicating research findings, a research report should be viewed as a first—not the last—step for researchers to engage in conversations with potential users, and thereby gain a broader and deeper appreciation of the meanings of research findings.

When interpretive differences exist on the meanings of research findings, then a more complex semantic boundary of "knowledge translation" must be crossed. At this boundary, speakers and listeners engage in conversations and discourse to mutually share, interpret, and construct their meanings of research findings. Speakers and listeners become co-authors in mutually constructing and making sense of their interactions. At the knowledge translation boundary, conversation is the essence and the product of research.

Knowledge transfer and translation may surface conflicting interests among parties. Crossing this even more complex pragmatic communication boundary requires parties to negotiate and politically transform their knowledge and interests from their own domain to a collective's. As Carlile (2004: 559) states, "When different interests arise, developing an adequate common knowledge is a political process of negotiating and defining common interests." Although social scientists tend to shy away from political discourse, developing such skills is clearly needed to communicate research knowledge at the political boundary.

The persuasiveness of a message is in the "eyes" of the listener (not just the speaker) and requires appreciating the context and assumptions of the audience. For example, Davis (1971, 1986) argues that what influences readers to view a theory as interesting or classical is the degree to which the writer challenges the assumptions of the reader. In a nutshell, a classic work speaks to the primary concerns or assumptions of an audience, while an interesting theory speaks to the secondary concerns of an audience. Interesting theories negate an accepted assumption held by the audience and affirm an unanticipated alternative. The key rhetorical message is that knowledge transfer is not only a function of the logic and data supporting a message, but also the degree to which the speaker is viewed as a credible witness and is able to stir the human emotions of listeners. Hence, from a rhetorical perspective, a researcher can increase the likelihood of influencing his or her intended audience by going beyond logos (the logical, technical research findings) to include pathos (persuasiveness and incentives) and ethos (the ethical and appropriateness) of the findings in research presentations, discussions, and reports.

Designing the research as a collaborative learning community

Engaged scholarship is not a solitary exercise; instead, it is a collective learning achievement. Engagement means that scholars step outside of themselves and participate with others to learn about different interpretations in performing each step of the research process: problem formulation, theory building, research design, and problem solving. This form of collaborative learning requires a fundamental shift in how researchers define their relationships with the communities in which they are located, including faculty and students from various disciplines in the university and practitioners in relevant professional domains. Edward Zlotkowski, a leading proponent of engaged scholarship in American higher education, captures the identity and empathy of an engaged scholar:

> It's about faculty members having a profound respect for those other than themselves, whether they be practitioners or students. ... There is a profound emphasis on the concept of deep respect and, I might even say, humility vis-à-vis other kinds of knowledge producers. Not because we don't have an important and distinctive role to play in knowledge production, but because we don't have the exclusive right to such production. As we begin to engage in partnerships with both our students and outside communities of practice on the basis of such deep respect, we allow ourselves to become real-world problem solvers in a way that is otherwise not possible. Indeed, I would suggest that unless we learn to develop deeper respect for our non-faculty colleagues, we run the risk of becoming "academic ventriloquists"—speaking for our students, speaking for the communities we allegedly

serve—but not really listening to them or making them our peers in addressing the vital issues that concern all of us.

(Edward Zlotkowski, quoted in Kenworthy-U'Ren, 2005: 360)

Engagement is a relationship that involves negotiation and collaboration between
researchers and practitioners in a learning community; such a community jointly
produces knowledge that can both advance the scientific enterprise and enlighten
a community of practitioners. Instead of viewing organizations and clients as
data collection sites and funding sources, an engaged scholar views them as a
learning workplace (idea factory) where practitioners and scholars co-produce
knowledge on important questions and issues by testing alternative ideas and different views of a common problem. "Abundant evidence shows that both the
civic and academic health of any culture is vitally enriched as scholars and practitioners speak and listen carefully to each other" (Boyer, 1996: 15).

Conclusion

In conclusion, this chapter has introduced an online course on engaged scholarship, and summarized it as a collaborative kind of research that is undertaken for
the purpose of advancing knowledge for both theory and practice. We discussed
four key tasks of problem formulation, theory building, research design, and
problem solving, and the different roles and skills that academics and practitioners need to jointly engage in these tasks. The roles and skills include how to:

* negotiate the research relationship;
* formulate the research problem and question;
* compare alterative models or propositions that address the research
  question;
* communicate and use the research findings in ways that change how academics and practitioners think about the research question and problem; and
* design the research as a collaborative learning community of scholars and
  practitioners with diverse perspectives.

The chapter has also reviewed various ways to practice engaged scholarship,
including basic, collaborative, evaluation, and action research as illustrated in
Figure 7.4, and to use the approach that best addresses the research question.
Most doctoral students and junior faculty begin their research career addressing
basic questions devoted to describing, explaining, or predicting various phenomena. I encourage young researchers to do this basic science with stakeholder
advice because such engagement produces more significant advances to knowledge than when researchers do their studies alone. Moreover, I suggest that
researchers do *not* go it alone—engage and rely on senior and experienced
colleagues for mentoring, networking, and accessing potential research sites
and stakeholders. Engaged scholarship is a collective and developmental
achievement. As researchers learn the technical and social skills of engaging

stakeholders in basic science, then they can begin to address additional challenges of finding mutual interests, boundary spanning, power sharing, and task coordination between academics and practitioners in the other forms of engaged scholarship. A personal reflection on my own experiences in "Learning to become an Engaged Scholar" is available as a video clip in the last session of the course.

Note

1 I also think that too many scholars dilute their competencies by conducting an eclectic and unrelated series of cross-sectional studies in their careers.

References

Bartunek, J. M., Rynes, S. L. & Ireland, R. D. (2006). What makes management research interesting and why does it matter? *Academy of Management Journal*, 49(1), 9–15.

Beyer, J. M. (1997). Research utilization: Bridging a cultural gap between communities. *Journal of Management Inquiry*, 6(1), 17–22.

Boyer, E. L. (1996). *Scholarship Reconsidered: Priorities for the Professoriate.* San Franciso, CA: Jossey-Bass.

Brief, A. P. & Dukerich, M. (1991). Theory in organizational behavior. *Research in Organizational Behavior*, 13, 327–52.

Carlile, P. R. (2004). Transferring, translating, and transforming: An integrative framework for managing knowledge across boundaries. *Organization Science*, 15(5), 555–68.

Collins, H. (2004). Interactional expertise as a third kind of knowledge. *Phenomenology and the Cognitive Sciences*, 3(2), 125–43.

Davis, M. (1971). That's interesting! Towards a phenomenology of sociology and a sociology of phenomenology. *Philosophy of Social Sciences*, 1(4), 309–44.

Davis, M. (1986). "That's classic!" The phenomenology and rhetoric of successful social theories. *Philosophy of Social Sciences*, 16(3), 285–301.

Dewey, J. (1938). *Logic: The Theory of Inquiry.* New York: Holt.

Edmondson, A. (2011). Crossing boundaries to investigate problems in the field: An approach to useful research. In Mohrman, S. A., Lawler, E. E. III & Associates (Eds.) *Useful research: Advancing Theory and Practice.* San Francisco, CA: Berrett-Koehler.

Kenworthy-U'Ren, A. (2005). Towards a scholarship of engagement: A dialogue between Andy Van de Ven and Edward Zlotkowski. *Academy of Management Learning and Education*, 4(3), 355–62.

Kilduff, M. & Kelemen, M. (2001). The consolations of organization theory. *British Journal of Management*, 12(Special Issue), S55–S59.

Lewin, K. (1951). *Field Theory in Social Science.* New York: Harper

Osborn, R. N. & Hagedoorn, J. (1997). The institutionalization and evolutionary dynamics of inter-organizational alliances and networks. *Academy of Management Journal*, 40(2), 261–78.

Pettigrew, A. M. 2001. Management research after modernism. *British Journal of Management*, 12(Special Issue), S61–S70.

Rogers, E. M. (2003). *Diffusion of Innovations* (5th ed.). New York: Free Press.

Rousseau, D. M. & Boudreau, J. W. (2011). Sticky evidence: Research findings practitioners find useful. In Lawler, E. E. & Mohrman, S. A. (Eds.) *Useful Research 25 Years Later*. San Francisco, CA: Berrett Koehler.

Rynes, S. L., McNatt, D. B. & Bretz, R. D. (1999). Academic research inside organizations: Inputs, processes, and outcomes. *Personnel Psychology*, 52(4), 869–98.

Starbuck, W. H. (2005). What the numbers mean. Retrieved July 25, 2005 from www.stern.nyu.edu/wstarbuc/whatmean.html.

Van de Ven, A. H. (2007). *Engaged Scholarship: A Guide for Organizational and Social Research*. Oxford: Oxford University Press.

Weick, K. (1989). Theory construction as disciplined imagination. *Academy of Management Review*, 14(4), 516–31.

Weick, K. (1995). *Sense-making in Organizations*. Thousand Oaks, CA: Sage Publications.

8 Practices for leveraging the paradoxes of engaged scholarship

Paula Jarzabkowski, Marianne Lewis, and Wendy Smith

* All three authors have contributed equally to this chapter, as reflected by the alphabetic order of authorship

Engaged scholarship offers us an incubated laboratory to apply and test our own theories. Working with practitioners can generate some of the most relevant and rigorous insights (Van de Ven, 2007; Van de Ven Chapter 7 in this volume). Yet our learning extends beyond just the content of our interactions with "real world" people, to address our *processes* of working together. As scholars of paradox theory, we study the nature and management of contradictory, yet interdependent demands (Lewis, 2000; Schad, Lewis, Raisch & Smith, 2016; Smith & Lewis, 2011). Paradoxes permeate our efforts to both study and learn with practitioners, including tensions between rigor and relevance, short-term demands and long-term processes, simplicity and complexity, etc. As scholars of practice theory, we look to understand and address these paradoxes in our everyday activities (Jarzabkowski, 2004; Jarzabkowski, Balogun & Seidl, 2007). Engaged scholarship therefore offers an opportunity where we can apply and extend our own theories.

Our goal in this chapter is to help academics generate valuable knowledge and spark high quality connections by working more effectively with practitioners. To do so, we integrate both paradox theory and practice theory with our own experiences to develop insight about effective practices for "engaged scholarship." Bringing together paradox theory and practice theory, we suggest that more creative, thriving academic–practitioner relationships depend on:

- adopting a paradox mindset;
- differentiating practices that respect distinctions between academics and practitioners; and
- integrating practices that enable synergies and linkages between academics and practitioners.

As authors, we use ourselves as subjects, demonstrating our own practices to effectively engage with practitioners in the context of action research (Marianne), executive education (Wendy), and field research (Paula).

We conclude by exploring how our experiences with engaged scholarship can extend and challenge insights in paradox and practice theory.

Adopting a paradoxical approach to engaged scholarship

Heated debates among academics reveal different approaches—an "either/or" separation approach versus a "both/and" paradoxical approach—to engaging practitioners. One approach regards academia and practice as separate domains (Beyer & Trice, 1982; Pelz, 1978) pursuing divergent objectives, with little to say to each other. Academia stresses rigorous inquiry into challenging questions that can surface reliable, valuable and generalizable insights. Practitioners seek ideas that can solve their immediate problems, influence practice, and deliver improvements. These distinctions raise differences in overall logics, time horizons, identities, language, processes/practices, and rewards/incentives. In their recent work, Bartunek and Rynes (2014) offer an extensive review of these tensions.

Scholars adopting an either/or approach suggest that, in light of these distinctions, the domains be kept apart. For example, Seidl (2007) conceptualized academia and practice as distinct systems, the integrity of each depending on their purposeful separation. We have distinct journals for each audience with different publication criteria. Those adopting a separation agenda denigrate as "science fiction" (Nicolai, 2004) efforts to conclude scholarly articles with implications for practice. In classes, we assign academic journal articles to our doctoral students, and managerial journal articles to our MBA and executive students. Scholars emphasizing separation defend their right to "blue skies research" (see Spee & Jarzabkowski, 2017), and stress rewards based primarily (or solely) on academic accomplishments; practitioner publications can be viewed as neutral or even detrimental for promotion.

This either/or approach that keeps academia and practice separate sparks defensive responses and vicious cycles (Jarzabkowski, Le & Van de Ven, 2013; Lewis, 2000; Smith & Lewis, 2011). In the extreme, the lack of engagement with leaders and managers can diminish the value of resulting insights and disenfranchise the academic who does not see the impact of their scholarly efforts. Moreover, these efforts reduce the relevance of our teaching. In the over US$200 billion spent annually on executive education, only US$1 billion is earned by business schools (Scheurer, 2015), showing that, paradoxically, business leaders do not turn to researchers to help them understand and adopt best practices.

In contrast, other scholars highlight the paradoxical interplay between academia and practice. From this perspective, these realms are complementary and interdependent (Jarzabkowski, Mohrman & Scherer, 2010). Business school academics teach tomorrow's (and often today's) leaders in their undergraduate, graduate and executive programs (Bennis & O'Toole, 2005; Mintzberg, 2004). Research is similarly complementary, conducted in the very firms and contexts in which these students are or will be employees, with results then incorporated into the classroom. Assuming interdependence, scholars seek synergies between research and practice (Bartunek & Rynes, 2014). For example, scholars may advocate Mode 2 research, conducted in collaboration with practitioners who help shape the object of inquiry and the ways of knowing it, over Mode 1 research, in which academic questions are developed and knowledge is produced without recourse to practice (Gibbons, Limoges, Nowotny, Schwartzman, Scott & Trow, 1994). Yet taken to the extreme, emphasizing synergies without recognizing differences can lead to detrimental vicious cycles. Academics may find practice-driven research questions too narrow. They may feel pressured to reveal results too quickly, without a rigorous investigation, or find their results clouded by practitioner bias. Such research can compromise academic freedom, scientific integrity, and research quality, which can ultimately diminish a scholar's motivation and energy.

A paradox mindset appreciates *both* the differences and the synergies between academia and practice (Miron-Spektor, Ingram, Keller, Smith & Lewis, 2017). As Bartunek and Rynes (2014: 1191) noted, in the context of academic–practitioner relations:

> It does not, on the surface at least, make sense that rigor and relevance can be both compatible and incompatible, yet they are. It does not, on the surface, at least, make sense that academics and practitioners can be both compatible and incompatible, yet they are.

In this mode, scholars recognize practice as *both* distinct *and* valuable. Numerous special issues of management journals (e.g., BJM, JMS, Organization Studies) adopt a paradoxical perspective to such challenges, recognizing the distinctions while also debating how we can address what are often referred to as the "double hurdles" (Pettigrew, 1997) of both rigor in our science and relevance in our findings. The roles of scholars and practitioners can be both distinct and interdependent. These roles can be held by different individuals—the professor vs. the manager/leader—yet these roles can also overlap. Professors engage in leadership, while leaders often profess (Crosina & Bartunek, 2017). Others live in the "liminal" spaces between multiple identities (Creed, Dejordy & Lok, 2010; Empson, Chapter 12 in this volume). In addition, terminology such as rigor and relevance indicate a commitment to paradoxical thinking (Smith & Lewis, 2011), a *both/and* logic that has also given rise to terms such as "engaged scholarship" (Van de Ven, 2007) that reframe the two as interdependent and complementary.

Differentiating and integrating practices to enable the paradoxes of engaged scholarship

Leveraging a paradox mindset, practices of differentiation and integration help scholars engage the academic–practitioner divide. It is within practices that people can instantiate taken-for-granted structures that, reciprocally, shape practice. Academic and practitioner practices often remain separate. For instance, doing research with solely an academic audience in mind, and, at best, paying lip service to its practical implications, perpetuates defensive approaches. By contrast, collaboratively framing research questions with practitioners can enable, from the outset, the structures within which we can generate research outcomes of relevance to both academic and practitioner audiences.

Research finds that effectively engaging paradox involves accepting and engaging competing demands, rather than trying to resolve them. Doing so depends on two types of practices: differentiating and integrating (Andriopoulos & Lewis, 2009; Miron-Spektor, Gino & Argote, 2011; Smith & Lewis, 2011; Smith & Tushman, 2005). Differentiating involves activities to separate poles and value each side, whereas integrating surfaces connections, linkages, and synergies. Clearly depicted in the Taoist yin–yang symbol, the distinction between the dark and light slivers emphasize differentiation, while the alternative shaded dots, as well as the overarching fit between slivers depict integration (see Figure 8.1). Studies find the value of these dual practices for managing paradoxes at the level of individuals (Miron-Spektor et al., 2011; Smets, Jarzabkowski, Burke & Spee, 2015), teams (Andriopoulos & Lewis, 2009), and senior leadership (Smith, 2014). In the context of academic/practitioner partnerships, differentiating might involve segmenting time and space for each agenda, surfacing distinct goals, missions, and rewards, linking with unique stakeholder groups, and engaging conversations in distinct outlets. Integrating practices might involve clarifying a shared higher purpose that involves both domains, highlighting linkages between alternative demands, and managing a portfolio of activities.

Effectively managing paradox requires adopting both differentiating and integrating practices (Smith, 2014; Smith & Lewis, 2011). Either alone is not only limited, but detrimental (Smith, 2014). Differentiating supports and respects individual agendas, but without integrating, these distinctions often incite intractable conflict and struggles between opposing sides. Integrating, without differentiating, proves equally problematic. Emphasizing overarching identities and a higher purpose can smooth over conflicts, but without recognizing unique

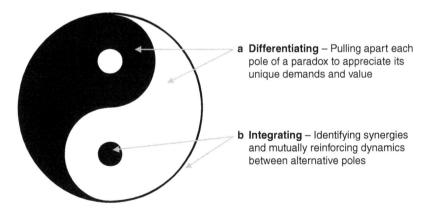

a Differentiating – Pulling apart each pole of a paradox to appreciate its unique demands and value

b Integrating – Identifying synergies and mutually reinforcing dynamics between alternative poles

Figure 8.1 Differentiating and integrating practices.

elements of each pole this can lead to false synergies, as one pole overpowers and dominates the other. Both differentiating and integrating are vital, highlighting that effectively engaging paradox is paradoxical (Cameron & Quinn, 1988).

Leveraging the paradoxes of engaging scholarship

In the following section, we draw from our own experiences to illustrate the nature and responses of academic–practitioner paradoxes. We highlight practices for addressing these tensions in three integrative spaces:

- action research;
- executive education; and
- field research.

Table 8.1 summarizes these practices.

Action research: Marianne Lewis

Action research offers a paradoxical method for engaging the academic–practice divide. Action research provides a rigorous means of deepening insight alongside practitioners, so that the outcomes benefit both theory and practice. According to Reason and Bradbury (2001: 1), action research "seeks to bring together action and reflection, theory and practice, in participation with others, in the pursuit of practical solutions to issues of pressing concern to people." Intensive, collaborative interventions help managers make sense of tensions, while managers and researchers can develop, test, and iteratively refine rich insights. The process can be mutually beneficial, creating a positive, virtuous cycle. This method is particularly valuable when fitting shared desires for learning. For practice, action research best suits organizational members who genuinely seek to learn through and take action based on the intervention (Eden & Huxham, 1996). For researchers, this approach most effectively addresses latent dynamics: interactions, understandings, and interpretations that might, using more detached methods, confound "espoused theories" and "theories-in-use" (Argyris, 1993).

My experience with action research proved exceptionally insightful and challenging. I joined a colleague who had been working for over two years with the LEGO Corporation. She had chosen action research as the research design to enable deep access to managers' sense-making process. Joining my colleague's effort, I came to quickly develop a deep respect for the method. At times, however, such close interactions with the strained managers sparked our anxiety as well as theirs, raising challenges for managing our own varied defenses.

Diving deeper into our experience of action research highlights differentiation and integration practices at its core. While specifics vary by researchers and research settings, at LEGO we came to view our action research as a process of paradoxical inquiry. Differentiation entailed segregated periods of either intervention or reflection. Interventions are highly collaborative, and, at LEGO, came

Table 8.1 Differentiating and integrating practices to engage academic–practitioner paradoxes

Forum	Paradox mindset	Differentiating practices	Integrating practices
Action Research	Value action research as means of engaging and leveraging the academic–practice divide	Iterating between intervention and reflection Cultivating varied perspectives that canvas internal (immersed in interactions) and external (detached from interactions)	Theory building as the emerging theory integrates varied perspectives, and links periods of intervention and reflection
Executive Education	Value executive education as a bridging space that allows for both sharing and learning new insights	Using different language to describe the research questions and key findings Publishing research in different outlets, that have different expectations as far as timing, validity, contributions, and style	Developing an overarching identity emphasizing *impact* of ideas Leveraging stories from managers to help make the academic research come alive; leveraging research from scholarship to help validate the ideas for practitioners
Field Research	Value field research as an opportunity for co-production of theoretically interesting and practically relevant findings	Maintaining sufficient professional distance as a researcher that you can observe critically, without over-privileging an "us" and "them" approach. Ensuring academic rigor in conduct of the field work and its analysis, and insisting that industry participants wait for robust results, despite their natural tendency to want rapid solutions to their very real problems	Working with practitioners in designing the research problems and conducting the research, during which both academics and practitioners influence and shape each other Developing presentations and reports written in industry-approachable language, so that important theoretical insights developed from the findings are not lost in academic jargon

to be called "sparring sessions" as in our intensive interactions with the managers we sought together to surface understandings of existing practices as well as deep-seated tensions and potential responses. Such sessions occurred one to one and in groups, and were recorded, in audio and sometimes video, and transcribed. For some sessions, an outsider observed while the second author consistently remained distant from any interactions. Reflection periods, in contrast, were researcher-focused, enabling our triangulation of perspectives. Bringing together the transcription and experience of the engaged researcher with outsider perspectives helps researchers explore what was said, understood, and learned. Analysis during reflection focuses on both the intervention results and the research process. At LEGO, as we identified patterns, the emerging theory and research process became increasingly interwoven. We became aware not only of the managers' and our own sense-making but also the varied impact of different types of researcher questioning. In sum, the emerging theory became the vehicle for integration. Sharing the emerging theory with the managers, central concepts and relationships served as fodder for subsequent sparing sessions, further testing, and refining the theory.

Publishing this work for academics, however, proved an even greater challenge, as we sought to integrate academic and practitioner experiences into one journal article. Over seven years, we tried top journal after top journal. Reviewer responses signaled their discomfort with our methods of working so closely with practitioners as they consistently questioned the "objectivity" and "generalizability" of our work, yet offered scarce feedback on the findings or potential contributions. We occasionally received a "revise and resubmit," and after rewriting the article several times, we had a nearly new and, indeed, a far stronger manuscript. So we finally went back to *AMJ*, our first journal attempt, where we benefitted from an editor who saw the potential in both the paradoxical findings and method. His guidance helped us leverage the constructive, often intense, reviewer criticisms into the final publication. The result was an academic manuscript as much about learning through action research as it was the managers' process of working through paradox (Luscher & Lewis, 2008).

Our hope is that action research will become increasingly accepted, in turn further reducing tensions and resulting defensiveness among academics and practitioners. Indeed the effectiveness of action research grows from an awareness that rigor enables relevance, while relevance motivates rigor (Susman & Evered, 1978). Painstaking iterations between data collection and analysis push researcher and subject to consider, question, and refine their understandings. Theory-building thereby becomes a collaborative, cyclical process. As a result, the academia–practice divide can be leveraged and bridged.

Executive education: Wendy Smith

Executive education offers another bridging space: a forum where academics and practitioners can meet, connect, and learn from one another. Managers pose problems and scholars use their research tools to collect, analyze, and interpret data from the practitioners to solve these problems. The executive education classroom offers a forum for sharing the result, gaining feedback, and using the discussion to refine the answers and develop new questions. Academics benefit by gaining access to relevant questions as well as data that helps address important, real world problems. Practitioners benefit by gaining insights that directly confront their core challenges. Together, this interaction involves generating and applying novel insights, effectively leveraging the paradoxical tensions inherent in academic–practitioner relationships. As Tushman and colleagues argued, executive education is a "context where research is linked to real managerial issues, and where faculty relationships with firms, in turn, enhance the quality of our research and teaching" (Tushman, Fenollosa, McGrath, O'Reilly & Kleinbaum, 2007: 346). Executive education enables the potential for a positive synergy.

Academics and practitioners, however, rarely realize the full potential of executive education, stymied by the gulf between the two worlds. Tushman et al. (2007) argue that academics frequently view executive education only as an additional source of income, and seek to do so with as little time as possible. Yet the more that we bring our same teaching material to executive education, the less chance we have to learn new ideas, generate fresh insights, and become inspired.

Traditional either/or assumptions underlie a limited view of executive education. Consistently assumptions emphasize executive teaching and research as opposing activities and identities. Others suggest that scholars cannot be great at both. As a junior scholar, I remember feeling quite proud when a senior colleague commended my high teaching ratings, noting "Teaching seems to really energize you." My pride quickly subsided when he followed up with, "Yeah, I don't get energized by teaching, I get energized by research." His either/or assumption suggested that one could not be energized by, and talented at, both. His backhanded compliment of my teaching challenged my research capabilities.

Our identity assumptions are compounded by scarce resource expectations. Executive education takes time. In a zero-sum world, time for teaching comes at the expense of research time. Before earning tenure, I was consistently warned by senior colleagues to make sure my research did not suffer from the time I spent with executive education. Looking to minimize this scarce temporal resource, academics often resort to teaching well-developed content—the case we've taught a million times before. While some of this is inevitable, even valuable, at the extreme, such content can become generic and divorced from the participant's actual challenges. Managers become wary. Failing to see the clear value academics offer, they seek education elsewhere.

In contrast to these approaches, a paradox mind-set allows us to effectively leverage tensions. In my own experience, I benefitted as an academic from the executive education feedback loop. As a doctoral student, my first field project with IBM senior leaders emerged from a collaborative executive education research project. I was lucky to be working with Mike Tushman as an adviser.

IBM faced critical questions about how senior leaders could effectively manage "ambidexterity," and turned to Mike and his colleagues for answers. As part of Mike's arrangement with IBM, I collected, analyzed and interpreted data from these senior leaders to surface their best practices and generate insights, and used these insights to inform executive education sessions with them. It was through this project that I first turned to the paradox literature to articulate the experience of these leaders as they struggled to explore and exploit. These insights helped inform the insights we shared with IBM senior leaders in their executive education sessions. Feedback from the IBM leaders then helped shape future research. For example, in one project, executives in another organization became interested in diagnosing and expanding paradox mind-set among their middle managers. Based on conversations with the executives, our research team developed a paradox mind-set scale. Field data from the firm helped validate the scale while also serving as the basis for direct feedback in executive seminars.

Effectively leveraging executive education involves both differentiating and integrating practices. Differentiating begins with using distinct language when addressing different stakeholder groups. In my project with IBM, I told my academic colleagues that I was exploring how *top management teams* addressed the *paradoxical* challenges of *exploring* and *exploiting* to enable *ambidexterity*. However, when talking with executives, I talked about studying how *senior leaders* addressed challenges of *managing today's existing product* and *developing innovations for tomorrow*. An academic colleague recently depicted this language gap to me, noting that, while academics appreciate Latin words (i.e., more sophisticated language), practitioners benefit more from Anglo-Saxon words (i.e., more simple and straightforward language). When sharing our research on paradoxes with senior leaders, we shift the academic terms *differentiating* and *integrating*, to *separating* and *connecting*.

Differentiating also involves producing multiple outputs that differ in response time, focus, and journals. Publishing an article in a high quality academic journal can take years by the time we effectively collect and analyze the data to satisfy validity demands. In contrast, practitioners want insights that can address their present challenges as quickly as possible. I remember feeling stumped when an IBM general manager turned to me at the end of a meeting I was observing and asked, "So what did you learn so far that you can share with our leaders?" To turn data round quickly for practitioners, I wrote white papers or conducted feedback sessions with emerging insights. Although I often felt anxious sharing ideas that we not yet fully substantiated, these opportunities proved useful: leaders provided feedback and reactions to my emergent ideas that significantly strengthened my findings.

I further had to translate the style and nature of the output. To publish my findings in the *AMJ*, I created a detailed boxes and arrows model that not only addressed questions of *what*, but also *how* and *why*. I worked to show how my findings were situated in and advanced existing theory (see Smith, 2014). To publish these findings in the *Harvard Business Review*, I developed simple models that stressed what, but without detail about the how and why. I worked to tell good stories to help illustrate and situate these findings within real world experiences (see Tushman, Smith & Binns, 2011). I also created different presentations for feedback sessions. My academic presentations were text and citation heavy, while my practitioner presentations involved few words and lots of images. On several occasions, I hired Powerpoint experts to help make my slides more graphically appealing for practitioner audiences, a practice I deemed unnecessary, even extravagant, for academic audiences. Indeed, practitioners are offering a compliment when they describe executive education sessions as "not too academic."

Working with these distinct stakeholders could lead to a highly bifurcated experience, and I personally felt demands pulling my time and attention in opposite directions. Integrating practices help to continue to see how these activities can benefit one another. Integrating practices often start with an overarching identity, a passionate commitment to a higher purpose that unites conflicting ideas. As an academic, I value impact—generating useful and applicable ideas. Inspired by Kurt Lewin's (1951) proclamation that there is nothing as practical as a good theory, and Roethlisberger's (1977) depiction of good theory as walking sticks that can organize thoughts and guide actions, I value my in-depth interactions with practitioners' surface novel insights that allow more thoughtful and ultimately more useful theories. The time and energy I spend on executive education results in deeper, more impactful ideas.

I further recognize how efforts focused on one audience can translate to another, and often minimize time and effort; for example, executive education offers fast and easy access to data. When collecting data to validate our survey, my colleagues and I approached one organization to conduct the survey to their middle managers. Multiple rounds of conversations across several months ultimately resulted in no data. However, several months later, an organization contacted me to teach paradoxical thinking to middle managers. We handed out the surveys, and used them as foundation for the session. Motivated to collect the data in advance of the session, we ended up gaining access to hundreds of surveys with minimal challenges. I found other spillover effects. My presentations to academic audiences pull in more stories, graphics, and illustrations to help make the research come alive, something that I know I always value in colleagues' presentations. My presentations to practitioners include more references to others' books, research, and insights that they can follow up with on their own. Participants have often told me that they end an executive education session having created a whole reading list for the future.

As the adult education market grows, business schools hope to capture some of that value. Paradoxical thinking might offer a new approach to more effectively engage this community and generate greater insights.

Field research: Paula Jarzabkowski

Increasingly government funding for research in the UK, particularly within business schools, has emphasized the importance of both highest scientific quality and also demonstrable impact upon practice and policy. Research grant applications must now provide a three-page statement specifying their pathways to impact, alongside the six-page statement of their scientific case. Such impact is assessed one year from the end of the study, in a separate reporting statement that constitutes one evaluation of the success of the completed research. From its initial design through to its evaluation, funded research must now, therefore, be conducted with a view to incorporating both scientific and practical outputs. Further, the Research Excellence Framework, by which the quality of research in UK universities is periodically judged for block funding, now requires not only evidence of top publications but also "impact cases"—in which one top impact case is reportedly evaluated as equivalent, for ranking purposes, to eight top publications. This government impetus is supporting a change in practice within UK universities and within academics.

In this environment, I have been awarded a number of Economic and Social Research Council (ESRC) research grants that had an explicit remit to generate both top publications and practically relevant outputs. For example, I received an ESRC/Advanced Institute of Management mid-career fellowship grant from which I was expected to both publish top journal articles and also produce reports for practice and run workshops with senior managers to discuss my findings. At this stage I adopted a differentiation approach—essentially producing findings and then working out how to make them accessible to managers. This was a useful lesson in translation as I began to learn the "language games" (Astley & Zammuto, 1992) of explaining my findings in practitioner-friendly terminology and inviting managers to debate those findings, so translating my academic concepts into their language.

However, my subsequent grants, two ESRC Business Partnership grants, put me in the position of working with a steering committee of high-ranking practitioners including CEOs and Chief Risk Officers, initially on a monthly and then a quarterly basis, to co-produce the research questions and shape the evolving research design, as we discussed the emergent findings. I had to move from my initial differentiation of my language and theirs to finding a point of integration. The initial meetings were very "paradoxical" and tense, as we spoke at cross-purposes. Indeed, I often referred to the early meetings as "sandpaper" sessions because the experience was so abrasive. Why couldn't these obviously intelligent people understand what I was telling them? And, yet, they clearly had something useful to tell me if I could work out how to bridge the language gap.

The problem was that I was used to differentiating between my academic findings and my engagement with practitioners, only translating findings into something that practitioners valued or understood after the fact. Now integration was necessary, as we worked together in developing the research questions and conducting the work. I was truly stunned to find that words like "actors," "scripts," and "institutionalized norms" were neither understood nor accepted. They were alienating and it was little use to be defensive about how obtuse my "actors" were in sticking to their own well-rehearsed "scripts." Rather, I learnt to stop hiding behind my academic language. At the same time, I had to educate them in how academic research proceeds. For example, in our initial meeting a Chief Risk Officer asked me when my ethnography would begin adding to their bottom line. I was amazed at this expectation. In the context of ethnographic research, we clearly had some paradoxical tensions to bridge between my talk of cultural norms and their discussion of bottom lines.

The onus was on me. While I could not offer quick fixes or five general principles, I learned to use their field terms to make my own language more evocative. I would begin with their terms to introduce and explain my concepts and then invite them to reflect on those concepts from their experience of the industry. For example, on one occasion I was explaining a type of heuristic I had observed by which people in their industry came to rapid judgments that seemed to negate the quantitative data-mining nature of their work. In discussing the findings, they suggested that social situations such as playing golf and drinking with each other contributed to these heuristics, so allowing me to further theorize about how social interactions contributed to commercial decision-making, which later became the basis of both industry reports and academic papers. At the same time, managers were intrigued to have frameworks on which to hang their native understandings and give them opportunities for reflection on their industry. As integration grew, I began to bring partial findings or an early framework to these meetings and we interacted together in co-producing findings that were both relevant to industry and also theoretically interesting. It was hard work, building the bridges into their world and gaining sufficient credibility that I could begin to educate them in my language. However, the collaboration was exciting, resulting in widely disseminated and adopted industry reports and master classes that became part of their lingua franca for discussing their industry, even as I improved the quality of my findings.

Integration increased, as companies I had worked with used my research frameworks in their strategic reports to their investors and clients, or used them to restructure and generate more strategic value from their client relationships. Indeed, the research won a research council award for Outstanding Impact on Business. At the same time, theoretical differentiation blossomed. I really "knew" this industry as I had never understood an industry before and it provoked my best theorizing. While my academic papers went beyond the frameworks and diagnostics I had developed for industry, they were also informed by the deep understanding I had generated through collaboration. A research monograph published by Oxford University Press was reviewed in the business media and key academic journals for its academic and industry credibility (Jarzabkowski, Bednarek & Spee, 2015), while academic papers also flowed (Bednarek, Burke, Jarzabkowski & Smets, 2016; Smets et al., 2015; Spee, Jarzabkowski & Smets, 2016).

Constructing and maintaining a transcending identity

Van de Ven (2007) developed principles of engaged scholarship to inspire academics to reach across the great gulf and effectively work with practitioners, transcending the tensions, and overcoming the vicious cycles. It was a response to a more disengaged approach, an approach where academics worked alone to solve problems and generate insights. Engaged scholarship has the potential to generate valuable insight to important problems. As our world becomes more volatile, complex, and uncertain, new challenges consistently arise. Organizations have the potential to address many of these "grand challenges" or "wicked problems" (Colquitt & George, 2011). Doing so, however, requires researchers who can integrate rigor and relevance, scholarship and engagement, whilst acknowledging the differentiation between academics and practitioners that enables each to offer the other insight, wisdom, and guidance along the way. In this piece, we sought to extend our collective understanding of engaged scholarship by highlighting its paradoxical nature and developing specific practices to address these paradoxes. Doing so has offered us a chance to reflect personally. We hope these insights inspire fruitful engagement with practitioners.

Our experiences with engaged scholarship also offer insights to extend paradox and practice theories. For example, all our experiences highlight the interwoven and emergent nature of paradoxes. Moving between different activities, such as developing research questions, collecting data, analyzing data, and providing feedback, surfaced new challenges, and required nuanced and varied responses.

These experiences emphasize the dynamic nature of managing paradoxes—new situations surfacing tensions and demanding emergent practices. Understanding of these dynamics will benefit from longitudinal and processual methods (Langley, 1999; Tsoukas & Chia, 2002). Yet such methods and subsequent insights about the paradoxes and associated practices of conducting engaged scholarship remain underdeveloped, providing valuable avenues for future research (see Schad et al., 2016). In addition, all of our experiences suggest that our own approaches evolved and developed over time as we "bumped up" against challenges, surfaced new paradoxes, muddled through our responses, and reflected on our experiences. That is, we each learned over time. Again, capturing the art of learning the practices of paradox further remains underdeveloped and important for future research (Le & Bednarek, 2017).

Engaged scholarship has offered us our own laboratory—a chance to generate insights from observing practitioners, but also from observing ourselves as we work with these practitioners. We hope our insights offer fodder that can continue to develop both rigorous and relevant research.

References

Andriopoulos, C. & Lewis, M. W. (2009). Exploitation-exploration tensions and organizational ambidexterity: Managing paradoxes of innovation. *Organization Science*, 20(4), 696–717.

Argyris, C. (1993). *Knowledge for Action: A Guide to Over-coming Barriers to Organizational Change.* San Francisco, CA: Jossey-Bass.

Astley, W. G. & Zammuto, R. F. (1992). Organization science, managers, and language games. *Organization Science*, 3(4), 443–60.

Bartunek, J. M. & Rynes, S. L. (2014). Academics and practitioners are alike and unlike: The paradoxes of academic–practitioner relationships. *Journal of Management*, 40(5),1181–201.

Bednarek, R., Burke, G., Jarzabkowski, P. & Smets, M. (2016). Dynamic client portfolios as sources of ambidexterity: Exploration and exploitation within and across client relationships. *Long Range Planning*, 49(3), 324–41.

Bennis, W. G. & O'Toole, J. (2005). How business schools lost their way. *Harvard Business Review*, 83(5), 96–104.

Beyer, J. M. & Trice, H. M. (1982). The utilization process: A conceptual framework and synthesis of empirical findings. *Administrative Science Quarterly*, 1, 591–622.

Cameron, K. & Quinn, R. (1988). Organizational paradox and transformation. In Quinn, R. & Cameron, K. (Eds.) *Paradox and Transformation: Toward a Theory of Change in Organization and Management* (pp. 1–18). Cambridge, MA: Ballinger.

Colquitt, J. A. & George, G. (2011). Publishing in AMJ—part 1: Topic choice. *Academy of Management Journal*, 54(3), 432–5.

Creed, W. E. D., Dejordy, R. & Lok, J. (2010). Being the change: Resolving institutional contradiction through identity work. *Academy of Management Journal*, 53(6), 1336–64.

Crosina, E. & Bartunek, J. M. (2017). Unpacking a paradox of rigor and relevance: How academics can learn from relevant skilled practitioners. In Lewis, M. W., Smith, W. K., Jarzabkowski, P. & Langley, A. (Eds.) *Oxford Handbook of Organizational Paradox*. Oxford: Oxford University Press.

Eden, C. & Huxham, C. (1996). Action research for management research. *British Journal of Management*, 7(1), 75–86.

Gibbons, M., Limoges, H., Nowotny, H., Schwartzman, S., Scott, P. & Trow, M. (1994). *The New Production of Knowledge: The Dynamics of Science and Research in Contemporary Societies.* London: Sage Publishing.

Jarzabkowski, P. (2004). Strategy as practice: Recursiveness, adaptation and practices-in-use. *Organization Studies*, 25(4), 529–60.

Jarzabkowski, P., Balogun, J. & Seidl, D. (2007). Strategizing: The challenges of a practice perspective. *Human Relations*, 60(1), 5–27.

Jarzabkowski, P., Mohrman, S. A. & Scherer, A. G. (2010). Organization studies as applied science: The generation and use of academic knowledge about organizations introduction to the special issue. *Organization Studies*, 31(9–10), 1189–207.

Jarzabkowski, P., Le, J. & Van de Ven, A. H. (2013). Responding to competing strategic demands: How organizing, belonging and performing paradoxes co-evolve. *Strategic Organization*, 11(3), 245–80.

Jarzabkowski, P., Bednarek, R. & Spee, P. (2015). *Making a Market for Acts of God: The Practice of Risk Trading in the Global Reinsurance Industry*. New York: Oxford University Press.

Langley, A. (1999). Strategies for theorizing from process data. *Academy of Management Review*, 24(4), 691–710.

Le, J. & Bednarek, R. (Eds.). (2017). *Paradox in Everyday Practice: Applying Practice Theoretical Principles to Paradox*. Oxford: Oxford University Press.

Lewin, K. (1951). *Field Theory in Social Science: Selective Theoretical Papers*. New York: Harper.

Lewis, M. W. (2000). Exploring paradox: Toward a more comprehensive guide. *Academy of Management Review*, 25(4), 760–76.

Luscher, L. & Lewis, M. W. (2008). Organizational change and managerial sensemaking: Working through paradox. *Academy of Management Journal*, 51(2), 221–40.

Mintzberg, H. (2004). *Managers, not MBAs: A Hard Look at the Soft Practice of Managing and Management Development*. San Francisco CA: Berrett-Koehler.

Miron-Spektor, E., Gino, F. & Argote, L. (2011). Paradoxical frames and creative sparks: Enhancing individual creativity through conflict and integration. *Organizational Behavior and Human Decision Processes*, 116(2), 229–40.

Miron-Spektor, E., Ingram, A. S., Keller, J., Smith, W. K. & Lewis, M. W. (2017). Microfoundations of organizational paradox: The problem is how we think about the problem. *Academy of Management Journal*, March, doi: 10.5465/amj.2016.0594.

Nicolai, A. T. (2004). The bridge to the "real world": Applied science or a "schizophrenic tour de force"? *Journal of Management Studies*, 41(5), 951–76.

Pelz, D. C. (1978). Some expanded perspectives on use of social science in public policy. In Yinger, J. M. & Cutler, S. J. (Eds.) *Major Social Issues: A Multidisciplinary View* (pp. 346–57). New York: Free Press.

Pettigrew, A. M. (1997). The double hurdles for management research. In Clarke, T. (Ed.) *Advancement in Organizational Behavior* (pp. 277–96). Lebanon, LH: Dartmouth Press.

Reason, P. & Bradbury, H. (2001). *Handbook of Action Research*. London: Sage Publishing.

Roethlisberger, F. 1(977). *The Elusive Phenomenon*. Cambridge, MA: Harvard University Press.

Schad, J., Lewis, M., Raisch, S. & Smith, W. (2016). Paradox research in management science: Looking back to move forward. *Academy of Management Annals*, 10(1), 5–64.

Scheurer, W. 2015. The exec ed action plan, BizEd: AACSB International. Retrieved April 1, 2017 from www.bizedmagazine.com/archives/2015/6/features/exec-ed-action-plan.

Seidl, D. (2007). General strategy concepts and the ecology of strategy discourses: A systemic–discursive perspective. *Organization Studies*, 28(2), 197–218.

Smets, M., Jarzabkowski, P., Burke, G. T. & Spee, P. (2015). Reinsurance trading in Lloyd's of London: Balancing conflicting-yet-complementary logics in practice. *Academy of Management Journal*, 58(3), 932–70.

Smith, W. (2014). Dynamic decision-making: A model of senior leaders managing strategic paradoxes. *Academy of Management Journal*, 57(6), 1592–623.

Smith, W. K. & Lewis, M. W. (2011). Toward a theory of paradox: A dynamic equilibrium model of organizing. *Academy of Management Review*, 36(2), 381–403.

Smith, W. K. & Tushman, M. L. (2005). Managing strategic contradictions: A top management model for managing innovation streams. *Organization Science*, 16(5), 522–36.

Spee, P. & Jarzabkowski, P. (2017). Agreeing on what? Creating joint accounts of strategic change. *Organization Science*, 28(1), 152–76.

Spee, P., Jarzabkowski, P. & Smets, M. (2016). The influence of routine interdependence and skillful accomplishment on the coordination of standardizing and customizing. *Organization Science*, 27(3), 759–81.

Susman, G. I. & Evered, R. D. (1978). An assessment of the scientific merits of action research. *Administrative Science Quarterly*, 23, 582–603.

Tsoukas, H. & Chia, R. (2002). On organizational becoming: Rethinking organizational change. *Organization Science*, 13(5), 567–82.

Tushman, M. L., Fenollosa, A., McGrath, D. N., O'Reilly, C. & Kleinbaum, A. M. (2007). Relevance and rigor: Executive education as a lever in shaping practice and research. *Academy of Management Learning & Education*, 6(3), 345–62.

Tushman, M. L., Smith, W. K. & Binns, A. (2011). The ambidextrous CEO. *Harvard Business Review*, 89(6), 1700–706.

Van de Ven, A. H. (2007). *Engaged Scholarship: A Guide for Organizational and Social Research*. Oxford: Oxford University Press.

9 Is there anybody in there?

Reconceptualizing "action" in action research

Donald MacLean and Robert MacIntosh

Introduction

Whilst broader acceptance of engaged scholarship is perhaps growing in the light of ever increasing calls for "impact" in research, tensions, and debates inevitably recur around the definition of "academic professionalism" and the practice of action research with practitioners. This chapter is primarily concerned with one such tension in particular—the balance between creativity and control in research.

More pointedly, the chapter challenges the idea that the researcher is, or ought to be, in control of his or her research, its questions, participants, outcomes, mechanisms, etc. Questions such as:

- "Is it possible to be 'professional' whilst 'in charge' of processes and resources over which one has limited, often very limited, control?"

or, the corollary,

- "Can it truly be called research where everything is delivered just as it said on the research proposal—was all that work really necessary if the activities and outcomes were so obvious and predictable that they could be spotted far in advance?"

And so on.

In this chapter, we hope to introduce some ideas, particularly that of "creative action" in the belief that they will seriously challenge our preconceptions of what it means to be a "professional researcher"—indeed we will argue that many of what might be considered the symptoms of "unprofessional research" are in fact the unacknowledged hallmarks of good research when creative partnership working is a key feature.

A major theme of our argument is that in the conduct of research into human beings' behaviors, we must "rehumanize" ourselves—as human-being researchers. Personal attributes, experiences, biographies, aesthetic sensitivities, logics, imaginations, intuitions, hopes, fears, etc., play major roles in our lives as researchers—yet they are barely acknowledged.

Our purpose here is to draw attention to the aspects of research practice that most accounts seem not to reach—namely, complexity, full-bodied people, and multifaceted creative action.

Given this purpose, what follows draws heavily on our own shared experiences as researchers. Our own embodied experiences gleaned over two decades of working in creative partnership with practitioners (and occasional trench warfare with academic colleagues) will form a kind of running case. We hope this doesn't seem too self-indulgent on our parts and that by the end of the chapter you will see that it "stacks-up" with our argument and furnishes some value. These descriptions of our "field work" will alternate with our "back at the ranch" theorizing as we try to create some insights of more general value concerning research process.

In the more theoretical sections we will aim to show how our thinking about research has travelled—from its origins influenced by our early experiences of methodology in "hard" science, through ideas of research informed by complexity theory, onwards (we think!) to concern with the embodied researcher expressing creative action. By necessity, our reflections contain more by way of self-citation than may normally occur. This is simply to signpost our evolving thinking—any self-indulgence or vanity is a mere bonus (sorry!), unintended consequence, of course. We hope you enjoy the ride!

Field work 1: the best laid schemes...

We were both trained in the methodology of the natural sciences—one as a physicist (Donald), the other (Robert) as an engineer. We both drew upon experience from industry—as engineers and managers. For us, methodology was something of a non-question. We were professionals—we had to be objective (none of that subjective distortion) and we had to conduct our research in ways that introduced no disturbance whatsoever (no contamination through intervention). So we needed a clear aim for our work: we should follow well-rehearsed protocols that ensured the generation of reliable, generalizable, and valid findings. And all of this should be captured in a design that took account of the various factors in the environment that might undermine any of the above: ends, means, and conditions.

As young strategy researchers, we couldn't believe our luck. This rational approach to research was in complete accord with our understanding of strategy itself—the alignment of intent, capability and environmental factors (MacIntosh & MacLean, 2015): ends, means, and conditions. Perfect consistency!

So off we went. We had succeeded in finding the CEO of a small to medium-sized enterprise (SME) who had major challenges in his or her recently inherited business and was intrigued/reckless/desperate enough to agree to an experiment that might help to transform it (and his or her fortunes). Between the three of us we devised a plan which combined conventional strategy stuff with a dash of organizational learning and business process re-engineering, both highly fashionable at the time.

It was quite an elaborate plan combining lectures, simulations, experiential exercises, factory redesign, and more (MacIntosh & MacLean 1999). Needless to say, things didn't go according to plan.

As an alternative to one of our increasingly frequent theory squabbles—where we tried to figure out whether organizational learning or BPR was responsible for the lack of discernible progress—we decided to visit our practitioner partner and colleagues at their plant. The news on arrival shocked us. The BSE[1] food crisis in the UK—and a sudden blanket ban on certain foods—had essentially knocked out the business's main market overnight. Bizarrely, at the same time, they had succeeded with one of their key aims—selling into major supermarkets some newer products that flowed from our experimenting. So it was bad, but, with optimism, promising.

Just as significantly, "the plan" had assumed its rightful place atop the controversial if invisible "abandoned-plan mountain" and was smouldering pointlessly out of sight somewhere. In its wake, the factory had erupted into a new crisis-induced form of operation. Teams were springing up, combining some of the stuff we had rehearsed with other new stuff made up on the spot; some initiatives worked, some didn't; some folks seemed to be thriving—others not (one or two left). It was turbulent, but maybe just what was needed. In spite of our plan, or because of it? Or, weirdly, both? We couldn't tell, which in itself was telling. We retreated to the academic ranch to think this through.

Back at the ranch 1: research, complexity, and emergence

Perhaps to reassure ourselves that we were still in control of the situation, we set to work on an explanation. (As we busied ourselves, the factory appeared to be finding its feet, indeed rising to its many challenges). Somewhere in the recesses of his PhD memories, Donald recalled an array of laser diodes which one supervisor had dismissed as "pathological" whilst another celebrated the unexpected patterning of their output as "self-organization."

To cut a long story short, our digging around unearthed complexity theory and, suitably recontextualized as a metaphor, it seemed to help us understand, in a new way, what might be going on in our partner's factory.

In broad terms, complexity theory offers an alternative to the Newtonian universe characterized by equilibrium and a tendency towards decline in mechanisms. Change is typically governed by some grand design or plan (divine or otherwise) aided (or impeded) by thermodynamics' second law, which states that all mechanisms typically proceed from order to disorder.

By contrast, the Nobel prize-winning work in physics of Ilya Prigogine and colleagues (Prigogine & Stengers 1984), and subsequent work in a range of fields including biology (Kauffman, 1993), zoology (Goodwin, 1994), and economics (Arthur, 1989), turned scientific thinking on its head with theories and evidence that pointed towards the prevalence of disequilibrium and emergent, spontaneous self-organization in complex adaptive, sometimes "living" systems (see Coveney & Highfield, 1996, for a comprehensive review of the development of complexity theory).

So, little by little we viewed our experience (and our data) of the factory's apparent transformation through the lens of complexity theory and, in particular, Prigogine's idea of spontaneous transformation in "dissipative structures" (MacIntosh & MacLean, 1999).

Perhaps unwittingly, an implicit position on our parts, namely that our methodological stance had to be consistent with our substantive focus and/or theoretical apparatus, necessitated a rethink on method.

We had begun to explore the idea that organizations could helpfully be viewed as complex adaptive systems, and that strategic change in particular might be better understood using complexity theory: if organizations were thus just unpredictable networks of interacting elements, shouldn't our desire for consistency require us to view our research teams and partnerships in the same way?

Couldn't/shouldn't research be better understood as a complex and unpredictable dynamic, capable of expressing unpredicted emergent properties at any time, spontaneously transforming from time to time, and, as such, impervious to the attempts of any individual or group to control it (MacLean & MacIntosh, 2003)? Conversely, if management research was "controllable," didn't that mean it was being styled as some sort of mechanism? What were the potential costs of reducing a rich social dynamic to mechanism through the imposition of protocols from the natural sciences? What might we be missing, or repressing even?

Field work 2: is there anybody in there?

Now genuinely intrigued by complexity theory, we continued to research and set about publishing and we scored a few successes. Nevertheless, we had some concerns about both method and strategy when viewed and practiced from a complexity perspective. We were not alone. Even our complexity-theory "colleagues" (e.g., Stacey, 1995) were skeptical about some of our claims. By and large these centered round our claims that complex processes could be somehow "managed" towards desired outcomes in broad terms, albeit through a form of management very different from the traditional plan-then-do approach. Several complexity "converts" openly stated that we were thinly disguised charlatans who obviously understood nothing of complexity if we were seriously suggesting anything could be "managed."

Now on the back foot, we appealed to many of our practitioner friends to help deepen our understanding of working from a complexity angle. The response was positive—we were surprised by the appetite to get involved. In a relatively short period of time we had assembled a network of around 30 representatives of organizations of all shapes and size—multinational corporations, government bodies, consultancies, third-sector bodies, and SMEs.

The aim was simple: to conduct the network in accordance with our understanding of how complex social systems "ought to be" managed—and take it from there. In practice this meant agreeing some basic things that we wanted to explore (in this case managerial expressions of complexity concepts such as disequilibrium, interconnectedness, positive feedback) and some basic principles about how we would do that (meet regularly as a group, conduct experiments off-line, discuss off-line action research interventions before and after, help each other to make sense of what was happening, use theory to develop our understanding of complexity-based management principles, and share experience to help answer questions in practice).

Again to cut a long story short, we think we made some progress: some businesses reported successes whilst we published on both method—which we increasingly accounted for in terms of Mode 2 (MacLean & MacIntosh, 2003, 2015; MacLean, MacIntosh & Grant, 2002)—and other (unpredicted) topics relating to strategic change such as paradox (Beech, Burns, Caestecker, MacIntosh & MacLean, 2004), conflict (Beech, MacIntosh, MacLean, Shepherd & Stokes, 2002), and organizational health (MacIntosh, MacLean & Burns, 2007).

However, our celebration of the arrival of a promising new management paradigm was tempered by an equally new batch of disconcerting questions which themselves arose out of the practitioner research network:

- If organizations are complex systems, what are the elements of such systems?
- If, as most seem to assume, the elements are human beings, what are the consequences of elements belonging to several systems at the same time?
- Moreover, how could you draw boundaries around such a multiplicity of interacting elements and systems?
- If you can't define the elements or boundaries of your systems, what are you using the term "system" for?!

Perhaps the critical event to tip us into a new line of enquiry in theoretical terms came when we were answering post-presentation questions at a conference in Cambridge. Someone in the audience expressed some surprise that our presentation seemed to be trying to convince them that the logic of mechanistic rationalism applied to strategy was wrong, that there was an alternative logic based on complexity theory but that there were real difficulties associated with its use in human settings and we had some serious questions to answer. That, our erstwhile interrogator quickly added, was not what bothered them. What did bother them was the apparent "battle of logics" and how we seemed to be implying that all of this was intellectually driven—which didn't seem very far at all from the rationalism which we seemed to be critiquing. What, they questioned, of phenomena such as intuition, the influence of other people, mood, emotion, etc.?

Somewhat wrong-footed by this unreasonable line of questioning, we cleared our throats as we prepared to defend ourselves in relation to this suddenly glaring blind spot. Before we could muster a reply, however, we were stopped in our tracks by our practitioner-partner who had "jumped in" with an answer: "Yes, I agree with the questioner." Apparently overlooking his co-authorship (and complicity), he added:

Donald and Robert have presented an over-sanitized account of what happened. Too clean, too tidy. It was much messier than that—and it certainly wasn't all comprehended intellectually at the time. In the thick of it we spent a lot of time stumbling around—a lot of guess work, intuition, compromise, and emotional intensity. Robert and Donald's description might be accurate in terms of how it looked from the outside, but inside, I can tell you, it was much more emotionally driven.

We stood before our audience, stunned. "From the inside…" … "emotion" … "intuition." Could one talk about things like that in strategy? Or in complexity theory? Certainly we never had!

Again, to gloss over the protracted agonizing, we eventually (under the influence of a debate in the related systems theory of autopoiesis (Luhmann, 1984) and the insight that the idea of system may be an unhelpful reification) decided to suspend the idea of humans belonging to things called systems. Instead we went straight to the heart of the matter—the *actions* of human beings—with their unruly emotions, disturbing idiosyncrasies, biographies, and, perhaps most unnerving of all for a couple of "techies," interacting human bodies.

Back at the ranch 2: enter the human (in full embodied technicolor)

So with complexity theory on hold whilst we explored *actual* human beings in a bit more detail, our (now highly overlapping) enquiries into strategic change and action research slowly revealed two highly particular caricatures of the human actor. On the one hand, there was a dominant view of the human actor as a highly, if not exclusively, rational individual. On the other, the human actor took the form of indistinguishable member of a socially structured collective. Pure reason or pure culture.

We have written at some length on theories of human action (implicit or otherwise) in the strategy literature (MacLean & MacIntosh 2012, 2015, MacLean, MacIntosh & Seidl, 2015) but have only begun to address the issue in relation to research method (MacIntosh, Bartunek, Bhatt & MacLean, 2016). So, whilst an extensive review of the literature remains to be done, our experience never the less would suggest that the same basic pattern applies—our notions of research are dominated by views of the researchers as rational problem-solvers or culturally driven clan-members.

In more detail, the cultural view of human action, which social theorist Hans Joas (1996) has dubbed "normative," emphasizes the role of shared social structures such as values, rules, and cultural norms in configuring what we do and how we do it. One can see this in particular in the form of research protocols, the increasing emphasis on training in particular techniques and methods, and a growing drive to ensure that researchers are doing what they "ought" to if they want to "belong" to a community of researchers and have their work regarded as legitimate. The point of drawing a normative view of action into a fuller view is to point out that research, under this view, is primarily driven by social structures, the needs of folk to "belong" to something, and a desire on the part of all members of a collective to sustain their sense of who they are together—largely, it must be said, a conservative process.

On the other side of the "think–act" Cartesian coin, however, we have a different, and probably dominant, view of human action: the rational view. By "rational" we mean simply that action is straightforwardly viewed and explained in terms of ends, means, and conditions as outlined above. In typical research settings the appropriate means (resources, methods, etc.) are enlisted or engaged to deliver on clearly predefined ends (questions, aims, objectives, and the like) in any given context (the field). We think it through, then we mechanically execute our plans.

Fortunately (or otherwise) in research these two theories of action are mutually supportive—the very protocols that are promoted as social norms are typically rational in flavor, and it is seen as rational to employ normatively structured protocols in pursuit of findings. Thus our communities of enquiry are supposed to deliver insights which are not only appropriate to the prior question and effective in terms of resource utilization, but broadly acceptable in social terms to interested stakeholders. To borrow from the strategy literature (Johnson, Whittington, Scholes, Angwin & Regnér, 2013) research strategies (increasingly in vogue) are seen to be suitable, feasible, and acceptable.

The parallels with strategy are not only striking but inevitable. In a fascinating essay on ideology and methodology in the social sciences, philosopher Alasdair MacIntyre (1998) accounts for the similarities between the dominant, positivistic orthodoxies of enquiry, bureaucracy, and strategy as different contextual expressions of the same phenomenon—an ideologically structured process of bureaucratic control. Consider first his observation:

> Methodology then functions so as to communicate one very particular vision of the social world and one that obscures from view the fundamental levels of conceptualization, conflict, contestability, and unpredictability as they constitute and operate in that world.
>
> (MacIntyre, 1998: 65)

The reasons for such a rationally structured control process may be manifold and understandable—accountability, predictability (reliability, generalizability, validity, etc.) to mention but a few—and the fruitful alignment with Newtonian mechanics is obvious. The problem for us is that in styling the actor as rational (and the process as mechanical) we are implicitly subscribing to an ideology which seeks to eliminate (as some undesirable form of Newtonian friction) the very things to which we as management researchers might need to attend. The methodologically obscured "conceptualization, conflict, contestability, and unpredictability" we would argue are the hallmarks of good action research in particular.

So, for us, questions around what view of human action we subscribe to in our use of the term action research became highly important. What if we didn't agree with the limitations imposed by rational or normative views? What if we wanted a view that both aligned with complexity theory but allowed us to view emergence from the "inside" as participants in the creation of novelty—such as new meanings, new understandings and possibilities? What if research is therefore first and foremost a form of creative (inter)action?

Joas's (1996) work, heavily influenced by American philosophical pragmatism, seeks to move his readers towards a view of creative action which he claims is much better suited to the times in which we live—more concerned with individual expression and innovation, and better able to deal with MacIntyre's "obscured levels" of contestability, emergence, unpredictability, etc. In seeking to account for human creativity, Joas depicts a view of action which, as an alternative to the ends–means–conditions framework of rationalism, is organized around situated social interaction, embodied expression, and emergent intention (Figure 9.1).

So, according to this view, research action is seen somewhat differently as a three-dimensional dynamic. We will briefly outline these dimensions below (for more detail see MacLean et al., 2015; MacLean & MacIntosh, 2012, 2015).

Interactive identity formation

As human beings, processes of relating reaffirm our own identity and satisfy the quintessentially social nature of our being. Who we are, and who we are becoming, are under constant iteration whilst interacting with others in organizational settings. Our identity is at least partly socially constructed—thus our identities as researchers will bear directly on our experience of research and vice versa.

Emerging intention

For us as individuals, it is these identity processes of interactive sense-making with each other which helps us to create and feel a real sense of meaning in our

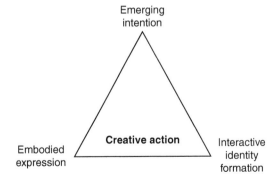

Figure 9.1 The three dimensions of creative action.
Source: After Joas, 1996.

activities. The obvious implication of this in organizational settings is that creative action requires our individual intention to be in meaningful dialogue with
that sense of joint enterprise with others which defines the organization at that
point in time. Research should thus allow for the ongoing development of individual and collective intentionality, recognizing that it is its dynamism rather
than "fixedness" (i.e., slavish enactment of set goals) which signifies creativity
and vitality.

Embodied expression

As researchers, as humans, our biographies are literally embodied in us at any
given point. How we feel about ourselves and those we interact with determine
the course of events that we experience, though perhaps not in simple-to-
understand cause and effect ways. In particular, we have to recognize the expressive dimension of the human body—seeing it as something that moves and
creates in its own right rather than simply as some instrument at the beck and
call of the intellect. The emotional and embodied aspects of our organizing have
a bearing on what we do, what we notice, what we create, what things mean to
us, etc. Emotional expression, intuition, imagination, sensorial engagement, and
sensitivity to our aesthetic faculties are all facets of the creative actions and
meaning-making which underpin research practice. It is these faculties in particular that we feel are missing from the way we (as a community of researchers)
typically think about, or account for, our research—and which we will tend to
highlight in the remainder of this chapter. At this stage all we would like to do is
point out that we feel we have found a "human-level counterpart" to the "system-
level" ideas of complexity—i.e., we can begin to conceptualize our actions in
research in a way that aligns with complexity themes such as uncertainty, interaction, paradox, and the emergence of novelty.

Field work 3: the plot (or the mist) thickens

Now 15 years or more into our ongoing enquiries in strategy process, we had put
a considerable distance between ourselves and our starting positions. Far from
working in terms of strategy, and strategy research, as objective, personality-
independent, rational, mechanistic processes, we had somehow stumbled (out of
our depths) into the possibility of researching actual human beings in interaction.
Bodies, gut-feelings, politics, delusions, etc.: the lot! Terrifying! However, we
had one thing on our side: we had all of these things ourselves.

Eventually, we found ourselves back in another engagement—a new one.
Bizarrely, the head of the partner-organization was a long-standing member of
our research network who not only had an interest in complexity theory, but, as
a consultant clinical psychiatrist, was keen to open up the black box of complex
adaptive systems somewhat and explore the emotional and psychological dimensions of emergence from the "inside"—i.e., rather than from the outside looking
out for systems-level emergent-properties. She was keen to explore emergence

as experienced by living human beings—complexity meets creative action, just what we were contemplating.

So, armed with a new resolve to "background" some of our research baggage, and just be "ourselves," we immersed ourselves in an 18-month project. We had agreed with all involved to have regular reflections together on the emotional, intuitive, and other "non-rational" (as opposed to irrational) aspects of any particularly striking events, decision, activities, exchanges, or episodes. As the project gained momentum and through many work and social get-togethers, we got to know each other and eventually trusted—and liked—each other enough to share fairly private thoughts, feelings, and hunches, not just about ourselves but about each other and the project as a whole.

A particular feature of the project was a tendency, initially prompted by the leader of the organization, but eventually by most of us, to "press pause" every now and again and ask the simple question "What's really going on here, what is this really about—thoughts, feelings, impressions, hunches, possibilities?" These reflection sessions were fascinating in the way that they could reveal how we might construct a variety of partial and sometimes fragmentary narratives corresponding to our experience and then, as these were shared, contested, and iterated, we could collectively reach some agreed sense of what was going on and what to do next. Occasionally, the apparent emergence of shared meaning was sudden rather than gradual and galvanized by a particularly resonant style of contribution—often taking the group by surprise and accompanied by a somewhat more intense emotional "atmosphere"—which we called "generative dialogic encounters" (Beech, MacIntosh & MacLean, 2010).

What was particularly interesting in this work was not just the way in which it was characterized by the intensified occurrence of some of the phenomena in which we had become interested—such as emotion, personalities, intuition, emergent intention, paradox—but how the transformation of the situation in question seemed to draw on human faculties that lie beyond the reach of logic and science altogether—regardless of whether that science is modern or postmodern. We were at something of a loss to explain our own experiences.

Back at the ranch 3: people, paradox, and poetry

At this stage it could be probably said that our work was (and is) wandering well off the beaten track of strategy research—and research method. Whilst we continue to work in partnership with fairly typical (if somewhat adventurous) private and public sector organizations, an increasing quotient of work with arts organizations, artists, and designers sustains a healthy challenge to the more familiar situations in which rationality is more or less taken for granted and creative artistic expression is seen as belonging somewhere else. We were trying to find out what was going on in these "generative dialogic encounters" and had a growing hunch that possible answers might lie beyond our normal scientific borders—possibly beyond scientific thinking itself; perhaps this was as much art as science.

However, even in science things appeared to be shifting as regards the dominance of rationalism:

- developments in neuro- and cognitive science are casting new light on how we as humans think and act; and,
- on our part at least, we increasingly question the cultural specificity of a view of organization predicated on rationality and efficiency (i.e., with no real appreciation of artistic practice as anything other than ornament or entertainment) (MacIntosh & MacLean 2015).

Touching first on cognition, in his review of narrative in strategy, Freedman (2013) introduces the distinction between system 1 and system 2 decision-making from the field of cognitive science. Both types of decision-making operate in most of us, but we are only beginning to learn about the former, so the latter is dominant in our representations of (and education about) decision-making. System 2 decisions are described as "conscious, explicit, analytical, deliberative, more intellectual and inherently sequential" and "just what was expected of strategic reasoning." System 1 processes, on the other hand, are more holistic, instantaneous, complex, and personal. To illustrate, Freedman relates to a quote by philosopher Isaiah Berlin:

> a capacity for integrating a vast amalgam of constantly changing, multi-coloured, evanescent, perpetually overlapping data, too many, too swift, too intermingled to be caught and pinned down and labelled like so many individual butterflies. To integrate in this sense is to see the data (those identified by scientific knowledge as well as by direct perception) as elements in a single pattern, with their implications, to see them as symptoms of past and future possibilities, to see them pragmatically – that is, in terms of what you and others can or will do to them, and what they can or will do to others and to you.

> (Freedman, 2013: 613)

In the context of our work, we were struck by the way in which this description of system 1 cognition resonated with the possibilities of creative action in any given situation—in which people are experiencing the emergence and creation of novelty "from the inside"—as creative participants in the forming of whatever is taking shape (as opposed to external observers of that which has formed); a form of real-time pattern-recognition and generation that spontaneously draws on all of our embodied faculties and socializes them into new shared meanings and possibilities for action.

There is something about this description that strikes us as highly resonant with our experience of the reflective conversations and experiences with our research-partners at times. Just too many perspectives and competing ideas to tie anything down though linear rational thought. Situations and accounts of them are often, when most interesting, characterized by paradox, mystery, and an almost overwhelming proliferation of possibilities. And yet often consensus on how to look back or move forward is nevertheless reached in many cases. Interestingly, in our experience, this is often aided by a charismatically delivered insight or contribution, often visual, or stylized prose, or (melo-)dramatic performance. And perhaps performance is the key word here. The thing that "tips" opinion in a particular direction is often the stylized performance of an individual or group rather than a compelling conceptual structure or analytical movement. In terms of creative action, intention emerges in the situation as individuals interact—responding to the "pre-reflexive urges" (Joas 1996) of their embodied historical bodies in pursuit of positive identity experiences (Beech, 2008) together.

The critical point here is that, in response to being struck by a potentially overwhelming, surprising, mystifying, paradoxical, or otherwise challenging difficulty in action research, it may be artistic creative social processes that come to the fore. It may have as much to do with "making" and "expressing" as revealing, unfolding or discovering.

Research capability may thus include the capacity for collective, artistically inspired, creative action—and, of course, collective creative action is not necessarily best accessed through scientific thinking. Indeed, developing our second point above, about the cultural specificity of organizing, in the current times it may strike us as odd today that strategic action, collective enquiry, and social order were in some places and times promulgated through art, stories, and poetics in many of our traditional cultures. Berlin's description above could equally fit the processes that might have been used by historical poets and bards as they sought to make sense of complex social phenomena in order to create reassurance, hope, social cohesion, and collective action.

In the words of Brendan Lehane (2005: 28–9), "bards kept alive the ancient stories of a race, dramatized new events, and entertained the courts with their long stylised narratives." Becoming a bard involved training that was "long and hard" (Chadwick, 2002) so this class of work was neither informal nor on the sidelines. Bards helped to sustain social order and the cultural life of their clan. Lehane's term "stylised narrative" is interesting.

Is there any room for this kind of thinking in relation to our roles as action researchers? Could the skilful researcher–practitioner in action research operate at least partly as a "bard"—who spots possibilities, scatters them as social seeds in stylized delivery, then has the patience to let them germinate in a myriad of situations which, in turn, give rise to further development and elaboration of the emerging narrative. Are we as researchers at least part story-maker, story teller? Storytelling is in this sense an iterative process; stories are part retrospective sense-making (Weick, 1995) and part aspirational in the context of the strategy statements crafted at the outset.

Holding this tension between what has passed and what has still to come, Alastair McIntosh (2004: 121) suggests that the bard is continually required to "step outside of the consensus trance reality, observe the psychodynamics of individual or social disease, and then step back in to protest for change." For us, now, research is increasingly something we see as often very far from the objective distanced non-disturbing scientific discovery process. In stark contrast, our research is a creative human process whose created artifacts reflect the emerging intentions, artistic capabilities, and political skills of those involved in what is an uncertain and unpredictable complex dynamic. As researchers we make things, we change things—with others. The extent to which we succeed in our endeavors depends partly on how we influence those we work with—and vice versa.

People matter. For many years the leadership literature has been fascinated by the role of transformational leaders (see Burns, 1978) who inspire those around them to "do more than they originally expected to do" (Fu, Tsui, Lui & Li, 2010). We are struck by the similarities from a more ancient tradition where bards engage in purposeful action, glimpse emerging patterns, and engender collective responses acting as a midwife to the (re)birth of the organization. Using stories, they spread awareness and engagement through commanding oratory, compelling visions, and imagery and, above all, as McIntosh suggests, "stepping back in" to agitate for change. Isn't that what happens in action research—at least some of the time?

Discussion and conclusion

So our extended, somewhat rambling journey has seen us move from an initial view of management research as a rational, designed mechanistic sort of process to a complex, creative, emergent dynamic in which we draw on artistic as well as logical faculties. This is *not* to say that research plans and designs have no place—of course they do. We are just drawing attention to the possibility, or perhaps eventuality, of things not turning out according to plan. Or, perhaps more specifically, that plans themselves are transient products of creative human process of interaction, temporary crystallizations of emerging intention—and that as the action moves on, and the situations, contexts, concerns, and available resources develop, so, in turn, plans evolve and are iterated as we negotiate and renegotiate with one and other just what we are doing and indeed who we are as people in this situation.

In line with complexity theory, the research "system" gives rise to unpredictable emergent properties that are always in the process of forming and reforming; in terms of creative action, we humans experience this as part of a negotiated political dynamic into which we express our intentions, aspirations, intuitions, and emotional expressions—along with our logics, theories, methods, and protocols—and whilst we aim to influence what we create together, we are never really in control of it.

This unpredictable, uncontrollable, creative, and expressive dimension of research draws as much on our artistic capabilities as on our abilities as scientists. Perhaps this is because, in accordance with both complexity theory and art, our research experiences are frequently paradoxical and even occasionally mysterious (Beech et al., 2004).

John Shotter (2006a, 2006b, 2008), drawing in particular on the later Wittgenstein, has written extensively about the tendency of those engaged in enquiry, under the influences of our rationally oriented educational processes, to treat every difference we experience as "problems" that have "solutions." So, when faced with a "felt" difficulty, we tend to conceptualize the difficulty as a problem and set about finding the solution—in our case, perhaps, the answer to a research question. However, he goes on to argue that, in many cases, the difficulty is actually a "difficulty of inter-personal relating" rather than a "difficulty of the intellect," and that, in intellectualizing it, i.e., conceptualizing the difficulty it as a "problem," we abstract ourselves from the very same difficulty which is exercising us—often exacerbating it by turning away from the very personal matters that comprise it—the interactions of our embodied human biographies. To return to the distinctions introduced at the start of the chapter, this may of course reflect and reveal the nature of what it means to be "professional."

For Shotter, possible progress lies not in the relentless march of rationalism, but in a heightened awareness of the paradoxical and sometimes confusing nature of experience, research experience or otherwise, and thus the engagement of each other in creative dialogue (Shotter, 2008) that resolves the difficulty, or transforms the paradox (Beech et al., 2004) instead of seeking always to solve a problem or answer a question. He links the ability to do this to a form of "withness thinking" (Shotter, 2006a) where we work "with" each other rather than "on" a problem—an ability which is not traditionally at the top of our research methods training courses.

Sensitivity to imagination, intuition, aesthetics, paradox, and mystery draws on creative faculties that most research writing (at best) overlook. Non-rational does not necessarily imply irrational. A more acknowledged role for art, poetry, "social poetics," and non-conceptual expression/imagery in the workings of our research may lead us into somewhat neglected and unfamiliar but nevertheless fertile territory. It may also mean that we need to open up a little, break out of our existing confines—work with artists, poets, performers, for example—and rethink what it means to be "professional"—both for ourselves and, perhaps more importantly, those entering the field.

Finally, we have increasingly come to recognize some exciting possibilities of research as creative practice informed by both logic and science and by art, poetry and aesthetics.

With our research cycle in Figure 9.2 below, we attempt to represent visually what we think happens in practice. Research may begin anywhere in the cycle, but typically with a rational design or plan often framed as an initial question. As the research begins, this gives way to an emergent phenomenon enabled by the kinds of reflective, sense-making, and (re)planning conversations with which we are all familiar. Together, these two parallel processes interact, feeding into the creative processes of emergence and "bardically" stewarding the emergence of insights and new knowledge as the project progresses.

Each of us is different—different strengths, leanings, blind-spots, and so on. Where we think our visual might help is as part of a team conversation about

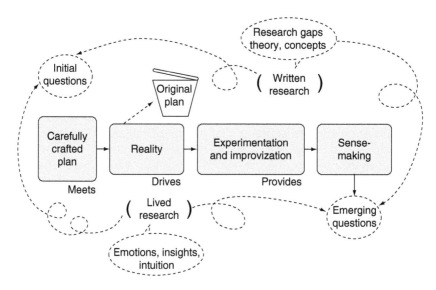

Figure 9.2 The complexity of the research cycle.

any particular research project—who does what, how, and, ideally, in encouraging you and others to think about how, when, where in the cycle you consider bringing your "art" into what we (currently) call action research!

Note

1 Bovine spongiform encephalopathy (BSE) is more commonly known as mad cow disease. In 1996 the UK government ordered a cull of all potentially infected herds which led to the slaughter of over four million animals to try to eradicate the problem. During the crisis, sales of products containing processed meat fell sharply as public confidence in the safety of such products was eroded.

References

Arthur, W. B. (1989). Competing technologies, increasing returns and lock-in by historical events. *Economic Journal*, 99(394), 106–31.

Beech, N. (2008). On the nature of dialogic identity work. *Organization*, 15(1), 51–74.

Beech, N., MacIntosh, R., MacLean, D., Shepherd, J. & Stokes J. (2002). Exploring constraints on developing knowledge: On the need for conflict. *Journal of Management Learning*, 33(4), 459–75.

Beech, N., Burns, H., Caestecker, L. D., MacIntosh R. & MacLean, D. (2004). Paradox as invitation to act in problematic change situations. *Human Relations*, 57(10), 1313–32.

Beech, N., MacIntosh, R. & MacLean, D. (2010). Dialogues between academics and practitioners: The role of generative dialogic encounters. *Organization Studies*, 31(9), 1341–67.

Burns, J. (1978). *Leadership*. New York: Harper & Row.

Chadwick, N. (2002). *The Celts*. London: Folio Press.

Coveney, P. & Highfield, R. (1996). *Frontiers of Complexity*. London: Faber and Faber.

Freedman L. (2013). *Strategy: A History*. New York: Oxford University Press.

Fu, P. P., Tsui, A. S., Lui, J. & Li, L. (2010). Pursuit of whose happiness? Executive leaders transformational behaviours and personal values. *Administrative Science Quarterly*, 55(2), 222–54.

Goodwin, B. (1994). *How the Leopard Changed Its Spots*. London: Phoenix Giant.

Joas, H. (1996). *The Creativity of Action*. Chicago, IL: University of Chicago Press.

Johnson, G., Whittington, R., Scholes, K., Angwin, D. & Regnér, P. (2013). *Exploring Strategy: Text and Cases* (10th ed.). Harlow, UK: Pearson.

Kauffman, S. A. (1993). *The Origins of Order: Self Organization and Selection in Evolution*. Oxford: Oxford University Press.

Lehane B. (2005). *Early Celtic Christianity*. London: Continuum.

Luhmann, N. (1984). *Soziale Systeme*. Frankfurt am Main: Suhrkamp.

McIntosh, A. (2004). *Soil and Soul*. London: Autumn.

MacIntosh, R. & MacLean, D. (1999). Conditioned emergence: A dissipative structures approach to transformation. *Strategic Management Journal*, 20(1), 297–316.

MacIntosh, R. & MacLean, D. (2015). *Strategic Management: Strategists at Work*. London: Palgrave.

MacIntosh, R., MacLean, D. & Burns, H. (2007). Health in organization: Toward a process-based view. *Journal of Management Studies*, 44(2), 206–21.

MacIntosh, R., Bartunek, J., Bhatt, M. & MacLean, D. (2016). I never promised you a rose garden: Reflections on the evolution of research questions. In Shani, A. B. & Mouair, D. (Eds.) *Research in Organizational Change and Development: Proceedings of the Academy of Management*, Vol. 24 (forthcoming).

MacIntyre, A. C. (1998). Social science methodology as the ideology of bureaucratic authority. In Knight, K. (Ed.) *The MacIntyre Reader*. London: Polity Press.

MacLean, D. & MacIntosh, R. (2003). Complex adaptive social systems: Towards a theory for practice. In Mitleton-Kelly, E. (Ed.) *Complex Systems and Evolutionary Perspectives on Organizations: The Application of Complexity Theory to Organizations* (pp. 149–65). Amsterdam: Elsevier Science BV.

MacLean, D. & MacIntosh, R. (2012). Strategic change as creative action. *International Journal of Strategic Change Management*, 4(1), 80–97.

MacLean, D. & MacIntosh, R. (2015). Planning reconsidered: Paradox, poetry and people at the edge of strategy. *European Management Journal*, 33(2), 72–8.

MacLean, D., MacIntosh, R. & Grant, S. (2002). Mode 2 management research. *British Journal of Management*, 13(3), 189–207.

MacLean, D., MacIntosh, R. & Seidl, D. (2015). Rethinking dynamic capabilities from a creative action perspective. *Strategic Organization*, 13(4), 340–52.

Popper, K. R. (1972). *Objective Knowledge*. Oxford: Oxford University Press.

Prigogine, I. & Stengers, I. (1984). *Order Out of Chaos: Man's New Dialogue with Nature*. New York, Bantam.

Shotter, J. (2006a). On the edge of social constructionism: Wittgensteinian inquiries into organizations and management. *Qualitative Research in Organizations and Management: An International Journal*, 1(3), 189–203.

Shotter, J. (2006b). From minds hidden in the heads of individuals to the use of mind–talk between us: Wittgensteinian developmental investigations. *Journal for the Theory of Social Behaviour*, 36(3), 279–97.

Shotter, J. (2008). Dialogism and polyphony in organizing theorizing in organization studies: Action guiding anticipations and the continuous creation of novelty. *Organization Studies*, 29(4), 501–24.

Stacey, R. (1995). The science of complexity: An alternative perspective for strategic change processes. *Strategic Management Journal*, 16(6), 477–95.

Weick, K. E. (1995). *Sense-making in Organizations*. Thousand Oaks, CA: Sage Publishing.

10 Learning the craft

Developing apprentice scholars with the capacity to integrate theory and practice

Claire Collins and Richard McBain

Introduction

The aim of this chapter is to consider the development of the apprentice scholar in the context of a Doctor of Business Administration (DBA) Program in a UK business school. This program allows mid- to senior-career professionals working in a range of organizations and contexts to develop rigorous academic research capabilities which will complement their advanced practitioner experience and expertise, and it does so in a way that provides an opportunity to engage faculty with real-world problems impacting practice and research.

Our focus will be on the individual's journey from practitioner to researcher; the development needed to enable them to hold these two worlds together and to gain a deeper understanding of how each world contributes to the other, bringing rigor and relevance in both cases. Three key interrelated themes which are encountered on this journey will be explored in this chapter:

*   identity—developing an identity as an engaged scholar;
*   competence—the practitioner as researcher; and
*   community—a community of academic faculty and practitioner researchers to support the transition to practitioner researcher.

First, we will outline the context.

Context

The presence of a gap between theory and practice or between academics and practitioners has been a focus of both public policy and research (Sandberg & Tsoukas, 2011). Typically this gap is considered to be problematic and requiring action. For example, Bennis and O'Toole (2005: 2) argue that business schools "need to strike a new balance between scientific rigour and practical relevance" and also point out that institutional pressures promote the current position of separating theory and practice. Evidence suggests that research incentives promote rigor not relevance (Flickinger, Tuschke, Gruber-Muecke & Fielder, 2014). Underpinning this theory and practice divide may lie more fundamental issues relating to philosophical stances and it has been argued that scientific rationality and empiricism have encouraged a detachment from practice (Raelin, 2007; Sandberg & Tsoukas, 2011).

More research into the issue of exploring and meeting this gap may be justified (Kieser, Nicolai & Seidl, 2015) but for Bartunek and Rynes (2014) the tensions inherent in the dichotomy between academics and practitioners, which may include different logics, time dimensions, communication styles, rigor and relevance, interests and incentives, may be underpinned by paradoxes that should be open to generative exploration, but they may also result in new research and practice. The concept of "engaged scholarship" (Van de Ven & Johnson, 2006) offers a way of approaching the problem of producing knowledge that flows between the theory–practice divide, whilst recognizing that there are also issues of knowledge and arguments that theory and practice are distinct forms of knowledge. They define "engaged scholarship" as: "a collaborative form of enquiry in which academics and practitioners leverage their different perspectives and competences to produce knowledge about a complex problem or phenomenon that exists under conditions of uncertainty found in the world" (Van de Ven & Johnson, 2006: 803).

Research activity in a DBA program operates in the space between scientific rigor and practical relevance and embraces these two positions (Bradbury & Lichtenstein, 2000). Professional doctorates are relatively recent innovations in higher education, originating in the USA but now widespread, and have been developed to better meet the needs of practitioners and provide a vehicle for relevant and rigorous research.

The DBA and professional doctorates

Both authors of this chapter have been Directors of the DBA program at Henley Business School, University of Reading: Richard McBain in 2007–11 and Claire Collins from 2011 to the present. The Henley DBA first enrolled Research Associates in October 1992 and has graduated some 186 since then. In 2008, the structure of the DBA changed from being a single award to a double award, the first part of which, at the beginning, is an MSc in Business and Management Research. Recognizing that all doctoral candidates undergo methodological training, the rationale for creating an additional award was to ensure that those candidates who had been away from academic study for a while would be well supported in gaining the research skills necessary at this level. Effectively we translated the methodological training element into an award that is *a requirement* to start the DBA, so the students see themselves as working towards a doctorate, but they accumulate credits from required assignments towards a new award to encourage structured understanding and practice of the different aspect of research skills at masters level before extending those skills at doctoral level. This is an important contribution to building confidence and knowledge.

The MSc is a structured taught program and transitions the individual from a position of, typically, Master's level study to an understanding of the requirements of doctoral level research. Therefore, the structure takes them from the context of research through to advanced methodological skill development. There are two more elements to this first part of the program:

- the exploration and development of a range of holistic competences including research, personal, teaching, and consultancy competences (AMBA, 2015); and
- the building of strong, mutually supportive networks, for the more independent phase of DBA study.

Encouragement for building strong networks helps to catalyze the practitioner–researcher transition. This is generally facilitated through community-building, by sharing experiences at workshops, participating in research colloquia, and engaging with social media and other social networking vehicles.

Initially, the Research Associate is supported by a mentor who is broadly knowledgeable in the subject domain, but also supports the candidate's pastoral needs, including the important practitioner–researcher transition. Towards the end of the MSc, a provisional supervisor takes over. By the start of the DBA phase, a second supervisor will also be in place. This supervision team will be experts in the research area and in the chosen methodology, so as to comprehensively support the candidate through to completion of their thesis. The supervision structure is in line with the requirements of the university for the support of doctoral candidates and no differentiation is made between the PhD and the DBA in this regard, or in the requirements for outputs. Therefore, a unique contribution to knowledge is required and in addition, for the DBA, a unique contribution to practice. The doctorate will produce either a monograph or collection of papers which will fulfill the requirements of the university.

In order to generate a holistic view of the academic journey, the DBA deliberately addresses wider issues of development. There are four workshops in the MSc phase of the study which step the candidate through a developing understanding of research techniques, from the philosophical underpinnings of research to more detailed technical skills development. These are assessed to ensure learning adherence. There are regular opportunities to present current work to their supervisors and peers at Research Colloquia. Integrated into the program is a process of personal development which complements the technical development with progression of thinking about the self in a number of ways. At the start of the MSc, each student works with a mentor who is skilled in knowledge expansion and the early stages of transition and combining identities. Towards the end of the MSc, the supervisory team is introduced to progress the research into the doctoral phase and on to completion.

The characteristics of the post-Humboldtian doctorate epitomise the structure of the DBA. Some of these characteristics include (Lee, 2011):

- multi-national, diverse;
- the student acts as consumer or co-producer of knowledge;

- typically part-time study;
- multidisciplinary, collaborative;
- external involvement/stakeholders;
- production of human capital for knowledge economies; and
- political, governmental, or commercial accountability.

The development of the apprentice researcher

Within the overall context of the applied research domain, the apprentice researcher needs to develop cognitive, emotional, and practical skills to hold the two worlds of practice and research together simultaneously in order to deliver optimum outcomes for each and, as importantly, develop the deep understanding of how each can contribute in order to bring rigor and relevance to the other.

For those embarking on a DBA, a specifically applied doctorate in Business Administration, this is the requirement that the educator has to manage in the design of the program so as to support the development of the individual, as well as the individual having to manage their own transitions. The challenge, or opportunity, to hold the roles of senior manager, consultant, or teacher alongside the role of apprentice researcher is a skill to master and a mind-set to be imbibed.

For a PhD researcher, a number of possibilities are presented. It is more typical that a PhD applicant will come directly from a Master's program and may well be targeting a career in academia. Therefore, their motivation is likely to be based on theoretical contributions more than on immediate impact. Post-experience PhDs could, however, be in a similar situation to the DBA researcher, in that they hope to solve real world problems and build knowledge drawn from experience as well as theory. DBA candidates are typically mature people who have been working in organizations or for themselves over a number of years and are coming to the research arena to fulfill some gap in their ambition. This gap can range from a personal development desire, to role transition, to a requirement of their industry in order to differentiate themselves from others. There is also a group of PhD researchers who begin their research directly from Master's or even undergraduate study. This chapter will largely concern itself with the former groups: those who are embedded in a mind-set of practitioner engagement and senior management, where they may be inculcated in a leadership echelon with the familiarity of seniority, delegation, and strategic level decision-making.

These different constituencies, if they are undertaking "engaged scholarship" (Van de Ven, 2007), may have very different paths to researcher–practitioner maturity. Some of the elements of these paths will be discussed below. Specifically, the DBA must fulfill guidelines as set down by various accreditation bodies for example, the Association of MBAs (AMBA, 2015), which clearly state the dual and unique contributions to theory and practice that the research must achieve.

Alongside these technical requirements, the prospective DBA researcher may come to embark on their research journey for any number of reasons: career progression, curiosity, thirst for knowledge, transition from one life state to another, or a desire to change something. Therefore, their view of the research may be guided by the outcomes they hope to achieve. They will need to acquire some technical skills along the way, such as competence or even excellence in academic writing, critical thinking, and synthesis of ideas. An open mind-set (Dweck, 2006) will be essential as they suspend old habits and lay themselves open to new ideas and processes. Indeed, their seniority at work may have habituated them into a mind-set of the expert manager or technical master in which they are accustomed to being the decision-maker and leader in terms of knowledge and expertise.

There are numerous texts to support the technical development of the novice researcher (Blaikie, 2010; Crotty, 2003), which include familiarization with the logic of social enquiry, the role of social theory in this research area, and an introduction to the major research approaches and designs. The former of these texts has been specifically developed for mature candidates with diverse academic backgrounds.

The experienced manager encounters boundary conditions in learning to become a researcher. The nature of that boundary is a person–society dialectic created by the different role expectations that apply to researchers and practicing managers. These require a level of transformative learning to evolve the learner's identity. Since the emphasis of outputs is shifted towards practice as well as theory, the researcher will potentially encounter a role within the person–society dialectic (Tennant, 2006). Indeed, as the transition to researcher maturity progresses there will be an interaction between the developing person and their social environment, whether that is within organizations, groups, or societies as a whole. This dialectic process and the role of society in the shaping of the individual learner's identity sits within the Transformative Learning theories of, for example, Mezirow (1991).

The transition beyond senior manager to researcher may be seen as a process of transformation of the self, in order to achieve a level of skill in a new cognitive space and to be an instrument for broader social change (Tennant, 2006). A question which arises, therefore, is how much we participate in our own self-formation and to what extent do we interact with the social context? It may be useful to think of identity as a narrative approach to this imbedded change process. In this sense, the role of the doctoral supervisor is key to guiding helpful enculturation and interpreting the story of the researcher to achieve the appropriate transition.

Integrated in the role of the researcher is to understand their "view of the world" in terms of their consideration of ontology and epistemology. This process, for the post-experience doctoral student, must be contemporaneous with their personal world view development, concerned with developing a "replacement" narrative of their identity which serves them better in the research world (McAdams, 1996).

Identity and the transition path

Over the course of the twentieth century there was a developing understanding that, within organizations and between work and social life, a distinction between the different roles being undertaken was emerging (Ashforth, 2001). This dispersion means that people increasingly act as "role occupants" rather than as individuals. The movement between these roles may be seen as continuous. However, there needs to be a clear view of transitioning between roles and this may also mean exiting one persona and entering another. These transitions intersect roles and identities. For the novice researcher coming from senior organizational life the existence of different roles or identities may be apparent, but the transition process may be unexpected and discontinuous.

The identity transition may combine elements of Social Identity Theory (Tajfel, 1979) and Identity Theory (Stryker & Burke, 2000); that is, the oscillation between the perceptions formed by others or groups of others and the self-perception of identity. The transitions between these states are not always recognized and even when there may be an apparent transition from practitioner to researcher/practitioner, the movement may not be instantaneous. Ashforth (2001: 23) offers the example of a medical intern having become a resident one day and not comprehending the fact that they would now be a role model, teacher, and mentor to a group of which yesterday they were one of the members. In making this transition, the individual must address issues of self-coherence, that is, internal integration and consistency.

Cognitive structures, such as scripts or schemas which are bodies of knowledge, including expectations about roles, may help the researcher–practitioner to facilitate this transition (Ashforth, 2001; Fiske & Taylor, 1991). The researcher–practitioner develops from a binary state to a combined state and from individual identity states into the combined state of the "engaged scholar" (Van de Ven, 2007). The schema is the cognitive framework that creates the persona of the engaged scholar, but what are the characteristics, attributes, and behaviors that indicate success in this identity?

The competence to build these scripts and schemas requires the attributional ability to combine different mind-sets. It flows from this that the notion of paradox (Smith & Lewis, 2011), that is, holding both the mind-set of practice and that of research, is able to operate during and as a consequence of this transitional state. The tension that is produced as a result of inhabiting two spheres at the same time (Cameron & Quinn, 1988; Smith & Lewis, 2011) is recognized in the context of the individual and of organizations.

Based on the evidence of our experience as DBA directors, another aspect of the monitoring process and of tracking levels of transition is to set up methods of uncovering and supporting the identity shifts (Laura Empson outlines the experience of a mature academic in Chapter 12) and focus more on the personal conditions of change that exist and change during the transition process. For example:

- *Ignorance* is intended to indicate a necessary pre-condition for conscious change and is the polar opposite of awareness. What we are unaware of forms the field of our ignorance. There could be said to be two types of ignorance. One is where you simply don't know, and unawareness is just an unconscious absence (e.g., "blind spot"?). The other is where you choose not to know, and unawareness is more consciously imposed (e.g., "ignorance is bliss"?) or "wilful blindness," as described by Heffernan (2011).
- *Insecurity* explores the feelings and emotions associated with entry (or re-entry) to the academic learning environment, and the way that students deal with the unknowns that this entails.

At this point, the value of Reflective Practice emerges (Merriam & Bierema, 2014). The skill associated with this is that of the curious assumption-seeker. Reflective practice may be seen as an "organizing concept" (Schön, 1983) and can be pre- or post-experience, or contemporaneous with it, and a solo exercise or done in collaboration with teachers or peers, in order to capture rich texture in real time. The purpose is to process assumptions and beliefs and transmute these into tools for future assimilation.

- *Interaction* is the development of communities of practice to share, debate, and facilitate mutual support and learning. In this sense, a community concerns the spaces between groups of like-minded people. Embedded in this process is the quest to find that community which may be the cohort for the early student, or an academic "tribe" as knowledge maturity grows. There will be a journey in itself for finding this tribe: the people who speak the common language, have a similar foundation in terms of domains of literature, and methodological paradigm, and come to know the boundaries of the community of inquiry that make it distinctive; in which people can share their practice, their weaknesses and problems openly and without fear of ridicule (Gulati, 2007). A developmental attribute in this stage is to become comfortable with sharing ideas with others and having the confidence to challenge existing knowledge or offered opinions.
- *Interdependence* moves forward another step to where the cohort, community of practice, or tribe provide a mutual learning environment. Similarity of style may still exist between them and they are being more active with offering guidance to others. The relationship with supervisors and other interested parties is changing too, where previous one-way relationships are becoming more mutual and learning is being enacted on both sides.

At this stage Action Learning (Pedler & Abbott, 2013) may be used to stimulate problem solving, critical thinking, and learning agility. The technique of Action Learning, through critical questioning of real practice assumptions by others who may not share the same world view, but with similar experience and diverse expertise, values the use of different perspectives to stimulate problem solving, critical thinking, and greater learning.

- *Individual integration* develops over time as the researcher–practitioner is applying both sets of knowledge and skills interchangeably to the problems and situations at hand. They are able to investigate and interrogate sources of knowledge and draw out, and critically apply, relevant techniques.

These transitions involve a process of loss from a former sense of self, first of all from the work-related identity (Conroy & O'Leary-Kelly, 2014), based on aspects of identity, role (Ashforth, 2001), and self-definition which are tied to particular activities and knowledge domains. After this, the transition from a conscious hybrid identity towards a more unconscious "engaged scholar" persona as envisaged by Van de Ven (2007). At each stage the transition requires a realignment of self-perception and triggers a need for a new sense of self. The phase of letting go of the former state and moving to the new involves a liminal process (Conroy & O'Leary-Kelly, 2014; Garsten, 1999; Pina e Cunha, Guimarães-Costa, Rego & Clegg, 2010; Tempest & Starkey, 2004). The liminal period is defined by the "dynamic process of self-construal" (Conroy & O'Leary-Kelly, 2014) so that the known person gives way to the person they are becoming. This liminal period can, in certain circumstances, be profound and the way in which individuals process this will be unique, and the significance of activities may not be fully appreciated until later—as may be the case when DBA associates find the pace of research methods training too slow at the outset of the program. However, these very same research associates will come back some six months to a year later to report that they now understand the way that things unfold and that they are really glad that they were able to take on the new skills at a pace where their professional transition was synchronized. Without this "keeping in step" the individual can experience "identity instability" (Conroy & O'Leary-Kelly, 2014), being cognitively and emotionally confused by the change. That the individual experiences liminality in redefining self towards a more research orientation, suggests that some sort of similar change will exist in their work and social personas.

In considering the transition process of the practitioner towards an orientation as the apprentice researcher, Figure 10.1 summarizes the three positions discussed

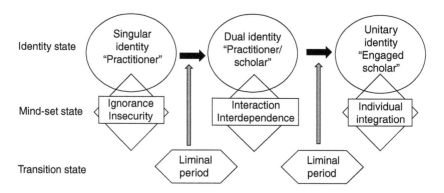

Figure 10.1 Normative identity transition in the practitioner–scholar maturity path.

Vignette 1

A young entrepreneur, 26 years old at commencement, came with great promise. He had been top of his MBA class and had thought of beginning a PhD at the age of 19. Initially, he appeared to fulfil the promise he brought with him. He was clearly excellent at statistics and had a ready-made source of access to the data he required for his study. However, very soon after completing his research training, he began to fall behind on the methodological elements of the program. Recently, he has been concentrating on one of his businesses which he hopes to float on the full market. Where was the problem? Was the research methods teaching too slow for him? Was he bored? On the other hand, could his stuttering progress be a question of lack of transition from business-owner and practitioner to researcher? Perhaps his unwillingness to accept a mind-set state of ignorance, and to experience insecurity in an academic setting, is coming from the fact that hitherto he has always been far ahead of his contemporaries. Might taking this into consideration aid his supervisors in bringing him forward in his research and supporting him to reach the end goal? In our model, this student has stalled at the second liminal point. He is distracted by pressing practitioner demands and has not moved to a point where his thinking has developed more critically.

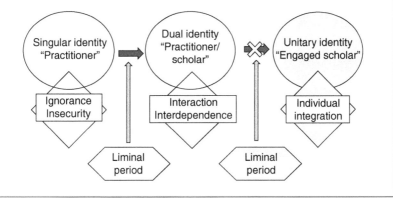

Vignette 2

The ability, or willingness of a doctoral student to make the transition from practitioner to researcher may be influenced by many things and the apparent manifestation of difficulty could be due to a number of factors. One candidate, a mature, senior public sector manager had much difficulty at the beginning of her doctoral journey with her assigned supervisor. Despite a change in supervision and acknowledgment of this difficulty, the candidate ceased to make progress, blaming this difficulty for disrupting her research. The new supervisors provided good and regular support, but progress was not forthcoming. What was the underlying reason for this? Could the surface manifestation of damage caused by supervisors been used to mask a lack of underlying confidence and "stuckness" in moving from the practitioner state to the researcher state? Might her seniority in practice be inhibiting her ability to adopt a growth mind-set in the academic world? This is clearly inhibiting her from creating opportunities to develop the deep connections and disjunctions between practice and theory which allow for inner debate and forward momentum. How might the supervisors have managed the process and relationship in order to understand any difficulties in the transition points and liminal period facing the candidate?

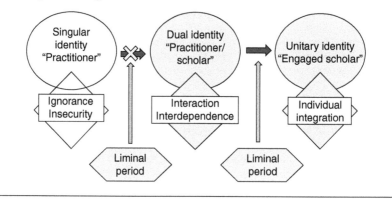

Vignette 3

The use of reflexivity as part of the research process has likely helped a DBA student who is conducting strategy-in-practice research on her own IT organization. The reflexive cycle, an important element of the grounded theory approach that she is taking, would support the transition from practitioner to researcher. An interesting added element is that she has to hold the ambidexterity of these two positions simultaneously in her mode of research and constantly flexes between the two as necessary, particularly during her data collection. This has been a successful process and she is reaching a state where she simultaneously occupies the role of senior practitioner and engaged scholar and has achieved individual integration which seamlessly translates personal and observed knowledge into data. The constant interaction and interdependence she practices in BOTH settings has helped towards the unitary identity that she was able to develop very quickly in her journey.

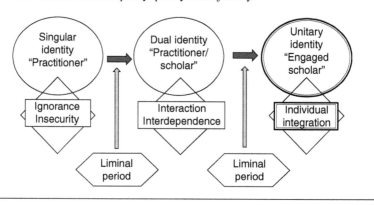

above. The identity transition from singular identity as the practitioner, through a dual or hybrid identity of practitioner–scholar towards a unitary identity of engaged scholar. This is linked to a mind-set change from ignorance/ insecurity, through interaction/independence towards individual integration. These changed states are traversed by entering a liminal process where loss of the previous identity causes some level of trauma before the new self-meaning is taken on.

Educating engaged researchers

The nature of the research undertaken by this cohort of apprentices also plays a part in their developing understanding of identity and role. It is commonly described that the type of research that is being undertaken to combine successfully the academic and practitioner worlds must possess rigour and relevance. This concept itself has undergone some scrutiny as to how to define and shape what this means (Bartunek & Rynes, 2014; Kieser et al., 2015). Kieser et al. (2015) examine in detail two themes: programmatic and descriptive literature, which present some of the shortcomings of conjoining academic rigour with practical relevance. They categorize these conceptual areas and propose that responsibility may lie in a number of places which include; the way that business schools teach research skills, the potential inability of the practitioner to grasp academic outputs (see Bartunek and Rynes, Chapter 6) and the relationship that researchers have with external stakeholders. All of which adds pressure onto the shoulders of the applied researcher to meet a number of demanding expectations at once.

Using the programmatic view, the assumption may rest in the notion of a simple transfer of knowledge where the complexities of the knowledge acquisition and translation are not recognized (Nicolai & Seidl, 2010). By contrast, the descriptive literature may offer greater potential for systematic use in management research, though a further, more holistic view may yet be developed taking into account the context of the knowledge being generated (Brown & Duguid, 1991) and acknowledging that knowledge and context are not separate (Van de Ven & Johnson, 2006). The DBA becomes particularly relevant in addressing these issues.

Developing competence

In developing the competence of the practitioner researchers we need to take account of theories of adult motivation and learning. Adult motivation to learn is influenced by psychological, anthropological, and sociological factors (Merriam & Bierema, 2014). A modern theory of motivation, self-determination theory (Ryan, Connell & Deci, 1985), identifies three needs that are necessary for the psychological health of all humans: competence, autonomy and relatedness (see Smith & Lewis, 2011, on relatedness). If a desire for competence is thus universal it is important to create the right conditions for the development of competence for the practitioner–researcher. Self-efficacy beliefs have been shown to influence behavior and performance. Self-efficacy "concerns people's beliefs in their capacities to mobilize the motivation, cognitive resources and courses of action needed to exercise control over events in their lives" (Wood & Bandura, 1989: 364). Self-efficacy thus underpins motivation and four principal ways of developing self-efficacy beliefs have been identified:

* mastery of experiences;
* modeling;
* social persuasion; and
* knowledge of one's own physical and mental states.

The DBA program employs several mechanisms for the development of self-efficacy. The structure of the program, i.e., MSc stage, is intended to provide an achievable first target, regular colloquia provide the opportunity to develop mastery experiences and gain feedback, but above all the relationship with mentor and supervisor are vital for the development of self-efficacy Table 10.1 shows how the assessments on the MSc map across to the development of self-efficacy through these different mechanisms.

The practitioner needs support during his or her transition to practitioner–researcher and this support is provided primarily by mentors and supervisors. The role of the mentor is to support the research associate as they progress through the MSc, complete their competence development process and begin to prepare their research proposal; the supervisor's role is to provide academic guidance, in both content and methodology, to the research associate as they complete their research. Mentoring is a key developmental relationship providing professional and psychosocial support for individuals, particularly through periods of transition (Kram, 1988). The distinction between mentoring and coaching is not always easy to draw, and many skills are shared between the roles, but typically the mentor, unlike the coach, will have had relevant experience.

The role of the mentor/supervisor is, therefore, critical in the transitional phases of the apprentice researcher. In the early stages in particular, the role of

Table 10.1 The MSc assignment events which demonstrate self-efficacy development

Self-efficacy development mode	MSc assignment which develops this
Mastery experience	Literature review, Pilot study, Research proposal
Modelling	Thesis critique
Social persuasion	Personal development, Research development, Qualitative and Quantitative techniques
Knowledge of self	Personal development journey

the mentor/supervisor can have a great influence in the formation of an apprentice researcher. Lee's thesis (2011) is that this transition is facilitated by the academic through a holistic teaching and learning approach. A number of facets of learning can be explored in the supervision relationship: creativity (Kleiman, 2008), critical thinking (Watkins & Earnhardt, 2015), academic writing, and so on. The different approaches available to a supervisor are given in Table 10.2 (Lee, 2011).

Whilst we may dwell on the skills that the apprentice researcher has yet to develop, it is worth recognizing that the more mature, experienced individual has skills and knowledge to bring to the situation which don't exist in a pre-experience doctoral candidate. They will surely have numerous management competences, such as: networking, planning, project management, decision-making, and leadership. These skills are likely to become blended with new skills as the transition takes place. It can be surprising and fulfilling to the candidate to realize that the benefits that they get from developing and strengthening research skills to sit alongside their management skills begins very early in the program. Whilst people inevitably develop and change at different paces, transition begins to happen quite quickly and the effects are felt by the influence of management on research and by research on management.

These transitions may equate to the "liminal periods" described above (p. 166) and in Figure 10.1 (Conroy & O'Leary-Kelly, 2014; Garsten, 1999; Tempest & Starkey, 2004). Using Lee's (2011) framework above (Table 10.2), the mentor or supervisor can influence the development of the research associate during these liminal periods. Just as when a leadership style is adopted for appropriate circumstances, then the agile mentor or supervisor might adopt a particular supervision style to be appropriate for the identity state or transition position of the research associate. The mentor and the supervisor thus act as models to show the apprentice researcher that it is possible to hold the tension between the contradictory demands of theory and practice, rigor and relevance, short-term and long-term orientation, and work through them to come up with a holistic response that can satisfy both demands in their thesis.

The above, in turn, requires a level of mastery on behalf of the mentor or supervisor. The importance of supervision is apparent to a number of stakeholders in the research process (Collins, 2015; Lee, 2008; McCallin & Nayar, 2012; Neumann, 2007). The lack of pedagogic acuity and theoretical underpinning leaves some ambiguity in the processual nature of supervision (Åkerlind & McAlpine, 2015; Grant, 2003), therefore supervisors must support learning action as well as content development. Training programs differ in the emphasis given to supervisory competence and often concentrate on the requirements stated in University Postgraduate Research guidelines regarding issues such as roles of the supervisor, joint supervision, and requirements of the doctorate. It would certainly seem that the combined factors of supervisory support and the structure of the program are inextricably linked in giving

Table 10.2 Supervisory interventions to develop competence (from Lee, 2011)

Professional —————————————————————→ *Personal*

	Functional	*Enculturation*	*Critical thinking*	*Emancipation*	*Relationship development*
Supervisor's activity	Rational progression through tasks Consultation Techno–rational	Gatekeeping Introductions to people Exemplars of high quality work	Evaluation Challenge Enquiry-based partnership	Mentoring Supportive constructivism	Supervising by experience Developing a relationship team
Supervisor's knowledge and skills	Directing Leading Negotiating Project management	Diagnosis of deficiencies Coaching	Argument Analysis Synthesis	Facilitation Reflection	Managing conflict Emotional intelligence
Possible student reaction	Logical Information giving Organized Obedient	Role modeling Apprenticeship	Constant enquiry Synthesis Fight or flight	Personal growth Reframing	A good team member Emotional intelligence

optimal guidance, development support, and intellectual challenge. As Grant (2003: 175) notes:

> supervision differs from other forms of teaching and learning in higher education in its peculiarly intense and negotiated character, as well as in its requirements for a blend of pedagogical and personal relationship skills. These differences arise because supervision is not only concerned with the production of a good thesis, but also with the transformation of the student into an independent researcher.

The supervisor should, therefore, undertake appropriate training to ensure that a range of skills and techniques are available. The role of the supervisor is crucial to the transitionary journey of the apprentice researcher. According to Halse and Malfroy (2010: 79) doctoral supervision is "theorized as *professional work* [their emphasis] that comprises five facets: the learning alliance, habits of mind, scholarly expertise, techne, referring to the architectural input of research design and contextual expertise." This may be an important point to make to supervisors who may regard that particular role as an "add-on," or "necessary evil," of their academic work.

The relationship aspect of supervision should be highlighted. As with other dyadic relationships such as mentoring (Kram, 1988; Ragins, Cotton & Miller, 2000); or coaching (Whitmore, 2009), there are different facets to the relationship which lead to positive outcomes. These may include "support" (Gatfield, 2005), the "learning alliance" (Bordin, 1979; Halse & Malfroy, 2010), and "research relation orientation" (Franke & Arvidsson, 2011). Supporting the apprentice researcher through liminal periods, therefore, requires a fruitful relationship with their supervisor, who in turn is well-equipped to observe, diagnose, and manage the transition in an agile manner.

Building community

Building a community of academic faculty and DBA practitioner–researchers is important for several reasons. To begin with, Van de Ven and Johnson's (2006) concept of "engaged scholarship" involves a collaborative activity involving academics and practitioners, which implies community, in order to address the knowledge production aspect of the theory–practice divide. In addition, involvement in this community helps to provide support and motivation that facilitates the development of competence and development of identity in the transition to practitioner researcher.

The DBA program employs a range of methods of community-building. Research associates join a cohort which follows the same schedule of workshops and submissions in the MSc phase and this helps to build support networks. In addition, research colloquia are held four times per year at which research associates present their research ideas to other research associates and a panel of faculty. Research associates are required to present at least once per year and mentors and supervisors are present. These opportunities help to build self-efficacy and competence, as well as creating networks between faculty and the practitioner–researchers.

However, holding colloqiua doesn't imply that faculty will attend and be willing to be involved in the DBA program. To achieve this, appropriate incentives and training should be in place for those who wish to become involved in mentoring or supervising, and, more broadly, the value of practitioner knowledge and achieving both rigor and relevance needs to be recognized alongside academic knowledge.

Conclusion

The aim of this chapter is to demonstrate the contribution the professional doctorate, in this case the DBA, can make to the development of applied research skills and the journey of practitioner to a blended persona of practitioner–researcher.

By using the conceptual framework in Figure 10.1 it is suggested that the structure and process of the DBA can contribute significantly to the emancipation of research using the practitioner voice and experience. Furthermore, this research can be commissioned by and have impact on the domain of the practitioner and their organization, or of society more generally, through policy development and implementation.

The development process occurs in the liminal spaces between ignorance and insecurity, interaction and interdependence, and finally to individual integration. The achievement of the final stage represents an ability to undertake research which calls upon real-life context to develop impactful results.

References

Åkerlind, G. & McAlpine, L. (2015). Supervising doctoral students: Variation in purpose and pedagogy. *Studies in Higher Education*, 1–13.

AMBA (2015). Criteria for the Accreditation of DBA Programmes. Retrieved April 7, 2017 from www.mbaworld.com/en/Accreditation/~/media/41EC0250BCF349E78E90 E0E1CD75A901.ashx.

Ashforth, B. (2001). *Role Transitions in Organizational Life: An Identity-based Perspective*. Mahwah, NJ: Lawrence Erlbaum Associates.

Bartunek, J. M. & Rynes, S. L. (2014). Academics and practitioners are alike and unlike: The paradoxes of academic–practitioner relationships. *Journal of Management*, 40(5), 1181–201.

Bennis, W. G. & O'Toole, J. (2005). How business schools lost their way. *Harvard Business Review*, 83(5), 96–104.

Blaikie, N. (2010). *Designing Social Research*. Cambridge, UK: Polity Press.

Bordin, E. S. (1979). The generalisability of the psychoanalytic concept of the working alliance. *Psychotherapy: Theory, Research and Practice*, 16(3), 252–60.

Bradbury, H. & Lichtenstein, B. M. B. (2000). Relationality in organizational research: Exploring the space between. *Organization Science*, 11(5), 551–64.

Brown, J. S. & Duguid, P. (1991). Organizational learning and communities-of-practice: Toward a unified view of working, learning, and innovating. *Organization Science*, 2(1), 40–57.

Cameron, K. & Quinn, R. (1988). Organizational paradox and transformation. In R. Quinn & K. Cameron (Eds.) *Paradox and Transformation: Towards a Theory of Change in Organization and Management*. Cambridge, MA: Ballinger.

Collins, B. (2015). Reflections on doctoral supervision: Drawing from the experiences of students with additional learning needs in two universities. *Teaching in Higher Education*, 20(6), 587–600.

Conroy, S. A. & O'Leary-Kelly, A. M. (2014). Letting go and moving on: Work-related identity loss and recovery. *Academy of Management Review*, 39(1), 67–87.

Crotty, M. (2003). *The Foundation of Social Research*. London: Sage Publications.

Dweck, C. S. (2006). *Mind-set: The New Psychology of Success*. New York: Ballantine Books.

Fiske, S. T. & Taylor, S. E. (1991). *Social Cognition*. New York: McGraw Hill.

Franke, A. & Arvidsson, B. (2011). Research supervisors' different ways of experiencing supervision of doctoral students. *Studies in Higher Education*, 36(1), 7–19.

Flickinger, M., Tuschke, A., Gruber-Muecke, T. & Fielder, M. (2014). In search of rigor, relevance and legitimacy: What drives the impact of publications. *Journal of Business Economics*, 84(1), 99–128.

Garsten, C. (1999). Betwixt and between: Temporary employees as liminal subjects in flexible organizations. *Organization Studies*, 20(4), 601–17.

Gatfield, T. (2005). An investigation into PhD supervisory management styles: Development of a dynamic conceptual model and its managerial implications. *Journal of Higher Education Policy and Management*, 27(3), 311–25.

Grant, B. (2003). Mapping the pleasures and risks of supervision. *Discourse: Studies in the Cultural Politics of Education*, 24(2), 175–90.

Gulati, R. (2007). Tent poles, tribalism and boundary spanning: The rigor–relevance debate in management research. *Academy of Management Journal*, 50(4), 775–82.

Halse, C. & Malfroy, J. (2010). Retheorizing doctoral supervision as professional work. *Studies in Higher Education*, 35(1), 79–92.

Heffernan, M. (2011). *Wilful Blindness*. London: Simon and Schuster.

Kieser, A., Nicolai, A. & Seidl, D. (2015). The practical relevance of management research: Turning the debate on relevance into a rigorous scientific research program. *The Academy of Management Annals*, 9(1), 143–233.

Kleiman, P. (2008). Towards transformation: Conceptions of creativity in higher education. *Innovations in Education And Teaching International*, 45(3), 209–17.

Kram, K. (1988). *Mentoring at Work*. London: Lanham.

Lee, A. (2008). How are doctoral students supervised? Concepts of doctoral research supervision. *Studies in Higher Education*, 33(3), 267–81.

Lee, A. (2011). *Successful Research Supervision: Advising Students Doing Research*. Abingdon, UK: Routledge.

McAdams, D. (1996). Personality, modernity and the storied self: A contemporary framework for studying persons. *Psychological Inquiry*, 7(4), 295–321.

McCallin, A. & Nayar, S. (2012). Postgraduate research supervision: A critical review of current practice. *Teaching in Higher Education*, 17(1), 63–74.

Merriam, S. & Bierema, L. (2014). *Adult Learning: Linking Theory and Practice*. San Francisco, CA: Jossey-Bass.

Mezirow, J. (1991). *Transformative Dimensions of Adult Learning*. San Francisco, CA: Jossey-Bass.

Neumann, R. (2007). Policy and practice in doctoral education. *Studies in Higher Education*, 32(4), 459–73.

Nicolai, A. & Seidl, D. (2010). That's relevant! Different forms of practical relevance in management science. *Organization Studies*, 31(9–10), 1257–85.

Pedler, M. & Abbott, C. (2013). *Facilitating Action Learning: A Practitioner's Guide*. Maidenhead, UK: McGraw-Hill Education.

Pina e Cunha, M., Guimarães-Costa, N., Rego, A. & Clegg, S. R. (2010). Leading and following (un)ethically in "limen." *Journal of Business Ethics*, 97(2), 189–206.

Raelin, J. A. (2007). Toward an epistemology of practice. *Academy of Management Learning & Education*, 6(4), 495–519.

Ragins, B., R. Cotton, J. L. & Miller, J. S. (2000). Marginal mentoring: The effects of type of mentor, quality of relationship, and program design on work and career attitudes. *Academy of Management*, 43(6), 1177–94.

Ryan, R. M., Connell, J. P. & Deci, E. L. (1985). A motivational analysis of self-determination and self-regulation in education. *Research on Motivation in Education: The Classroom Milieu*, 2, 13–51.

Sandberg, J. & Tsoukas, H. (2011). Grasping the logic of practice: Theorizing through practical rationality. *Academy of Management Review*, 36(2), 338–60.

Schön, D. A. (1983). *The Reflective Practitioner: How Professionals Think in Action*. New York: Basic Books.

Shotter, J. (2006). Understanding process from within: An argument for "withness"-thinking. *Organization Studies*, 27(4), 585–604.

Smith, W. K. & Lewis, M. W. (2011). Toward a theory of paradox: A dynamic equilibrium model of organizing. *Academy of Management Review*, 36(2), 381–403.

Stryker, S. & Burke, P. J. (2000). The past, present, and future of an identity theory. *Social Psychology Quarterly*, 63(4), 284–97.

Tajfel, H. (1979). Individuals and groups in social psychology. *British Journal of Social and Clinical Psychology*, 18(2), 183–90.

Tempest, S. & Starkey, K. (2004). The effects of liminality on individual and organizational learning. *Organization Studies*, 25(4), 507–27.

Tennant, M. (2006). *Psychology and Adult Learning*. Abingdon, UK: Routledge.

Van de Ven, A. H. (2007). *Engaged Scholarship: A Guide for Organizational and Social Research*. Oxford: Oxford University Press.

Van de Ven, A. H. & Johnson, P. E. (2006). Knowledge for theory and practice. *Academy of Management Review*, 31(4), 802–21.

Watkins, D. V. & Earnhardt, M. P. (2015). Developing critical thinking within a master of science in leadership program. *Academy of Educational Leadership Journal*, 19(1), 184–94.

Whitmore, J. (2009). *Coaching for Performance* (4th ed.). London: Nicholas Brearley Publishing.

Wood, R. & Bandura, A. (1989). Social cognitive theory of organizational management. *Academy of Management Review*, 14(3), 361–84.

11 The capacity for *phronesis*

Building confidence through curiosity to cultivate conscience as central to the character of impactful scholarship

Elena P. Antonacopoulou

Introduction

The focus of this chapter is to explicate the capacity for *phronesis* (practical judgment), so central for engaged scholarship and collaborative research to be impactful. IMP-roving ACT-ion is the meaning attributed to impact (see Antonacopoulou, 2009, 2010a); therefore impactful scholarship goes beyond engagement in the drive to make a positive difference. It is scholarship that demonstrates consistency between what is preached and what is practiced and in doing so promotes curiosity to experiment with possibilities. It also inspires confidence whilst cultivating conscience in recognizing the implications of what is practiced for the common good. Put simply, impactful scholarship reflects the character of scholars who conduct themselves not just with competence but with care for improving actions by cultivating both their own curiosity, confidence, and conscience and that of others they engage in learning-driven collaborations.

This chapter draws on and extends previous accounts of engagement in collaborative management research as part of the GNOSIS research initiative (Antonacopoulou, 2010b, 2010c). It reflexively distils lesson learned from the collaboration with a prestigious think tank—ResPublica—in the production of a major report aimed at restoring trust across the professions (teaching, legal and medical) (Blond, Antonacopoulou & Pabst, 2015). Both the topic of the report and, the nature of the collaboration itself called for *phronesis*. Hence, the basis for explicating what a capacity for *phronesis* in impactful scholarship entails comes from a combination of evidence of its practice in other professions, reflection on the researchers experience, and theory.

The Aristotelian notion of *phronesis* has intrigued many scholars since its initial exposition in *Nicomachean Ethics* (for interpretations see MacIntyre, 1985; Noel, 1999). It has also received attention in management studies as a basis for rethinking leadership and management education and more recently managing change (Shotter & Tsoukas, 2014; Badham, Mead & Antonacopoulou, 2012; Antonacopoulou, 2012). Central to the analysis and treatment in this chapter are the processes that are integral to the act of *phronesis* itself: the role of discernment, practical syllogism, insight, wisdom, virtue, and moral excellence (Wall, 2003). *Phronesis* has been explicated as reflexive critique

(Antonacopoulou, 2010d), particularly in situations that cause uncertainty, present dilemmas, and invite choices about how to respond. Chapters 2 and 3 in Part I of this book consider further the conceptual foundations of this important characteristic.

Promoting *phronesis* as a *characteristic* (virtue) of impactful scholarship extends recent accounts of the meaning of a scholarly career (as a *care-er* of ideas see Antonacopoulou, 2016a) by demonstrating not only consistency in professional conduct (in adherence to ethical codes) but also a *care-full* approach in which impactful research fosters collaborations that support collective growth and wider human flourishing.

The chapter is organized in four sections:

- A brief overview of the GNOSIS approach to conducting management research lays the foundation for the essential principle of *phronesis* which could make such scholarship impactful.
- This is followed by a summary of the lessons learned from collaborative research with the think tank ResPublica, which produced a major report launched in the British House of Lords. The desired impact of the report was to restore trust in the professions.
- The lessons from this report are extended to apply to scholarship as a professional practice to legitimately promote virtue in professional practice.
- The capacity for *phronesis* was not just central to the report content, it also had to be exemplified in the production process.
- In the fourth section the focus of the analysis is on explaining the importance of "designing for impact" as a key focus of the ResPublica report. This notion of "designing for impact" will be extended to account for the implications of improving action—professional practice—and also forming the foundation for accounting what professionalism in impactful scholarship may mean.

The chapter will conclude by considering the implications of the capacity for *phronesis* in advancing and sustaining impactful scholarship as well as building on this capacity to restore trust across the professions.

Global research: the GNOSIS approach to impactful scholarship

Emphasizing the global character of research demands an important research capability: scholarship which can transcend boundaries. When management scholars collaborate across geographical contexts with business executives and policy makers, as well as other scholars from diverse disciplinary backgrounds within and beyond the management field, there are many boundaries to transcend. Global research, connects practitioners across *inter-national* (*contextual* boundaries), *inter-disciplinary* (scientific or *professional settings*) and *inter-active* (*fields of practice*) boundaries. Global research practice engages those who create ("producers") and use ("consumers") knowledge as *co-researchers*, focusing jointly on the *impact* that the knowledge co-creation can potentially generate. The knowledge co-creation process provides the necessary backdrop for explicating both how the capacity for *phronesis* is developed and how it complements and extends the capability of being a global scholar transcending boundaries of context, professional setting, or field of practice.

In my career as a scholar I have embraced this global character of management research, in founding and directing for over 15 years a research initiative—GNOSIS (the Greek word for knowledge—ΓΝΩΣΗΣ). GNOSIS offers a space to actively experiment with different modes of co-creating knowledge through collaborations that bring international scholars across disciplinary backgrounds together with business practitioners and policy makers. From this, I have derived a set of principles for impactful scholarship described as the *GNOSIS research* approach.

GNOSIS research is founded on two design principles for creating actionable knowledge:

- engage actively with *lived experience* so as to enhance *ways of seeing*; and
- build *confidence and capability* by focusing on the *character of performance* (Antonacopoulou, 2010b, 2010c).

To enhance ways of seeing, GNOSIS research engages research partners in activities that encourage them to confront issues causing blind spots (e.g., *hybris, hamartia,* and *anagnosis*: Antonacopoulou & Sheaffer, 2014). To this end, research partners are encouraged to identify the critical connections when they confront tensions embedded in competing priorities and to practise working through the professional dilemmas that arise from the paradoxical nature of management practice, for example where the connections are between short- and long-term priorities, strategic and operational activities, formal and informal procedures. The objective of GNOSIS research is to raise awareness of how these tensions, dilemmas, and paradoxes require judgment in pursuit of the common good, not merely financial targets. Thus, central to the GNOSIS approach is providing a place to practise *feeling safe being vulnerable* whilst learning to engage with the unknown and unknowable (Antonacopoulou, 2014). This process of practising has the potential to maximize the lasting impact of experiences encountered, both by distilling the lessons learned more explicitly, and by deploying a mode of experiential learning that expands the scope to experiment, exploit and explore when "*learning-in-practise*" (Antonacopoulou, 2006). Thus, "practising" is a mode of learning that can reconfigure patterns of action that form the core of everyday experiences.

Consequently, how practices are performed is at the heart of the second key design principle. Emphasizing the character of performance draws attention to the dynamics, which contribute to the tensions, dilemmas, and paradoxes experienced. Thus, the agents engaged in any complex situation are highlighted as contributors to its creation, making it critical to understand them in terms of their character and capabilities. Then through a commitment to reflexive critique, they build their confidence to make a difference with and through others. In other words, agents actively demonstrate what matters most when they are account-able for the value they add through the actions they take in a practicing mode. The character of performance explicates the underlying principles (axes, values: see Figure 11.1) that define one's conduct. Equally the character of performance widens the value proposition beyond measureable results and accounts for social, political, and environmental impact, as well as economic outcomes. In this sense, by practicing reflexively one expands the scope to make a positive difference to the common good.

These design principles, distilled from experiences of leading and participat-ing in *inter-national, inter-disciplinary*, and *inter-active* research collaborations previously discussed (see Antonacopoulou, 2010a) are incorporated into the research framework that constitutes the GNOSIS approach to impactful scholar-ship presented in Table 11.1.

The ResPublica report: restoring trust in professions

This section, illustrates the centrality of the capacity for *phronesis* in the process and outcomes of collaborating with a prestigious think tank—ResPublica—to produce a major report. The discussion focuses on the process of developing actionable knowledge for a policy audience and lobbying professional bodies in the medical, legal, and teaching professions to radically change their practices

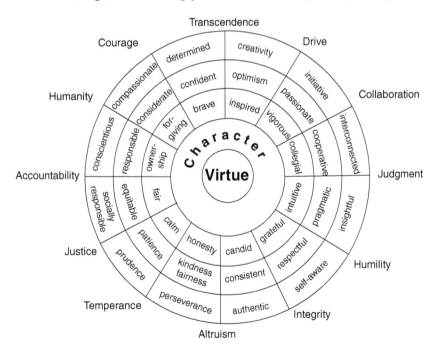

Figure 11.1 Code of chivalry in management as professional and scholarly practice.

Source: Adapted from Antonacopoulou, 2016.

Table 11.1 The characteristics of the GNOSIS approach

	THE CHARACTERISTICS OF THE GNOSIS APPROACH

Inter-National	Inter-Disciplinary	Inter-Active
Mobilizing or setting up networks to attract relevant experts, contributors, or participants in the research across geographical contexts enriches the pool of perspectives and versions of reality.	Some phenomena by their very nature call for multiple perspectives to inform the research revealing different dimensions and sensitizing us to the multiple ways in which a phenomenon may be manifested.	Investing in building relationships with executives and policy makers calls for exploring multiple modes of collaboration ranging from informal, systematic conversations on a variety of themes or on a specific theme, to a range of collaborative research engagements (e.g. Executive-in-Residence, Professor-in-Residence, etc.) either commissioned or part funded.
Investing time and energy to study other's research across international traditions of research practice, not just thematic relevance, cultivates sensitivity to contextual conventions of research practice.	Challenges are presented not only in terms of research practice but research identity which can make communication between researchers harder even if the same terminology is used but the meanings attributed to terms is very different.	Gaining access becomes a binding commitment towards working together with the industrial or policy partner(s) to address the issues that matter. It entails an active engagement in all aspects of the research process and often spills over through ongoing dialogue to new projects.
Co-designing the research strategy to ensure commitment and ability to deliver the research to agreed standards lays a basic foundation for the collaboration.	Variations in the ways in which the same subject/topic can be seen adopting different disciplinary lenses signals aspects of research identity which shapes research practice.	Being sensitive to industrial partners' concerns about corporate reputation calls for more than reassurances. It demands communicating findings with care.

Pulling together mutual and diverse interests and building on respective individual strengths to define and execute the research is critical.	Key aspects of research practice (*Practitioners*, *Phronesis*, *Purpose*, *Principles*, *Procedures*, *Place*, *Past*, *Present*, and *Potential* future projections, *Patterns of connection between them*, *Pace*, and *Promise*—Antonacopoulou, 2008) become more visible when openly debated at different stages of the research when critical decisions have to be made in the research process.	Securing endorsement by executives for high-profile research calls for removing the risk that they sponsor a project that may fail to deliver what it promises.
Open and active dialogical exchange exposes the variety of interpretations of what is considered "good research practice" even when a common research orientation is followed (e.g. qualitative research).	Disciplinary specializations are reflective of the way we chose to see the world. They also reflect the very myopia in doing so. By imposing our lenses we not only limit the ways we see the world, but we may deny in research the opportunity to broaden the horizons of our understanding.	It is critical at the onset to overcome the stigma that previous unpleasant research collaborations with academics may leave as reasons for executives and policy makers not wanting to participate in collaborative research.
A balance of flexibility and firmness is imperative when negotiating deviations from agreed research design to ensure that the quality of the research is not compromised.	To enable the research to progress may call for suspending agreement on certain issues with research partners, including how key terms, phenomena, processes are to be defined.	Genuine *engagement* can overcome differences in language between academics and executives, and differences in the time frame in conducting the research and delivering findings. This implies seeking actively to understand how the co-creation of knowledge adds value to those it engages in mutually beneficial ways.

continued

Table 11.1 The characteristics of the GNOSIS approach

Inter-National	Inter-Disciplinary	Inter-Active
Reviewing own research practice informed by the collaborators' orientations to research is part of the commitment to reflexivity. Learning to negotiate differences so that these are transformed from impediments to the research into key dimensions of its success.	Creating common experiences, including capacity-building initiatives that can expose the interdisciplinary research team to a very different practices, e.g., demonstrations by a Michelin chef, a theatre director of their practices as a useful foundation for building connections as opposed to allowing differences to dominate. Sharing experiences acts as a living metaphor enabling greater dialogue around issues that may otherwise be un-discussable.	*Re-search is a common practice* on which meaningful collaborative relationships can be developed even if performed for different ends. Executives are more inclined to research for solutions to problems rather than debate how to define a problem as academics do. Executives value more research that offers them insights that they can apply to address specific issues especially concerning the bottom line (i.e., financial profitability). Policy makers are more predisposed to understand how initiatives they undertake can deliver wider social and economic prosperity.
Instilling a learning culture within the research team to cultivate collective trust and respect towards individual preferences and orientations.	Creating through these shared experiences, an active/safe space of experimentation and improvisation of alternative ways of pursuing collaborative research in ways that engages all actors, because it gives voice to their ideas, interests, and research identity to *practice* their (research) practice.	Engagement in collaborative research needs to be founded on the principle of *connectivity*, which is also what engagement means: to connect. This focuses collaborative research on the power of association in developing the respective re-search practice of collaborators. This means that the research practice is not only a common practice, but a common space for connecting ideas that provide mutual development and learning.
Instigating a higher purpose under which collaborators can "unite." Such higher purpose could be founded on altruistic ambitions founded on pragmatic imagination of what can be accomplished collectively.	Co-existence of a multiplicity of disciplinary perspectives could build confidence in one's discipline to ensure it can continue to grow, and remain relevant and impactful by learning from other disciplines thus broadening capacity to attend to issues by seeing more and differently.	Creating powerful connections by *integrating knowledge for action* is less concerned with developing local recipes for how to act. It is more concerned with asking the "grand" questions that reflect global challenges relevant across boundaries with a view of broadening the repertoire of modes of action locally in different fields of management practice.

and instill virtue as a central characteristic. The production of the ResPublica report was a major capacity building activity for me, but also one that offers great opportunities to take stock of what it means to demonstrate capacity for *phronesis* not just by advising others to do so, but by actively demonstrating this first in one's own practice.

The opportunity to work with ResPublica arose out of research I published previously on virtue and *phronesis* (Antonacopoulou, 2004, 2010d) that I had shared with one of the long-standing GNOSIS collaborators, a business executive who was already building on our previous collaboration by acting as a commissioned researcher and consultant on another ResPublica report. This knowledge sharing gesture, typical among members of the GNOSIS network, led to an introduction to the Director of ResPublica and only a few weeks later an invitation for me to work as an Associate with the think tank to produce the report entitled "In professions we trust: Fostering virtuous practitioners in the medical, legal and teaching professions" (Blond et al., 2015).

As an "independent non-partisan" think tank, ResPublica seeks to establish:

> a new economic, social and cultural settlement for the United Kingdom … [through] interventions in public policy and public debate [so that their] ideas [are] adopted by politicians of all parties. [They] believe in the common good and the development of real wealth that promotes both social and economic flourishing.
>
> (ResPublica, 2016a)

"Virtue" is one of ResPublica's three core themes, the other two being "society" and "prosperity":

> "Virtue" charts a way of life that enables a person, community and nation to properly identify and fulfil the shared goals that they hope to achieve…. The exercise of virtue is a process of discernment that has an ambitious goal in mind: the flourishing of all humankind.
>
> (ResPublica, 2016b)

Aside from the production of influential reports and events that bring together relevant representatives across stakeholder groups, ResPublica also lobbies professional associations to promote social change beyond mere legislation and regulation. In the case of the virtue agenda it seeks to promote the depth of social and cultural change that can restore humanity and the pursuit of the "common good." This is stated in the ResPublica agenda:

> "Virtue" encompasses not simply an ethical code or guideline by which we measure ourselves and our institutions. It also entails a much deeper understanding of what it means to be human and why it matters to contribute to the "common good" …
>
> (ResPublica, 2016b)

This orientation towards "Virtue" relies on a practising orientation: living a "good life" is practiced systematically so as to become a habit rather than just an aspiration. Here is where the capacity for *phronesis* lies. Producing the ResPublica report can be considered as practising to explicate what this would mean for professions and professionals to be virtuous so that trust can be restored in their professional practices. This practising was approached with a commitment to understand the professional practice of the three professional groups (doctors, lawyers, and teachers) with what Shotter (2006) calls a "withness" orientation, so as to sense more actively what it feel like being a doctor, lawyer, or teacher. This practising was not only empathetic in orientation it was also compassionate in the sensitivity towards the sources of professional dilemmas that can lead to professional malpractice. For example, the all-too-prevalent emphasis on career and financial targets, especially in law (at least in public perception), is stifling attention on other priorities valued by their clients (such as care for justice). In medicine, technical knowledge confers power and ethical knowledge and the practitioner–patient relationship suffer. In teaching the diverse needs of pupils set against the rather rigid targets set makes creating an overarching good initially seem too utopian a task. Unsurprisingly, medical practitioners, teachers, and lawyers all face so many time constraints that they are, understandably, focused on task-oriented modes of professional conduct. Most worrying (especially in the teaching profession where issues of staff retention are most prevalent), being a professional (be it teacher, lawyer, or doctor) is fast losing the sense of joining a vocation whose values one lives by. Instead, the work pressures are too high and the standards that govern professional practice are becoming meaningless. These conditions are central to the level of disengagement among professionals, which underpins the *virtue gap* in professions (Blond et al., 2015).

Distilling the virtue gap in professions called for developing the capacity for *phronesis* in formulating a compassionate understanding towards the issues professionals experienced. It extended the knowing and practising that Beech, MacIntosh, Antonacopoulou and Sims (2012) promote through dialogical encounters. Although the timeframe for producing the report left limited scope for face-to-face discussions with professionals, there was still a commitment to dialogical exchange in the way recent published systematic research conducted by the Jubilee Centre for Character and Virtue (see Arthur, Kristjánsson, Thomas, Holdsworth, Confalonieri & Qiu, 2014; Arthur, Kristjánsson, Thomas, Kotzee, Ignatowicz & Qiu, 2015a; Arthur, Kristjánsson, Cooke, Brown & Carr, 2015b), with whom ResPublica closely collaborated, to account for the typical everyday dilemmas professionals experience. This as a central feature of our dialogic exchange focused on ways of connecting theory and practice as if professionals co-authored the report. This meant that the process of producing the report was guided by a capacity for *phronesis* not merely to speak on behalf of the professionals or about what professionals experience as dilemmas. Instead, it was produced as if professionals were engaged in co-authoring the messages of the report, accounting for both the practical and theoretical insights that informed our analysis.

Working on the report offered time and space to make sense of what it means to be virtuous as a professional, and by extension as a scholar appreciating what professionalism entails. The very substance of what constitutes professionalism was another critical point where capacity for *phronesis* was called for, because the report expressed a fresh view of professionalism that extends beyond expertise and competence. The choice to address this was informed by a dialogical exchange orientation which acknowledged that professionals are humans too and sensitizing professionals to realize their impact on the quality of life of the citizens they serve forms a critical step towards reassessing their professional conduct. In other words, this point calls for new modes of learning that address the typical professional dilemmas experienced which lie at the core of professional misconduct. The capacity for *phronesis* was central here as well, in the way recommendations were constructed. We had to make a choice to avoid formulating a report that was damning of professional practices but one instead that invited professionals to review their choices and to be phronetic in their conduct. To this end we focused in the report on acknowledging that the problems vary across the three professions that the ResPublica report examined. However, we captured the main common challenge as one we described as a "virtue gap." This was a judgment call in our effort to produce a report that made recommendations that were realistic and at the heart of addressing the issue pragmatically.

We noted from our discussions with professional bodies and the available research, that there is a *relational disengagement between professions and professionals and the users and citizens they serve.* The choice to name this relational disengagement as the "virtue gap" was an attempt to problematize professions and professionals to recognize their individual and collective *impact on social wellbeing.* In doing so, we did not want to offer prescriptions but to ignite their *curiosity* to be more *attentive* to this relational gap. We saw this as central to the capacity for *phronesis,* because we also wanted to build *confidence* in their ability to see more in their professional identity and practice. We therefore produced the report so that we can frame the challenge as a virtue gap to enhance their *alertness* about their professional *competence* and their personal responsibility in conducting themselves in line with their chosen character traits, thus becoming more aware how their *character* reflects their conduct. We also framed the challenge as a virtue gap to enhance their *appreciation* of the power of *conscience* and not only codes of ethical conduct as the means of redefining the essence of their professionalism.

All these dimensions of the process of producing the ResPublica report reflect the capacity for *phronesis* which the three author team (Phillip Blond, ResPublica Director, Adrian Pabst, and myself) were invited to demonstrate actively in the collaboration. For me as a scholar it was also a unique opportunity to live by my professional values/axes. In this sense, the capacity for *phronesis* outlined here in addressing the "virtue gap" in the professional practice (of doctors, lawyers, and teachers) was also a reflection of practicing impactful scholarship as detailed in the previous section and diagrammatically presented in Figure 11.2.

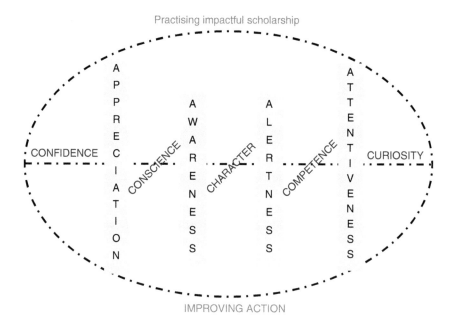

Figure 11.2 The principles of impactful scholarship.

Producing the ResPublica report explicates what it means to be a virtuous professional and what it takes for a profession to be virtuous. The professional practices of a virtuous professional within a virtuous profession ought to be governed by principles (values-in-use) that support leading a professional life, not merely applying professional ethical codes (espoused values). The latter are by definition insufficient to account for all the complexities professionals are confronted with, which vary not only across professions but also within professions and across specific incidents in professional life. Inspired by Aristotle's dictum that "We are what we repeatedly do. Excellence then, is not an act, but a habit," producing the ResPublica report called for *phronesis* in appreciating as central to addressing the virtue gap investing in creating the platforms (by giving priority, space, and time) for practising virtuousness across personal and professional life. Practising virtuousness calls for rethinking the process of learning to become professional and, second, introducing a mode of learning that fosters practising virtue reflexively.

Producing this report was for me a profound opportunity to practise impactful scholarship, not merely improve actions of other professions. It became a catalyst for me to practise the very ideas I have been advancing, and recognizing not only their practical value and relevance, but their impact in improving my own scholarly practice. In this respect, practising as a mode of learning embeds reflexive critique at its core (Antonacopoulou, 2010d; Beech et al., 2012). Practising impactful scholarship for me was becoming more *attentive, alert, aware,* and *appreciative* of the issues that the professions and professionals I was studying were experiencing. Building compassion towards the pressures that may lie at the core of malpractice was not only a sensitivity to their circumstances but a capacity for *phronesis* to consider how to address this challenge in a way that serves the common good. It was the capacity for *phronesis* which transformed the initial curiosity on the subject, and the scope to build on my competence as a scholar, that also gave me opportunity to express in producing this report my character traits and my conscience in serving the common good—social well-being. Therefore, I do not merely stand by the recommendations put forward by the report, I do so with clear conscience that they can add value and make a positive difference in restoring trust in professions, because I have confidence in my own professionalism as a scholar to have accounted for these recommendations and applied them to my own practice first.

One of the key lessons learned, therefore, in producing the ResPublica report, was that it is in practicing one's practice that one changes aspects of the practice and oneself (Antonacopoulou, 2008). This means that central to becoming a professional is the need to have space to experiment with multiple aspects of professional practice as it is in this process of practicing that the professional dilemmas will be experienced and insights will be gained about ways in which one can develop a virtuous response. Practicing is a mode of learning that entails change, because it helps practitioners to push the boundaries of their repertoire of action, by exercising their judgment more centrally than merely performing their practice as if it were a routine. What is afforded through practicing is transforming confusion into a drive for curiosity to restore clarity before one takes action. It is in this juncture of being curious to work with the unknown that the capacity for *phronesis* has the most potential to emerge and greatest significance in adding value to the quality of action taken. This is, fundamentally, because practicing sharpens *phronesis* (Antonacopoulou, 2008, 2016b).

In short, summarizing the highlights of the ResPublica report, demonstrates how scholarly research practice can be impactful when the capacity for *phronesis* invites other professionals (medical, legal, teaching professions) to see that this can be a means of restoring trust in their professional practices. It also shows that arriving at the recommendations and placing emphasis on practicing virtuousness as a key dimension around which a range of policy recommendations are delivered by the report is an illustration of the capacity for *phronesis*. This is so because the co-production of the research that informed the ResPublica report is not only the amalgamation of the ideas of the authors (reflecting different practitioners—scholars and policy makers). It is also an illustration of how these ideas come to life when they are designed to address practical issues and make a difference. Put differently, the recommendations of the ResPublica report were not simply compiled by reviewing relevant prior research, but by connecting the multiplicity of perspectives and integrating these with a whole range of issues in professional practice. This approach showed understanding and sensitivity to how these issues could be pragmatically addressed. Therefore, the recommendations offered are not only practical but are designed to deliver impact. That impact is more likely to emerge and transcend boundaries because it is positioned as a conversation piece with other professional bodies to stimulate further co-creation processes for application in different contexts.

Designing for impact: restoring professionalism in (scholarship as a) professional practice

The process of producing the ResPublica report provided scope to better understand how the impact of collaborative management research may be extended. Scholarly impact at the policy level calls for evidence that investment in science leads to returns in terms of societal, economic, political, and environmental impact. This is in line with calls for greater accountability and responsibility for the social contract between science and society (Chubb, 2014; Chandler, 2014).

The production of the ResPublica report demonstrates both in terms of content and process that actionable knowledge is impactful, and not only when it moves, energizes, and propels practitioners (be the academics, executives or policy makers) to act differently by reflexively critiquing their practices. Actionable knowledge is also impactful when it engages possibilities of acting in ways that demonstrate one's virtues and character. In other words, impact is about practising improving actions and steering such practising and associated improvements reflexively and in doing so critiquing not only one's actions, but how one chooses to act. This embeds the capacity for *phronesis* as a force integral to restoring trust in professional practice.

Practising virtuousness is not only what the ResPublica report invites professions and professionals (teachers, lawyers, doctors, and scholars) to do. It reflects that the collaboration between scholars and policy makers who produced the report also called for them to practice the virtuousness too in their capacity to breathe life into ideas in ways that build confidence in navigating the unknown and not only solve isolated moral problems or recommend another set of rules to replace existing standard operating procedures of codes of ethical conduct. What this fundamentally means is that the impact of the capacity for *phronesis* is not merely recognizing responsibility and accountability in how one chooses to act as a professional. It is also a reflection of the commitment to engage in actions that demonstrate virtuousness in the pursuit of the common good. This is the key message of the ResPublica report and the key learning in undertaking the collaboration. This key lesson enriches the substance of the GNOSIS approach to collaborative management research by demonstrating that impactful research "by design" reflects the commitment to serve the common good.

Conclusions

The analysis of the capacity for *phronesis* presented in this chapter draws on my experience of working with the ResPublica think tank to produce a report that actively seeks to deliver impact in restoring trust in professions. The discussion explicates not only the focus of the report and the process of building capacity for *phronesis* in its construction. It reinforces the GNOSIS approach to collaborative management research and indicates why collaborative research designed for impact not only demonstrates this capacity for *phronesis*, but transforms this capacity from mere professional competence to a demonstration of the character of professional practice (including scholarship) to add value to the social well-being by cultivating collective social conscience.

The chapter distils the importance of instigating confidence-building as an indicator of the impact of collaborative management research particularly when this offers scope to mobilize a stronger connection between competence, character, and conscience underpinned by the curiosity when practicing reflexivity.

The ResPublica report makes also the case for the *humanization* of professional service provision, which places the actual value of professional practice in the *relationship* between the provider and the user of professional services. This relational orientation towards co-creating value means that collaborative management research becomes the foundation of generating the impact desirable as a means of improving not only actions but the wider social well-being—the quality of life. Hence, virtuousness as a characteristic among professionals and across professions is about restoring altruism as the desire to make a difference in pursuing the common good (Antonacopoulou, 2016a).

Acknowledging the power of co-creating value when the ethos of professional and scholarly practice is assessed on the basis of its underlying principles radically shifts the focus of how value is assessed. The ethos of professionalism is what often defines the value of professional practice as that which serves the common good. Therefore, the impact of management scholarship is assessed and sustained for the value it contributes in supporting social well-being by restoring humanity in professional practice not least in demonstrating the capacity for *phronesis*.

Acknowledgments

I offer gratitude to Shelagh McNerney for our longstanding dialogue and collaboration on ideas in GNOSIS research and for being the catalyst for me to return to the earlier work on virtue. Sincere thanks are also extended to Philip Blond and the ResPublica team for the learning during our work on the report and the lessons distilled which form the foundation of the ideas presented in this chapter.

References

Antonacopoulou, E.P. (2004) On the virtues of *practising* scholarship: A tribute to Chris Argyris a "Timeless Learner". Special Issue "From Chris Argyris and beyond in organizational learning research," *Management Learning*, 35(4), 381–95.

Antonacopoulou, E. P. (2006). Working life learning: Learning-in-practise. In Antonacopoulou, E. P., Jarvis, P., Andersen, V., Elkjaer, B. & Hoeyrup, S. (Eds.) *Learning, Working and Living: Mapping the Terrain of Working Life Learning* (pp. 234–54). London: Palgrave.

Antonacopoulou, E. P. (2008). On the practise of practice: In-tensions and ex-tensions in the ongoing reconfiguration of practice. In Barry, D. & Hansen, H. (Eds.) *Handbook of New Approaches to Organization Studies* (pp. 112–31). London: Sage Publications.

Antonacopoulou, E. P. (2009). Impact and scholarship: Unlearning and practising to co-create actionable knowledge. *Management Learning*, 40(4), 421–30.

Antonacopoulou, E. P. (2010a). Beyond co-production: Practice-relevant scholarship as a foundation for delivering impact through powerful ideas, *Public Money and Management, Special Issue: The Politics of Co-production Research*, 30(4), S219–25.

Antonacopoulou, E. P. (2010b). Global research: Transcending boundaries by learning to collaborate and learning from collaboration. In Cassell, C. & Lee, W. J. (Eds.) *Management Research: Challenges and Controversies* (pp. 86–104). London: Routledge.

Antonacopoulou, E. P. (2010c). Advancing practice-relevant scholarship: Delivering impact. In Cassell, C. and Lee, W. J. (Eds.) *Management Research: Challenges and Controversies* (pp. 314–34). London: Routledge.

Antonacopoulou, E. P. (2010d). Making the business school more "critical": Reflexive critique based on *phronesis* as a foundation for impact. *British Journal of Management*, 21(Special Issue), S6–S25

Antonacopoulou, E. P. (2012). Leader-ship: Making waves. In Owen, H. (Ed.) *New Insights into Leadership: An International Perspective* (pp. 47–66). London: Kogan Page.

Antonacopoulou, E. P. (2014). The experience of learning in space and time. *Prometheus*, 32(1), 83–91.

Antonacopoulou, E. P. (2016a). Rediscovering paideia and the meaning of a scholarly career: Rejoinder to identifying research topic development in business and management education research using legitimation code theory. *Journal of Management Education*.

Antonacopoulou, E. P. (2016b). Practising innovating through Learning-in-Crisis: Realizing the impact of man-agement in HRM practice. In Sparrow, P., Shipton, H., Budwar, P. & Brown, A. (Eds.) *Human Resource Management, Innovation and Performance* (pp. 266–81). Basingstoke, UK: Palgrave.

Antonacopoulou, E. P. & Sheaffer, Z. (2014). Learning in crisis: Rethinking the relationship between organizational learning and crisis management. *Journal of Management Inquiry*, 23(1), 5–21.

Arthur, J., Kristjánsson, K., Thomas, H., Holdsworth, M., Confalonieri, L. B. & Qiu, T. (2014). *Virtuous Character for the Practice of Law*. Research Report. The Jubilee Centre for Character and Virtues, University of Birmingham. Retrieved March 15, 2016 from www.jubileecentre.ac.uk/userfiles/jubileecentre/pdf/Research%20Reports/Virtuous_Character_for_the_Practice_of_Law.pdf.

Arthur, J., Kristjánsson, K., Thomas, H., Kotzee, B., Ignatowicz, A & Qiu, T. (2015a). *Virtuous Medical Practice*. Research Report. The Jubilee Centre for Character and Virtues, University of Birmingham. Retrieved March 15, 2016 from www.jubilee centre.ac.uk/userfiles/jubileecentre/pdf/Research%20Reports/Virtuous_Medical_Practice.pdf.

Arthur, J., Kristjánsson, K., Cooke, S., Brown, E. & Carr, B. (2015b). *The Good Teacher: Understanding Virtues in Practice*. Research Report. The Jubilee Centre for Character and Virtues, University of Birmingham. Retrieved March 15, 2016 from www.jubilee-centre.ac.uk/userfiles/jubileecentre/pdf/Research%20Reports/The_Good_Teacher_Understanding_Virtues_in_Practice.pdf.

Badham, R., Mead, A. & Antonacopoulou, E. P. (2012). Performing change: A dramaturgical approach to the practice of managing change. In Boje, D. M., Burnes, B. & Hassard, J. (Eds.) *The Routledge Companion to Organizational Change* (pp. 187–205). Oxford: Routledge.

Beech, N., MacIntosh, R., Antonacopoulou, E. P. & Sims, D. (2012). Practising and knowing management: A dialogic perspective. *Management Learning*, 43(4), 373–83.

Blond, P., Antonacopoulou, E. P. & Pabst, A. (2015). In professions we trust: Fostering virtuous practitioners in teaching, law and medicine. Retrieved March 15, 2016 from www.respublica.org.uk/our-work/publications/virtuous-practice-professions/.

Chandler, C. (2014). What is the meaning of impact in relation to research and why does it matter? A view from inside academia. In Denicolo, P. (Ed.) *Achieving Impact in Research* (pp. 1–9). London: Sage Publications.

Chubb, J. (2014). How does the impact agenda fit with attitudes and ethics that motivate research? In Denicolo, P. (Ed.) *Achieving Impact in Research* (pp. 20–32). London: Sage Publications.

MacIntyre, A. (1985). *After Virtue: A Study in Moral Theory*. London: Duckworth.

Noel, J. (1999). On the varieties of *phronesis*. *Educational Philosophy and Theory*, 31(3), 273–89.

ResPublica (2016a). ResPublica. Retrieved on March 15, 2016 from www.respublica.org.uk.

ResPublica (2016b). Virtue. Retrieved on March 15, 2016 from www.respublica.org.uk/about-us/virtue/.

Shotter, J. & Tsoukas, H. (2014). In search of *phronesis*: Leadership and the art of judgment. *Academy of Management Learning & Education*, 13(2), 224–43.

Smith W. K. & Lewis M. W. (2011). Towards a theory of paradox: A dynamic equilibrium model of organizing. *Academy of Management Review*, 36(2), 381–403.

Wall, J. (2003). *Phronesis*, poetics and moral creativity. *Ethical Theory and Moral Practice*, 6(3), 317–41.

Part III

Becoming and being at home in both worlds

Introduction to Part III

The eight chapters in this third part of the book are case studies of successful academic–practitioner partnerships and, in one case, practice. Together they represent more than 80 years of accumulated experience working in academic–practitioner relationships. They are also representative of the diverse approaches that can be used to develop and maintain relationships at interfaces between academia and practice. Despite the diversity of practice, they echo the sorts of capability which authors in Part II described quite independently, and embody the foundational principles sketched out in Part I implicitly, if not explicitly.

In Chapter 12, Laura Empson offers a very personal account of her experience of liminality throughout her career. She shares the lessons learned from the part of her life spent at Cass Business School and running the Centre for Professional Service Firms. The rules of engagement she has evolved to guide her choices have allowed her to maintain the quality of her standing in the academic world at the same time as she has built a reputation for producing relevant material. Further, these rules of engagement are clearly practical principles that prevent her being torn in different directions by the contradictory demands on her time and attention. Empson's auto-ethnography shows how the liminal experiences of apprentice researchers, whom Collins and McBain attempt to develop, continue through the academic's life

It is hard to ignore the advice in Chapter 13, when it comes from Susan Albers Mohrman's 35 years of experience as a research scientist at The Center for Effective Organizations (CEO). Founded in 1978, by Ed Lawler, it is unlikely that the Center would have survived so long if their work was not producing both valuable academic output and relevant material for the organizations who join the consortia. The chapter describes the foundations of the CEO approach to research and then explains how that approach is enacted in a particular research program, using complexity theory as the theoretical foundation to examine how organizations can "design for sustainable effectiveness." There are some definite resonances here with MacLean and MacIntosh's Chapter 9 in Part II.

From London and California respectively in the first two chapters of Part II, we travel to South Africa to examine how Ralph Hamann and Kristy Faccer (Chapter 14) managed the collaborative relationships in the Network for Business Sustainability (NBS) and the South African Food Lab. Both collaborations were established to address sustainability problems in the developing world, but the comparison between them provides some interesting insights into the process of transforming knowledge beyond simply relevant content, and into applied research that really makes a difference. Despite extensive effort to establish a shared language and common understanding of purpose in NBS, translation was not enough: it is essential that researchers are open to learning and changing their own understanding as a result of interactions with practitioners. So the knowledge transformation that Carlile (2004) identifies is two way: not just interaction to adapt theory to the practical context, but also to revise theory based on practical evidence. Second, when the motivations and values underlying the researchers' identities fit with the purpose of the collaboration and research interactions occur *in the context of* meaningful practice as a means to an end, rather than research being the end in itself, it has a profound effect on impact. This echoes Antonacopoulou's chapter in Part II.

In Chapter 15 Carton and Dameron provide a useful typology of collaborative interfaces which have had major organizational impact. They analyze the development of various well-known conceptual frameworks that have changed business thinking for example, the Balanced Scorecard, Open Innovation, Blue Ocean Strategy and Business Model Canvas, and identify the different ways that the tensions which Bartunek and Rynes (2014) identified play out as a result of the way the interface between the academics and practitioners is constructed.

In Chapter 16, Landman, Glowinkowski and Demes reflect on the development of a rigorous quantitative global values indicator through a three-way relationship involving an academic, the head of a private organization, and a post-doc. research associate funded through the Knowledge Transfer Partnership (KTP) scheme in the UK. Such a triangular relationship is configured to permit the academic to uphold the concerns for rigor, the practitioner to uphold relevance and commercialization concerns, and the KTP associate to learn how to integrate both into the final output, which is another way of developing the paradoxical mind-set that Jarzabkowski, Lewis, and Smith examine in Part II. Clearly in this case it worked and the results are delivering recognizable and measurable impact.

Chapter 17, by McKenzie and van Winkelen, provides an example of how the different modes of Van de Ven's engaged scholarship outlined in Part II (Figure 7.4, Chapter 7) have been used to serve the varying interests of a changing organizational membership in the Henley Forum. As an interface between academia and practice, the Forum combines collaborative research with individual and organizational capability development. McKenzie and van Winkelen explain how, over 16 years, combinations of interactive research methods, action research, and basic research work in conjunction with developmental activities to address organizational problems associated with knowledge and learning. The choice of method is driven by the nature of the practitioner problem and variations in the tolerance for longer-term returns from the output of the research. Evaluation research has been used primarily to provide insights to improve academic practice in designing the interface between the business school and practitioners within member organizations and managing the relationships. The case illustrates how tensions associated with differences in logic, time horizons, communication styles, interests, and incentives, which Bartunek and Rynes (2014) identified, have been managed in the Forum and the importance of facilitation skills.

Chapter 18, the final chapter in this section and in the book, is unique in that it is written by a researcher working outside of academia. Personal conversations with Jennifer Kurkoski lead us to avoid calling her a practitioner. In her view, labeling those who work in organizations in a way that unnecessarily differentiates them exacerbates a sense of division, and does nothing to help them connect and relate. Kurkoski's experience of running the People Innovation Lab at Google is quite the opposite. She shows how research is fundamental to Google's approach to human resources and people management, and the ways in which the work of the People Innovation Lab actively connects with those parts of academia that see their work as contributing to wider societal benefit. The skills to transform the knowledge gained back into organizational practice are clearly evident in Kurkoski's work.

We commented in our overall introduction that there have been very few occasions for presenting a full portrait of the progress being made in *thinking* about academic–practitioner partnerships (Part I), in *developing the skills* to carry them out successfully (Part II), and in showcasing a wide range of *successful examples* of such partnerships (Part III), and that presenting these is the purpose of this book. We also stated that this book does not present a finished product, but a step on a path to enhanced possibilities for academic–practitioner collaboration.

The chapters in this section are important, because they do make evident how much is going on in academic–practitioner collaboration. The partnerships in operation do not follow only one philosophical foundation, but many of them, though these foundations are somewhat consistent with each other. They do not only represent collaborative research, but include multiple types of relationships and activities. They all require skills that have not always been recognized in discussion of such collaboration.

Overall Part III offers a rich resource to inspire anyone seeking to operate at the interface between the two distinct worlds of academia and organizational practice who is prepared to engage in the learning, relationship-building, and identity work required for engaging successfully in academic–practitioner partnerships.

References

Bartunek, J. M. & Rynes, S. L. (2014). Academics and practitioners are alike and unlike: The paradoxes of academic–practitioner relationships. *Journal of Management*, 40(5), 1181–201.

Carlile, P. R. (2004). Transferring, translating and transforming: An integrative framework for managing knowledge across boundaries. *Organization Science*, 15(5), 555–68.

12 My liminal life

Perpetual journeys across the research–practice divide

Laura Empson

Introduction

In 1967, when I was four years old, my family moved to Cyprus, a Mediterranean island divided by centuries of conflict between the Greeks and the Turks. During the week we lived in our large house in the capital city of Nicosia in the Greek Zone. At the weekend we travelled to our small cottage in the fishing village of Kyrenia in the Turkish Zone. Only a few people on the island were able to travel between the two embattled zones, but my father's senior diplomatic status gave us an "access all areas" pass.

Every Friday evening, as dusk began to fall, we made the journey. We crossed the Green Line, a zone which separated the Greeks and the Turks, passing through three military check points; and inspected first by Greek soldiers, then by United Nations peace-keeping troops, and finally by Turkish soldiers. As a little girl on her way to the seaside I was excited but also anxious, with three sets of armed guards examining our diplomatic identity cards carefully before giving us permission to pass. I remember leaving the hot and dusty city where everyone spoke Greek, driving through the mountains as the sun was setting, and arriving at the small fishing village where everyone spoke Turkish. The smells changed, from car fumes, to lemon groves, to fresh fish. And every Sunday evening we repacked the car and repeated the journey in reverse.

It occurred to me, as I sat down to write this chapter, that I have continued to enact this ritual throughout my career—moving regularly from the world of academia to the world of practice and back again, excited but anxious, fascinated by both worlds, and never fully belonging to either. I have lived my life in liminal space.

In "My affair with the 'other': Identity journeys across the research–practice divide" (Empson, 2013), I outlined the identity struggles I experienced during my evolution into a successful scholar of professional service firms who has maintained a life-long engagement with practitioners. Previous studies of the research–practice divide have remained at the institutionalized level but "My affair with the 'other'" focused on the causes and consequences of the divide at the individual level.

I outlined my experiences, first as a strategy consultant, then as a PhD student at London Business School, followed by ten years as a member of faculty at the University of Oxford, culminating in becoming a Professor at Cass Business School. Utilizing auto-ethnographic methods (i.e. analyzing my diary entries over several years), I explained how my identity as an academic had been affected by sustained engagement with practitioners through my dedication to researching professional service firms. Applying the metaphor of an affair to my three-year consulting relationship with a leading law firm, I sought to understand my experiences of excitement, affirmation, enjoyment, and escapism alongside confusion and guilt. Interwoven with this auto-ethnographic analysis, I discussed the more generalizable implications of my experiences, identifying factors which create and exacerbate identity conflict, the experience of identity conflict, and tactics for resolving identity conflict.

In this chapter I pick up where that narrative left off. I analyze my perpetual journeys across the research–practice divide through the concept of liminality in order to conceptualize the space that both separates and connects the worlds of academia and practice. I describe how I have constructed a "dwelling place" in this liminal space through the creation of my research centre, the Centre for Professional Service Firms (CPSF) at Cass Business School. The CPSF is founded on a commitment to conducting rigorous academic research and engaging with practitioners. I explain about my most tangible evidence of practitioner impact to date, my appointment to the Board of KPMG UK as Senior Independent Non-Executive. I conclude by outlining the personal rules I now attempt to live by when engaging with practitioners. My intention, as with "My affair with the 'other'," is to encourage fellow academics to cross the research–practice divide, to help you avoid the mistakes I have made, and to enable you to become well-informed travelers—open to new experiences and willing to take risks, but with sufficient insight to ensure those risks are carefully calculated.

Liminality: "betwixt and between" a dominant space

A dominant space has clear boundaries, and the practices within these boundaries are interwoven with social expectations, routines, and norms (Shortt, 2015). When I was a child I moved between the dominant spaces of the Greek and Turkish Cypriot zones. As an adult I have moved between the dominant spaces of academia and practice. It has been argued by numerous scholars that the social expectations, routines, and norms of these distinct communities are incommensurable (see Bartunek & Rynes, 2014, for an overview of this debate). A series of past presidents of the Academy of Management have raised concerns about our crisis of irrelevance as management scholars (Bartunek, 2003; Hambrick, 1994; Huff, 2000). Gulati (2007: 777) has referred to "two tribes on either side of a chasm" when referring to the ongoing hostilities between academics who seek to define themselves in terms of research and those academics who seek to sustain engagement with practice.

A liminal space lies at the boundary of two dominant spaces and is not fully part of either (Dale & Burrell, 2008). In my analogy, the liminal space is the Green Line that separates the Greek and Turkish Cypriots, where the United Nations peacekeepers live. By contrast, the research–practice divide is a "no-man's-land"—there are no established communities dwelling in this liminal space. With hindsight I can see how these conditions helped to create the problems I describe in "My affair with the 'other'" (Empson, 2013), and the feelings of depression, isolation, anxiety, exhaustion, confusion, and guilt I experienced as I journeyed across the research–practice divide. While I could pass freely backwards and forwards between the worlds of academia and practice, I felt isolated and vulnerable, so I did not feel that I could come to rest in this liminal space. In my exhausted state I reluctantly came to the conclusion that "I belonged to an outgroup of one, i.e., me" (Empson, 2013: 243).

According to Turner (1967, 1982), liminality represents a stage of reflection, part of a coming of age process. The liminar spends time outside society, "betwixt and between," in order to make a transition from their established social position, or identity, to their new one (Turner, 1982: 27). Beech (2011) and others have emphasized that an individual who spends extended periods of time in liminal space may experience feelings of anxiety and social separation— Jung's conceptualization of the dark phase of liminality where one is broken down before being made whole.

But liminal space may also be liberating as it can represent a space for freedom from structural obligations; it is a space where "anything might happen" (Turner, 1982: 27). When an individual is obliged to contend with an oppressive dominant space, liminal space can represent a transitory dwelling space that provides a sense of security and an opportunity for escape (Shortt, 2015). In "My affair with the 'other'," my engagement with practitioners enabled me to escape from the oppressive dominant space of my situation at Oxford. Talking about my consulting relationship with the law firm, I explain that, "I love doing it. It is fun. It is important. It puts everything else in perspective. When I am flying back from a meeting with them, nothing at the business school seems to matter" (Diary note, May 25, 2006, quoted in Empson, 2013: 240).

My experience of liminality as a child was not limited to my time in Cyprus. Throughout my childhood I lived in five different countries and attended ten different schools. In the process I developed survival skills which would prove extremely valuable in my future academic career. I worked out how to enter an alien environment and quickly identify and assess the norms of interaction and established power dynamics. The skills that stopped me from being bullied as the new British girl in yet another foreign playground have proven useful in my qualitative field work studying the leaders of elite professional service firms. From my earliest years as a PhD researcher I have been able to walk into a research interview with a high status individual and quickly build the necessary level of trust to enable them to feel comfortable disclosing confidential and highly personal information to me.

My experience of liminality has also taught me how to view the same situation from very different perspectives. So in a research interview I am both myself and not myself. Of course I bring my own subjective preoccupations, concerns, and prejudices into the interview. However, in order to build a rapport, I try to manage my thoughts and feelings so that I can genuinely empathize with the interviewee, regardless of who they are or what they are saying. As they open up to me, it becomes easier for me to see the world as they see it and I no longer have to pretend to be empathetic. But during the interview I am also in a third place, a liminal space, where I am attempting to maintain an objective position, informed by theory and my own reflexivity, in order to develop intellectually valid interpretations and judgments.

I wonder how many academics who have chosen to journey across the research–practice divide have similarly strong experiences of liminality in their past. Researchers seeking to cross the research–practice divide would do well to examine their own motivations that cause them to do this. The question is not what makes you want to start the journey? That is the easy part. *The important question is, what it is within you that makes you persist?*

Integrating the "other"

In 2007, after ten years on the faculty at Oxford, I was approached by Cass Business School in the City of London and asked to take up a position specially created for me as Professor in the Management of Professional Service Firms. They asked me to establish my own research centre, dedicated to researching professional service firms. One of Cass's strategic objectives was to become "a leading intellectual resource for professional service firms" (note the use of the words "resource for"—the intention was explicitly functional). I would be in the heart of Europe's financial centre, surrounded by the global headquarters of many of the world's leading professional service firms.

The Dean had previously been an investment banker and championed the professional service firm agenda and my work with great enthusiasm. He told me that I had a "blank sheet of paper" to decide how best to advance this initiative.

From the start I was determined that the centre would embody a commitment to conducting rigorous academic research and to engaging with professionals at all stages in the research process: from inception, design, execution, dissemination, to application. But I was also clear that it would always be us, the academics, who actually did the research—we would decide what to research and how to research it. So, shortly after I arrived at Cass, on what was literally a blank sheet of paper, I wrote the following:

The Cass Centre for Professional Service Firms:

- A place where academics make a difference—the Centre conducts rigorous research that aims to change the way that academics and professionals analyze and understand professional service firms.

- A place where professionals come to think—the Centre provides professionals with space and stimulus to explore the management challenges they face.
- A place where academics and professionals collaborate—the Centre brings academics and professionals together to challenge each other and create new ideas.

As I wrote in "My affair with the 'other'," with the establishment of the CPSF, "I have inadvertently created my own eclectic referent group to which I can belong" (Empson, 2013: 243). I have attracted very high quality PhD, post-doctoral, and visiting scholars from around the world and I have encouraged many of my colleagues at Cass from Organizational Behavior, Strategy, and Marketing to join. I have also recruited several distinguished retired Global Senior and Managing Partners, Chairmen and Chief Executives, of elite professional service firms to join us as Visiting Professors of Practice.

These senior professionals are typically individuals I have known for many years and whom I have come to respect as particularly intelligent, intellectually curious and personally reflexive. These are the crucial qualities I look for and value most highly in the practitioners I seek to work closely with.

The relationship may begin with an approach from the Chair of a global professional service firm, perhaps asking me to give keynote speech about my research at their firm's annual partner conference. After the event I remain in touch with them and subsequently ask them to speak at an event I am organizing at Cass. Or the relationship may begin with me getting to know them through my research in their firm. Thereafter, we remain in touch. Sometimes I ask them for advice about my research; sometimes they ask me for advice about their firm. Through a series of meetings and lunches over several years we develop a personal relationship. And, once they are due to retire, I "pop the question," asking them to join the CPSF, knowing that they will make a valuable contribution to our work because I have already learnt to value their insights.

For me one of the most personally rewarding aspects of running the CPSF is our monthly research meetings, which resemble "joint interpretation meetings," as described by Mohrman, Gibson and Mohrman (2001). These bring together our eclectic group of senior professionals, established faculty, and PhD students, to hear an academic colleague present work in progress. Because we meet every month we are able to get to know each other well and learn how to communicate effectively with each other. More generally we just have fun arguing about ideas—practitioners with practitioners, academics with academics, academics with practitioners—until it no longer matters who is what. My vision for the CPSF is validated when I am presenting my own research and a practitioner interprets my data differently through the lens of their own experience, when they ask a question which blows apart my carefully constructed piece of analysis, or see a relationship between two seemingly unconnected pieces of data I have presented, and offer me an explanation for the mechanism that connects them.

In terms of what other members of the CPSF get out of these meetings, Table 12.1 includes some of my colleagues' comments.

We have now raised many hundreds of thousands of pounds in prestigious research grants from research councils. One of the factors contributing to our success at winning these grants is our evidence of successful research dissemination and of engagement with academics and practitioners. We have organized an extensive program of research-focused events, including academic symposia,

Table 12.1 A sample of CPSF member views

Question: "Given the considerable demands on your time, why do you continue to come to CPSF research meetings?"

Senior practitioners
- "I love the exposure to new ideas and new ways of looking at things provided by academics who are actually keen to be challenged by non-academics. I always come away from a meeting having learnt something—and I can't say that about every meeting I attend."
- "Attending CPSF seminars is one of the most stimulating and satisfying things I get to do. There is a wonderful fusion or synthesis of views, evidence and experience. It feels creative and worthwhile."
- "I enjoy the sheer fun of intellectual debate in a multi-disciplinary non-hierarchical group. The CPSF provides a forum where we can constructively analyze and challenge why things happen the way they do, and how they can be done better."

PhD students
- "Every time I attend a CPSF meeting I come away with enhanced confidence and restored faith in my chosen career. It allows me to experiment with my changing identity without expecting me to choose sides and be either an academic or a practitioner. ... I was always interested in doing a PhD which might improve the lives of (even just a handful of) professionals."
- "I really treasure the opportunity to meet with practitioners who have been exposed to different experiences than the academics we doctoral students interact with on a daily basis. The CPSF is an important part of my PhD process, both in providing inspiration and in validation (or non-validation) of my research ideas."
- "It is interesting to observe the reactions of the practitioners to the research, including how they disagree *with each other* ... Regular meetings of the same small group can allow everyone to speak and argue in a 'safe' environment so that bonds can be formed and fledgling ideas can be shared."

Faculty
- "I've been a member of quite a few research groups, and this is the first (and only) one in which I've seen such a candid and generative ongoing conversation between academics and practitioners."
- "I am attracted by the chance to hear practitioners speak about that which is 'unsayable in public'. I find it interesting and very useful for developing my thinking. The group allows everyone to participate and to get to know each other for a relaxed exchange of ideas rather than for ego-driven debates and disagreements."
- "I recognize the difficulty of getting access to and studying professionals in their natural habitat, so it is always fascinating to hear about the ongoing projects of CPSF members. It becomes doubly interesting when deeply experienced practitioners validate and/or question our theoretical analyses and offer their perspectives, which often simplify and clarify the issues we identify."

---

early career researcher masterclasses, and practitioner discussion forums. At these discussion forums we present our emerging findings to a special invited audience of 100–150 senior professionals and invite Managing and Senior Partners, Chairmen and Chief Executives of professional service firms to debate our preliminary conclusions. Our research is improved by these interactions and ensures that our research begins to have an impact several years before it is published in academic journals. The relationships that we build through these events help us to gain access for subsequent research. In this way we have constructed a dwelling place within the liminal space which generates a virtuous circle of both research and practice.

Archetypes of problem practitioners

This book is intended to celebrate and encourage the interaction of academics and practitioners in the production of research that is both rigorous and relevant. But it is important to be realistic about the problems that can arise from these interactions. One consequence of the success of the CPSF is that each year I receive many dozens of requests for meetings with practitioners. Whilst I still remain passionately convinced of the value of practitioner interaction, over the years I have learnt to become much more selective about how I interact with them and who I interact with. I have identified four archetypal problem practitioners: the "Very Important Pontificator," the "Needy Student," the "Mental Leech," and the "Singing Siren." I explain below how I try to identify and respond to each one.

The Very Important Pontificator (VIP) has occupied a senior leadership role in a professional service firm, but is now retiring and looking for new interests (i.e., superficially just like the practitioners I invite to join the CPSF, but crucially different). A VIP might refer to their status as a distinguished retiring professional and suggest a meeting "as an opportunity to explore areas of mutual interest." Whereas the distinguished professionals in the CPSF are interested in learning alongside the academics, the VIPs are more interested in teaching them. Of course people like this may have a huge amount to offer the CPSF but too often I sense they are using the Centre to gratify their ego needs. A senior professional making a transition into retirement will be going through their own challenging liminal time and looking for new sources of validation. As senior leaders, they are used to being listened to by people who want the benefit of their wisdom, they need to find a new group of people to listen to them. A VIP does not understand, and is insufficiently reflexive to learn, that the norms of interaction in academia are very different, and that status is derived not from experience but from the quality of an individual's thinking. They do not understand why their hard-won insights may be banal or simply irrelevant in the context of our research. The challenge with the VIP is to extract yourself from the interaction before too much time is wasted and without causing offence to someone who, after all, was offering to help.

The Needy Student may also be coming to the end of, or taking a break from, a successful professional career, but their initial approach will be very different from the VIP. They are likely to talk explicitly about their desire to "collaborate on research." Rather than seeking to tell me the answer (as the VIP does) they come to me with questions. They are yearning for something they think academia can give to them—their views of academia are often based on nostalgic memories of undergraduate life. In the early days of the CPSF I was very receptive to these approaches—I was genuinely curious to experiment, to see how these kinds of relationship could contribute to the research life of the Centre. Over time I have realized that, even with the simplest, practitioner-oriented pieces of research, the Needy Student needs a great deal of help to frame their ideas, design their study, analyze their data, and write up their findings. Having created the reputation of the CPSF as an intellectually rigorous research centre, I need to safeguard it. The challenge with the Needy Student is to set expectations clearly up front, help them to recognize that you are not there to help them fulfill their fantasy of becoming an academic, and to explain (briefly) to them how they can negotiate their own path through the maze of academia.

The Mental Leech tends to be attracted by university marketing activities and networking events. Their initial approach they will often include an explicit request to "pick your brains." They often say they have read about my research, "found it very insightful," and want to discuss their organization with me. In the early days of the CPSF my response might have been: flattered that they liked my research, excited that they thought it might be helpful to them, and hopeful that this might translate into some kind of valuable opportunity. But the Mental Leech is a voracious feeder and is not willing to offer anything of value in return. A Mental Leech will always charge their clients for their time, yet assumes that academics will happily provide detailed advice for the price of a coffee. The challenge with the Mental Leech is working out how to distinguish them from valuable opportunities and how to keep them at bay, without undermining the goodwill that the university marketing activities have sought to generate.

The Singing Siren's Call can be heard from many different directions, such as university PR departments, executive education, journalists, and professional conference organizers. But they all sing the same song. They want you to speak about a particular topic of interest to practitioners and their assumption is that, because you have done a great deal of research into Topic A, you must be able to speak with authority on Topics B and C—after all, B and C are very close to A. It is important that we academics have the intellectual creativity to work out how to apply our hard-won insights in novel and interesting ways to new topics. But at what point do you stop being an authoritative expert on a topic and become a "rent a gob"? Some years ago my (practitioner) Dean asked me to give a talk on "the future of the legal profession" to a law firm he was keen to cultivate. I was reluctant to do this as I had not done any research on the topic but explained that, if I spent a few days preparing, I could probably come up with something interesting to say. "What fee was the firm offering?" I asked. "None," said the Dean, and, as it was a marketing activity, I should not spend much time preparing my speech. He emphasized, "You should learn to develop a Laura

Empson lite." My response was: "There is no Laura Empson lite. That's the whole point." I pointed out that the reason the law firm wanted to hear me speak was because they knew my reputation as a researcher and believed I would have something significant to say. As I did not have something significant to say, I refused to give the talk. Learning how to say "no" convincingly, courteously, and constructively to Singing Sirens is an important skill to cultivate—I am still working on it.

"Acts of pain"

Van Gennep (1961) describes liminality as the destructive stage in a rite of passage. According to Thomassen (2006: 322), the liminar initiands "live outside their normal environment and are brought to question their self and the existing social order through a series of rituals that often involve acts of pain." What takes place in the dark phase of liminality is a "process of breaking down ... in the interest of making whole one's meaning, purpose and sense of relatedness" (Shorter, 1988: 73). Just as the CPSF was becoming successful and well-established, something like this happened to me.

By 2011 I had been at Cass for four years and had invested a huge amount of time in establishing the CPSF. I had helped to achieve one of Cass's strategic goals to become globally recognized as a centre of excellence for professional service firms. I had also secured a substantial grant from the Economic and Social Research Council of Great Britain to conduct my own research into leadership dynamics and was deeply immersed in field work among the senior leadership groups of a series of elite professional service firms. I had consistently received top ranking on my appraisals but, in the midst of everything else I was doing, I had not had time to publish much. This was not a particular concern to the Dean or my Head of Faculty as they shared my commitment to practitioner engagement and recognized that the publications would come after I had completed my field work for the ESRC study.

Then everything changed and, within a short space of time, the university got a new Vice Chancellor, the business school got a new Dean, and I got a new Head of Faculty. This coincided with the run up to the REF (Research Excellence Framework), an exercise held every six years by the UK government to assess the quality of research at UK universities. Under the REF, universities need to justify the public funding allocated to them by providing evidence that funds spent have met the three Es: economy, efficiency, and effectiveness (Martin, 2011). This is part of the "regime of excellence" (Butler & Spoelstra, 2014) manifested in journal rankings and research assessments which is coming to increasing prominence in universities more generally. In the UK each participating university is required to submit an extremely detailed "return." The quality of these submissions is then assessed by an external panel. The REF panel award a score to each university department; the higher the aggregated score for the university, the more income awarded by the government for the following six years.

The REF process is highly controversial (Tourish, 2015). "The content and quality of a piece of work is less important for the purposes of evaluation than its performance according to purely quantitative criteria" (Butler & Spoelstra, 2014: 538). Willmott (2011: 430), himself a REF assessor and highly distinguished scholar, has referred to the "journal list fetishism and the perversion of scholarship" that has arisen in this environment.

The university decides which individual faculty to submit to the REF based on the number and quality of their publications. Faculty who are not submitted are deemed "non-REFable." In the run up to the REF deadline many UK universities engage in a frenzy of recruiting, similar to football's annual transfer market window (Lucas, 2006), as they outbid each other for "star" publishers (Clarke, Knights & Jarvis, 2012).

Thomassen (2006: 322) says that, through their "acts of pain," liminars "come to feel nameless." During the run up to the REF I felt that, from the university's perspective, my 20 years of scholarly endeavor had been reduced to a single number, my REF score.[1] What I experienced during this time was fairly widespread amongst UK academics, as many universities attempted to increase their REF ranking by "easing out" or "culling" faculty who were not "REFable," or forcing them to transfer to teaching-only contracts. Academic identities, which are inherently insecure (Gabriel, 2010), were rendered ever more fragile by the proliferation of increasingly stringent performance demands and penalties for underperformance (Knights & Clarke, 2014).

Within a short space of time, I shifted from being a star performer to a "question mark" as I did not yet have the required number of high quality publications to be included in my department's REF submission. I was told by the new regime that I should focus all my attention on achieving the necessary number of top ranked publications and should "stop wasting [my] time" on practitioner engagement.[2] The anxiety that ran throughout "My affair with the 'other'," suddenly returned. In the environment of the REF, where my employing institution had become an increasingly oppressive dominant space, the liminal space I had created no longer seemed secure. After years of practice at refusing to relinquish my British identity in yet another foreign playground, I should have been able to resist my employer's pressure to conform. But the bloody-minded determination had enabled me to stand up to playground bullies when I was a child deserted me when I was confronted with the institutionalized bully embodied in the REF. During the next 18 months, in order to make myself REFable, I worked harder and on a more sustained basis than at any time in my life. Toward the end of this time I experienced a double bereavement: the sudden death of my father and the rapid onset of my mother's dementia.

Mourning is another form of liminal space and I learnt an extraordinary amount during this bitter time of trial. This "process of breaking down" (Shorter, 1988) forced me to ask profound questions about my life. I was certain that a life devoted primarily to the production of REFable publications would be a sad and worthless waste. In the immediate aftermath of my father's sudden death, and of learning to care for my mother, I realized that my life was short and could end at any moment, so I might as well do whatever I wanted, and do it right now. I realized also that it made no sense whatsoever to comply with institutionally prescribed performance metrics because they could change overnight with the arrival of a new university Vice Chancellor or a new Minister of Education. What really mattered to me was the thrill of intellectual discovery, of learning and growing intellectually, of creating and crafting research insights, and of using those insights to make a positive difference in the lives of the people I cared about: professionals, fellow researchers, my students, and myself.

And, around the time I came to this conclusion, my fourth paper was accepted into a top ranked journal and I became REFable. "My affair with the 'other'" was one of the publications that helped me to achieve this goal.

"Making whole"

During the run up to the REF I turned down many professional service firms' requests for help as I needed to focus on developing my publications. However, I was intrigued when the Chairman of KPMG UK, one to the "Big Four" global accounting and advisory firms, asked me to join their Board as an Independent Non Executive (INE) and member of their Public Interest Committee.[3]

As with my childhood trips to the Turkish Zone, I approached the opportunity with a mixture of excitement and anxiety. The other three INEs at KPMG and their equivalents in the other major accounting firms were highly experienced practitioners (I would be the only academic amongst this august group). Most were already serving on the boards of major publicly quoted corporations and many had worked as corporate chairmen or very senior civil servants. Most were 10 to 20 years older than I, and many of them had knighthoods, reflecting their status as part of the "great and the good" of the British Establishment. I had felt like an outsider all my life so I could not conceive of myself becoming one of "them."

After three years of serving on the Board as an independent non-executive I have come to realize that my lack of experience in many key areas was more than compensated for by two decades of studying and advising professional service firms on leadership and governance. My experience of liminality, a longstanding feature of my academic life, had prepared me perfectly for the *ultimate liminal role* of the non-executive director.

We participate in Board meetings, advise the executive of the firm, and hold them to account. I also act as an informal sounding board to members of the Board. Our remit under the Audit Firm Governance Code explicitly encompasses the "public interest" and, in that capacity, we have particular responsibility for oversight of risk and quality issues within the firm. We meet regularly with the audit sector's regulator, the Financial Reporting Council (FRC), to discuss KPMG's activities in the context of public interest issues, and we also meet periodically with institutional investors.

Put in these terms, the work sounds rather dry and dull. It isn't. It is hard work and sometimes stressful, but it can also be fascinating and fulfilling.

I remember sitting in my first KPMG Board meeting with my hand over my mouth as I struggled to control the broad grin that kept spreading across my face. The Board members were looking very serious and I needed to look like one of them, but I was feeling utterly gleeful as I felt intellectual fireworks going off inside my head. One agenda item after another was connecting with the past 20 years of my research and I could feel ideas and insights bubbling up inside me. I had presented many times before at the Board meetings of other professional service firms but this experience felt entirely different. I was no longer simply an invited guest, visiting temporarily, but someone who had a right to be there, with significant ongoing responsibilities to the firm and the public interest.

Jung talks about the experience of liminality as a necessary precursor to "'making whole' one's meaning, purpose and sense of relatedness" (Shorter, 1988: 73). My role at KPMG has helped me to achieve that. It has provided me with a strong and alternative sense of affiliation and identity.

As an insider/outsider, the role of the independent non-executive is inherently liminal and very complicated in identity terms. On the one hand we must remain outsiders, in order to provide independent challenge and perspective—i.e., KPMG are "them." On the other hand, we need to become insiders if our voices are to be heard, understood, and respected[4]—so KPMG are "us." In Board meetings I think carefully about when to say "we" and when to say "you," depending on what I am trying to achieve with my comment (i.e., whether I want to gently build support or to provoke and disturb). Our insider/outsider status enables the INEs to offer a very robust challenge, to say things which are simply too difficult to articulate for people who have worked in the firm their entire careers.

My role at KPMG maps directly onto my current research into senior leadership dynamics but it also relates back to my previous research on governance in professional service firms. I participated in a meeting a while back where the Financial Reporting Council was proposing substantial revisions to the Audit Firm Governance Code. There were about 20 people sitting around a large table, including representatives of the regulator, the professional association, government, the largest accounting firms, their INEs, and investors. Having published on institutional work in a professional context, I sat there thinking "Wow! This is institutional work, happening right in front of my eyes." And when the Chief Executive of the FRC turned to me and said, "Laura, given your research on professional service firm governance, I am particularly interested to hear your views on the proposals," I thought, "Wow! This is me *doing* institutional work."

My Cass and KPMG identity cards give me "access all areas" to two very different spaces and I have learnt to move easily between them over the course of a single day. *I perform both roles better, precisely because I am performing both roles.* After two years as an INE I was asked to take over as Chair of the Public Interest Committee (to be become in effect the Senior Independent Non-executive Director) of KPMG. This has opened up a new phase of learning for me and new opportunities to have a positive impact. Turner argues that, at the conclusion of an enforced period of reflection, the liminar finds that they have acquired enhanced responsibilities and "powers." My time of "pain" in liminal space and my new-found responsibilities at KPMG have indeed given me enhanced "powers," by enabling me to operate with a greater degree of insight, confidence, and effectiveness in the realms of both academia and practice.

Rules of engagement

My aim in writing this chapter has been to encourage academics to keep crossing the research–practice divide. As with any form of adventure travel, the key is to prepare carefully, educate yourself about the risks, and to be open to what you may discover about yourself and the world along the way. Below are the rules of engagement which I have developed to enable me to do this. These are personal to me and I encourage you to develop some rules which work for you.

It is about them, not us—they are not objects but individuals

When we approach practitioners as people rather than as research objects, the quality of the data we gather is immeasurably improved. Here are two examples from my recent experience of how academics objectify practitioners and why this can undermine the quality of our research:

- An academic asked me recently: "How can I get a gig like yours at KPMG? I would love to sit at their Board table and observe those lab rats in their natural environment." I explained that this was precisely why he would not be invited to join the Board of any organization. If he ever wanted to get close enough to Board members to study them properly, then he needed to stop thinking of them just as research objects and recognize that they were also individuals struggling to do their jobs to the best of their ability.
- A PhD student told me recently about a series of elite interviews she had conducted where she had "messed up" because she had been overwhelmed with anxiety by the seniority of the professionals she was interviewing. I suggested that most interviewees, no matter how senior, will assume that someone studying for a PhD is more intelligent than they are and may be worried about their own ignorance or inadequacies being revealed in a research interview. I encouraged her to try to empathize with her interviewees, to lose sight of her own insecurities as she tapped into theirs, to encourage them gently to relax, and enjoy themselves as they opened up to her.

Learn to spot time wasters and users—and work out how to say "no" to them

I am always acutely aware that an hour wasted with the wrong practitioner is an hour I could have spent on research. Earlier in this chapter I explained how I try to spot time wasters and users so I will not say more here.

Always build in opportunities to learn something new—and remember to shut up and listen

At the end of a day of speaking to practitioners I sometimes wonder: if my commitment to engagement is genuine, then why do I feel used up? Why do I feel as though I have "given away" my expertise and have "received" nothing in return? When we have something that other people want, and which we want to share, how do we replenish ourselves intellectually? Every academic who wants to engage seriously with the world of practice needs to develop answers to these questions. I make it a rule, for example, that whenever I agree to give a speech to a professional service firm, I conduct a series of interviews with organizational members beforehand. This enables me to tailor my material directly to their concerns, and ensures that my speech has considerably greater impact. It also means that I am learning even as I am lecturing. By saying "no" to the majority of requests I receive for public speaking, I limit the amount of time I spend in "broadcast" mode and make sure I spend plenty of time in "receive."

Only agree to speak or offer advice where you have a deep expertise— and ruthlessly protect your academic legitimacy

The professionals I choose to work with are as intelligent and expert as I am in their chosen field and are an exceptionally demanding audience. Some years ago, as a way of overcoming my profound anxiety about public speaking, I made it a rule to only agree to speak to practitioners about topics where I was one of the world's leading authorities. Anyone with a PhD is by definition the world's leading authority on *something* and our academic careers are essentially a project in expanding the range of areas in which we can legitimately claim a unique expertise. The more we engage with practitioners, and the more we come to be seen as authorities with interesting things to say, the more we will be asked to talk outside our area, to over-simplify our message, to eliminate the nuances of our argument, and to tell practitioners what they want to hear. We are under pressure to become "public intellectuals," but I believe strongly that the word "intellectual" should always take precedence over the word "public." We should always be wary that our desire to engage with practitioners does not lead us to undermine our credibility as academics. Practitioners believe what we say because they assume we know what we are talking about. It is important we do not betray that trust.

Never do research for money—always charge well for consulting

I have always funded my research through research council grants and have never done contract research for organizations, or allowed a firm I am studying to pay my expenses. Because of the rigorous professional training I received in my previous career as a management consultant, I take the consultant/client relationship very seriously and maintain a clear separation between the services

I offer my clients and the data I gather from my research sites. The power relationships between consultant/client and researcher/research site are entirely different and, I believe, incommensurable. As a consultant, I am there to serve the client; as a researcher, the research site is there to serve the research. As a consultant, any insights I develop are confidential to the client; as a researcher, any insights I publish are a "public good." When working as a consultant, it is important to value yourself, to charge accordingly, and to be prepared to walk away from a lot of work that comes your way. Tacit knowledge is notoriously difficult to value and professionals use a variety of tactics, including pricing, to convince their clients that they have knowledge that is worth paying for. If we do not value the insights we offer practitioners, we cannot expect practitioners to value them either.

Conclusions

It is easy for academics to devalue themselves. We are required to submit to a relentless stream of increasingly intrusive and largely meaningless performance metrics, critiqued and rejected by anonymous colleagues through the peer review process, and subjected to continuous cuts in funding and administrative support. As we are de-professionalized, it is easy to internalize this de-professionalization (Knights & Clarke, 2014) and to see ourselves as just another group of wage slaves, no different from the practitioners we are studying. But to practitioners we *are* different. Academics know that PhD students are at the bottom of the academic food chain and that the status of Professors has been substantially devalued in recent years, but to practitioners a PhD student is an exceptionally clever individual and a Professor is someone who has scaled the heights of an erudite profession. Both academics and practitioners are correct.

While I would never advocate academic arrogance, I do think it is important for us to remember that our academic status lends weight and authority to what we have to say. Practitioners may object to our "ivory towers" and "academic navel gazing," but the strength of their criticisms reflects their disappointment in us. They want us to be wise and insightful, to have the answers to the questions that beset them, and they are frustrated and resentful when we fail them.

As many of the contributors to this book makes clear, academia is beginning to change. In the next REF, an increasing proportion of a university's ranking will be based on Impact Case Studies which will outline the impact of selected academics' research on practitioners. My work with KPMG and the FRC represents an ideal Impact Case Study. By enhancing the research ranking of my university under the REF, my engagement with practitioners should translate directly into substantial government funding for my institution. My relationship with my university has come full circle.

The nature of liminal space between research and practice is, therefore, changing. Academics who choose to journey backwards and forwards between the worlds of research and practice may continue to do so alone, but we are now more aware of our fellow travelers. This book in itself represents a dwelling place in the liminal space of the research–practice divide where we can "hang out" with like-minded colleagues engaged in similar journeys. However, we still have a long way to go before our endeavors become legitimized. Being invited to write a chapter for this book is an honor and a pleasure, but it does not "count" in terms of my university's performance metrics. To quote my earlier performance appraisal, it is "a complete waste of time." We must never lose sight of the importance of continuing to publish in "legitimate" academic journals.

Recently the CPSF established an alliance with Harvard Law School's Center on the Legal Profession and I have become a Senior Research Fellow at Harvard. This opens up a whole new realm of possibilities for research and engagement. As the academic environment starts to change, I hope that more and more researchers, who share a commitment to conducting rigorous research and making a positive difference to practitioners, will come together and collaborate. If we do so, the possibilities for impact will be infinite.

Notes

1 At my university, this calculation is based on a faculty member's four "best" publications over the six-year REF period, multiplied by the value accorded by the ABS (Association of Business Schools) to the journals in which they were published.
2 The 2014 REF included a section on "Impact" where universities were invited to submit Impact Case Studies, outlining how particular pieces of published research had had an impact on organization, society, and the economy more generally. Due to the REF rules I was unable to submit an Impact Case Study, in spite of the fact that my research had had significant impact in many organizations, because the research had been published while I was at Oxford and could not, therefore, be included in an Impact Case Study for Cass Business School.
3 According to the UK's Audit Firm Governance Code, the largest UK accounting firms are required to appoint independent non-executives. Their role is to safeguard the public interest. As these firms are partnerships, INEs are not technically board directors, but their roles are similar in other respects. The key distinction is that they have an expanded accountability to stakeholders rather than to shareholders (i.e., the public rather than simply the partners of the firm).
4 Partnerships are notoriously insular and resistant to outsider influence (Empson, Cleaver & Allen, 2013).

References

Bartunek, J. M. (2003). A dream for the Academy. *Academy of Management Review*, 28(2), 198–203.
Bartunek, J. & Rynes, S. (2014). Academics and practitioners are alike and unlike: The paradoxes of academic–practitioner relationships. *Journal of Management*, 40(5), 1181–201.
Beech, N. (2011). Liminality and the practices of identity reconstruction. *Human Relations*, 64(2), 285–302.
Butler, N. & Spoelstra, S. (2014). The regime of excellence and the erosion of ethos in Critical Management Studies. *British Journal of Management*, 25(3), 538–50.
Clarke, C., Knights, D. & Jarvis, C. (2012). A labour of love? Academics in business schools. *Scandinavian Journal of Management*, 28(1), 5–15.

Dale, K. & Burrell, G. (2008). *The Spaces of Organization and the Organization of Space: Power, Identity, and Materiality at Work.* London: Palgrave.

Empson, L. (2013). My affair with the "other": Identity journeys across the research–practice divide. *Journal of Management Inquiry*, 22(2), 229–48.

Empson, L., Cleaver, I. & Allen, J. (2013). Managing partners and management professionals: Institutional work dyads in professional partnerships. *Journal of Management Studies*, 50(5), 808–44.

Gabriel, Y. (2010). Organization studies: A space for ideas, identities and agonies. *Organization Studies*, 31(6), 757–75.

Gulati, R. (2007). Tent poles, tribalism and boundary spanning: The rigor–relevance debate in management research. *Academy of Management Journal*, 50(4), 775–82.

Hambrick, D. (1994). 1993 presidential address: What if the academy actually mattered? *Academy of Management Review*, 19, 11–16.

Huff, A. (2000). Changes in organizational knowledge production. *Academy of Management Review*, 25(2), 288–93.

Knights, D. & Clarke, C. (2014). It's a bittersweet symphony, this life: Fragile academic selves and insecure identities at work. *Organization Studies*, 35(3), 335–57.

Lucas, L. (2006). *The Research Game in Academic Life.* Maidenhead, UK: Open University.

Martin, B. (2011). The Research Excellence Framework and the "impact agenda": Are we creating a Frankenstein monster? *Research Evaluation*, 20(3), 247–54.

Mohrman, S., Gibson, C. & Mohrman, A. (2001). Doing research that is useful to practice: A model and empirical exploration. *Academy of Management Journal*, 44(2), 357–75.

Shorter, B. (1988). *An Image Darkly Forming: Women and Initiation.* London: Routledge.

Shortt, H. (2015). Liminality, space and the importance of "transitory dwelling places" at work. *Human Relations*, 68(4), 633–58.

Thomassen, B. (2006). Liminality. In Harrington, A., Marshall, B. L. & Muller, H. P. (Eds.) *Encyclopedia of Social Theory.* Abingdon, UK: Routledge.

Tourish, D. (2015). Rank irrelevance. *Times Higher Education*, March 19, pp. 32–3.

Turner, V. (1967). *The Forest of Symbols: Aspects of Ndembu Rituals.* Ithaca, NY: Cornell University Press.

Turner, V. (1982). *From Ritual to Theatre: The Human Seriousness of the Play.* New York: Performing Arts Journal Publications.

Van Gennep, A. (1961). *The Rites of Passage.* Chicago, IL: University of Chicago Press.

Willmott, H. (2011). Journal list fetishism and the perversion of scholarship: Reactivity and the ABS list. *Organization*, 18(4), 429–42.

13 Partnering to advance sustainable effectiveness at the center for effective organizations

Susan Albers Mohrman

The Center for Effective Organizations (CEO) in the Marshall School at the University of Southern California (https://ceo.usc.edu/) was founded in 1978 by Ed Lawler to embody the principles of collaborative, adaptive research, and to focus on key issues of organizational effectiveness. I have been a research scientist there since 1981.

The CEO's mission is to conduct research which generates knowledge that advances practice and academic understanding of organizations (Mohrman & Mohrman, 2011). Our publication strategy is to report the results of our research in both practitioner and academic outlets. Our dual focus combines a collaborative approach between academics and organizational practitioners (Shani, Mohrman, Pasmore, Stymne & Adler, 2007) with rigorous research methodologies that build on existing theory and knowledge while working to expand it and direct it to today's contexts and the critical problems that organizations are facing.

The CEO approach to research

Several elements of our approach stem from our intent not only to collaborate with organizational practitioners in the creation of knowledge, but also to ensure that the knowledge we partner to create is useful in practice. These include:

- a focus on how organizations are designed to address the challenges they are facing that stem from the rapid change in the market, societal, and environmental contexts in which they operate;
- the use of multimethod and multidiscipline collaborative approaches;
- concern with multi-stakeholder outcomes;
- problem-focused research;
- clarifying changing purposes; and
- being aware of the full value stream through which knowledge is produced and influences practice (Mohrman & Lawler, 2011).

Focus on organizational design

A major stream of the CEO's research has been guided by our interests in how organizations design themselves to accomplish their purposes, how they generate and incorporate knowledge, and how they continually reconfigure to accomplish desired outcomes and achieve the purposes of their stakeholders (Mohrman, 2007; Mohrman & Cummings, 1989; Worley & Mohrman, 2015). These interests reflect the perspective that organizations are social artifacts, built and changed by people to accomplish their purposes (Simon, 1969). The study of organizations thus can be conceptualized as the multilevel study of how people as individuals and collectives go about organizing to accomplish their purposes, making it impossible to truly understand organizations without understanding the purposes of their members, and how purposes change through time.

A constant focus in the CEO's organization design research has been to generate knowledge about how organizations learn and redesign themselves as they adjust to the changing context in which they operate. This naturally extends beyond the study of organizational forms to include a focus on collaborative research itself as a source of learning and of redesigning and on the dynamics of such research that are related to the application of the knowledge generated (Mohrman, Gibson & Mohrman, 2001).

The co-evolution of technological capabilities and the global economy, changes in geopolitical and societal contexts, and more recently the heightened awareness of constraints due to the limits of our natural environment have led to fundamental changes in the nature of organizations, even challenging deeply embedded assumptions about purpose. The many organizations with which we have partnered are seeking knowledge to help them become more agile to cope with the rapidity of these changes and with relentless pressures for new levels and types of performance that often require the development of new capabilities.

Multi-method and multidiscipline collaborative approaches

Our collaborative research studies take many forms. Action research, including the application of organizational knowledge to intentionally generate and implement design changes to achieve organizational purposes and the systematic assessment of impact, enable a deep understanding of how organizations reconfigure themselves to change their capabilities. In this design research, we look for "outliers"— organizations that are using or developing new organizational approaches to establish a performance advantage and/or to better achieve positive impact on stakeholders (Starbuck, 2006). Among the approaches they are using are:

- more directly engaging the workforce in the success of the business;
- developing new ways to collaborate within and across organizations, including new partnership relationships with customers and other stakeholders; and
- finding new ways to access and foster the growth and development of the knowledge and skills necessary in the rapidly changing world of work.

We establish loosely coupled consortia involving multiple companies and academic partners from several universities and several disciplines to investigate challenges occasioned at particular junctures in the evolution of companies. Examples have included multi-company investigations of the transition to increasingly lateral organizational forms accompanying the emergence of cross-functional team-based organizations (Mohrman, Cohen & Mohrman, 1995), and of the virtual work and geographically dispersed networks made possible by new technological capabilities (Gibson & Cohen, 2003).

The work of the research consortia includes case-based, exploratory action research in several companies to develop a deep understanding of the challenges of making these transitions, and of the organizational dynamics and design features that contribute to effectiveness. The research programs also include co-planned, multi-company longitudinal investigations of the organizational features that contribute to success in achieving the new ways of operating. Analytical approaches based on data from surveys and structured interviews, and performance assessment methodologies are used to measure impact on outcomes of interest (e.g., Mohrman, Mohrman & Finegold, 2003a). Consortia members come together periodically to collaboratively plan the studies, share and interpret the learnings, identify knowledge gaps that need to be investigated, and to co-plan further research activities.

The conduct of these field-based studies is of necessity collaborative. The academic participants bring an understanding of research methodology and theoretical foundations that guide research design to focus on key variables and their relationships. We rely on the deep knowledge of practice that comes from our organizational colleagues to navigate the meaning systems in their organizations and so make it more likely that we are actually studying what we set out to study. The company participants also help identify and develop the relationships with the appropriate parts of the organization to examine the phenomena of interest, to carry out the logistics of the study, and to help interpret the findings and share perspectives on relevance and further knowledge that is needed to apply them effectively to accomplish their purposes. Academics' purposes include the generation of both theoretical and practically useful knowledge. For organizational practitioners, the purpose is to gain knowledge to impact the organizational outcomes of concern (Mohrman et al., 2001). In the examples above, the knowledge generated was about team-based (Mohrman et al., 1995) and virtual work (Gibson & Cohen, 2003) and about the design features that are required for these approaches to be successful.

Problem-focused research

A problem-focused approach has guided much of the work we have done at CEO. Our topics have roots in our own experience-based and theoretical interests in organization, but they emerge and are shaped in close interaction with practitioners. Problem-focused research provides a natural home for and evokes a need for collaboration that brings together multiple perspectives, including those of theory and practice. Many important problems are not readily resolvable within any single community of practice. They call for the combination of knowledge from multiple perspectives, types of expertise, and disciplines (Stokes, 1997; Van de Ven, 2007). Problems create a context in which practitioners are likely to be open to influence from research. Problems represent anomalies, and present a need to step outside the daily reality that is driven by implicit theories and existing solutions, and to try to achieve a detachment that enables the search for new understandings that can guide action (Argyris, 1996; Schön, 1983; Weick, 2003).

Concern with multi-stakeholder outcomes

We have kept a constant focus on the impact of organization on multiple stakeholders, including owners, customers, employees, and increasingly the communities, societies, and natural environment in which organizations operate. Early in the history of our research center we used approaches such as union–management collaboration to research ways of increasing the stake and involvement of workers in the organizations in which they are employed (Lawler, 1982). In the past decade, our studies have involved many stakeholders and multiple organizations, often from different sectors, that are partnering with each other to understand how to organize both within and across organizations to collectively address complex societal problems.

The problem of increasing access and effectiveness of healthcare is an example. Addressing the challenge of driving down costs to a sustainable level while delivering needed population health care involves insurance companies, health care delivery systems, professional groups, the government, the companies that employ and provide healthcare benefits to the majority of our population, and the behavior of individual patients and their families (Mohrman & Shani, 2012). Solutions to such mega-problems extend well beyond improving the organizational effectiveness of any one actor and involve intertwined organizational and individual behavior changes. These problems are situated in deeply intertwined but loosely coupled complex systems.

The problems and challenges that organizations face are increasingly systemic, including:

- operating efficiently and effectively across multiple cultures and societies;
- embracing, adjusting to, and preserving the diversity that must be the wellspring of human progress;
- dealing with the issues of social justice; and
- operating sustainably in a world characterized by resource constraints and climate change impacts.

Large companies are increasingly dominating the distribution of resources and wealth and shaping the prevailing behavior patterns and distribution of benefit in society (Waddock, 2015). How they organize and the purposes they pursue have an outsized impact on their stakeholders, and on the interests that receive attention and whose purposes are addressed. This fact, when added to considerations of justice and sustainability, calls out for an expansion of both company and academic focus on a broad set of stakeholders and their outcomes (Freeman, Harrison, Wicks, Parmar & DeColle, 2011). In our view, it also calls for research consortia that include multiple stakeholders, in order to assure that their voices are heard and that the knowledge and purposes that are incorporated are not artificially constrained and shaped by narrow interests, thereby limiting purchase on the problems.

Clarifying and aligning purposes

Today's challenges can't be addressed by single companies trying to find approaches that give them a competitive advantage and make them winners or by lone academics pursuing individual research programs. Rather, we believe that to be viable and relevant in the future, companies must expand their purposes and design themselves to add value to society beyond wealth and jobs creation, and academics must consider complex systemic interactions among system dynamics and the achievement of multiple purposes.

Organizations are increasingly facing, and often contributing to, resource and environmental constraints and degradation, and backlash due to concerns for social justice. NGOs and governments in many parts of the world are taking measures to ensure that companies' licenses to operate depend on their social responsibility in the face of pressing social and environmental challenges. Single companies and individuals cannot gain significant purchase on these large systemic issues. At best they can become more sustainable individually (Ehrenfeld & Hoffman, 2013). As in all complex systems, changes in the overall outcomes of the system require changing the interaction patterns of its many agents (Holland, 2014). Similarly, isolated pockets of knowledge generation activity, even when crystallized in peer reviewed articles and in practitioner publications, have very little influence on how organizations are evolving as systems and on whether they are meeting the needs of humanity. To have such influence will require shared purpose and collective knowledge generation to align the focus of academic researchers and their practitioner partners to yield ways of organizing to address redefined outcomes.

Concern with the full knowledge value stream

We have come to believe that in order to be useful, knowledge has not only to be collaboratively created and formalized, but also has to find pathways to practice that transcend the participants in particular research consortia or research partnerships. The generation of useful knowledge, like the generation of other products and services that are consumed by and that shape society, can be thought of as a value stream from inputs to making that knowledge accessible to and usable by its consumers. Each step of the value stream contributes value to the whole flow. Particular participants can be involved in some or all of the elements of the flow, but if the value stream stops short of the intended beneficiaries of the flow, the outputs are neither useful nor used.

Figure 13.1 shows this flow as we have come to conceive of it (Mohrman & Lawler, 2011). It starts with connecting and combining the knowledge from multiple academic disciplines and organizational practices that are collaborating and creating synergies in the conduct of problem-focused research. The remainder of the value stream has not traditionally been a concern of academic researchers, but our view is that awareness of how knowledge can and does travel from research to practice is a prerequisite for useful research. Producing knowledge that is "potentially" useful to address real world problems and even partnering with practitioners in its generation are insufficient to lead to broad application. Through close collaboration with our corporate research partners, we have learned that they have difficulty applying knowledge even from collaborative studies if the results aren't translated into language and action frameworks that enable organizational members to understand its relevance to issues they confront (Mohrman et al., 2001). The full value stream includes this translational work.

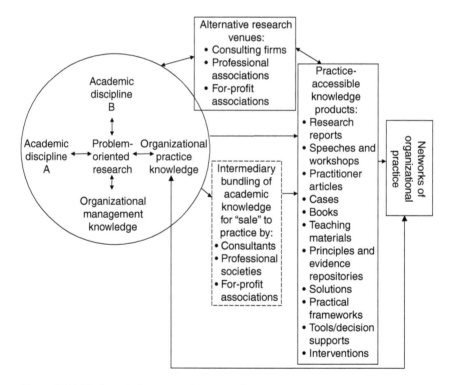

Figure 13.1 The knowledge-generating network.

Source: Adapted from Mohrman et al., 2011.

Figure 13.1 points out that impact is achieved only if the research network connects to actors who are farther down the value stream, including to those who ultimately incorporate the knowledge into their practice. Knowledge can't be tested and extended until it is applied. Feedback to researchers about how and whether the knowledge works in practice is an input to future research. The feedback loop from application in practice to the research community is particularly important given the dynamic and systemic nature of organizations. Adopting new knowledge enables changes to how organizations operate and thus substantively changes phenomena being studied in ways that can't be completely anticipated. Knowledge is applied in contexts that are themselves continuously changing so that applicable knowledge has to be continuously updated to reflect the new realities.

This view of the useful research value stream has led us to expand our network of collaboration to include connection to internal and external consultants and members of professional societies who are concerned with the development of broadly available guidance to practice through such mechanisms as practice-oriented webinars, publications, workshops, and learning networks. These groups are closely connected to shifting organizational contexts.

Purposefully assembled consortia of researchers and practitioners may be established to combine different knowledge bases to carry out a problem-focused research program. These may be built to connect to the translational processes of converting research-generated knowledge into practice. The collaborative research can generate broad learnings that can be captured in principles for practice, and create prototypes of new forms of organization such as through action research. The CEO's early work exploring organizations' use of purposefully designed internal and external learning networks to enable the scale up of large-scale work system innovations applied such an approach (Mohrman, Tenkasi & Mohrman, 2003b). The research collaboration involved multiple companies and a team of academics interested in the role of networks in knowledge creation and dissemination. Based on the research findings, models and frameworks were created by our research partners to communicate to others in their companies and in their professional societies.

In the remainder of this chapter, I will describe a research program that examines Design for Sustainable Effectiveness in which we are working with many colleagues in a collaborative research approach tailored to fit with the systemic nature of today's sustainability challenges. Our collective aspiration is to accelerate the generation of knowledge to address seemingly intractable systemic problems.

Design for sustainable effectiveness: a research program

The Design for Sustainable Effectiveness research program has its genesis in the pressing need to develop new organizational approaches to address the complex sustainability problems that threaten humanity and the earth. Academia, commercial, and civil society organizations, individuals in many companies, communities throughout the world, and governments have played roles in defining and trying to address this emergent focus. The challenges include:

- climate change and its attendant risks and financial and human costs;
- environmental degradation;
- population growth beyond the carrying capacity of the earth;
- global economic growth and associated resource shortages;
- demographic shifts in both developed and developing nations that threaten the capability of nation states to deliver important infrastructure and services;
- social and economic inequities and unrest; and
- changes in expectations and aspirations around the globe that are putting an ever-increasing demand on the limited resources of the earth.

This research program focuses specifically on how organizations can design for sustainable functioning, contributing to the economic, social, and environmental outcomes necessary for the viability of humanity and our planet. Corporations have played an integral role in creating and maintaining the global economy that is tightly linked to the unsustainable status quo. Many scholars and practitioners believe that a significant bend toward greater global sustainability cannot occur unless companies play a central role in the transition. Many corporate leaders also believe that companies are going to have to learn to operate differently to take a leadership role to address social and environmental challenges and a future where resources are scarce (Hayward, Lee, Keeble, McNamara, Hall, Cruse, Gupta & Robinson, 2013). Because the term sustainability is used in many ways, we use an expansive definition: fostering sustainable effectiveness involves increasing the value that is delivered to stakeholders, while decreasing the resources that are consumed in the process.

Our research collaboration to investigate this domain of concern began in 2008, with institutional and personal collaborations between researchers at CEO, Cal Poly San Luis Obispo, Politechnica di Milano, and Chalmers University in Gothenburg, Sweden. Researchers in each of these academic institutions were already conducting collaborative field research with organizations that were embarking on different approaches to increase sustainability. Together we formulated an approach to build a network to achieve synergy between related collaborative knowledge-generating activities that had been going on independently and in parallel in these institutions and others.

The network is formed and maintained by convening topical conferences that involve academic researchers and their practitioner partners in collaborating organizations to share systematic, theory-driven and methodologically sound case analyses of approaches that are being taken to become more sustainable and the outcomes that are being achieved. Systematically coding and integrating the themes and knowledge that emerge from the different conference cases frames the publication of the cases and learnings in a volume in Emerald Press's *Organizing For Sustainable Effectiveness* series (Series Editors: Susan Albers

Mohrman, Abraham (Rami) Shani & Christopher Worley). In the final chapter of the volume, important issues and knowledge gaps are identified to guide future research, including, we hope, research by academics beyond those who are part of the consortium. Our goal is to operate on a yearly cycle. Each volume of the book series has editors who are particularly interested in the focus of the conference upon which it is based. They solicit and identify the case roster for the conference, and commit to the integration of the knowledge from the conference. They take the lead in crafting a volume that is theoretically framed, includes rich case descriptions and theoretical analyses, and is written to be accessible to academics and reflective practitioners.

Little is known about organizational design for sustainability. The vast majority of organizational research has been conducted in organizations working within a traditional wealth optimization paradigm, and we are just beginning to understand how the assumptions, variables of interest, and dynamics underpinning organizational science will have to be modified to accommodate the expansion of the objective function. We seek a diversity of academic disciplines, functional membership, organizational settings, and organizing approaches to learn about achieving multiple outcomes. This diversity of approaches and theoretical foundations is intended to cumulatively and rapidly provide rich accounts of different approaches being taken by organizations to achieve sustainability, and of different theoretical lenses that can provide leverage in developing knowledge to guide both theoretical and practical progress in this relatively new field of exploration. Sharing multiple diverse cases provides the opportunity for cross-case comparisons that enable the discovery of important commonalities in substantive and organizational approaches, and examination of organizational factors related to effectiveness.

For the academic participants, the work presented at the conference is part of their broader research programs. In essence they bring the knowledge from their own network of collaborators and activities to the consortium, and their own positioning in the value stream of knowledge generation. This includes other studies and academic- and practitioner-oriented publications, and sometimes partnerships with downstream consulting firms or professional societies, offering diverse pathways through the value stream to influence practice. This broadens the network of connectedness and potential impact of the knowledge that stems from this consortium. In the following sections we will examine the theoretical frame for this consortium approach, how the network grew and developed, and the dissemination strategies.

The theoretical frame for this approach to knowledge creation

Both the research approach and our overall framing of the domain of organizing for sustainability is based on complexity theory. It views organizations as actors in complex interdependent environments (Holland, 2014). Actors, both independently and interdependently, adapt in order to carry out their purposes, and in so doing have both intended and unintended impacts on the contexts in which they operate. System-level outcomes and problems cannot be addressed within the confines of single organizations. The system overall can only be sustainable if organizations individually and collectively learn new ways of operating and interacting. System-wide outcomes cannot be centrally driven, but depend on the relationships that develop within the system to manage the full value stream for the consumption of fewer resources and the delivery of greater value to stakeholders, and on the learning that occurs that enables accelerated improvement in both.

The knowledge production approaches in this research program reflect our view of complexity, and our view that current academic knowledge-generation processes are too fragmented and too slow to create the knowledge required to inform ongoing fundamental change. New ways of examining organizations and new models of organizational effectiveness are required. Similarly, new approaches to knowledge generation are required that support collective learning and the invention of solutions. How individuals, organizations, groups of organizations, networks, and communities are learning to operate in a sustainable manner is a major focus of the research. We believe that research partnerships between academics and organizational practitioners can be an element of how this learning happens.

We have employed several approaches to try to address the sustainability of the research program itself, considering it a dynamic set of relationships in the larger emergent system of organizational and academic actors addressing the domain. Our broad definition of sustainability is one such approach, inviting actors with many different perspectives and purposes into the conversation. This fits with our view that redirecting toward sustainability entails a continuous dynamic adaptive process of individuals, organizations, and systems striving to be proactive, and moving upstream and downstream in interaction with each other to identify issues and improve and develop organizational and inter-organizational processes. The consortium is itself an emergent system, and its work must likewise be agile, including shifting membership in forums for co-learning, and the regular sharing of knowledge to advance and refocus the collective research agenda. Although this approach may not be viewed as fundamentally different from more traditional academic communities, it is the collaboration across the network, and the consideration of knowledge and purposes of multiple communities of practice that differentiates it and grounds it firmly in the nexus between theory and the practices of academics and organizational practitioners, allowing solutions to emerge.

The consortium includes a fluid assembly of multiple actors, disciplines, functions, and sectors that are involved in generating solutions to sustainability challenges. The collaborative research mirrors the richness of the focal eco-systems by including varied theoretical and methodological approaches. Although all the projects shared at the consortium are collaborative field-based projects, they employ different research approaches. Some use qualitative interview and observation-based data collection and analysis to find patterns and develop theory about the dynamics of the transition to more sustainable functioning. Others use action research and quantitative evaluation research methodologies for applying and testing theory during the design and implementation of new organizational forms. The research teams investigating the generation of new practices and designs include members who have knowledge of organizational design principles, change and development theory, or of specific content focuses such as leadership, strategy implementation, financial measurement, and inter-organizational collaboration. A stronger sense of the membership can be gleaned by viewing the co-authors of the various chapters in the Emerald *Organizing for Sustainable Effectiveness* series.

Developing and growing the network and its focus

Our first network meeting in 2008 included ten case examples from healthcare organizations, cities, natural resources companies, consumer products companies, transportation companies, the Port Authority of Los Angeles, waste and recycling companies, and manufacturing companies. These organizations were implementing and testing a broad variety of approaches both individually and in cross-organizational partnerships, and in so doing were learning how to operate in a more sustainable manner. Each organization was already connected to academics and/or consultants who were partnering with them to study and learn from their sustainability initiatives. Although both academics and organizational practitioners attended the conference and were involved in the analysis and discussion of the cases, the case presentations were made by the organizational practitioners in order to stay grounded in their empirical reality and purposes. This same approach has been followed in subsequent conferences.

At each conference, presentations of the projects are grouped by similarity of approach and focus. For example, three action research projects that entail collaboration between corporations and NGOs may be presented on one morning, followed by cross-project break-out groups discussing and then combining the knowledge themes that they have pulled from these projects. The second and subsequent segments will have cases with different focuses and approaches and will similarly be followed by cross-project discussions of learnings. In this way multiple perspectives are involved in the interpretation of the data. Participants spend the last half day of the conference building on the themes that have emerged from each segment of the conference, and drawing out overall common themes, identifying gaps of knowledge, and talking about their hopes for future work by the consortium.

The foundational conference yielded key themes in the transition to sustainable functioning captured in Volume 1 of the Emerald series and provided a platform for the articulation of future directions of the consortium. One theme is the inherently cross-functional and cross-organizational nature of sustainability approaches and the need to learn more about how organizations can design to align multiple functions and organizations around shared sustainability objectives. A related theme is that moving to a more sustainable way of functioning entails the integration of processes along the full value stream, including the upstream and downstream portions of the value stream that may not be controlled by the organization of focus. Another theme focuses on the change in the nature of leadership to include being a catalyst for the development of expanded purpose, and building the capacity for shared leadership in the organization. The cases also yield an appreciation of the extent to which putting in place explicit change and learning approaches needed for the organization to become more sustainable is itself a key component of organizing for sustainable effectiveness.

The research program is recursive, as the knowledge from each conference is the basis for the definition of the focus of the next. The researchers and interested practitioners are invited for a third day of integration of learnings from the previous two days, with an eye to framing the volume that will be written based on this conference, and collectively defining the focus for the next conference. Participants also identify additional sustainability researchers and specific projects that could be brought into the next conference to enable empirically based learning in areas that were identified as important to making progress in understanding the domain.

An expanding set of international researchers and practitioners from different disciplines and functions in many universities, companies, governmental bodies, and NGOs have participated in this consortium. Increasing the empirical base, the breadth of problems being addressed, and methodological approaches being utilized deepens and increases the scope of knowledge that is both the input to and the output from the collaborative knowledge-producing consortium. This dynamic network collaboration approach is intended to increase relevance and speed of knowledge generation, sharing, and dissemination to better address the urgent sustainability challenges we face.

The consortium develops based on the energies and learnings of its members. For example, at the first conference, several healthcare organizations were particularly eager to quickly explore the themes that had been identified. Healthcare is a key sustainability domain for most of the countries of the world. It also provides an empirical laboratory for examining the cross-functional, cross-organizational, and transformational theoretical knowledge about change to a more sustainable organizational model. Ten healthcare systems were easily identified that had a significant focus on becoming more sustainable by delivering greater value to stakeholders using fewer resources, and that were already partnering with academic researchers. Thus, our second conference (and second volume) focused on the healthcare domain, while investigating the themes that had emerged from the foundational conference and discovering additional thematic focuses.

The learnings from this second conference were viewed by the participants as so valuable theoretically and practically that the participants in that 2010 conference decided to take the lead in organizing our fourth conference, which specifically focused on the required eco-system transformation of healthcare, and brought in five additional healthcare systems with collaborative inter-organizational research projects underway. In the interim, consortium members organized and participated in several more focused conferences to quickly investigate and make progress with respect to the generation and dissemination of healthcare specific knowledge. An example is a conference run by Cornell University in 2010: Healthcare Delivery System Reform and the Implications for the Workforce. It examined the role of the healthcare labor force in moving to a more sustainable way of delivering healthcare. It included five collaborative teams from the original consortium meeting, as well as many other teams from other healthcare projects. Knowledge from those parallel conferences was shared with the expanding group of research teams.

The collaborative research network isn't unfolding linearly in a neat and tidy way. It emerges as it builds on the enthusiasm of its members, who now have a model and framework for proceeding in multiple related directions. While some members were focusing on pulling together the healthcare conferences, other members of the consortium pulled together the third consortium conference, focused on cross-organizational, trans-sectoral, and system-level change initiatives. It brought additional researchers, organizations, and sectors, and a whole new set of empirical examples into the consortium. This conference generated input knowledge for the next two conferences. Conference four (2013) examined changes in the eco-system for healthcare. Conference five (2015) examined approaches being used to achieve a sustainable food chain. It was hosted at Politechnica di Milano specifically to build connections with other sustainable food supply knowledge-generating activities in conjunction with the 2015 Food Expo hosted by Italy and held in Milan. This conference introduced a new dimension for exploration, contrasting global approaches to creating a sustainable food chain with place-based approaches focusing on creating a local food chain. Understanding the impact of local and global organization has emerged as a key focus for knowledge generation about how to craft sustainable solutions.

For both the academics and organizational practitioners, being a member of this consortium was an extension of their learning journeys and of their professional networks. It provides opportunities to share and get feedback, and to exchange learnings and collectively generate knowledge. Each of these conferences expanded the consortium, and built expanded network connections to other forums to enable dissemination and cross-learning.

Dissemination

Conference case write-ups and most of the chapters in the Emerald volumes are written collaboratively by the researchers and the involved organizational practitioners (e.g., Doolin & Hamer, 2014; Steele & Feyerherm, 2013). The presenters in the conferences agree to author chapters in the Emerald Press series. They also agree that their chapters will include a clear statement of the sustainability problem, the case example, and their theoretical framework for investigating it and understanding it. The chapters are case and cross-case analyses, generally including measurement and quantitative analytic assessments of the impact of organizational approaches.

Each of the five volumes has begun with a chapter by the volume editors that describes the overall critical challenges and reviews what is known about the domain of focus for the volume. The volume includes eight to ten systematic cases, and ends with a chapter drawing out the key integrative themes that emerged during and after the conference through a systematic coding. The final chapter also includes a discussion that identifies areas that were identified as needing further exploration, with attention to both practical and theoretical knowledge gaps.

Beyond the Emerald volumes, the learnings from each of the cycles of the work of the consortium have been leveraged into a larger network. They have been the basis for symposia and workshops in professional societies, such as the Academy of Management meetings, EURAM, or more practitioner-oriented professional forums such as the Organization Design Forum. These workshops and symposia at large professional gatherings have been supplemented by the smaller very topical targeted conferences and exchanges aimed at further disseminating the findings from the consortium, and bringing a broader swath of collaborators and perspectives into the conversation. An example is a two-day conference, based largely on the findings from the first foundational meeting of our consortium, held at Cleveland State University in 2011. This meeting brought together interested academics, practitioners, and civic leaders from the Cleveland area who were engaged in sustainability work. The framework of knowledge from our foundational conference was used to critically assess the somewhat fragmented initiatives going on in the city with an eye to determining how creating connections and synergy could accelerate progress. The initiatives captured in several chapters of later volumes in the Emerald series had their genesis in this and other loosely connected forums. These very focused conferences are closer to practice, and often involve individuals further down the value stream than is depicted in Figure 13.1. They provide a feedback loop to the collaborative research network.

Discussion

The rhythm of activity in the Design for Sustainable Effectiveness research network is shown in Figure 13.2. It reflects our understanding of sustainable functioning of the knowledge-generating network, fostering acceleration, efficiency, leverage, and effectiveness of the knowledge generation and dissemination process through coordination, exchange, and synergy across organizations and stakeholders. This approach reflects the spirit of Van de Ven's (2007) framework for establishing research partnerships to address large problems. Extending his treatment, our network has been built of nested sub-networks of many collaborative teams designing and enacting studies and getting together to share, interpret, derive knowledge from cumulative projects in an accelerated fashion, and identify important focuses for future research. Further, our publication strategy reflects the intent to reach multiple communities of practice, academic and organizational.

The conferences and volume focuses are recursive. In many cases it becomes apparent from one conference that additional theoretical perspectives and

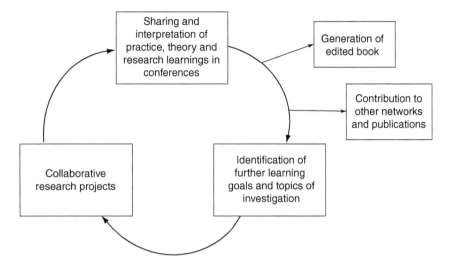

Figure 13.2 The knowledge-generating cycle in the design for sustainable effectiveness research program.

empirical examples will be required for a rich investigation of the research focuses that have been identified. Thus, each research conference and each volume reflects an expanded and evolved set of topics and settings for research projects and an expanded network of multidisciplinary and multi-stakeholder contributors.

Further, the network consists of many stakeholders and a variety of academic participants. The latter range from experienced and relatively new academics carrying out focused projects examining particular aspects of sustainability in specific settings to more senior and seasoned field researchers often engaged in multiple collaborative studies and working with teams of researchers and partners. Although it may be unrealistic for an early career academic to play a leadership role in a research consortium, participation in this network is a good way for researchers who are in the early stages of their careers to develop an understanding of how their work can fit into a more systemic framework for generating and disseminating knowledge to address the problems they care about.

Finally, the organizing activities required to build and keep the consortium healthy and growing are substantial, as are the logistics of securing funding for and organizing conferences. This consortium has benefitted from the fact that its founders are located in institutions that are supportive of building connections between academics and practitioners, and of the conduct of field-based research partnerships. It has also benefitted from the fact that the participants in the consortium care deeply about its purpose: to yield knowledge that enables the design of organizations and inter-organizational networks that contribute to a more sustainable world.

In conclusion, creating a sustainable world requires organizations to expand both their focus and the way they apply resources to include outcomes beyond financial success. Similarly, combining systematic collaborative research partnerships to study how this can occur requires academic researchers to expand their own focus and "objective function" to include the impact of their research on organizational outcomes beyond the tacitly accepted single focus on creation of wealth for owners. It does not mean abandoning rigor or academic publication. It does mean expanding focus and purposes, and finding ways to do research such that knowledge flows to practice. Just as organizations have found that sustainability depends on finding connections and leverage between functions and organizations, we believe that doing research that impacts practice is enabled by similar changes in the way academic researchers connect to the other stakeholders in the eco-systems they are studying, and to each other.

References

Argyris, C. (1996). Actionable knowledge: Design causality in the service of consequential theory. *Journal of Applied Behavioral Science*, 32(4), 390–406.

Doolin, B. & Hamer, A. W. (2014). Network-based transformation of cardiac care in New Zealand. In Mohrman, S. A. & Shani, A. B. (Eds.) *Reconfiguring the Ecosystem for Sustainable Healthcare* (Organizing for Sustainable Effectiveness, Vol. 4) (pp. 69–100). Bingley, UK: Emerald Group Publishing.

Ehrenfeld, J. & Hoffman, A. (2013). *Flourishing: A Frank Conversation on Sustainability*. Palo Alto, CA: Stanford University Press.

Freeman, R. E., Harrison, J. S., Wicks, A. C., Parmar, B. L. & DeColle, S. (2011). *Stakeholder Theory: The State of the Art*. Cambridge, UK: Cambridge University Press.

Gibson, C. & Cohen, S. (2003). *Virtual Teams that Work: Creating Conditions for Virtual Team Effectiveness*. San Francisco, CA: Jossey-Bass.

Hayward, R., Lee, J., Keeble, J., McNamara, R., Hall, C., Cruse, S., Gupta, P. & Robinson, E. (2013). Architects of a better world: CEOs on accelerating the journey from plateau to peak on sustainability. *Accenture and the UN Global Compact Report on Sustainability* 5(3), 1–60. Retrieved April 7, 2017 from www.ingentaconnect.com/content/ungc/ungcr/2013/00000005/00000003/art00001.

Holland, J. H. (2014). *Complexity: A Very Short Introduction*. Oxford: Oxford University Press.

Lawler, E. E. (1982). Strategies for improving the quality of work life. *American Psychologist*, 37, 486–93.

Mohrman, S. A. (2007). Designing organizations to lead with knowledge. In Cummings, T. (Ed.) *The Handbook of Organization Development* (pp. 519–38). Thousand Oaks, CA: Sage Publications.

Mohrman, S. A. & Cummings, T. G. (1989). *Self-Designing Organizations: Learning How to Create High Performance*. Reading, UK: Addison-Wesley.

Mohrman, S. A. & Lawler, E. E. (2011). Research for theory and practice: Framing the challenge. In Mohrman, S. A. & Lawler, E. E., III (Eds.) *Useful Research: Advancing Theory and Practice* (pp. 9–35). San Francisco, CA: Berrett-Koehler.

Mohrman, S. A. & Mohrman, A. M., Jr. (2011). Collaborative organization design research at the Center for Effective Organizations. In Mohrman, S. A. & Lawler, E. E.,

III (Eds.) *Useful Research: Advancing Theory and Practice* (pp. 57–80). San Francisco, CA: Berrett-Koehler.

Mohrman, S. A. & Shani, A. B. (Eds.) (2012). Organizing for sustainable healthcare: The emerging global challenge. In Mohrman, S. A & Shani A. B. (Eds.) *Organizing for Sustainable Healthcare* (pp. 1–39). London: Emerald Press.

Mohrman, S. A., Cohen, S. G. & Mohrman, A. M., Jr. (1995). *Designing Team-Based Organizations: New Applications for Knowledge Work.* San Francisco, CA: Jossey-Bass.

Mohrman, S. A., Gibson, C. B. & Mohrman, A. M., Jr. (2001). Doing research that is useful to practice. *Academy of Management Journal*, 44(2), 347–75.

Mohrman, S. A., Mohrman, A. M., Jr. & Finegold, D. (2003a). An empirical model of the organization knowledge system in new product development firms. *Journal of Engineering and Technology Management*, 20(1–2), 7–38.

Mohrman, S. A., Tenkasi, R. V. & Mohrman, A. M. (2003b). The role of networks in fundamental organizational change: A grounded analysis. *The Journal of Applied Behavioral Science*, 39(3), 301–23.

Schön, D. A. (1983). *The Reflective Practitioner: How Professionals Think in Action.* San Francisco, CA: Jossey-Bass.

Shani, A. B., Mohrman, S. A., Pasmore, W. A., Stymne, B. & Adler, N. (Eds.) (2007). *Handbook of Collaborative Management Research.* Thousand Oaks, CA: Sage Publications.

Simon, H. A. (1969). *The Sciences of the Artificial.* Cambridge, MA: MIT Press.

Starbuck, W. H. (2006). *The Production of Knowledge: The Challenge of Social Science Research.* Oxford: Oxford University Press.

Steele, B. & Feyerherm, A. (2013). Loblaw Sustainable Seafood: Transforming the seafood supply chain through network development and collaboration. In Worley, C. G. & Mirvis, P. H. (Eds.) *Building Networks and Partnerships* (Organizing for Sustainable Effectiveness, Vol. 3) (pp. 101–32). Bingley, UK: Emerald Group Publishing Limited.

Stokes, D. E. (1997). *Pasteur's Quadrant: Basic Science and Technological Innovation.* Washington, DC: Brookings Institution Press.

Van de Ven, A. H. (2007). *Engaged Scholarship: A Guide for Organizational and Social Research.* New York: Oxford University Press.

Waddock, S. (2015). Stewardship of the future: Large system change and company stewardship. In Mohrman, S. A., O'Toole, J. & Lawler, E. E., III (Eds.) *Corporate Stewardship: Achieving Sustainable Effectiveness.* Sheffield, UK: Greenleaf Publishing.

Weick, K. (2003). Theory and practice in the real world. In Tsoukas, H. & Knudsen, C. (Eds.) *The Oxford Handbook of Organization Theory: Meta-theoretical Perspective* (pp. 453–75). New York: Oxford University Press.

Worley, C. & Mohrman, S. A. (2015). Designing for sustainable effectiveness: The role of embeddedness and agility. In Mohrman, S. A., O'Toole, J. & Lawler, E. E., III (Eds.) *Corporate Stewardship: Achieving Sustainable Effectiveness* (pp. 112–33). Sheffield, UK: Greenleaf Publishing.

14 Mind the transformation gap

Knowledge exchange, interests, and identity in research–practice collaboration

Ralph Hamann and Kristy Faccer

Introduction

We aim to better understand the factors that influence knowledge exchange and co-production in collaborations between researchers and practitioners. So while Bartunek and Rynes (2014) suggest that there is "truth" in both scholarly camps arguing either for or against such collaborations, our premise is that productive interactions between researchers and practitioners may be more likely in some circumstances than in others, and that context matters (see Nonaka, Toyama & Konno, 2000). We do this by analyzing two such collaborative initiatives—the Network for Business Sustainability (South Africa) and the Southern Africa Food Lab—in which we have been intimately involved.

We make two overarching arguments:

- First, we argue that knowledge co-production across the research–practice boundary (Van de Ven & Johnson, 2006) will likely be frustrated unless the intersection between knowledge and participants' underlying interests is understood and catered for. That is, in Carlile's (2004) terms, if knowledge transformation in such collaboration is not addressed, even the more modest objective of knowledge translation may remain elusive.
- Second, we argue that an initiative is more likely to achieve this if participants' individual identities and the initiative's organizational identity involve some hybridity between research and practice, and allow for a pluralist approach to knowledge.

We proceed by providing some theoretical background for our analysis, motivating for and describing Carlile's (2004) knowledge-exchange model and salient features of the identity literature. We then briefly describe our two case studies and how we analyzed them. In the fourth section, we develop our first argument on the intersection between knowledge and interests and the need for knowledge transformation. In the fifth section, we explain our second argument on the role of interests and context. We then discuss our arguments and close with a conclusion.

Theoretical framing

While it is not a new topic (e.g., see Jantsch, 1970; Whitehead, 1928), there is a growing chorus of scholars and policy makers emphasizing both the need for and feasibility of closer collaboration between researchers and practitioners. This has been particularly pronounced in efforts to enhance the contribution of science to pressing social and ecological problems (e.g., Gibbons, Limoges, Nowotny, Schwartzman, Scott & Trow, 1994; Hirsch Hadorn, Hoffmann-Riem, Biber-Klemm, Grossenbacher-Mansuy, Joye, Pohl, Wisemann & Zemp, 2008; Kates, Clark, Corell, Hall, Jaeger, Lowe, McCarthy, Schellnhuber, Bolin, Dickson, Faucheux, Gallopin, Grubler, Huntley, Jager, Jodha, Kasperson, Mabogunje, Matson & Mooney, 2001). It has also featured prominently in the management field, where there has been some anxiety about the extent or manner in which management scholars' work influences managers (e.g., Ghoshal, 2005; Gulati, 2007; Hambrick, 1994, 2007; for more recent overviews, see Bartunek & Rynes, 2014; Kieser, Nicolai & Seidl, 2015). Even so, empirical work on such partnerships remains limited, especially in the management literature (Bartunek, Rynes & Daft, 2001; Kieser, Nicolai & Seidl, 2015; see also Bartunek and Rynes, Chapter 6 in this volume).

Bartunek and Rynes (2014) point out that much of this debate has been among scholars only, and it has been normative and partisan (see also Gulati, 2007). Scholars such as Van de Ven and Johnson (2006) call for greater collaboration, arguing that the differences between researchers and practitioners can be fruitfully exploited through "intellectual arbitrage." Others feel that these differences are insurmountable and any attempt to bridge research and practice will dilute scholars' quest for objectivity—hence McKelvey's (2006: 825) memorable response to Van de Ven and Johnson: "consulting addles the scientific mind." Bartunek and Rynes (2014) suggest that both camps have elements of "truth" and this paradox ought to be used to motivate and frame fresh perspectives and research on the topic.

We propose that such research ought to give greater attention to the contexts and circumstances that might influence whether and how collaboration and knowledge co-production between researchers and practitioners manifest over time. We also draw inspiration from scholars who have applied theory in their analysis of research–practice collaborations (e.g., as in the use of institutional logics by Kieser & Leiner, 2009; Swan, Bresnen, Robertson, Newell & Dopson, 2010). Specifically, we focus on frameworks developed in the literature on knowledge exchange across domain boundaries, and on identity. These choices were inspired by the literature and also our personal, multi-year experience in research–practice collaborations.

Knowledge exchange across domain boundaries

Recurring references have been made to the role of communication challenges and divergent interests among researchers and practitioners (Bartunek & Rynes,

2014; Kieser, Nicolai & Seidl, 2015). Indeed these are more general features of knowledge exchange between different domains. Carlile (2004) argues that there are three successively complex levels of such knowledge exchange. Mirvis (2008) applies this three-level framework to characterize managers' and researchers' learning in three collaborative management research forums. In this chapter, we build on this to arrive at a more (self-)critical conclusion about knowledge exchange in research–practice collaborations.

According to Carlile (2004), at the most basic level of exchange, knowledge may be *transferred* when a common syntax exists and there are no clashes of interests. But when this pool of common knowledge is limited and when there is novelty and change that make the meaning of words ambiguous and priorities unclear, such transfer of knowledge starts to break down. Knowledge *translation* becomes necessary. Face-to-face interactions and brokering roles for particular individuals are often important to negotiate new, shared meanings and to make tacit knowledge explicit.

The next level of complexity arises because actors in different domains are likely vested in the knowledge that they rely on. This is because they have spent a lot of effort building up this knowledge, and because their interests (and identities) are tied up with the use of this knowledge. The interdependence of knowledge domains in a shared project will give rise to tensions and trade-offs, and so actors will need to carefully negotiate not just their interests but also the underlying assumptions and concepts. This gives rise to the need for knowledge *transformation*. These three levels of knowledge exchange are summarized in Table 14.1.

In Carlile's (2004) example of a car-design process, all three levels of complexity had to be catered for. Until the 1980s, coordination and negotiation between the different engineering teams were supported by the use of a clay model. As time pressures and quality demands increased, the clay model was replaced by a computer-generated three-dimensional model. Having the 3-D tool calculate drag (and other important outcomes) highlighted the interdependencies and trade-offs between the knowledge domains. For instance, if the engine team's preferred motor raised the hood too much, and hence created drag problems, the team would need to reconsider its premises and approach. Tools such as the 3-D model thus become "boundary objects" that allow the creation of shared meaning and even knowledge transformation, when actors in different knowledge domains adjust their understanding with respect to and in negotiation with other domains. But they remain just that, tools, and cannot replace the often-difficult negotiation between actors from different domains. Carlile's three-level framework is useful because it alerts us to different forms that knowledge exchange can take in research–practice collaborations, and the complexities, opportunities, and challenges associated with them.

Table 14.1 Summary of Carlile's (2004) three levels of knowledge exchange

Level	Novelty and complexity	Nature of the knowledge boundary	Nature of the knowledge exchange
Transfer	Increasing novelty and complexity	*Syntactic boundary*: Differences and dependencies between actors are known; a common lexicon exists to share knowledge; novelty and change are limited.	*Knowledge transfer* relies on existing lexicon and information processing capacities. Challenges are related to processing larger amounts of information.
Translation		*Semantic boundary*: Differences and dependencies between actors are unclear; a common lexicon does not exist.	*Knowledge translation* relies on learning and the creation of shared meanings, often in cross-functional teams and involving boundary spanners. Challenges are related to making tacit knowledge explicit and to find agreement on shared interpretations.
Transformation		*Pragmatic boundary*: Differences and dependencies between actors are unclear, and they involve different interests that are "tied up" with actors' knowledge.	*Knowledge transformation* relies on negotiation involving significant practical and political effort, possibly assisted by the collaborative creation and prototyping of boundary objects.

Individual and organizational identities

The second theoretical framework that we use to support our analysis has to do with identity. Gulati (2007: 277) emphasizes how different scholars identify themselves as members of "tribes," depending on their views on the rigor-relevance relationship, and how this gives rise to "sometimes brutal identity warfare." How researchers identify themselves will thus likely influence whether and how they engage in research–practice collaborations.

Indeed, trying to work across the academic–practice boundary can involve significant identity conflicts, as described by Empson (2012; see also Chapter 12 in this volume). On the other hand, Lam (2010) finds in her study of researchers' approaches to university–industry partnerships that most researchers seem relatively comfortable in creating for themselves and operating within hybrid identities situated in between the extremes of "Ivory Tower Traditionalists" and "Entrepreneurial Scientists." Yet this also depends on the kinds of knowledge involved, and scientists' corresponding identification: "applied" scientists were more likely to be comfortable with such hybridity than "pure" scientists.

Over and above this prominent role for individual identity, our own experience suggests that the initiative's purpose and its organizational identity also influence whether and how researchers and practitioners engage within it. Organizational members and their identities have an important role in constructing an organizational identity (Gioia, Price, Hamilton & Thomas, 2010; Scott & Lane, 2000), and founders are likely to have a particularly prominent influence (Powell & Baker, 2014). At the same time, organizational identity influences members' responses to organizational challenges (Dutton & Dukerich, 1991). Kreiner, Hollensbe and Sheep (2006) consider when individual and organizational identities may be considered complementary and there is a "fit" between them. According to their suggested framework, there seems to be something akin to a Goldilocks effect: fruitful complementarity requires an overlap between individual and organizational identities that is just right—neither too low, nor too high.

We may thus expect that the interplay between researchers' and practitioners' individual identities and the organizational identity of a collaborative initiative will have some bearing on the degree and manner, in which these different participants become involved. But how this plays out in researcher–practitioner collaborations has not been considered explicitly, to our knowledge.

Our cases and analysis approach

Our analysis focuses on two initiatives: the Network for Business Sustainability (South Africa) (NBS-SA) and the Southern Africa Food Lab. Ralph co-founded and played a leading role in both initiatives, while Kristy worked as knowledge manager at NBS-SA for two years. The fact that we have been closely involved in both initiatives provides us with in-depth knowledge, and our leadership role in both also means that possible leadership effects do not add variance across the two cases, thus assisting our comparison.

The Network for Business Sustainability (South Africa)

NBS-SA was established in 2013 as an affiliate of the Canada-based Network for Business Sustainability (see Bansal, Bertels, Ewart, MacConnachie & O'Brien, 2012), whose mission is to enable "business sustainability by fostering collaboration and co-creating knowledge through research and practice." NBS-SA initially adopted and adapted the structures and processes that had been developed and refined by our Canadian colleagues. Senior managers in some 15 South African companies with strong sustainability commitments were enrolled to participate in our "Leadership Council."

Each year, this group met to identify between eight and ten research questions that represented priority knowledge needs for the managers. Two of these were chosen for dedicated attention in annual "flagship" research projects, in which we commissioned competitively selected research teams to conduct a systematic review of the scholarly literature. Outputs included a systematic review report targeted at other researchers and a short executive report targeted at practitioners. (These reports are available on the NBS website: http://nbs.net). The reports should include models, charts, or diagrams that could function as boundary objects—that is, they would synthesize salient concepts and practical guidance in a way that would make sense to both researchers and practitioners, and facilitate communication among and between them.

To support the research teams, a "Guidance Committee" consisting of four or five members of the Leadership Council participated in short, regular teleconference calls (every six weeks) to discuss progress and next steps. Our own role in this process was to act as brokers and so, for instance, we chaired the annual Leadership Council meetings and the Guidance Committees' teleconference calls.

In our Leadership Council meetings and also in various informal conversations, we continuously sought participants' feedback in order to adapt and improve our processes and outcomes. The emerging insights are discussed in more detail below. They led to the inclusion of more face-to-face interactions between the Guidance Committees and the research teams, and a greater focus on emergent practices—rather than only scholarly literature—in project outputs. One of the research teams in 2015 took the additional step of including a practitioner from the Leadership Council in their team.

The Southern Africa Food Lab

The Southern Africa Food Lab is a multi-stakeholder initiative focused on the "wicked problem" of food insecurity and hunger (Hamann, Giamporcaro, Johnston & Yachkaschi, 2011). It was established in 2010 following a multi-stakeholder workshop attended by participants from academia, business, government, and civil society. There was broad agreement at this workshop that some kind of cross-sector dialogue was necessary on food security and a small yet diverse group of participants formed a steering group. A funding proposal that envisaged a year-long "change lab" process inspired by "Theory U" (Scharmer, 2009) was written and found support.

The "U" process consisted of three phases:

- The first was focused on different role-players including participating researchers "co-sensing the system," that is, gaining an understanding of the various organizations, perspectives, and relationships that are involved in the production, distribution, and consumption of food. This involved numerous "dialogue interviews" which sought to discuss not only cognitive understanding of the food security problem, but also personal motivations and commitments. It also involved two three-day "learning journeys," in which participants travelled to important sites in the food system, such as farms, fresh produce markets, production facilities, retail distribution centers and stores, and street vendors in low-income areas.

- The second phase was meant to allow participants to reflect on their and each others' understanding of challenges and opportunities in addressing food insecurity, and to identify issues on which they were committed to work together. This was achieved in a two-day workshop in early September 2010, which resulted in the formation of "innovation teams" focused on issues including smallholder agricultural production and the need for a "national conversation" on food.
- In the third phase, these teams then discussed specific opportunities for affecting positive change with regard to their target issue, with a focus on designing and implementing experimental pilot projects.

The group focusing on smallholder farming obtained funding and facilitated another "U" process focused on this topic in 2012–13, including five learning journeys to explore smallholder farming areas and associated supply chains. A second project resulted in a "Transformative Scenarios Process" implemented during 2014–15, following principles and guidelines proposed by Kahane and Van Der Heijden (2012). This was meant to complement the smallholder farming work with a high-level, national dialogue on possible futures for the food system (Freeth & Drimie, 2016; see also the Food Lab website, www. southernafricafoodlab.org).

Data collection and analysis for this chapter

As noted, we were intimately involved in establishing and facilitating both initiatives. We thus take an interpretivist approach and make use of our own reflections, extensive personal notes, and countless conversations. We complement these reflections on our experiences with an analysis of interviews with diverse participants in these initiatives that we conducted for the purpose of this chapter, and we also analyzed diverse reports prepared by others. Finally, we also invited reviews of earlier drafts by insiders and outsiders.

Together with friends and colleagues working with us, our roles explicitly included continuously learning about what was working well or not so well, and responding with adjustments. While engaging with and brokering between researchers and practitioners in both initiatives to learn more about the initiatives' substantive content—corporate sustainability in the one, food security in the other—we also endeavored to continuously learn about the process of research–practice collaboration. In other words, both projects were action-learning projects focused on both content and, as far as we were concerned, process.

Thus, over and above our own reflections and conversations about what was going on, we collected substantial data about what participants thought about the structures and processes of both initiatives. This took the form of semi-structured interviews and informal conversations (which would often cover content and process of the initiatives), workshop reports, and email communication. In NBS-SA, Kristy conducted in-depth interviews with ten Leadership Council members and we distributed two annual questionnaires to annual meeting participants. In the Food Lab, consultants conducted a similar study, and two MBA groups investigated the initiative for class projects.

These interview transcripts, survey responses, workshop reports, and third-party reports collected over six years in the Food Lab and three years in NBS-SA add up to over 1,000 pages. In addition, as preliminary coding and discussions gave rise to our emergent focus on different levels of knowledge exchange and the role of identities, we also conducted dedicated interviews or email correspondence in order to probe these themes directly. Such interactions took place with four participants in the Food Lab and two participants in NBS-SA.

Analysis of this information involved several iterations, but essentially there were two phases:

- Given the broad thematic scope of our data, the first round of coding highlighted those sections of interview transcripts or notes or workshop reports that dealt with or had some bearing on structures and processes of research–practice collaboration. An analysis of these sections, coupled with a review of the literature, gave rise to our focus on types of knowledge exchange and the role of identities.
- We then returned to our data to find evidence in interviewee comments, events, or interactions that reflected different levels of knowledge exchange, or expressed how identities came to bear. This analysis gave rise to two arguments, which we explain below.

The knowledge transformation gap

Our first argument is that knowledge co-production between researchers and practitioners involves all three types of exchange identified by Carlile (2004), and initiatives that do not respond to the particularly challenging demands of knowledge transformation are likely to stumble. One of our NBS-SA projects offered a particularly clear illustration of this. The question identified by our practitioner members for more detailed investigation was, "How do we measure and value social capital?" The research team selected for the project had demonstrated experience and published work on social capital in well-regarded management journals. The initial interactions of the research team and the practitioners in the Guidance Committee were courteous and stimulating, but it was clear that communication between these groups was difficult. We explained this to ourselves, and in our conference calls, as a result of the technology and researchers' emphasis on clearly defined research questions and scope, which the practitioners struggled to appreciate.

Two months later it was still apparent that the practitioners and researchers were struggling to understand each other. Ralph suggested that a face-to-face meeting might help so he arranged a lunch meeting between a practitioner and a member of the research team. The two of them talked for 40 minutes and suddenly it became clear why they kept talking past each other: They were using fundamentally different definitions and interpretations of the term that was at the core of the project—"social capital." For the researchers, this definition was based on the scholarly literature, which emphasizes the character and value of relationships and networks between individuals or groups. For the practitioners, however, the term was used in a more pragmatic and inclusive sense. For them, it had to do with the social impacts of business activity. Social capital is one of the six "capitals," which need to be reported on as inputs and outputs of a company's business model in its integrated report—something all our Leadership Council member companies were working on (Cheng, Green, Conradie, Konishi & Romi, 2014; Eccles & Saltzman, 2011; see also http://integratedreporting.org).

Our response to this realization was to emphasize to the research team the need to directly address these various uses of the term in the hope of developing a shared understanding. This was not an easy task, because the integrated reporting requirements faced by companies, and the mostly gray literature that had developed around them, were largely unknown to the scholars. We thus saw this as a valuable knowledge-translation opportunity: our project should help practitioners grapple with scholarly knowledge on relationships and networks, while the researchers would integrate an understanding of practitioners' priorities in their discussion of this.

Through this process and in our resulting outputs, we thought that we had succeeded in our knowledge-translation ambition, clarified the "true" meaning of social capital, and provided an evidence-based set of recommendations on how to measure and value it. Yet we learnt that this was not the case. In discussion with our practitioners in one of our workshops the following year, Leadership Council members were still defining social capital in the "practitioners' way"—that is, as a broad category of social impacts of business activity.

We were dumbfounded. But after further reflection and with the benefit of Carlile's (2004) framework, we realized that we had focused our attention on knowledge translation without recognizing the need for knowledge transformation. Without the latter, we were constrained in achieving the former. Despite the many interactions between researchers and practitioners in our process, we failed to recognize and cater for the need to consider underlying interests of the groups on either side of the knowledge boundary. As Carlile (2004) points out, knowledge is "at stake" for people and there are costs associated with adopting new knowledge and giving up knowledge that has been useful.

For the scholars, the primary interest was to remain faithful to the literature that they were reviewing, and this was also motivated by the desire to possibly publish in the scholarly literature some of the results of their work. For the practitioners, however, the primary interest was to understand whether or how the emerging ideas would influence their decisions and practices. Some of them highlighted their specific motivation to gain practical advice on how to report on social capital in their integrated reports, but noted that this was not forthcoming in the project outputs or in their interactions with the researchers.

Responding more directly to the practical interests of practitioners was not just a challenge for the researchers. As one of the researchers who reviewed a previous draft of this chapter pointed out, we—the authors and knowledge brokers—were also adamant that scholarly rigor was needed in the process and its outcomes. We were thus directly involved in heightening the tensions between researchers' and practitioners' interests. Because these interests and their entanglement with the knowledge we were hoping to share or translate were not carefully considered and discussed, the researchers held on to the academic definition of social capital, and while the practitioners considered the project outputs interesting, they held on to their broader and pragmatic definition of social capital.

So we paid insufficient attention to the way that knowledge was tied up with diverging interests among researchers and practitioners and the stakes involved in giving up this knowledge. In addition, the format of our process was not conducive for this kind of communication to take place. Most of the interactions were on conference calls using telephone conferencing facilities or Internet platforms such as Skype, and often these were hampered by bad sound quality or even interruptions. In listening to recordings of these calls, it is clear to us—that is, the NBS-SA chairs of the conversations—that we often spent too much time talking, and much of the rest of the time was dedicated to the researchers. We gave too little time to the practitioners, motivated as we were by a desire to translate researchers' knowledge for the practitioners and produce high-quality, rigorous outputs. We thus gave too little attention to practitioners' views and underlying interests. The medium of the teleconferencing and the format we implemented in hosting the calls thus did not allow for nuanced communication and it also did not allow for the development of interpersonal relationships and trust that would be helpful in expressing underlying interests (which was ironic given the topic of the project!).

The result of this failure to address interests and knowledge transformation is that we were constrained in our knowledge-translation ambition. The practitioners learnt that there was a certain academic way of talking about social capital. But they did not adopt core aspects of this—including the definition of "social capital"—as part of the "shared knowledge" (Carlile, 2004) that would be necessary for effective communication across the research–practice boundary.

There are other experiences in some of the other projects, as well as interview data, which support our argument that we did not sufficiently address underlying interests and knowledge transformation needs in NBS-SA. For instance, one of the researchers in 2015 argued, "What the practitioners want from us is just too different to what our journals want from us; it's tricky to do both or find a middle ground." In the same project, one of the members of the Leadership Council described the emerging outcomes: "This is interesting, but I don't know how this will help us just yet; it's still too abstract." Speaking about the NBS-SA outputs more broadly, another Leadership Council member noted that, even if she found the reports useful and interesting, she was cautious about assuming that her colleagues would do so, as well: "I didn't pass on the reports [within my firm]. They were too heavy. It wasn't that they weren't interesting, it's just that we are very cautious about how we position ourselves [as 'sustainability' managers within the firm]."

As we discussed these challenges among ourselves, with our members and our affiliated researchers, and with our Canadian colleagues, we made changes to our NBS-SA model that we think are helping to reconcile diverging interests and the associated knowledge "stakes." The experience outlined above provided important motivation and insights for these changes. We had learnt that aspiring to knowledge translation was not enough. More thorough, deliberate, and open-ended interactions between researchers and practitioners were called for, and knowledge transformation was the more generative aspiration and framing for such interactions. A significant part of this was adopting a stronger learning orientation among our researchers, and involving practitioners more directly in the learning process. Thus some of the subsequent changes involved more direct immersion by researchers in member companies' operations and challenges, and much closer, iterative, and ongoing interactions between researchers and practitioners. One of the latter describes the benefits of this: "It resulted in me certainly looking at things differently because of the different perspectives ... it is the contact and working together [more directly] that is important."

The role of identities

Our first argument—outlined above (p. 239)—is that knowledge co-production goes beyond knowledge transfer and translation, and that knowledge transformation and its associated challenges are involved. Our second argument is that personal and organizational identities, and their inter-relationship, play an important role in influencing whether there is sufficient commitment for and engagement in knowledge transformation.

The above discussion has suggested that it is important for research–practice collaborations to recognize and respond to the entanglement of participants' interests and their knowledge "stakes," and to facilitate the kinds of interaction and relationships that allow for effective communication on such potentially awkward issues. The design principles of the Food Lab were arguably more attuned to such requirements than our early efforts in NBS-SA. For instance, the "dialogue interviews" that were conducted during the inception of the Food Lab in 2010, and in early stages of both the smallholder and scenarios projects, were designed and implemented to reveal respondents' feelings and motivations related to the problem of food insecurity and the proposed collaboration to address this problem. The learning journeys, innovation workshops, and subsequent working groups were facilitated with the intention of bringing participants' "whole selves" into conversation.

This intention and process design likely contributed to participants highlighting a relatively effective exchange of knowledge among and between researchers and practitioners. For instance, one participant highlighted a particular experience, in which researchers offered a typology of smallholder farmers:

> On one of the learning journeys, [a leading academic in the field] outlined the profile of different kinds of smallholder farmers. This opened the eyes of

everyone, and we realized we need to be more specific about which farmers can be linked to commercial agriculture, and that other farmers require different kinds of support.

Yet this was not a straightforward or one-way transfer of knowledge. As explained by a member of the facilitating team for the smallholder support program:

> We were able to hold onto key nuggets [of knowledge], and translate this—like the typology [of smallholder farmers]. So it might have been missed the first time it was presented, [but] we made sure it was continuously brought into discussions.… There is some subtle translation going on. The terms get put up by the researchers and possibly not fully understood, and through us discussing them there's been a lot more definition of what those terms mean … [The Food Lab] has allowed [the researchers] to refine their thinking. I think they have benefited a lot from these interactions and from the environment [in the Food Lab] in general.

Notably, such knowledge exchange was never an explicit priority or purpose for the Food Lab and therefore the stakes involved in shifting or adapting this knowledge or ambiguous language were, relatively speaking, lower than in NBS-SA. Rather, its purpose was focused on a shared problem, which had a visceral urgency due to the suffering caused by hunger. The purpose and organizational identity of the Food Lab thus had the co-creation and exchange of knowledge as a means to an end, and in fact knowledge per se was not part of its vision or mission.

This is despite the fact that research and academic participants played a vital role throughout the Food Lab's work. Ralph and his co-founder were both employed as academics when they helped establish the Food Lab. Both were motivated to do so by research they had been conducting, and this research directly fed into the early discussions of the Food Lab. Similarly, the Supporting Smallholder Agriculture project was established in order to build on a research program implemented by a team of researchers at the University of the Western Cape. This team of researchers continues to play a vital role in informing the Food Lab discussions, and also integrates the outcomes from these discussions into its research. In the case of the Transformative Scenarios Process, the participants motivated for the development of a systematic review of the scholarly literature, in order to inform the creation of the scenarios. This review played a formative role on the scenarios process and it has also become a much-used reference for a variety of actors in the South African food system (an adapted version was published as Pereira & Drimie, 2016).

Yet, despite the vital role of research and of researchers throughout the Food Lab process, research has always been a means to an end, rather than an explicit part of the initiative's purpose and identity. This has been an important factor in motivating a diverse array of participants, for whom knowledge per se is not a prominent part of their personal or professional ambition.

Relatedly, the boundary between research and practice was never a very clear or pronounced one during Food Lab discussions, especially when compared to our early efforts in NBS-SA. Over and above the pragmatic orientation of the Food Lab itself, this was also because of participants' personal identities. A prominent theme in our interviews or correspondence with Food Lab participants in researching this chapter was hybrid identities of individuals. A member of the facilitating team exemplified this when she embarked on a PhD in 2015. She reflected on her own identity and that of others involved in the Food Lab as follows:

> As I look at particular individuals [in the Food Lab] I see them as both practitioners and researchers, and so this separation is sometimes an artificial one, because people are straddling different roles and different relationships to knowledge, in the context of food. If I look at Bertha (not real names), she produces research, she commissions research, she works on an empirical basis; and she is a campaigner and a manager [at an NGO]. If I think of Lance, his background is in corporate practice, in management practice in the retail industry, and that's where his networks are, and [at the same time] he has done a lot of research. I cannot think of anyone right now who is one or the other.

Similar views were shared by other interviewees. These hybrid personal identities were dynamically connected to the Food Lab's organizational identity. As argued by an interviewee:

> Perhaps because of how the Food Lab started to frame its purpose, it became a useful vehicle for both [research and practice]; well, not only for both, but for people who are hybrids, who seek a change agenda and who see research as one of the ways through which change can happen, but not to the exclusion of the kind of dialogue platform that the Food Lab was proposing.

Hence, for the academics involved in the Food Lab as founders and/or participants, their disciplinary training and ambitions had a significant overlap with the Food Lab's problem-oriented identity. They are generally focused on development- and policy-related research, which they publish in corresponding journals that are less devoted to theory than in the management field. For instance, research that motivated and provided a basis for the Food Lab, or for particular programs within the Food Lab, has been published in development or agrarian change journals (Hamann et al., 2011; Neves & Toit, 2013), and the Lab and the kind of collaborative governance it seeks to foster have featured in broader analyses in policy journals (e.g., Pereira & Ruysenaar, 2012). Perhaps as a result, there has been a notable absence of concerns expressed by researchers in the Food Lab about a lack of fit between their publishing ambitions and their contributions to the Food Lab.

This fit between the researchers' identities and the Food Lab's identity was not only important to ensure the researchers' ongoing involvement and commitment. It also mattered to the practitioners. For instance, an official at the national government's agriculture department highlighted the importance of researchers' immersion and interest in local, practical concerns and how this gave them legitimacy in his eyes when discussing policy-related matters:

> The Food Lab has influenced our policy making a lot … When we spoke to people from the Food Lab, it became clear that they had gone to Mopane [a remote rural area] and had seen things first-hand and worked with farmers.

That is not to say that the role of researchers has always been easy in the Food Lab; some researchers' knowledge stakes and corresponding personal identities were clearly at odds with it. For example, an academic found the scenarios workshops very difficult and ended his involvement vocally, arguing that expert opinion and research should be the basis of the scenarios and that the "wishy-washy" discussion was creating implausible scenarios. The Food Lab's emphasis on dialogue between diverse perspectives was also criticized by academics emphasizing a more critical analysis of food insecurity. At the launch of the scenarios, for instance, a well-known critical sociologist argued that the scenarios paid insufficient attention to the role of power and that the process leading up to the scenarios was inherently flawed due to corporations' involvement.

A key dimension of participants' identity hence had to do with their attitude towards knowledge and dialogue. Participants that felt at ease in the Food Lab often highlighted the inherent value of dialogue and they considered knowledge to be situated within contexts. In other words, they adopted a pluralist approach to knowledge. Those that felt uneasy in the Food Lab, or criticized it from outside, often argued that dialogue could not supplant the existence of fundamental "truths" of a scientific or political nature. This is a tension that is orthogonal to the research–practice tension; that is, these different perspectives cut across researchers and practitioners. As explained by an interviewee:

> I think all of [the participants in the Food Lab] have brought this strongly: the idea that there are multiple ways of knowing, and multiple sources of knowledge; and all of them deserve to be heard and valued and part of the conversation, in order to make a difference.… So at the launch event [of the scenarios] … there was a brewing disagreement, and there was a very provocative address by [the above mentioned critical sociologist]; it was accusatory; there was the potential for us to all go back into our various camps and corners … [But then another participant] spoke about the importance of being able to argue, the freedom to argue; and how the Food Lab as a platform and how the scenarios as a tool for generating—whether you want to call it stories, new knowledges; how invaluable it was that we were able to argue across our boundaries.

So even though it may be premature to assess the Food Lab's contribution to the knowledge transformation with much conviction, there are indications that participants' interactions were sufficiently "deep" and deliberative to address not just cognitive aspects, but underlying interests and stakes, as well.

Discussion and conclusion

In Table 14.2 we provide an overview of the stories about the two case studies that we have analyzed here. We focus on two dimensions: the form and focus of interactions between researchers and practitioners, and their identities. In the early days of NBS-SA, interactions were limited to the annual workshop and occasional teleconferences and email correspondence. The focus of these interactions was primarily on knowledge needs and content. Researchers' and

Table 14.2 Overview of our case studies with regard to interactions, identities, and outcomes

Dimension		NBS-SA (early days)	Food Lab
Interactions	Format and frequency	Face-to-face workshop once a year Occasional teleconference meetings Occasional email correspondence	Face-to-face workshops and/or learning journeys three to six times a year Occasional email correspondence
	Focus and character	Focus on knowledge content and cognitive expertise and discussion	Focus on "whole-person" involvement, including feelings and motivations, and dedicated opportunities for reflection
Identity	Personal	Participants mostly identify distinctly as researcher or practitioner	Participants mostly identify as hybrid research-practitioners
	Organizational	Focused on knowledge translation (knowledge as an end)	Focused on action and social change (knowledge as a means to an end)
	Fit (personal–organizational)	Practitioners struggle to identify with knowledge focus and academic rigor Researchers struggle to identify with practical needs	Hybrid research–practitioners identify with action-oriented purpose and design of the initiative
Knowledge co-production outcomes		Limited face-to-face interactions and identity mismatches lead to limited knowledge transformation, and this constrains knowledge translation	Intensive face-to-face interactions and identity fit contribute to at least some knowledge transformation, and this supports knowledge translation

practitioners' identities were largely distinct, and these personal identities were not strongly aligned with the initiative's organizational identity focused on knowledge translation. The practitioners struggled to identify with the emphasis on rigor and the researchers struggled to identify with practical needs. As a result, the entangled knowledge-interests were not addressed and thus knowledge translation also stumbled. These experiences helped us revise our approach to enable closer and more iterative interactions between researchers and practitioners, which are furthermore more embedded in participating organizations' processes.

In the Food Lab, interactions involved more intensive face-to-face encounters, at times in unusual contexts during learning journeys, and there was an explicit focus on a "whole person" approach, in which the sharing of feelings and motivations was encouraged. There was no clear distinction between researchers and practitioners, with many participants comfortable with a hybrid identity. This allowed for a stronger alignment with the initiative's action-oriented, yet knowledge-informed, organizational identity. These interactions and identity alignments created conditions conducive to knowledge transformation to take place, and this also facilitated clear instances of knowledge translation.

We are thus making two contributions in this chapter. First, by applying Carlile's (2004) three-level model of knowledge exchange across domain boundaries in an analysis of two research–practice collaborations we have illustrated the important role of knowledge transformation in such collaboration. Neglecting the role of participants' underlying interests and the way in which knowledge is tied to these interests, we argue, will likely undermine research–practice boundary spanning initiatives, even if their ambition is not transformation per se, but the more modest objective of knowledge translation. That is because participants' knowledge "at stake" will prevent them from adopting or committing to the "shared knowledge" that is necessary for knowledge translation to take place.

What does it mean for a research–practice collaboration to recognize and address the transformation gap? For a start, it is necessary to recognize and understand this intersection of knowledge and interests. The collaboration needs to be designed and facilitated in such a way that participants can bring their interests "to the table." This is not easy or automatic, partly because this is likely to generate discomfort and possibly conflict. Addressing such conflict in a creative and constructive manner is thus a vital element of "engaged scholarship" (Van de Ven & Johnson, 2006). It likely requires repeated, longer-term, and face-to-face interactions for interpersonal relationships and trust to develop. This trust is necessary for underlying interests to be expressed and conflict to be managed constructively. We thus add to Van de Ven and Johnson's treatise on engaged scholarship by explaining the need for constructive responses to conflict on the basis of in-depth case studies and the transformation gap idea.

Second, we have highlighted the role of personal and organizational identity in influencing whether and how the "transformation gap" may be addressed in research–practice collaboration. In doing so, we build on the burgeoning work on identity in organizations and specifically those authors focusing on identity in research–practice interactions (Empson, 2012; Gulati, 2007; Lam, 2010) and on the interface between individual and organizational identities (Gioia et al., 2010; Kreiner et al., 2006; Powell & Baker, 2014).

We argue that research–practice collaboration is more likely to achieve knowledge exchange and co-production objectives if there is a "fit" between participants' personal identities and the initiative's organizational identity, and if this entails a hybrid approach to role definitions straddling "researcher" and "practitioner," as well as a pluralistic approach to knowledge. In our experience, this is more likely if the initiative is founded, structured, and implemented in a way that has a pragmatic and inclusive orientation, but this requires further investigation. An initiative focused primarily on (or entirely exclusive of) knowledge creation may be less likely to attract the commitment of practitioners (or researchers).

The fruitful role of hybrid personal identities in our analysis may be seen to be at odds with Van de Ven and Johnson's (2006) suggestion that the differences between researchers and practitioners can be put to good use through "intellectual arbitrage." We still feel that such arbitrage is at the core of effective research–practice partnerships, but suggest that it is more likely if the underlying differences are not too pronounced. We thus expect something akin to the Goldilocks effect, again: knowledge transformation requires carefully designed and well-facilitated interactions between researchers and practitioners who are sufficiently different to bring complementary perspectives to the table, but not so different that the interests underlying their knowledge claims are too far apart.

Acknowledgments

We are grateful to Tima Bansal, Stephanie Bertels, Rebecca Freeth, Jane McKenzie, and Jess Schulschenk for comments on draft versions of this chapter (though we could not respond comprehensively to all of them). We are also grateful to the people we interviewed for this chapter and the many colleagues and friends that have contributed in diverse ways to the two initiatives discussed herein. This includes as funders and hosts GIZ, Ford Foundation, and the MTN Solutions Space at the UCT Graduate School of Business. We also thank the UCT African Climate and Development Initiative and the South African National Research Foundation for funding that supported this writing project.

References

Bansal, P., Bertels, S., Ewart, T., MacConnachie, P. & O'Brien, J. (2012). Bridging the research–practice gap. *The Academy of Management Perspectives*, 26(1), 73–92.

Bartunek, J. M. & Rynes, S. L. (2014). Academics and practitioners are alike and unlike: The paradoxes of academic–practitioner relationships. *Journal of Management*, 40(5), 1181–201.

Bartunek, J. M., Rynes, S. L. & Daft, R. L. (2001). Across the great divide: Knowledge creation and transfer between practitioners and academics. *Academy of Management Journal*, 44(2), 340–55.

Carlile, P. R. (2004). Transferring, translating, and transforming: An integrative framework for managing knowledge across boundaries. *Organization Science*, 15(5), 555–68.

Cheng, M., Green, W., Conradie, P., Konishi, N. & Romi, A. (2014). The international integrated reporting framework: key issues and future research opportunities. *Journal of International Financial Management & Accounting*, 25(1), 90–119.

Dutton, J. E. & Dukerich, J. M. (1991). Keeping an eye on the mirror: Image and identity in organizational adaptation. *Academy of Management Journal*, 34(3), 517–54.

Eccles, R. G. & Saltzman, D. (2011). Achieving sustainability through integrated reporting. *Stanford Society Innovation Review Summer*, 59.

Empson, L. (2012). My affair with the "other": Identity journeys across the research–practice divide. *Journal of Management Inquiry*, 22(2), 229–48.

Freeth, R. & Drimie, S. (2016). Participatory scenario planning: From scenario "stakeholders" to scenario "owners." *Environment: Science and Policy for Sustainable Development*, 58(4), 32–43.

Gioia, D. A., Price, K. N., Hamilton, A. L. & Thomas, J. B. (2010). Forging an identity: An insider-outsider study of processes involved in the formation of organizational identity. *Administrative Science Quarterly*, 55(1), 1–46.

Ghoshal, S. (2005). Bad management theories are destroying good management practices. *Academy of Management Learning & Education*, 4(1), 75–91.

Gibbons, M., Limoges, C., Nowotny, H., Schwartzman, S., Scott, P. & Trow, M. (1994). *The New Production of Knowledge: The Dynamics of Science and Research in Contemporary Societies*. London: Sage Publishing.

Gulati, R. (2007). Tent poles, tribalism, and boundary spanning: The rigor–relevance debate in management research. *Academy of Management Journal*, 50(4), 775–82.

Hamann, R., Giamporcaro, S., Johnston, D. & Yachkaschi, S. (2011). The role of business and cross-sector collaboration in addressing the "wicked problem" of food insecurity. *Development Southern Africa*, 28(4), 579–94.

Hambrick, D. C. (1994). What if the academy actually mattered? *Academy of Management Review*, 19(1), 11–16.

Hambrick, D. C. (2007). The field of management's devotion to theory: Too much of a good thing? *Academy of Management Journal*, 50(6), 1346–52.

Hirsch Hadorn, G., Hoffmann-Riem, H., Biber-Klemm, S., Grossenbacher-Mansuy, W., Joye, D., Pohl, C., Wisemann, U. & Zemp, E. (Eds.). (2008). *Handbook of Transdisciplinary Research*. Berlin: Springer.

Jantsch, E. (1970). Inter- and transdisciplinary university: A systems approach to education and innovation. *Policy Sciences*, 1(1), 403–28.

Kahane, A. & Van Der Heijden, K. (2012). *Transformative Scenario Planning: Working Together to Change the Future*. San Francisco, CA: Berrett-Koehler.

Kates, R. W., Clark, W. C., Corell, R., Hall, J. M., Jaeger, C. C., Lowe, I., McCarthy, J., Schellnhuber, H. J., Bolin, B., Dickson, N. M., Faucheux, S., Gallopin, G. C., Grubler, A., Huntley, B., Jager, J., Jodha, N. S., Kasperson, R. E., Mabogunje, A., Matson, P. & Mooney, H. (2001). Sustainability science. *Science*, 292(5517), 641.

Kieser, A. & Leiner, L. (2009). Why the rigour–relevance gap in management research is unbridgeable. *Journal of Management Studies*, 46(3), 516–33.

Kieser, A., Nicolai, A. & Seidl, D. (2015). The practical relevance of management research: Turning the debate on relevance into a rigorous scientific research program. *The Academy of Management Annals*, 9(1), 143–233.

King Committee on Corporate Governance & Institute of Directors (South Africa). (2009). *King Report on Corporate Governance for South Africa, 2009*. Institute of Directors in Southern Africa.

Kreiner, G. E., Hollensbe, E. C. & Sheep, M. L. (2006). On the edge of identity: Boundary dynamics at the interface of individual and organizational identities. *Human Relations*, 59(10), 1315–41.

Lam, A. (2010). From "ivory tower traditionalists" to "entrepreneurial scientists"? Academic scientists in fuzzy university/industry boundaries. *Social Studies of Science*, 40(2), 307–40.

Mirvis, P. (2008). Academic–practitioner learning forums: A new model for interorganizational research. In Shani, A. B., Mohrman, S. A., Pasmore, W. A., Stymne, B. & Adler, N. (Eds.) *Handbook of Collaborative Management Research* (Vol. 1: pp. 201–24). Thousand Oaks, CA: Sage Publications.

McKelvey, B. (2006). Response: Van de Ven and Johnson's "engaged scholarship": Nice try, but … *Academy of Management Review*, 31(4), 822–29.

Neves, D. & Toit, A. (2013). Rural livelihoods in South Africa: Complexity, vulnerability and differentiation. *Journal of Agrarian Change*, 13(1), 93–115.

Nonaka, I., Toyama, R. & Konno, N. (2000). SECI, Ba and leadership: A unified model of dynamic knowledge creation. *Long Range Planning*, 33(1), 5–34.

Pereira, L. & Drimie, S. (2016). Governance arrangements for the future food system: Addressing complexity in South Africa. *Environment: Science and Policy for Sustainable Development*, 58(4), 18–31.

Pereira, L. M. & Ruysenaar, S. (2012). Moving from traditional government to new adaptive governance: The changing face of food security responses in South Africa. *Food Security*, 4(1), 41–58.

Powell, E. E. & Baker, T. (2014). It's what you make it: Founder identity and enacting strategic responses to adversity. *Academy of Management Journal*, 57(5), 1406–33.

Scharmer, C. O. (2009). *Theory U: Learning from the future as it emerges*. San Francisco, CA: Berrett-Koehler.

Scott, S. G. & Lane, V. R. (2000). A stakeholder approach to organizational identity. *Academy of Management Review*, 25(1), 43–62.

Smith, W. K. & Lewis, M. W. (2011). Toward a theory of paradox: A dynamic equilibrium model of organizing. *Academy of Management Review*, 36(2), 381–403.

Swan, J., Bresnen, M., Robertson, M., Newell, S. & Dopson, S. (2010). When policy meets practice: colliding logics and the challenges of "Mode 2" initiatives in the translation of academic knowledge. *Organization Studies*, 31(9–10), 1311–40.

Van de Ven, A. H. & Johnson, P. E. (2006). Knowledge for theory and practice. *Academy of Management Review*, 31(4), 802–21.

Whitehead, A. N. (1928). Universities and their function. *Bulletin of the American Association of University Professors*, 14(6), 448–50.

15 How to develop scholar–practitioner interactions

Lessons from management concepts developed through collaboration between research and practice[1]

Guillaume Carton[2] and Stéphanie Dameron[3]

Introduction

For more than 20 years, the academic literature has encouraged scholar–practitioner collaborations to produce management knowledge that is both academically rigorous and practically relevant (Bartunek & Rynes, 2014). Several frameworks have thus been developed to integrate practitioners' viewpoints in academic research. For instance, the British Academy of Management has been developing since 1998 propositions based on Gibbons, Limoges, Nowotny, Schwartzman, Scott and Trow's (1994) Mode 2 framework (see Starkey & Madan, 2001; Tranfield & Starkey, 1998). Later on, in the USA, Andrew Van de Ven suggested the development of an "engaged scholarship" (see Chapter 7). Many other prescriptive frameworks have been developed to foster practitioners' involvement in academic research (e.g., Avenier & Cajaiba, 2012; Louis & Bartunek, 1992) as well as edited books giving practical insights on how to develop knowledge that would be more relevant for practice (e.g., Dameron & Durand, 2011; Mohrman & Lawler, 2011; Shani, Mohrman, Pasmore, Stymne & Adler, 2008). However, despite this important amount of academic discussions and debates, Bartunek (2011) takes the example of Mode 2 to lament the fact that the framework is rarely mobilized in empirical research. There is consequently still a need to find ways to reconcile research with practice (see also Bartunek & Rynes, 2014; Kieser, Nicolai & Seidl, 2015).

A recent explanation of these difficulties lies in the intrinsic tensions underlying the academic–practitioner relationships (Bartunek & Rynes, 2014). Even if they may be seen as fruitful for the advance of knowledge, it seems that they have discouraged more than one scholar–practitioner relationship. Bartunek and Rynes (2014) enumerate five of them:

- difference in *logics* between research and practice due to their self-referential;
- differing *time dimensions* as academics' timelines are seen as much longer than practitioners';
- differences in terms of their *knowledge representation* (communication style);

- *rigor and relevance* which are seen as opposed, complementary, or orthogonal; and
- scholars and practitioners' different *interests and incentives* that divert them from working together.

To better understand how scholars and practitioners face these tensions while interacting, this chapter differentiates four types of interactions. For the purpose of this chapter, we illustrate each of them with developmental processes from five management concepts. The concepts include Balanced Scorecard (Kaplan & Norton, 1996), Blue Ocean Strategy (Kim & Mauborgne, 2005), Business Model Canvas (Osterwalder & Pigneur, 2010), Disruptive Innovation (Christensen, 1997) and Open Innovation (Chesbrough, 2003).[4] Their authors have all been recognized as being among the best management thinkers[5] and the books that have disseminated their concepts have sold more than a million copies as well as being taught throughout the world. In other words, the concepts are recognized as having reached a huge impact both in academia and practice. The construction of the developmental process of each concept is based on interviews conducted with the people who took part in it (i.e., Henry Chesbrough, Alexander Osterwalder, Yves Pigneur) and on secondary data (i.e., recorded conferences,[6] academic articles, book chapters).

The chapter is organized as follows. We first review each of the four interaction modes we found.[7] For each interaction mode, we define the interaction itself, present the concept we chose for illustration, develop two narratives, and suggest key learnings from them. We then conclude the chapter by generalizing our illustrative vignettes to show how tensions between research and practice can be managed. In particular, we discuss how technology may foster some interactions while only changes in academics' incentives may improve others.

Collaboration between academics and practitioners for the development of major management concepts

Partnership interactions

Scholar–practitioner partnerships are based on interactions aimed at producing shared knowledge. They contribute to building common reasoning and exchanges of verbal messages through turn-taking sequences (Tsoukas, 2009). If the dialogue is productive, each interlocutor potentially makes the other realize the limitations of his focal awareness and stimulates a search for an ever broader one. We illustrate the partnership interaction through the developmental process of the Balanced Scorecard model as two successive but different partnerships occurred during its developmental process: one highlighting the necessity for curiosity with the other, and the other one, the complementarity in terms of skills between academics and practitioners.

Balanced Scorecard

Named in 1992 after the eponymous article, the Balanced Scorecard is a strategy performance tool used by managers to keep track of the execution of activities by the staff within their control (see Kaplan & Norton, 1996). It is widely acknowledged that the prototype of the Balanced Scorecard emerged in 1987 within the Analog Device Inc., a semiconductor company based in Norwood, Massachusetts (Kaplan, 1998). Arthur Schneiderman, Vice President of Quality and Productivity Improvement, was in charge of the implementation of Total Quality Management (TQM). As he was the process owner for non-financial performance measurement, he created the scorecard between 1986 and 1987. However, it was not until Arthur Schneiderman had worked with Robert Kaplan, the Harvard Business School professor of accounting, that the scorecard was broadly diffused to the public at large.

Schneiderman–Kaplan partnership as curiosity-driven

As Schneiderman had read *Relevance Lost* (Johnson & Kaplan, 1987), he was aware of the work of Robert Kaplan. He asked him for help in the implementation of Activity-Based Costing within Analog Device. When entering the firm, Kaplan heard about the *half-life system*, an innovation measuring the rate of improvement of the company's TQM program that Schneiderman had accidentally discovered in 1984. Interested in the approach, Kaplan developed with the help of Schneiderman a teaching case and published it in 1990 under the title "Analog Devices, Inc.: The Half-Life System." As Kaplan and Schneiderman were discussing that innovation, they got to know each other better. That is how Kaplan heard about the scorecard Schneiderman had developed earlier on. The professor thus invited the practitioner to join a yearlong project led by the Nolan, Norton & Co group, which gathered several companies to work on performance measurement. As Analog Device's corporate scorecard captured the interest of participants, all the participants experimented on using the scorecard in their organizations and reported back to the project on the results. It led to a publication from the leaders of the projects, Kaplan and Norton (1992), the second partnership that continued the development of the Balanced Scorecard.

Norton–Kaplan partnership as a working team

That first publication in *Harvard Business Review* illustrates the beginning of a partnership that continued for more than a decade. David Norton is a consultant from Nolan, Norton & Co specialized in information systems. Even if he holds a Doctorate of Business Administration (DBA) from Harvard Business School, Norton has always been interested in applied science as attests his consulting career spent in several consultancies. The Norton–Kaplan partnership builds on a common respect of their differing role boundaries.[8] Kaplan is the one who focuses on concept development and writes the books and articles while Norton provides Kaplan with real cases, implements the balanced scorecard in organizations, and develops the tools. Their differing skills and distinctive roles allow them to complement each other. "There are few tandems with this unity" expresses a consultant who took part in the development of different management concepts. Their partnership led to the publication of more than nine articles published in the HBR since the 1992 article, five co-authored books, and the implementation of many projects throughout the world.

Key learnings from the Balanced Scorecard case

Even though they are contrasted, the two successive Balanced Scorecard partnerships exemplify some of their benefits:

- First, the Schneiderman–Kaplan interaction illustrates the necessity for scholars to construct strong ties with practitioners while entering fields of research. Here, it has allowed a move from a proprietary in-house innovation to an academic innovation shared with a broad community.
- Second, both interactions have occurred with mutual respect, each proponent of the partnership recognizing the other's competencies and respecting the other's boundaries. It has helped reconciling their different representations of management knowledge (see also Chapters 3, 14 and 16 in this volume).

Ambidexterity interactions

Markides (2007: 764) defines ambidexterity for an individual as doing contrary things at the same time. In the interactions occurring between research and practice for an individual, doing contrary things at the same time means acting both as a practitioner and a researcher. The illustration in this book developed by Laura Empson, in Chapter 12, illustrates the discomfort it creates in one person. People can do it in several ways. On the one hand, scholars may engage in practice through experiments in real-life organizations. For instance, a full array of research paradigms have developed to foster ambidexterity, the most emblematic ones being *action science* (Argyris, Putnam & Smith, 1985) or *process consultation* (Schein, 1969). Conversely, Schön (1983) acknowledges that practitioners' actions may be generalized to contribute to management knowledge as their reflections-in-action makes them act as researchers.

We will show how ambidexterity interactions can also occur within research paradigms different from action research and process consultation. For that purpose, we take the cases of Disruptive Innovation and Open Innovation where doctoral studies have given a sense of rigor to a lived experience and where staying close to the phenomenon under study has improved the relevance of an academic work.

Disruptive innovation and open innovation

Disruptive innovation is defined as a new practice or technique for creating "a simpler, more convenient product that sells for less money and appeals to a new or unattractive customer set" (Christensen & Raynor, 2003). On the other hand, open innovation is defined as "a distributed innovation process based on purposively managed knowledge flows across organizational boundaries, using pecuniary and non-pecuniary mechanisms in line with the organization's business model" (Chesbrough & Bogers, 2014). Both concepts offer appealing examples of ambidexterity interactions because Clayton Christensen and Henry Chesbrough, the two innovators behind those concepts, have both oscillated between academia and practice throughout their lives, first by entering academia after a substantive business experience and second by practicing consulting activities and giving advice to firms in parallel to their academic activity (see similar illustration in Chapters 9 and 16).

Doctoral studies as a gateway to academia

Ten years after he graduated from Harvard Business School in 1979 with an MBA, Christensen went back to pursue a DBA. In between, he spent time working as a consultant at BCG, for the US government, and as an entrepreneur. He based his dissertation on the historical study of the disk drive industry, where he had previously worked. His work gained in rigor by duplicating over time the concept of disruption from the disk drive industry to the excavating equipment industry and later to the steel industry. He also got credential from practitioners as his work had been empirically tested in different situations.

Similarly to Christensen, Chesbrough undertook doctoral studies after a first professional experience. He began his PhD at Haas School of Business (University of California, Berkeley) in 1992 after seven years spent working for Quantum, a firm operating in the disk drive industry whose division was acquired in 2001 by Maxtor (later bought by Seagate). By comparing the US and Japanese disk drive industries, Chesbrough noticed that a disruption phenomenon was taking place in the first territory while it was not happening in the latter. He explains it by the presence of many start-ups in the US that are not present in Japan, that play the role of agents of disruption. After defending his dissertation in 1997, Chesbrough was hired as an assistant professor at Harvard Business School where he benefited from different connections that helped him go beyond the disk drive industry to explore other contexts. As he was denied tenure in 2003 because of his lack of academic publications in the allotted time, he went back to Haas School of Business as an adjunct professor and published *Open Innovation* (Chesbrough, 2003), a book modeling a phenomenon he had experienced during his professional experience, and matured during his PhD and upcoming experience at Harvard.

*Practicing an advice activity to stay close to the phenomenon
under study*

As Christensen had published his ideas both in academic and practitioner outlets (e.g., Bower & Christensen, 1995; Christensen & Bower, 1996), companies became interested in his work. For instance, in 1996 he met Andy Grove, the CEO of Intel, to explain to him the concept of disruptive innovation. It seems that Grove understood from that discussion that disruption could also happen in the microprocessor industry as the company put the Celeron processor on the market to avoid disruption from Cyrix and AMD, who were making cheap and low-performance chips. Celeron quickly became the highest-volume product in the company. As the *Innovator's Dilemma* (Chesbrough, 1997) encountered a tremendous success, he launched Innosight in 2000, a consultancy that would dispense advice based on Disruptive Innovation. In 2007, he also founded Rose Park Advisors, an investment company that utilizes research based on Disruptive Innovation to make investments decisions.

On his side, after the publication of *Open Innovation*, Chesbrough has continued to oscillate between research and practice. As his first book and practitioner-oriented articles (all published the same year in *Harvard Business Review*, *MIT Sloan Management Review* and *California Management Review*) had received some echo among practitioners, he spent time with companies to answer to their questions related to the application of Open Innovation, either through consulting assignments or through workshops. In parallel, he enriched the academic side of the concept by organizing a Professional Development Workshop at the annual meeting of the Academy of Management in 2004, whose content was published as a handbook (Chesbrough, Vanhaverbeke & West, 2006). The same year, an article published by Laursen and Salter (2006) in the *Strategic Management Journal* participated in legitimating the concept in academia. Over time, Chesbrough has continued working on Open Innovation by acting both as a practitioner and a researcher, publishing books (Chesbrough, 2006, 2011), and regularly meeting with practitioners. He has been meeting with firms through the center he has developed at Berkeley (cf. section on "mediation"), and, in parallel, he has improved the academic grounding of the concept by mobilizing a community as exemplified by the published handbook (Chesbrough, Vanhaverbeke & West, 2014) and the World Open Innovation Conference that has been organized since 2014. As he recognizes himself,[9] he is a boundary spanner between industry and academia. His knowledge of academic research in certain fields gives him the academic credentials while, as he deeply interacts with industries and cares by being useful to them, he also feels he is part of practice.

*Key learnings from the Disruptive Innovation and Open
Innovation cases*

The examples of Disruptive Innovation and Open Innovation, first, express the complementarity of knowing a field from both practitioner and academic perspective. By exploring the same phenomenon in different industries with a scientific method, both Christensen and Chesbrough have been able to unravel things they were not able to make sense of as practitioners. Second, throughout their career, they have addressed practitioners' interests in different ways on the phenomenon they have discovered.

Mediation interactions

Mediation interactions take place when knowledge is co-constructed between academics and practitioners through media that enable a dialogue and knowledge exchanges between the two counterparts. Knowledge is refined and improved continuously. Again, the cases of Disruptive Innovation and Open Innovation offer interesting illustrations. To improve their concept, both Christensen and Chesbrough rely on the classroom and on forums gathering professionals.

Mobilizing the classroom to benefit from students' interactions

To improve his theory of Disruptive Innovation, Christensen relied on the Building and Sustaining a Successful Enterprise (BSSE) class he developed at Harvard Business School for his MBA students (Christensen & Carlile, 2009). As the traditional case study method was hardly helping them understanding the theory of disruption, Christensen had to develop this class where, instead of acquiring knowledge through inductive case studies, students would rather learn through a deductive course architecture. For each class, students are assigned readings on a theory about a dimension of a general manager's job and a case about a company facing a problem that is relevant to that theory. In class discussions, students look through the lens of the theory and test whether it adequately explains what happened in the firm. If it does well, students are able to suggest recommendations taken from the theory. If it does not, it means that they found anomalies that the theory cannot explain. In this way, in the next class they are given a new theory and a new case. To each new case they apply all the theories they have already learnt and find either recommendations or anomalies. By enrolling some 160 MBA students each semester, the BSSE class helped Christensen develop and improve the theory of Disruptive Innovation. For instance, he found that neither Holiday Inn nor McDonald's have been able to disrupt five-star hotels and restaurants. Those insights helped Christensen figure out that disruption has a technological core and he led on several publications. Apart from improving the rigor of the concept of disruption, the classroom also allowed the publication of practitioner-oriented articles (e.g., Christensen & Bever, 2014; Christensen, Kauffman & Shih, 2008). It shows how the classroom interactions can contribute to raising insights among practitioners.

Chesbrough also relied on his MBA classes to improve the concept of Open Innovation but the mechanism differs from Christensen. In a class taught to MBA students and dedicated to Open Innovation, after explaining and illustrating the concept, Chesbrough assigns each student to write a 15- to 20-page final paper where he or she would develop his or her own example of Open Innovation. By scanning different situations that he would never be able to find by himself, Chebrough has been able to figure out how the concept would work in fields he did not know much about, such as financial services or healthcare. In other words, he mobilized his students as very good eyes and ears to find new applications of the idea. Those insights helped to replicate the concept in other contexts and in turn to better understand the phenomenon.

Developing third places to push thematic interactions and organize regular exchanges with professionals

Christensen also relied on mediation interactions through the creation in 2007 of the Innosight Institute to apply his ideas to healthcare and education. It later became the Clayton Christensen Institute for Disruptive Innovation. According to its website, it aims to "work to shape and elevate the conversation surrounding these issues through rigorous research and public outreach."[10] It offers a forum for discussion for policy makers, community leaders, and innovators by distilling and promoting the transformational power of disruptive innovation. To reach their purpose, members of the think-tank participate in conferences all around the world and write blog posts as well as white papers in order to bring scientific knowledge to political debates. In a nutshell, this mediation place allows debates on key societal themes by using Christensen's concept.

In the case of Chesbrough, since his book quickly became a hit, he received a lot of requests on Open Innovation. After a couple of months, as companies were repeatedly asking the same questions, he decided to find a way to better address these questions all at once. It took the shape of a membership group of companies gathered within what he called the Berkeley Innovation Forum, which contributes to research for the Center for Open Innovation he runs at Berkeley. People meet twice a year to exchange practices among non-competing companies, to listen to outside speakers, and to talk about the challenges they encounter while managing innovation. From ten companies in 2005, the Forum had grown to some 30 company members by 2016. Running that forum allows Chesbrough to listen and talk to companies on an ongoing basis. It has become a very good way for him to conduct research on problem-finding rather than problem-solving.[11]

Key learnings from the Disruptive Innovation and Open Innovation cases

Both Disruptive Innovation and Open Innovation offer interesting illustrations of mediation interactions. We showed that the classroom is an interesting way for academics to test theories and get feedbacks from practitioners and more specifically executives[12] who have accumulated experiences and knowledge from a plurality of industries and countries. This way, it improves and refines theories.

Mediation interactions can also use rigorous knowledge to improve an area that is seen as relevant for society and focus on problem-finding to address relevant issues (see also Chapter 7).

Popularization interactions

We call popularization an interaction constituted by a one-way exchange of knowledge between academics and practitioners. Knowledge is produced by one counterpart and is then diffused to the other. From research to practice, it is the "transmission of scientific knowledge from scientists to the lay public for purposes of edification, legitimating and training" (Whitley, 1985: 3 cited in Schulz & Nicolai, 2015). On the other hand, from practice to research, it takes the form of relevant feedback effects from popularization media to scholarly journals that influence the degree of scholarly attention certain topics receive as well as influence the content of research (Schulz & Nicolai, 2015; Chapter 3). We develop this interaction by taking two successive examples: Blue Ocean Strategy, which took a typical North American popularization strategy, and Business Model Canvas, which relied heavily on social media.

Blue Ocean Strategy and Business Model Canvas

Blue Ocean Strategy is a strategy concept defined as the simultaneous pursuit of differentiation and low cost to open up a new market space and create new demand by targeting non-customers. Business Model Canvas is a strategic management and entrepreneurial tool that allows the description, the design, and the invention of a business model. Both concepts are very popular among academics and practitioners, *Blue Ocean Strategy* (Kim & Mauborgne, 2005) and *Business Model Generation* (Osterwalder & Pigneur, 2010) being sold at more than a million copies.

Blue Ocean Strategy: an archetype of North American popularization

The recipe of the popularization of *Blue Ocean Strategy* mixes different ingredients. After an academic career focused on publishing in the most rigorous outlets at the University of Michigan, Ross School of Business, W. Chan Kim and Renée Mauborgne moved to INSEAD in 1992 and disseminated the Blue Ocean Strategy concept in a sequel of nine articles published in *Harvard Business Review*. This is an astonishing number of articles because academics who disseminate knowledge to practitioners usually publish a book after two (or three) subsequent *HBR* articles. One may guess that the suspense it created participated in the success of the book.

   Second, the authors have devoted a lot of time to improve the diffusion of the concept to faculty and students. As it is currently taught in more than 1,800 universities over more than 100 countries,[13] efforts have been spent on ensuring its teaching quality rather than on co-creating knowledge with practitioners (for that purpose, see the "mediation" section above). It involves the development of teaching materials such as a syllabus for Blue Ocean Strategy electives and the creation of appealing paper and video cases. For instance, after Justin Trudeau's victory in the Canadian elections in late 2015, Fares Boulos, an Affiliated Professor at INSEAD, developed a case study for MBA students on Trudeau's election victory that he assimilates as "blue ocean politics." It also implies relying on new pedagogical techniques such as developing simulation games, or developing applications for computers, tablets, and smart phones.

Third, the book is the cornerstone of the popularization of Blue Ocean Strategy. Its name is appealing for the reader: would you rather fight among sharks or dive in the Caribbean Sea? Everyone chooses the blue ocean![14] It also relies on a high degree of rhetoric and persuasion.[15] For instance, at the beginning of the book, the authors put a figure explaining that, while Blue Oceans account for only 14 percent of the business, they represent 38 percent of the revenue and more importantly 61 percent of the profit (in comparison with red oceans that respectively account for 86 percent of the business launches, 62 percent of revenue, and only 39 percent of profit). It aims at convincing readers that they have in their hands a book that will help them generating revenue and profits. Finally, the book is made easy to work through. It guides the reader page after page by having a chapter upfront dedicated to explaining all the tools and frameworks in a systematic way and keeping the academic anchoring and justification for the end of the book. Much time has also been spent on the language to make it appropriate for practitioners (see also Chapter 17). The book is also illustrated with cases selected for their relevance and originality. In a sense, one may even wonder if Cirque du Soleil did not become successful thanks to all the MBA students who have heard about the show during their Blue Ocean Strategy classes.

Fourth, the concept has benefited from promotions orchestrated by the authors themselves: they have been involved in promotion tours, written articles in business newspapers, and given speeches all around the world to corporations, governments and so on. For instance, in 2002, they specifically targeted the management strategy community by being guest speakers at the Paris-held Strategy Management Society conference that gathers academics, businessmen and consultants. This is where the phrase "Blue Ocean Strategy" was heard by the public at large for the first time. They went one step further by taking advisory positions with governments. For instance, W. Chan Kim worked with the prime minister of Malaysia to launch a National Blue Ocean Strategy in 2012 and Renée Mauborgne has been a board member of the White House Initiative on Historically Black Colleges and Universities since 2012.

Fifth and last, the concept has been popularized through the Blue Ocean Strategy Network, a gathering of consultants that has applied the concept within firms. As the practitioners involved in the network had a stake in the development of the concept, they would not want to misuse it. To ensure the quality of the consulting activity to outsiders and in order to prevent people from falsely representing themselves as experts, W. Chan Kim and Renée Mauborgne also created a certification process.

Business Model Canvas: popularizing knowledge through social media

The concept of Business Model Canvas was developed a decade after Blue Ocean Strategy, as part of Alex Osterwalder's dissertation conducted at HEC Lausanne under the supervision of Yves Pigneur (Osterwalder, 2004). The thesis offers the theoretical building of a conceptual model of a business model accompanied with guidelines on how to implement it as a tool.

Popularization first took place through the mobilization of social media. As Osterwalder had participated in academic conferences during his PhD, he noticed that the topic of business modeling was drawing the attention of both the academic and business communities. After finishing his PhD, he put his manuscript on the University of Lausanne's website. Again, it attracted public interest. He then began blogging and tweeting on the business model while applying his concept within firms. These practices greatly contributed to advertising his work. In the meantime, he shared online his ongoing work including his professional presentations, using Creative Commons licenses. At that time, the community of people following his work was growing. Consequently, when Osterwalder and Pigneur decided to publish their book and launch their first set of conferences in 2008, they had immediate interest.[16]

The book also played an important role in popularizing the concept. It was constructed and published through an innovative business model. It was co-created with the help of 470 contributors, and self-published before being published by Wiley (Osterwalder & Pigneur, 2010). The authors paid attention to both illustrations and text. For that purpose, Alan Smith was hired as a graphic designer for the book and Tim Clark, one of the contributors, also helped to turn the text into "pure US-based English."[17] To advertise their book, Osterwalder and Pigneur made 80 pages of it freely available on the Internet. They also put a one-page Business Model Canvas registered under the Creative Common license that has been downloaded more than six million times and reproduced on many other websites. The book has been translated into more than 29 languages and has sold over one million copies. And they continued publishing their concept. In 2012, Tim Clark decided to use the Business Model Canvas to apply it to the self. So *Business Model You* (Clark, Osterwalder & Pigneur, 2012). And most recently *Value Proposition Design* (Osterwalder, Pigneur, Bernarda & Smith, 2014) has been published. The concept is currently taught all around the world and an online course is also offered on the Business Model Canvas website.[18]

Even if Osterwalder and Pigneur already had the opportunity to organize workshops, it was not until 2009 that they took the important step of popularizing the concept:

- The ideas were first developed as two-day workshops addressed to independent or small consultancies, entrepreneurs, and coaches. These workshops later reached people from corporations, such as intrapreneurs or business developers, and even top management teams and whole firms' divisions. Gradually, the concept diffused through word of mouth within these communities. More recently, online courses have developed with a similar objective.
- Both Osterwalder and Pigneur worked to increase the recognition and legitimacy of the concept. through two-hour keynotes aimed at diffusing and selling the book. In 2013, they also organized the Business Design Summit where they invited ten prominent scholars such as Steve Blank and Rita McGrath. The association with top management scholars certainly contributed to Osterwalder and Pigneur's visibility and recognition.[19]
- They developed a process for building a community that would continue to popularize the concept beyond the involvement of its creators. In 2013, they developed a specific Train the Trainer workshop aimed at certifying business model trainers to deliver their own workshops. There are now about 30 certified trainers who can in turn popularize the business model canvas throughout the world.
- Finally, tools played a significant role in the popularization of the concept with Osterwalder and Pigneur developing a computer-based program to construct a business model canvas which was released in 2012. However, the challenge remains to integrate the tool with other software to ensure its use in the long run.

*Key learnings from the Blue Ocean Strategy and Business Model
Canvas cases*

These two illustrations show that, to get academic knowledge accepted by practitioners, it is necessary to focus on particular outlets (i.e., books, bridging journals), to use metaphors, and to mobilize a rhetoric. Social media and word of mouth are also key to attracting the interest of an engaged community.

Discussion and conclusion

As we have reviewed the different frameworks that have been developed within academia to better link academia with practice (e.g., engaged scholarship, Mode 2 research, dialogic model, insider/outsider research teams), we lamented the fact they are rarely mobilized by academics or practitioners to undertake management research. For that purpose, this chapter offers a fine-grained model of collaboration between academics and practitioners by showing the different interactions that can occur between them and by taking illustrations from five major management concepts.

We have explained how to actually create scholar–practitioner collaborations by detailing the different possible forms of interactions. Interestingly, among the four modes of interactions that we have developed, we shed light on a populari-zation interaction relying on social media, a way of interacting that has been overlooked in research on academic–practitioner collaborations. We also show that interactions between academics and practitioners are necessary throughout the development of a concept. For instance, we showed that both Christensen and Chesbrough have been ambidextrous for their whole academic journey, focusing both on rigor and relevance by addressing both academic and practi-tioner communities. Furthermore, as we have shown elsewhere (Carton & Dameron, 2015), management concepts are developed by relying on a complex mix of the four interactions succeeding over time. In that sense, relevance is instilled in academic research throughout the development of management con-cepts by relying on different scholar–practitioner interactions. Finally, we have highlighted that a common respect between scholars and practitioners is neces-sary to develop fruitful interactions (see also Chapters 17 and 18).

Based on the illustrations from this chapter, Table 15.1 summarizes our find-ings by showing how it is possible to navigate through the different tensions inherent in scholar–practitioner interactions:

- Importantly, to manage tensions through ambidexterity, an individual has to change his or her mindset to address the counterpart's objective, as Henry Chesbrough and Clayton Christensen have done throughout their academic journey to span the academic–practice boundary.
- Second, to face tensions through mediation, a specific place, such as the classroom or a forum, has to be specifically designed to address expecta-tions from both parties.
- Third, to face tensions through partnership, mutual trust as well as a respect for the other party is necessary to allow each counterpart to specialize in its domain.
- Fourth and last, if an academic want to popularize knowledge to practition-ers, he/she has to adapt his/herself to the practitioner's audience, using their own language and media.

We did not intend in this chapter to develop a complete list of the different practices that can be put in place to favor scholar–practitioner interactions. In fact, with the rise of the digital era, we may expect novel interactions. In terms of medi-ation, we have just witnessed the development of online classes, either MOOCs or online classes such as HBX, the experiment developed by Harvard Business School.[20] They may offer feedback for academics from a broad range of people coming from all around the world. Popular social media such as Facebook, Twitter, or Pulse on LinkedIn may also provide quick feedbacks with a less-focused audience. To compensate, one can develop more confined and thematic areas as Gary Hamel did by developing Management Innovation eXchange.[21]

In terms of popularization, we may expect open access policies to facilitate interactions between research and practice. New technologies may also develop ways of consuming knowledge such as the experiment that the philosopher

Table 15.1 Solutions to face tensions taking place at the scholar–practitioner interface

Tensions/interactions	Ambidexterity	Mediation	Partnership	Popularization
Practices developed	Consulting activity by an academic (OI, DI), creation of a consultancy (DI), PhD/DBA (DI, OI)	Classroom theory-testing (DI), case development through assignments (OI), exchange forum (OI), think-tank (DI)	Case development, elective affinity (BSC)	Popular press (BOS), social media (BMC), conferences and workshops (BMC, BOS), essay (BMC, BOS), cases and teaching material (BOS), professional certification (BMC, BOS), consultancy (BOS), creation of tools (BMC, BOS), advisory work (BOS)
Different logics	Change of mindset to shift between communities	Gathering of the two communities in a common logic	Negotiation of common goals	Academics' efforts to anchor their work in practitioners' logic
Different time dimensions	Research apprehended as a long-term objective addressing both short-term practitioners' demand and long-term academic needs	Negotiation of a project with a delimited time frame and using a specific platform, in order to satisfy both parties	Negotiation of a common long-term objective with differing time span (e.g., intermediate deadlines)	Academics' efforts to address practitioners' shorter time span by using specific outlets
Different communication styles	Ability to change the communication style thanks to a knowledge of both academia and practice	Development of a common language to build knowledge on that basis	Assignment of complementary roles with differing communication styles	Academics' efforts to specifically address practitioners by translating knowledge (writing style, outlet choice)
Rigor vs. relevance	Change of mindset to change the criteria of rigor and relevance depending on the target audience	Development of common criteria of rigor and relevance	Assignment of complementary roles to complement rigor with relevance	Academics' efforts to turn academic rigor into relevant knowledge
Different interests and incentives	Change of mindset to respond to the interests/incentives of the other part	Gathering of the two communities within a specific platform gathering common interests and incentives	Negotiation of common goals	Academics' efforts to specifically address practitioners' issues

Notes

BOS: Blue Ocean Strategy; BSC: Balanced Scorecard; BMC: Business Model Canvas; DI: Disruptive Innovation; OI: Open Innovation.

Bruno Latour did by launching a website playing the role of a serious game with his book, *An inquiry into modes of existence.*[22] Finally, we have witnessed in these past few years many business schools developing websites or quarterly publications aimed at popularizing their knowledge to the public at large, following the example of Knowledge@Wharton[23] or of the *Harvard Business Review*. As Andrews (1977: 1) explains, the recipe for the success of such publications lies in "the ideal HBR article [being] original, analytical, and useful. It is not usually hair-raising, funny, artificial, superficial, or pointlessly academic."

Even if technology may help in developing new forms of mediation and popularization interactions, it hardly solves managerial issues. In fact, developing ambidexterity and partnership interactions largely rests on the development of incentives from business schools to favor scholar–practitioner collaborations. For instance, from hands-off methods of research, research in management may turn into more qualitative traditions of research, through which Chesbrough and Christensen have conducted their research. Furthermore, universities may also partner with firms to develop teaching case studies as a first port of entry to the firm, following the Balanced Scorecard's exemplar development. However, this change rests mainly on scholars' evaluations, especially tenure requirements, that do not currently favor such investments with practice.

Notes

1 This chapter is based on Guillaume Carton's PhD dissertation defended in December 2015, supervised by Stéphanie Dameron and entitled "la production des connaissances managériales: du rapport de la recherche à la pratique" (the production of management knowledge: on the relationship between research and practice).
2 Institut Supérieur de Gestion (France). Corresponding author: guillaume.carton@isg.fr.
3 PSL-Université Paris-Dauphine (France).
4 Their authors may be seen as Intellectual Shamans in the sense of Sandra Waddock (see Chapter 6).
5 For instance, they are among the Thinkers 50 ranking that has classified the 50 best management thinkers every other year since 2001.
6 See for instance www.youtube.com/watch?v=WJzYTxXH7R0.
7 To go further into how these four interactBon modes have been built, see Carton and Dameron (2015).
8 This is based on an interview conducted in August 2012 with a consultant who has closely worked with them.
9 This is based on an interview conducted in February 2014.
10 See www.christenseninstitute.com.
11 This is based on an interview conducted in February 2014.
12 For mediation interactions occurring during executive education, see Tushman, O'Reilly, Fenollosa, Kleinbaum and McGrath, 2007.
13 According to blueoceanstrategy.com.
14 A body of research has developed on metaphors in management (i.e., Cornelissen & Kafouros, 2008; Oswick, Keenoy & Grant, 2002; Tsoukas, 1991).
15 These arguments have been developed elsewhere for similar books (e.g., Nørreklit, 2003).
16 This interaction also had a mediation role as Alex Osterwalder and Yves Pigneur benefited from interactions with practitioners to improve their concept (cf. previous part).

17 This is based on an interview conducted with Tim Clark in 2013.
18 See Strategyzer.com.
19 This is based on an interview conducted with Yves Pigneur in 2013.
20 See hbx.hbs.edu.
21 See managementexchange.com.
22 See modesofexistence.org.
23 See knowledge.wharton.upenn.edu.

References

Andrews, K. R. (1977). Letter from the Program Chairman. *Harvard Business Review*, 55(5), 1.

Argyris, C., Putnam, R. & Smith, D. M. (1985). *Action Science.* San Francisco, CA: Jossey-Bass.

Avenier, M. J. & Cajaiba, A. P. (2012). The dialogical model: Developing academic knowledge for and from practice. *European Management Review*, 9(4), 199–212.

Bartunek, J. M. (2011). What has happened to Mode 2? *British Journal of Management*, 22(3), 555–8.

Bartunek, J. M. & Rynes, S. L. (2014). Academics and practitioners are alike and unlike: The paradoxes of academic–practitioner relationships. *Journal of Management*, 40(5), 1181–201.

Bower, J. L. & Christensen, C. M. (1995). Disruptive technologies: Catching the wave. *Harvard Business Review*, 73(1), 43–53.

Carton, G. & Dameron, S. (2015). A four-developmental stage model of management innovation through academic–practitioner interactions. Paper presented at the Strategic Management Society (SMS), Denver, USA.

Chesbrough, H. (2003). *Open Innovation: The New Imperative for Creating and Profiting from Technology*. Boston, MA: Harvard Business Press.

Chesbrough, H. (2006). *Open Business Models: How to Thrive in the New Innovation Landscape*. Boston, MA: Harvard Business School Press.

Chesbrough, H. (2011). *Open Services Innovation: Rethinking Your business to Compete and Grow in a New Era*. San Francisco, CA: Jossey-Bass.

Chesbrough, H. & Bogers, M. (2014). Explicating open innovation: Clarifying an emerging paradigm for understanding innovation. In Chesbrough, H., Vanhaverbeke, W. & West, J. (Eds.) *New Frontiers in Open Innovation* (pp. 3–28). Oxford: Oxford University Press.

Chesbrough, H., Vanhaverbeke, W. & West, J. (2006). *Open Innovation: Researching a New Paradigm.* Oxford: Oxford University Press.

Chesbrough, H., Vanhaverbeke, W. & West, J. (2014). *New Frontiers in Open Innovation.* Oxford: Oxford University Press.

Christensen, C. M. (1997). *The Innovator's Dilemma: When New Technologies Cause Great Firms to Fail*. Boston, MA: Harvard Business School Press.

Christensen, C. M. & Bever, D. v. (2014). The capitalist's dilemma. *Harvard Business Review*, 92(6), 60–68.

Christensen, C. M. & Bower, J. L. (1996). Customer power, strategic investment, and the failure of leading firms. *Strategic Management Journal*, 17(3), 197–218.

Christensen, C. M. & Carlile, P. R. (2009). Course research: Using the case method to build and teach management theory. *Academy of Management Learning & Education*, 8(2), 240–51.

Christensen, C. M. & Raynor, M. (2003). *The Innovator's Solution: Creating and Sustaining Successful Growth.* Boston, MA: Harvard Business Review Press.

Christensen, C. M., Kauffman, S. P. & Shih, W. C. (2008). Innovation killers. *Harvard Business Review*, 86(1), 98–105.

Clark, T., Osterwalder, A. & Pigneur, Y. (2012). *Business Model You: A One-Page Method For Reinventing Your Career.* Hoboken, NJ: John Wiley & Sons.

Cornelissen, J. P. & Kafouros, M. (2008). Metaphors and theory building in organization theory: What determines the impact of a metaphor on theory? *British Journal of Management*, 19(4), 365–79.

Dameron, S. & Durand, T. (Eds.) (2011). *Redesigning Management Education and Research: Challenging Proposals from European Scholars.* Cheltenham, UK: Edward Elgar.

Gibbons, M., Limoges, H., Nowotny, H., Schwartzman, S., Scott, P. & Trow, M. (1994). *The New Production of Knowledge: The Dynamics of Science and Research in Contemporary Societies.* Thousand Oaks, CA: Sage Publications.

Johnson, H. T. & Kaplan, R. S. (1987). *Relevance Lost: The Rise and Fall of Management Accounting.* Boston, MA: Harvard Business School Press.

Kaplan, R. S. (1998). Innovation action research: Creating new management theory and practice. *Journal of Management Accounting Research*, 10(10), 89–118.

Kaplan, Robert S. (1990) *Analog Devices, Inc.: The Half-Life System.* Boston, MA: Harvard Business School Case 190-061. Retrieved March 27, 2017 from www.hbs.edu/faculty/Pages/item.aspx?num=345.

Kaplan, R. S. & Norton, D. P. (1992). The Balanced Scorecard: Measures that drive performance. *Harvard Business Review*, 70(1), 71–9.

Kaplan, R. S. & Norton, D. P. (1996). *The Balanced Scorecard: Translating Strategy into Action.* Boston, MA: Harvard Business Review Press.

Kieser, A., Nicolai, A. T. & Seidl, D. (2015). The practical relevance of management research: Turning the debate on relevance into a rigorous scientific research program. *The Academy of Management Annals*, 9(1), 143–233.

Kim, W. C. & Mauborgne, R. (2005). *Blue Ocean Strategy. How to Create Uncontested Market Space and Make the Competition Irrelevant.* Boston, MA: Harvard Business Review Press.

Laursen, K. & Salter, A. (2006). Open for innovation: The role of openness in explaining innovation performance among UK manufacturing firms. *Strategic Management Journal*, 27(2), 131–50.

Louis, M. R. & Bartunek, J. M. (1992). Insider/outsider research teams: Collaboration across diverse perspectives. *Journal of Management Inquiry*, 1(2), 101–10.

Markides, C. (2007). In search of ambidextrous professors. *Academy of Management Journal*, 50(4), 762–68.

Mohrman, S. A. & Lawler, E. E. (2011). *Useful Research: Advancing Theory and Practice.* San Francisco, CA: Berrett-Koehler Publishers.

Nørreklit, H. (2003). The Balanced Scorecard: What is the score? A rhetorical analysis of the Balanced Scorecard. *Accounting, Organizations and Society*, 28(6), 591–619.

Osterwalder, A. (2004). The business model ontology: A proposition in a design science approach. Dissertation, University of Lausanne, Switzerland: 173.

Osterwalder, A. & Pigneur, Y. (2010). *Business Model Generation: A Handbook for Visionaries, Game Changers, and Challengers.* Hoboken, NJ: John Wiley & Sons.

Osterwalder, A., Pigneur, Y., Bernarda, G. & Smith, A. (2014). *Value Proposition Design: How to Create Products and Services Customers Want.* Hoboken, NJ: John Wiley & Sons.

Oswick, C., Keenoy, T. & Grant, D. (2002). Metaphor and analogical reasoning in organization theory: Beyond orthodoxy. *Academy of Management Review*, 27(2), 294–303.

Schein, E. H. (1969). *Process Consultation: Its Role in Organization Development.* Reading, MA: Addison-Wesley.

Schön, D. A. (1983). *The Reflective Practitioner: How Professionals Think in Action.* New York: Basic Books.

Schulz, A. C. & Nicolai, A. T. (2015). The intellectual link between management research and popularization media: A bibliometric analysis of the Harvard Business Review. *Academy of Management Learning & Education*, 14(1), 31–49.

Shani, A. B. R., Mohrman, S. A., Pasmore, W. A., Stymne, B. & Adler, N. (Eds.) (2008). *Handbook of Collaborative Management Research.* Thousand Oaks, CA: Sage Publications.

Starkey, K. & Madan, P. (2001). Bridging the relevance gap: Aligning stakeholders in the future of management research. *British Journal of Management*, 12(Special Issue), S3–S26.

Tranfield, D. & Starkey, K. (1998). The nature, social organization and promotion of management research: Towards policy. *British Journal of Management*, 9(4), 341.

Tsoukas, H. (1991). The missing link: A transformational view of metaphors in organizational science. *Academy of Management Review*, 16(3), 566–85.

Tsoukas, H. (2009). A dialogical approach to the creation of new knowledge in organizations. *Organization Science*, 20(6), 941–57.

Tushman, M. L., O'Reilly, C., Fenollosa, A., Kleinbaum, A. M. & McGrath, D. (2007). Relevance and rigor: Executive education as a lever in shaping practice and research. *Academy of Management Learning & Education*, 6(3), 345–62.

16 Making values matter

An academic and private sector collaboration

Todd Landman, Steve Glowinkowski,
and Kali Demes

Background to the collaboration

In the spring of 2010, the Registrar of the University of Essex, who had a portfolio that included regular communications with local businesses, convened a meeting between Professor Steve Glowinkowski (Founder and Managing Director of Glowinkowski International Ltd), David Wilson (Researcher at Glowinkowski International Ltd), David Physick (Principal Consultant at Glowinkowski International Ltd) and Professor Todd Landman (Director of the Institute for Democracy and Conflict Resolution at the University of Essex). Professor Landman had been developing a portfolio of work for the Institute for Democracy and Conflict Resolution, which included working papers, contract research, consultancy, and business development across the areas of democracy, mediation, conflict resolution, and other areas of expertise at the University of Essex. Glowinkowski International Ltd (GIL) offer a range of tools developed in-house, for organizational development, change management, and personal direction setting and development within large organizations. Initial meetings between these parties involved scoping discussions and mapping common interests, sharing of research interests and research findings, and the development of working relationships.

From this initial relationship a number of themes have emerged over the years in relation to engagement between the University of Essex and GIL. This includes the development of a program for internships and student placements within GIL as well as recruitment of permanent employees from the university's graduate pool. There has been collaborative work between GIL and the university in terms of publications, conference papers, and the implementation of the Glowinkowski tool kit in a leadership development program within the university. In addition, Glowinkowski practitioners have contributed to a number of the university's degree programs.

The practitioner

Glowinkowski built a business on the application of psychological models of human behavior within organizations based on his career as an organizational psychologist in companies such as ICI and Barclays in the 1980s and early 1990s. He captured these experiences and developed models to measure behavior and managerial "styles of engagement" in ways that provided critical insights to large organizations undergoing periods of change. This approach is based on over 35 years of research looking at the factors which differentiate outstanding from average performance at the level of the individual, teams, and organizations. This work has been multi-sector and international in reach. The GIL database contains data from over 60,000 leaders/managers and their respective employee groups.

Based on this research and analysis, Glowinkowski has developed a series of measures and techniques which are capable of assessing critical themes within organizations including Predisposition, Behavior and Organizational Climate. Through his work Glowinkowski has demonstrated how these themes integrate with one another to shape and drive the culture and performance of organizations. In many respects, the intellectual underpinnings of this approach lie in the pioneering work of Kurt Lewin (1951). It was he who said "there is nothing so practical as a good theory." Building upon Lewin's teachings, Glowinkowski emphasizes the importance of utilizing methodologies that are both practical and valid. In other words, at the heart of Glowinkowski's work is an approach which seeks to utilize methods that have "psychometric" proven or established validity and reliability that are crucially packaged and presented in a way that makes intuitive sense and is of practical value to people and organizations.

Glowinkowski's work has been published in two popular business books entitled *It's Behaviour Stupid* (Glowinkowski, 2009) and *Strategy, People, Implementation* (King & Glowinkowski, 2015) both of which draw upon the rich experience of working with executive leadership and senior leadership teams across a variety of sectors including power and energy, brewing, financial services, meteorology, education, and religion. His work combined the collection and analysis of individual level data, 360 degree feedback data, and qualitative data from hundreds of one-to-one feedback sessions. This led to the construction of the Glowinkowski "Integrated Framework," which shows the relationships between:

- the vision, purpose, and values of an organization;
- its strategic objective;
- individual predispositions, motivation, and personal values;
- organizational structure, behaviors, and processes;
- climate; and
- business performance (see Figure 16.1).

The academic

Landman built his research and teaching career at Essex on comparative political methodology (Landman, 2000, 2003, 2008), measuring and comparing human rights (Foweraker & Landman, 1997, 1999; Landman, 2002, 2004, 2005, 2006,

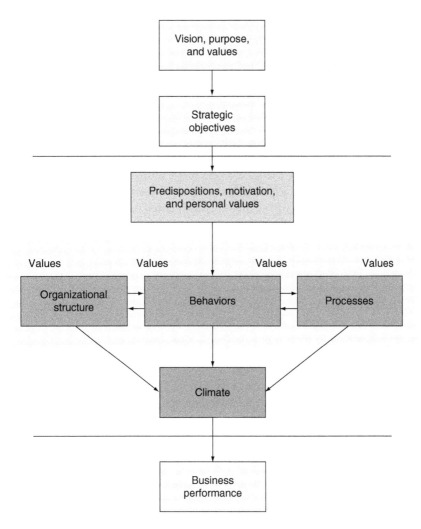

Figure 16.1 The Glowinkowski "integrated framework."

2012, 2016; Landman & Carvalho, 2009; Landman & Larizza, 2009), and on international consultancy delivering capacity building, contract research, evaluation, and teaching. His research has been on the relationship between social movements and citizenship rights (Foweraker & Landman, 1997, 1999), international human rights treaty ratification and the protection of human rights (Landman, 2005), inequality and human rights (Landman & Larizza, 2009), and advanced statistical applications to human rights (Landman & Gohdes, 2013; Landman, Kernohan & Gohdes, 2012).

Evolution of the partnership

At the beginning, while it was not immediately obvious how Landman and Glowinkowski would work together collaboratively, it was clear that both shared a keen interest in the measurement and analysis of human behavior, the use and testing of empirical models, and the application of their analysis and findings to real world problems. Glowinkowski's interests concern how individuals behave in different organizational settings and Landman's concern how individuals behave in different country contexts. Both sets of interests share much common ground, setting the stage for a mutually beneficial partnership (see Chapter 3 for Coghlan's insights into the foundations for academic–practitioner collaborations).

This relationship started to take shape more formally in February 2011 as Landman took part in an accreditation program to learn how to use the Global Predisposition Indicator (GPI) system, a tried, tested and validated method for measuring the natural predispositions that people have. Landman was intrigued with the tool itself and saw it as means to expand his knowledge and skills in ways that would contribute to his work on mediation, conflict resolution, and leadership. The formal accreditation led to a series of continuous engagements between Landman and Glowinkowski with a widening network of clients, and included direct interventions with senior leadership teams, where Landman and Glowinkowski led workshops, away days, and training programs. Once Landman became Executive Dean of the Faculty of Social Sciences at the University of Essex in 2013, he introduced the use of the GPI into the leadership training for the university's "Future Leaders" and "Strategic Leaders" programs.

In addition to the above, Landman worked with other Principal Consultants at Glowinkowski on the development of a training program for young people called "Crafting Confidence," which was deployed in a series of high schools in the United Kingdom. Landman worked with lower sixth form students in Milton Keynes, Cambridge, and Norwich in building confidence and providing insight into their own sets of predispositions. These engagements with young people fed into the work for "Unleashing Potential," a training and development program for the Executive Leadership Team and Senior Leadership Team in a large utilities company in the UK. Landman not only deployed the GPI, but also drew upon his experiences and the challenges associated with academic leadership and how common sets of concerns over people, budgets, and deliverables contain valuable lessons for most large organizations. These private sector experiences fed back into Landman's role as Executive Dean in crafting new educational programs, carrying out strategic reviews, and improving levels of financial sustainability across eight social science departments.

How the values theme emerged

These engagements between Landman and Glowinkowski took place over a period of three years and included additional meetings with a large number of stakeholders from education, human resource management, financial services, coaching, energy, accounting, management consulting, and insurance. At one such meeting at Mazars in London in 2012 (the UK's eighth largest accounting firm), Landman and one of the Glowinkowski Principal Consultants, David Physick, heard a young woman speak about values in business. She had been employed by a major financial institution as a fresh graduate from university, and was thrilled with the job, the salary, and the lifestyle. However, over time she had become increasingly frustrated and disillusioned with the actual products she was selling. She resigned from the company and took a job that was much more in line with her values, even though it meant she would receive a smaller salary and enjoy a somewhat less luxurious lifestyle.

Physick and Landman discussed this young woman's intervention at length and started to brainstorm on how values could be introduced into the Glowinkowski tool kit and how values could become more prominent in the Integrated Framework (see Figure 16.1). These discussions took place during a crucial period for the business world. Values-driven business ideas and the notion of "transformational capitalism" (as opposed to "transactional capitalism") were increasingly capturing public attention after the financial crisis in 2008, a series of corporate scandals that hit large firms in the US and UK, and an emerging consensus on using values, norms, and international guiding principles to shape current and future business practices. The collapse of Lehman Brothers, the BP Gulf disaster, the Payment Protection Insurance (PPI) scandal, and the Libor fixing scandal, among others, suggested that the departure from value commitments within corporate boardrooms had become widespread and had created significant and costly liabilities for firms across many different sectors.

In keeping with this theme, around this time Landman started teaching on the Judge Business School program on Sustainability Leadership at the University of Cambridge, where participants were drawn from middle to upper management from large global corporations engaged in fulsome discussions about the importance of values for business. He heard first-hand how such key managers across a wide range of sectors were increasingly interested in how an attention to values is important for business. Landman lectured on the international human rights regime and how human rights scholars and practitioners turned their attention to business. He set out the main international human rights instruments, the newly articulated "Ruggie Principles" for human rights and business and how they mapped onto the existing literature on corporate social responsibility. He complemented this with formal lectures and case study sessions on Shell in Nigeria, Starbucks, and the toxic waste scandal involving Trafugura (Amnesty International & Greenpeace, 2012).

Throughout 2012 and 2013, Landman and Glowinkowski organized a series of workshops with academics, management consultants, human resource professionals, and experts on corporate social responsibility, values, ethics, and inclusion in business organizations. These discussions proved highly fruitful and led to the proposition that a greater adherence to values would lead to greater bottom line performance of a large organization. The proposition itself needed further specification and operationalization, but the previous work carried out by

Glowinkowski had shown a link between improving "directed and concerned" leadership styles within large organizations and their overall business performance. The discussion groups postulated that placing values at the heart of the Glowinkowski Integrated Framework would enhance its toolkit and provide the means to test how values can make a difference for business.

The Knowledge-Transfer Partnership

The discussions described above took shape in the form of a joint application between the University of Essex and GIL to Innovate UK (formerly Technology Strategy Board) in 2013 for a Knowledge-Transfer Partnership (KTP) to develop a Global Values Indicator (GVI) that would measure values in large organizations and provide an appropriate diagnostic tool for a change management program that would address values gap identified through the diagnosis. The assumption behind the project was that closing any "gaps" would make an organization more authentic, a more desirable place to work, raise staff morale, and increase organizational performance (Jonsen, Galunic, Weeks & Braga, 2015; O'Reilly, Chatman & Caldwell, 1991; Sharma, Borna & Stearns, 2009; Valentine, Godkin, Fleischman & Kidwell, 2011). Given these objectives and the key stakeholders involved, the KTP seemed the most appropriate way to find support for developing the project (see Chapter 2 for Shani, Tenkasi and Alexander's historical take on academic–practitioner partnerships through Collaborative Management Research).

KTPs, launched in 2003 and replacing the Teaching Company Scheme (1975), are sponsored by Innovate UK, an executive Non-Departmental Public Body reporting to the Department for Business, Innovation and Skills. The aim of a KTP is to facilitate the transfer of knowledge and skills from the UK Knowledge Base (academic institutions) to industry settings in order to help small and medium-sized businesses grow by enhancing their competitiveness and performance. Across the UK there are over 800 KTPs running at any one time and each comprises three partners: the company (in this case GIL), the knowledge-base (here, the University of Essex), and a recent university graduate, known as a KTP Associate. The role of the Associate is to transfer knowledge, skills and expertise from the Knowledge Base to the company through a strategic project lasting one to three years. The Associate is placed within the company, effectively operating as an employee of the company with supervision provided from both the Knowledge Base partner and company partner. Innovate UK figures state that for every £1 million spent on KTP projects, the industry partner can expect an average annual increase in profit of £4.25 million before tax, the Knowledge Base can expect an average of two research papers to be generated, and the Associate can anticipate increased employability prospects (60 percent accept a job offer from the industry partner following the completion of the project).

Our bid was successful and we received a grant for £162,000 for a 30-month period starting from February 2014. We appointed Kali Demes as the KTP

Associate in that month, a social psychology PhD graduate from the University of Essex. Prior to her KTP appointment, Demes worked on an Economic and Social Research Council (ESRC) funded multinational study on "The Impact of Living Abroad." Through this project, over 2,500 international exchange students from over 40 different countries, travelling to one of over 50 different host destinations were monitored though nine online surveys at stages before, during, and after a year spent abroad. Demes managed this project, from survey design and construction, to project partner and participant communication, data collection, data cleaning and analysis, write up, and dissemination (Demes & Geeraert, 2015; Geeraert, Demoulin & Demes, 2014). Notably, through this work Demes and colleagues developed a series of successful measurement tools to assess key acculturation constructs (Demes & Geeraert, 2014), which are now being widely used by acculturation researchers (e.g., Kubovcikova, 2016; Ozer & Schwartz, 2016; Weber, Appel & Kronberger, 2015). The research, statistical, and project management experience gained through this work made Demes the ideal candidate for this KTP role. This collaboration between the University of Essex and GIL has led successfully to the creation of the GVI, which has been piloted at a British university, a British utility company, and in a university in the United States.

It is instructive that the evolution of our collaboration took three years before we bid for the KTP. We progressed from not knowing entirely how academics would collaborate with the private sector, to looking at how to commercialize social science and social psychological academic knowledge, to unleashing public funding to develop our tool, to deploying and refining it in ways that make it ready for the market. In Chapter 9 MacLean and MacIntosh present a view of academic–practitioner collaboration through a creative action perspective. The following section discusses our model.

Developing a values framework

The KTP team developed a values framework that would combine academic research with the insights and tools developed by GIL. This development was based on a review of relevant literature, crafting a new framework and tool from that review, and then subjecting the tool to a wide range of discussion from key stakeholders drawn from the network of experts known to the University of Essex and GIL. Considering what is a value, we look to Rokeach (1973: 2), who defines values as "standards or criteria to guide not only action but also judgment, choice, attitude, evaluation, argument, exhortation, rationalization, and … attribution of causality." Rokeach argued that values underlie all human phenomena and from this it follows that values have a role to play in organizational behavior (see also Chapter 11, where Antonacopoulou explores the role of virtue and ethics in advancing and sustaining impactful research). The objective of this KTP was to create a tool to assess the values present in a corporate setting along two key dimensions:

- the extent to which values are *demonstrated* in practice; and
- the *importance* assigned to these values by employees.

To begin, we set out to establish a framework for organizational values, a workable set of definitions and attributes of values that could be operationalized for analysis within organizations.

Reviewing the values literature

Through the literature review conducted by Demes, the KTP Associate, we examined virtue ethics, that is, what constitutes a moral or virtuous character (Annas 2011; Aristotle, 2009; Flyvbjerg 2011; Flyvbjerg, Landman & Schram, 2012; Hursthouse, 2013; for more on virtue ethics see Chapter 4 for Nielsen's Aristotelian interpretation of academic–practitioner activities). We also explored deontological approaches, which focus on the morality of actions in and of themselves (Alexander & Moore 2012; Kant 1785; Johnson 2014) and consequentialist approaches, which focus on the morality of actions on the basis of their consequences or outcomes (Sinnott-Armstrong, 2014; see also Jeremy Bentham, 1789; John Stuart Mill, 1863; Henry Sidgwick, 1907). We reviewed how, in moral psychology, these two approaches are examined in terms of "quandary ethics," with research focusing on situational factors in solving quandaries with regard to such issues as pro-social behavior (Batson, O'Quinn, Fulty, Vanderplass & Isen, 1983; Isen & Levin 1972), obedience (Milgram 1963), and bystander intervention (Latane & Darley 1970).

We explored how values have been defined and assessed in academic models, specifically in social psychology, such as Rokeach's (1973) theoretical framework of 18 "instrumental" (desirable modes of behavior) and 18 "terminal" (desirable end states) values and the operationalization of this framework through the Rokeach Values Survey (RVS). Schwartz (1992) drew upon this work and through extensive international research found that the values measured could be clustered into ten types, the structure of which has since been replicated in countless studies (e.g., Schwartz & Boehnke, 2004; Schwartz, Melech, Lehmann, Burgess, Harris & Owens, 2001; Schwartz & Sagiv, 1995; Vauclair, Hanke, Fischer & Fontaine, 2011).

In the field of political science, Inglehart and Welzel (2010) developed the idea of "post materialist values," the value set attributable to generations of people who had grown up under conditions of material security in post-industrial societies (i.e. more than 50 percent of the work force is employed in the tertiary sector). The resultant World Values Survey has now been used across an increasingly large number of countries, yielding a large number of studies examining the economic, social, and political causes and consequences of values (Inglehart, 1977, 1990, 1997; Inglehart & Norris, 2003; Inglehart & Welzel, 2005; Welzel, 2013).

Moving away from values examined at the level of individuals, directly concerning the economic, social, and political consequences of values, is the literature on business ethics and corporate social responsibility (CSR). This research has focused on how corporations are "doing good" across a wide range of business practices and operations, in relation to both internal stakeholders (i.e., employees) and external stakeholders including suppliers, customers, and the local communities within which businesses operate (Porter & Kramer, 2006, 2011). This focus on CSR has more recently been augmented by the international human rights community, which has sought to provide guiding principles for corporations to uphold in the areas of human rights, labor, the environment, and anti-corruption (e.g., United Nations, 2010). Both CSR and human rights approaches to business place new forms of external accountability on corporations and focus on both the positive and negative externalities of business activities.

Taken together, these trends from virtue ethics, moral and social psychology, political science, business studies, and business and human rights illustrate a strong and growing importance of values for organizing social life, legal and political institutions, and business organizations. Too often, however, corporations that have articulated their values publicly have been met with derision in the face of known or revealed unethical, immoral, or illegal acts, and events of the kind that have characterized the period since the 2008 financial crisis. Our approach takes these value commitments at "face value" and aims to measure them in order to provide new ways to understand the gap between the importance individuals in organizations place on values and the degree to which they believe these values are being demonstrated in practice.

Reviewing corporate values

Following the academic literature review, the KTP Associate collected the value statements from over 150 top corporations in the world (FTSE 100 and FT Global 100 companies) and examined them alongside values terms identified in various survey-based values models (Hofstede, 1980; House, Javidan & Dorfman, 2001; Rokeach, 1973; Schwartz, 1992; Welzel & Inglehart, 2010), more broad models found in moral philosophy (Allport, Vernon & Lindzey, 1970; Haidt, 2001; Keenan, 1996; Shweder, Much, Mahapatra & Park, 1997), and international guidelines and principles on corporate responsibility (ISO, 2010; OECD, 2011; United Nations, 2010, 2011).

Consolidating the review

This qualitative data was processed in a number of stages. First, the KTP Associate analyzed the gathered text using qualitative data analysis software. The most frequently appearing word among the review of all text for example was *integrity*, listed in 80 different sources, 70 of these instances representing corporations who listed this as one of their organizational values (see Figure 16.2). Following this initial word frequency analysis, words sharing a similar meaning or concept were manually sorted into common themes (e.g., inclusion and inclusive, collaboration and teamwork), a process verified by the both academic and company supervisors, Glowinkowski and Landman.

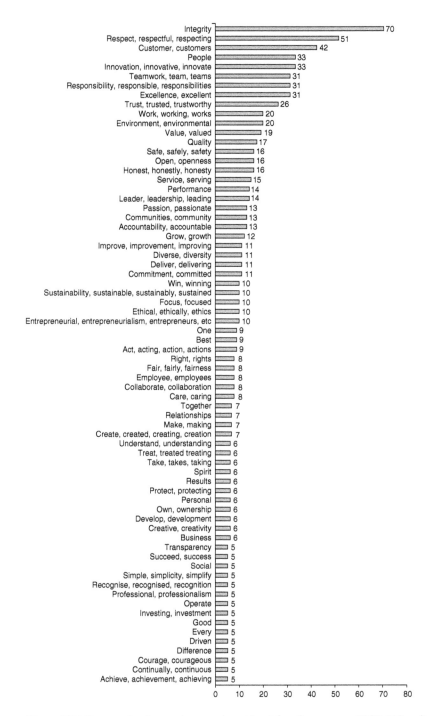

Figure 16.2 Frequencies for words appearing at least five times across FTSE 100 and FT Global 100 company values sets.

These values concepts and themes were then discussed with an advisory group panel of social researchers and organizational development professionals. This group was established for the purpose of sharing, progressing and soliciting feedback on the values work from industry experts. The members of this panel were business contacts and colleagues of Glowinkowski and Landman with interests in employee engagement, inclusion, and organizational development more broadly. They were invited to join this group, to meet for one day on a quarterly basis to discuss ongoing progress of the project. Importantly, these members volunteered their time to contribute to these discussions and proved an invaluable resource and key success factor for this work, its practical relevance and validity.

In sum, the first several months of the project were dedicated to producing and refining the values framework through a combination of independent work by Demes, the KTP Associate, fortnightly meetings with Glowinkowski and Landman, the company and academic partners, and larger group meetings with the project advisory group. This work resulted in the identification of 18 values for our framework, grouped in six core values groups:

- innovation;
- collaboration;
- excellence;
- accountability;
- integrity; and
- respect (see Table 16.1).

Work over the next few months focused on operationalizing the values framework, as discussed next.

Operationalizing the model

Having established a values framework we generated a number of survey items to serve as indicators of each of the 18 values (6×3 values). In the first instance respondents to the survey were asked to evaluate the extent to which their organization demonstrates in practice a commitment to the behaviors described in the items (*demonstration dimension*). In the second instance they were asked to rate each of the items according to how important it is to them that their organization demonstrates in practice a commitment to these behaviors (*importance dimension*). Assessing the values from these two different angles provides three distinct insights:

- how well an organization is demonstrating these values in practice;
- how important it is to employees that each of the values are demonstrated; and
- the discrepancy or "gap" between values demonstration and their importance.

Table 16.1 Global Values Indicator (GVI) framework and essence statements

Core value	Indicator value	Essence statement
INNOVATION	knowledge	makes use of specialist knowledge and technology
	novelty	is creative and fresh in their thinking
	adaptability	is flexible and open to change
COLLABORATION	teamwork	works together as a team
	inclusion	values the contribution of each individual
	relationships	promotes positive relationships at work
EXCELLENCE	performance	strives to be the best in what they do for customers/clients
	improvement	looks for ways to exceed standards
	recognition	recognizes and rewards good performance
ACCOUNTABILITY	thought	thinks and deliberates carefully before taking action
	transparency	communicates openly and clearly
	responsibility	takes responsibility for their actions
INTEGRITY	ethics	is ethical and does what is right
	trust	is honest and trusted
	authenticity	follows through on promises and commitments
RESPECT	environment	limits their environmental impact
	community	is considerate to local communities
	people	cares for the well-being, safety, and satisfaction of employees and suppliers/contractors

In this way, we capture a richer sense of organizational values, which can be further analyzed and broken down across different attributes of respondents in our samples, including age, gender, and organizational departments.

Trialing the values survey

At the time of writing this tool has been trialed with employees at a British university, with the staff body of a British university's Students Union, and with employees of a large British utilities company. The GVI is also currently being deployed in a university and medical school in the United States. Across all studies, we have found strong internal consistency of the items (see Table 16.2 for data from the utilities company), that the tool captures the importance of values, the demonstration of values and the gap or alignment between these two dimensions (see Figure 16.3) and that perception varies as a function of various individual differences.

Table 16.2 Cronbach's alpha (α) reliability statistic demonstrating the internal consistency of each set of three items designed to measure the 18 values of the GVI

	Demonstration	Importance		Demonstration	Importance
INNOVATION			**ACCOUNTABILITY**		
knowledge	0.75	0.87	thought	0.82	0.85
novelty	0.82	0.86	transparency	0.84	0.86
adaptability	0.80	0.86	responsibility	0.87	0.88
COLLABORATION			**INTEGRITY**		
teamwork	0.80	0.88	ethics	0.82	0.87
inclusion	0.84	0.88	trust	0.87	0.84
relationships	0.85	0.89	authenticity	0.87	0.88
EXCELLENCE			**RESPECT**		
performance	0.80	0.85	environment	0.81	0.88
improvement	0.86	0.89	community	0.64	0.78
recognition	0.91	0.90	people	0.87	0.90

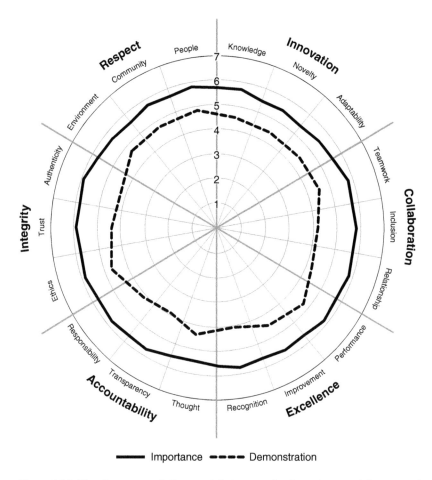

Figure 16.3 Mapping gaps and alignments between value importance and demonstration.

Visualizations

Reliability analysis also supports examining organizational values at the composite level (aggregated across all 18 values). Figure 16.4 shows a scatterplot of individual respondents' evaluations of the importance and demonstration of values overall in the utilities company. There is considerable variation in respondents ratings, but a general positive and significant association between the demonstration and importance dimensions ($r=0.35$, $p<0.001$). A particularly large grouping (68 percent) of data points are located in the upper right quadrant (i.e., strong importance and a high degree of demonstration). The larger dot in that quadrant depicts the aggregate score for the whole corporation, which means on balance that employees place high importance on values and think they are being demonstrated to a moderate to large extent on average. It is also intriguing

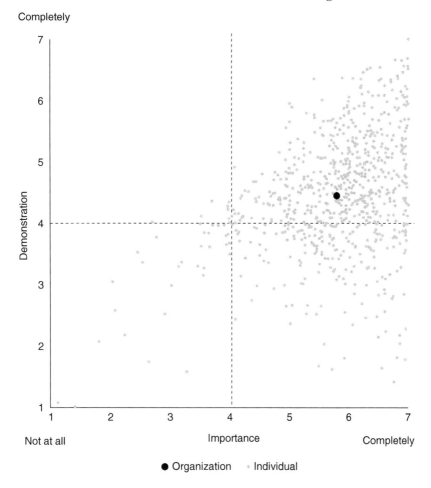

Figure 16.4 Scatterplot of respondents' evaluation of value importance and demonstration in a utility company.

to see, however, that just over a quarter (27 percent) of individuals are placed in the lower right quadrant highlighting a sizeable gap between the importance and demonstration of values in the organization.

Branding

Working together with GIL's graphic designer, branding for the tool, a color scheme, and data visualizations were developed for client-facing communications, reports, and feedback. One such of these visualizations is depicted in Figure 16.3 (minus the color scheme here), which visualizes the data using a "radar" chart that plots the mean score for each value for the *importance* and *demonstration* dimensions of analysis. The figure shows that the values with largest importance and demonstration gaps in this organization are recognition, transparency, responsibility, and inclusion.

Lessons and the future

This chapter has described the evolution of a collaborative working relationship between an academic institution and a private sector organization, the successful application for public funding for innovation, and the development of a tool that measures values in large organizations. It is clear from our discussion that the development of a productive relationship between academics and business people can take time, where ideas are developed, explored, and changed, and where opportunities come and go. For us, the project has been a success in that we now have a working tool that has been tested across three different organizations and is being deployed in a fourth. The tool effectively differentiates values in theory and in practice, and has a business-friendly way of visualizing the outputs of the analysis, which are underpinned by rigorous socio-psychological approaches to measurement and analytical techniques. The key factors for this success are many:

- The firm was in close proximity to the university with its offices only five miles away, where ample space was provided to host academics and Demes, the KTP Associate.
- Landman and Glowinkowski were intellectually and methodologically interested in a behavioral approach to studying the social world with a primacy on measurement and analysis of individual level data and the application of advanced statistical methods.
- The project was successful in recruiting a KTP Associate who had a good understanding of the main project aims and objectives together with the methodological training and skills to develop and operationalize the values model.
- Finally, both Glowinkowski and Landman brought pre-existing networks to the project, including key stakeholders willing to advise on the progress of work and key organizations prepared to participate in trialling the values tool.

Our next steps for the project are the collection and analysis of data from the US university and further development of our change management program. We recognize that any change management process begins with creating a sense of dissatisfaction with the status quo, which then motivates change agents to work on making the organization better. Our values tool provides a great diagnostic method for capturing the state of values in an organization, the challenges associated with the largest gaps between importance and demonstration, and a route for closing these gaps with a view to enhancing organizational performance. The full change management program has an initial measurement phase, followed by a change phase with specific projects carried out by employees across the organization, and a second moment of values measurement to gauge the degree to which change has taken place. Throughout the process we envisage a critical dialogue with the data and in-depth discussions at all levels within the organization for employees and leadership teams to learn why and how real commitment to values can bring about business success.

References

Alexander, L. & Moore, M. (2012). Deontological ethics. In Zalta, E. N. (Ed.) *The Stanford Encyclopedia of Philosophy.* Retrieved April 9, 2014, from http://plato.stanford.edu/archives/win2012/entries/ethics-deontological/.

Allport, G. W., Vernon, P. & Lindzey, G. (1970). *Study of Values* (3d ed. and test manual). Chicago, IL: Riverside.

Amnesty International & Greenpeace (2012). *The Toxic Truth.* Retrieved July 28, 2016 from www.greenpeace.org/international/Global/international/publications/toxics/Probo Koala/The-Toxic-Truth.pdf.

Annas, J. (2011). *Intelligent Virtue.* Oxford: Oxford University Press.

Aristotle (2009). *The Nicomachean Ethics.* Oxford and New York: Oxford University Press.

Batson, C. D., O'Quinn, K., Fulty, J., Vanderplass, M. & Isen, A. M. (1983). Influence of self-reported distress and empathy on egoistic versus altruistic motivation to help. *Journal of Personality and Social Psychology*, 45(3), 706–18.

Bentham, J. (1789). *An Introduction to the Principles of Morals and Legislation.* Oxford: Clarendon Press.

Demes, K. A. & Geeraert, N. (2014). Measures matter: Scales for adaptation, cultural distance and acculturation orientation revisited. *Journal of Cross-Cultural Psychology*, 45(1), 82–100.

Demes, K. A. & Geeraert, N. (2015). The highs and lows of studying abroad: A longitudinal analysis of sojourner stress and adaptation in 50 countries. *Journal of Personality and Social Psychology*, 109(2), 316–37.

Flyvbjerg, B. (2011). Case study. In Denzin, N. K. and Lincoln, Y. S. (Eds.) *The Sage Handbook of Qualitative Research* (4th ed.) (pp. 301–16). Thousand Oaks, CA: Sage.

Flyvbjerg, B., Landman, T. & Schram, S. F. (2012). Important next steps in phronetic social science. In Flyvbjerg, B, Landman T. & Schram S. F. (Eds.) *Real Social Science: Applied Phronesis* (pp. 285–97). Cambridge, UK: Cambridge University Press.

Foweraker, J. & Landman, T. (1997). *Citizenship Rights and Social Movements: A Comparative and Statistical Analysis.* Oxford: Oxford University Press, paperback edition 2000.

Foweraker, J. & Landman, T. (1999). Individual rights and social movements: A comparative and statistical inquiry. *British Journal of Political Science*, 29(2), 291–322.

Geeraert, N., Demoulin, S. & Demes, K. A. (2014). Choose your (international) contacts wisely: A multilevel analysis on the impact of intergroup contact while living abroad. *International Journal of Intercultural Relations*, 38(Jan), 86–96.

Glowinkowski, S. (2009). *It's Behaviour, Stupid! What Really Drives the Performance of Your Organisation.* Cornwall: Ecademy Press.

Haidt, J. (2001). The emotional dog and its rational tail: A social intuitionist approach to moral judgment. *Psychological Review*, 108(4), 814–34.

Hofstede, G. (1980). *Culture's Consequences: International Differences in Work-Related Values.* Beverly Hills, CA: Sage.

House, R., Javidan, M. & Dorfman, P. (2001). Project GLOBE: An introduction. *Applied Psychology: An International Review*, 50(4), 489–505.

Hursthouse, R. (2013). Virtue ethics. In Zalta, E. N. (Ed.) *The Stanford Encyclopedia of Philosophy.* Retrieved April 9, 2014, from http://plato.stanford.edu/archives/fall2013/entries/ethics-virtue/.

Inglehart, R. (1977). *The Silent Revolution.* Princeton, NJ: Princeton University Press.

Inglehart, R. (1990). *Culture Shift in Advanced Industrial Societies.* Princeton, NJ: Princeton University Press.

Inglehart, R. (1997). *Modernization and Post-modernization.* Princeton, NJ: Princeton University Press.

Inglehart, R. & Norris, P. (2003). *Rising Tide.* New York: Cambridge University Press.

Inglehart, R. & Welzel, C. (2005). *Modernization, Cultural Change, and Democracy.* New York: Cambridge University Press.

Inglehart, R. & Welzel, C. (2010). Changing mass priorities: The link between modernization and democracy. *Perspectives on Politics*, 8(2), 55–67.

Isen, A. M. & Levin, P. F. (1972). Effect of feeling good on helping: Cookies and kindness. *Journal of Personality and Social Psychology*, 21(3), 384–8.

ISO (2010). *The International Organization for Standardization Guidance on Social Responsibility.* Retrieved February 5, 2016, from www.iso.org/obp/ui/#iso:std:iso:26000:ed-1:v1:en.

Johnson, M. (2014). *Morality for Humans: Ethical Understanding from the Perspective of Cognitive Science.* Chicago, IL: University of Chicago Press.

Jonsen, K., Galunic, C., Weeks, J. & Braga, T. (2015). Evaluating espoused values: Does articulating values pay off? *European Management Journal*, 33(5), 332–40.

Kant, I. (1785). *Groundwork of the Metaphysic of Morals* (H. J. Paton, Trans. 1964). New York: Harper and Row.

Keenan, J. F. (1996). *Virtues for Ordinary Christians.* Kansas City, MO: Sheed & Ward.

King, R. & Glowinkowski, S. (2015). *Strategy People Implementation: Taking Strategy to Action Through Effective Change Leadership.* St Albans, UK: Panoma Press.

Kubovcikova, A. (2016). Going through the motions: Testing the measurement perspective, dimensionality and internal consistency of the three-dimensional adjustment scale. *Journal of Global Mobility*, 4(2), 149–75.

Landman, T. (2000). *Issues and Methods in Comparative Politics: An Introduction.* London: Routledge.

Landman, T. (2002). Comparative politics and human rights. *Human Rights Quarterly*, 24(4), 890–923.

Landman, T. (2003). *Issues and Methods in Comparative Politics: An Introduction* (2nd ed.). London: Routledge.

Landman, T. (2004). Pinochet's Chile: The United States, human rights, and international terrorism. *Human Rights and Human Welfare*, 4(1), 91–9.

Landman, T. (2005). The political science of human rights. *British Journal of Political Science*, 35(3), 549–72.

Landman, T. (2006). *Studying Human Rights.* London: Routledge.

Landman, T. (2008). *Issues and Methods in Comparative Politics: An Introduction* (3rd ed.). London: Routledge.

Landman, T. (2012). Projecting liberalism in a world of realist states: David Forsythe and the political science of human rights. *Journal of Human Rights*, 11(3), 332–6.

Landman, T. (2016). Rigorous morality: Norms, values and the comparative politics of human rights. *Human Rights Quarterly*, 38(1), 1–20.

Landman, T. & Carvalho, E. (2009). *Measuring Human Rights.* London: Routledge.

Landman, T. & Gohdes, A. (2013). A matter of convenience: Challenges of non-random data in analyzing human rights violations during conflicts in Peru and Sierra Leone. In Seybolt, T., Aronson, J. & Fishoff, B. (Eds.) *Counting Civilian Casualties* (pp. 77–96). Oxford: Oxford University Press.

Landman, T. & Larizza, M. (2009). Inequality and human rights: Who controls what, when and how? *International Studies Quarterly*, 53(3), 715–36.

Landman, T., Kernohan, D. & Gohdes, A. (2012). Relativizing human rights. *Journal of Human Rights*, 11(4), 460–85.

Latane, B. & Darley, J. M. (1970). *The Unresponsive Bystander.* Englewood Cliffs, CA: Prentice Hall.

Lewin, K. (1951). *Field Theory in Social Science.* New York: Harper & Row.

Milgram, S. (1963). Behavioral study of obedience. *Journal of Abnormal and Social Psychology*, 67(4), 371–8.

Mill, J. S. (1863). *Utilitarianism.* London: Parker, Son & Bourn.

OECD (2011). *OECD Guidelines for Multinational Enterprises.* Retrieved February 5, 2016, from www.oecd.org/daf/inv/mne/oecdguidelinesformultinationalenterprises.htm.

O'Reilly, C. III, Chatman, J. & Caldwell, D. F. (1991). People and organizational culture: A profile comparison approach to assessing person–organisation fit. *Academy of Management Journal*, 34(3), 487–516.

Ozer, S. & Schwartz, S. J. (2016). Measuring globalization-based acculturation in Ladakh: Investigating possible advantages of a tri-dimensional acculturation scale. *International Journal of Intercultural Relations*, 53, 1–15.

Porter, M. E. & Kramer, M. R. (2006). Strategy & society: The link between competitive advantage and corporate social responsibility. *Harvard Business Review*, 84(12), 78–92.

Porter, M. E. & Kramer, M. R. (2011). Creating shared value. *Harvard Business Review*, 89(1/2), 62–77.

Rokeach, M. (1973). *The Nature of Human Values.* New York: The Free Press.

Schwartz, S. H. (1992). Universals in the content and structure of values: Theoretical advances and empirical tests in 20 countries. *Advances in Experimental Social Psychology*, 25, 1–65.

Schwartz, S. H. & Boehnke, K. (2004). Evaluating the structure of human values with confirmatory factor analysis. *Journal of Research in Personality*, 38(3), 230–55.

Schwartz, S. H. & Sagiv, L. (1995). Identifying culture-specifics in the content and structure of values. *Journal of Cross-Cultural Psychology*, 26(1), 92–116.

Schwartz, S. H., Melech, G., Lehmann, A., Burgess, S., Harris, M. & Owens, V. (2001). Extending the cross-cultural validity of the theory of basic human values with a different method of measurement. *Journal of Cross-Cultural Psychology*, 32(5), 519–42.

Sharma, D., Borna S. & Stearns, J. M. (2009). An investigation of the effects of corporate ethical values on employee commitment and performance: Examining the moderating role of perceived fairness. *Journal of Business Ethics*, 89(2), 251–60.

Shweder, R. A., Much, N. C., Mahapatra, M. & Park, L. (1997). The "big three" of morality (autonomy, community, and divinity), and the "big three" explanations of suffering. In Brandt, A. & Rozin, P. (Eds.) *Morality and Health* (pp. 119–69). New York: Routledge.

Sidgwick, H. (1907). *The Methods of Ethics.* London: Macmillan.

Sinnott-Armstrong, W. (2014). Consequentialism. In Zalta, E. N. (Ed.) *The Stanford Encyclopedia of Philosophy.* Retrieved April 9, 2014, from http://plato.stanford.edu/entries/consequentialism/.

United Nations (2010). *The Ten Principles of the UN Global Compact.* Retrieved February 5, 2016, from www.unglobalcompact.org/what-is-gc/mission/principles.

United Nations (2011). *Guiding Principles on Business and Human Rights.* Retrieved September 5, 2014, from www.ohchr.org/Documents/Publications/GuidingPrinciples BusinessHR_EN.pdf.

Valentine, S., Godkin, L., Fleischman, G. M. & Kidwell, R. (2011). Corporate ethical values, group creativity, job satisfaction and turnover intention: The impact of work context on work response. *Journal of Business Ethics*, 98(3), 353–72.

Vauclair, C.-M., Hanke, K., Fischer, R. & Fontaine, J. (2011). The structure of human values at the culture level: A meta-analytical replication of Schwartz's value orientations using the Rokeach Value Survey. *Journal of Cross-Cultural Psychology*, 42(2), 186–205.

Weber, S., Appel, M. & Kronberger, N. (2015). Stereotype threat and the cognitive performance of adolescent immigrants: The role of cultural identity strength. *Contemporary Educational Psychology*, 42, 71–81.

Welzel, C. (2013). *Freedom Rising: Human Empowerment and the Quest for Emancipation.* New York: Cambridge University Press.

Welzel, C. & Inglehart, R. (2010). Agency, values, and well-being: A human development Model. *Social Indicators Research*, 97(1), 43–63.

17 Sustaining the interaction

The Henley Forum for Organisational Learning and Knowledge Strategies

Jane McKenzie and Christine van Winkelen

Introduction

The Henley Forum exists to engage academics, managers, and leaders of large organizations in joint research and dialogue about two inter-related problems:

- generating knowledge; and
- learning in organizational life;

and harnessing both for performance and change.

It was founded in 2000 at Henley Management College (HMC), an *independent* UK business school offering only post-graduate and executive education to experienced managers. In 2008, HMC merged with the University of Reading to form Henley Business School.

From its foundation to this day, concern has been to design a space where academic–practitioner partnership could flourish and provide both rigorous research opportunities for business school academics and relevant organizational output. As two academics involved throughout in this paradoxical endeavor (Bartunek & Rynes, 2014), we offer, in this chapter, a distillation of 16 years' experience of sustaining such interactions. What follows is an analysis of how we worked with the tensions generated by differences between people managing organizations and academics studying them.

Initial steps in relationship building

The Forum was started to investigate knowledge management (KM) practice. In the late 1990s, following a long and successful consultancy career, the founder, Edward Truch, started a DBA. His basic research developed and quantitatively tested a model of alignment between business environment, strategic orientation to knowledge, knowledge management practices, and organizational performance. Edward connected with Professor David Birchall, then Director of Research at HMC. They co-authored a paper about KM research gaps for a conference in Cambridge UK and subsequently published it (Truch, Ezingeard & Birchall, 2000). Armed with the conference paper, Edward talked with companies about how a Forum for research and practice development could benefit them. Membership would be open only to large organizations to give a common ground for dialogue about the difficulties of effective knowledge sharing and collective learning in firms where complex structures, systems, cultures, and behaviors can obstruct knowledge flow. To stimulate learning and idea generation, they deliberately targeted a cross-sector mix of organizations. Cutting-edge thinking and practical value would be integral to *all* types of activity: workshops, research projects, interest groups, conferences, and publications. Critically, all aspects of engagement between theory and practice would be complementary and mutually supportive. The emphasis would be strategy, people, and process considerations, rather than the specifics of technology platforms. Although, technology was acknowledged as an enabler—Internet advances in the 1990s could not be ignored—it was the knowledge-based theory of the firm (Grant, 1996; Liebeskind, 1996; Spender, 1996), and its impact on organizational performance and human capital management, which distinguished KM from information management.

Edward's background and networking skills gave him access to senior people in major companies. Microsoft UK was persuaded to sponsor the Forum; they invited preferred business partners to join, providing a foundation of shared concern. Edward also asked Leif Edvinsson the world's first director of Intellectual Capital (IC) at Skandia and an early writer on IC measurement (Edvinsson & Malone, 1997) to be Honorary President. With ten highly regarded sponsors, Leif's involvement and Henley's reputation, the Forum became an attractive proposition for other organizations. Edward remained as Director of the Forum until 2003, taking Forum membership to a peak of 49 organizations, predominantly from the private sector. During this period, Christine (the second author of this chapter, but the one who originally started it) coordinated research activities, then became Forum Director from 2003 to 2008. She remains part of the Forum management team, leading research projects each year, giving much needed continuity of theoretical knowledge and most importantly understanding of Forum research history. Jane (the second author) championed one or more research projects every year since 2000. She became Forum Director in 2009, remaining in post until 2016. The Forum continues under new leadership today.

Evolutions in the Forum focus and the relationship management process

Under Christine's leadership, membership averaged 45 organizations, shifting to a mix of private and UK public sector bodies, as public sector interest in KM practice grew. Member turnover was low and relationships became more productive as social capital and trust grew (Adler & Kwon, 2002; Nahapiet & Ghoshal, 1998). Environmental jolts, such as the stock market crash in 2008 and 2010 significantly reduced organizational appetite for external research partnerships but the value of individual development activities was of greater interest.

Co-incidentally, the HMC/University of Reading merger changed strategic priorities, triggering academic staff turnover and altering workload patterns. This impacted both faculty availability and interest in engaging in collaborative research. Since the global recession in 2010, annual membership has averaged 22 organizations with the mix of private and public sector institutions continually shifting in response to economic pressures.

Close relationships are better conduits for sticky and tacit knowledge (Granovetter, 1973; McKenzie & Van Winkelen, 2004; Szulanski, 1996), so, as churn weakened ties, conversations between practitioners and academics became less productive. Design changes were needed to help new members absorb foundational knowledge, understand prior research, develop a common language for communication, and build the depth of social capital needed for meaningful tacit knowledge exchange. So the program of activities evolved to integrate member briefings, action learning sets, and a two-day advanced course, giving participants a foundational understanding of the strategic value of knowledge and learning and the challenges for practice. The course uses prior Forum research.

Figure 17.1 summarizes the Forum evolution. It illustrates how activities for members and the big questions guiding collaborative research with members, altered over 16 years to adapt to external membership trends, theoretical developments, and internal management changes: for example, in 2004 emerging academic interest in ambidexterity coincided with organizational concern for innovation and the dynamics of organizational learning, so research began to focus on dimensions of capability-building and the impact of interfaces and inter-relationships. When leadership influences on the environment for knowledge and learning became more topical amongst members in 2011, we seized this opportunity to build an internal relationship with a new research center in the university. Since 2014, interest in the connection between knowledge and learning and change has grown, shifting the research approach from collaborative to action research (see Figure 17.2) and prompting the development of a new course in Organizational Development. Viewing the Forum as an integrated package of activities allows us to alter the mix of research topics and the balance of developmental activities to suit changing priorities. Overall we view developmental activities as scaffolds (Vygotsky, 1978) for better collaborative research across contexts, because they prime people to make more mental connections between theory and practice.

Approaches to research

Figure 17.2 maps the different forms of research the Forum has engaged in against Van de Ven's typology of engaged scholarship (see Figure 7.4 in Chapter 7 of this volume). We have added the words "*(and explore)*" beneath the heading of the first column to indicate that collaborative Forum projects are often qualitative and interpretative using exploratory designs to establish early understanding of relative new conceptual domains where theory is limited (Hair, Money, Samouel & Page, 2007: 154). Exploratory research identifies patterns or themes

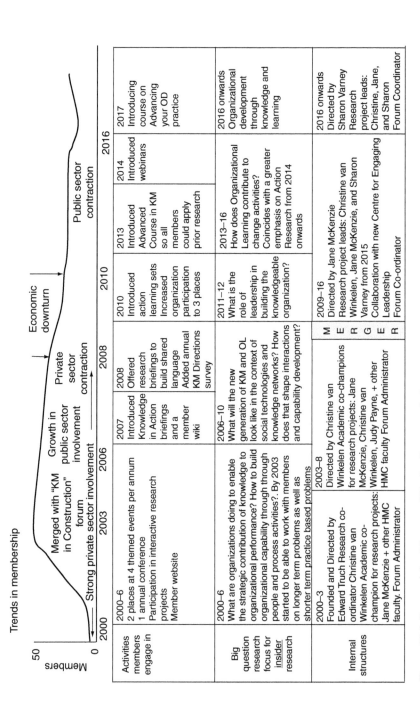

Figure 17.1 Summarizing 16 years of Henley Forum evolution.

Research question/purpose

	To describe/explain (and explore)	To design/intervene
Detached outside	**1. Basic research with stakeholder advice** 2000: 2 projects with only consultative participation producing doctorates 2015–16: 2 projects from a detached perspective with only stakeholder involvement in the interpretation	**3. Evaluation research for professional practice** 2013: Evaluation of member perceptions of engaged scholarship process 2008: Case comparison of other interorganizational community designs for evaluation purposes 2007: Evaluation of research relevance 2006: Evaluation of members perceptions of community 2002: Evaluation of interactive research design
Attached inside	**2. Co-produce knowledge with collaborators** 2009–13: 9 projects more focused on leadership, learning and how social technologies are changing organizations. Research format changed to concentrate stakeholder involvement and accommodate increased work pressures 2002–8: 23 further projects on aspects of knowledge strategy, ambidexterity and innovation plus 4 longer term projects building on deep shared understanding of a knowledge domain 2000–2: 14 interactive research projects to explore people and process considerations associated with delivery of organizational knowledge strategy	**4. Action/intervention research for clients** 2014–16: 5 out of 7 projects used Action Research to help member organizations deliver change

Research perspective (vertical axis label)

The evaluation projects in the grey box focused on Forum practice to provide feedback loops for improvement

Figure 17.2 Mapping Henley Forum projects against Van de Ven's framework of types of engaged scholarship.

across contexts to better understand dimensions of a larger research question (cf. Figure 17.1). Some topics pursued over several years (e.g., Communities of Practice) became explanatory or evaluative research projects, both of which rely more on theory and a detached objectivity to conduct research on systems, phenomena, or agents with limited stakeholder involvement.

Researching WITH

On the bottom row in Figure 17.2, academics aim to be insiders to the research context (Bartunek & Louis 1996). Thus research is done WITH practitioners, rather than being detached. In this space, we view academics and practitioners as equal knowers contributing differently to research; we explicitly acknowledge that the different motivations and interests (Bartunek & Rynes, 2014) of each constituency must be satisfied to sustain involvement. Not all practitioners have the same interests either, so *what* we focus on must excite a cross section of their interests: some want short-term actionable insights to improve practice, others value longer-term strategic topics and excel in critical thinking.

Researching ON

When we design more detached studies to research ON questions, it is mainly to evaluate Forum praxis (Figure 17.2, top right box). We have used independent coders, comparative cases, quantitative methods, or outsider investigations to examine how members experience Forum processes and relationships. This provides a feedback loop for redesigning the space and activities, as well as producing publications. On occasions, we have experimented with Basic Research (Figure 17.2, top left). However, as will become clear, it remains peripheral because it tends to negatively impact ongoing member engagement.

Cycles of research, adaptation, and learning

When and why did the research approach evolve to align interests and sustain relationships for 16 years? This section describes interlocking cycles of learning from researching *with* practitioners and *on* our own practice and how that shaped Forum design.

An early design for "researching with" practitioners

Edward was attracted by the potential of "interactive" research (Scott, Skea, Robinson & Shove, 1999; Skea, Robinson & Shove, 1998) to produce value and meaning in diverse organizational groups.

Interactive research is different from action research or participatory inquiry (Reason & Bradbury, 2001). It neither initiates change nor observes the consequences, nor does it involve longitudinal study of practice. It was designed for cross-sectional investigations of organizations at different stages of development to describe effective practice and occasionally prescribe improvements without researchers actually intervening. However, it does require regular interaction with those involved in the practice context. It uses a rhythm of collaborative discussions between academics and groups of practitioners at five stages of the research process:

- defining a researchable problem;
- formulating the research questions;
- collecting and interpreting the data;
- considering implications; and
- deciding how to communicate results.

This means differentiating responsibilities at every stage of research activity to make best use of each stakeholder's relevant knowledge whilst simultaneously giving academics and practitioners a contributory role. The goal is to use the plurality constructively to meet both constituencies' ends via similar means, without either party compromising their interests. Thus the paradoxical demands of rigor and relevance are handled *within* the regular discussions, rather than resolved at the end.

Each project has joint leadership: two co-champions, one an organizational participant the other a business school academic. A project group comprises the co-champions, a project researcher (a doctoral student or academic researcher at the business school) and volunteers from Forum member organizations. Each group meets for a half day approximately every six weeks at Henley. Co-champions often work through the rigor–relevance paradox in separate discussions.

After consultation, project outlines are crafted and circulated. If the initial loose framing of the problem excites a sufficient level of both academic and practitioner interest it becomes a research project. People volunteer to join. Academics summarise existing knowledge and debates around the focal topic (the equivalent of the literature review) are used to make concepts accessible, using everyday terms and graphical representations. This is positioned as a stimulus for discussion to encourage project participants to explore each other's perspectives and establish a common knowledge base so everyone can contribute. Practitioners challenge assumptions and increase critical evaluation by considering how theory fits with the reality of their practice. This helps to refine research questions and build practitioner commitment. Research design is an academic responsibility for obvious reasons; yet any methodology can benefits from practitioner critique of its potential to deliver meaningful results. Methodology would be modified where it did not compromise validity. Participants facilitate access to suitable respondents in organizations. Data may be collected by either practitioners or academics, depending on the study design and the importance of contextual independence during data collection process. Academics do the initial coding and analysis, but interpretation of findings and implications are considered in discussion with practitioners. This challenges academic assumptions in the interpretation process, and has positive benefits for considering relevance.

Using the interactive research approach

In the first year of the Forum, six research projects were selected from member concerns and priorities. They tackled tactical questions around virtual collaboration, managing customer knowledge, winning commitment to knowledge sharing, and strategic questions around KM strategy/organization fit. A project coordinator supported activities across projects and sought synergies between them. Sometimes that individual took more than one role.

Each project group was expected to present its findings within a year to an annual all-member conference and produce two distinct outputs: a fully referenced academic-style document—effectively a working paper—plus some output from project group discussions explaining potential implications and application of the findings, so other members could experiment with them. Early anecdotal feedback on research relevance came from the first KM Forum Annual Conference. Project findings were rated as "very useful," and "good quality research, frameworks will have practical utility."

We soon realized that the deeper learning generated by *active* participation in research projects would be harder to diffuse across the whole membership if delayed until conclusions were reached or if only communicated in text format. Cross-organizational learning was a critical priority for us, because we recognized how hard it would be to take thinking forward together over time without a foundation of common knowledge (Dixon, 2000).

Since Communities of Practice (CoP) (Wenger, 1998) were accepted learning mechanisms in KM practice and academics understood the theory, CoP principles were incorporated into the early Forum design. The merits of a "rhythm" to whole community interaction translated into quarterly "all member" workshops. We allocated unstructured time—"white space" to promote networking discussions around focal topics. Later renamed themed days, these quarterly workshops still remain the heartbeat of the community and core to the value proposition. Every member organization gets more than one "seat" at an event, so colleagues from different parts of the business can jointly discuss practice in the light of theory. This rationale was re-enforced by reading Gustavsen (2001), whose examination of the problems researchers encountered when diffusing action research results, surfaced the importance of a "mediating discourse" to connect theory and practice when working in relationships that straddle organizational boundaries.

A first cycle of "research on" Forum practice

After a year, we reviewed the interactive research approach to evaluate the extent and quality of interaction within the first six projects. Project meeting reports and participant interviews provided the data. Evidence of consistent engagement in dialogue, open exploration of issues and challenges, and regular idea generation was used to indicate the most-active participation. Least-active participation was classified by a passive process of receiving information and endorsing others' ideas.

We assessed interaction at each stage of the research cycle. The findings suggested that:

- projects developing conceptual frameworks or using quantitative methods produced the lowest levels of practitioner participation. Academics had to work harder to sustain involvement in abstract projects or detached outsider investigations;
- contrary to advice that interactive research needs "strong and focused research leadership" (Skea et al., 1998), too dominant an academic agenda reduced interaction and practitioners' interest in staying the course. On one particular project two doctoral researchers were using it to support their studies. Their clear (and openly acknowledged) academic agenda so shaped direction that practitioners switched off, despite the fact that the output would address a relevant practitioner problem. Even the co-champion structure, designed to balance theoretical and practical interests was insufficient to compensate. The project with the lowest degree of interaction (the term consultative participation might be more appropriate) was the one with the strongest and most focused research leadership; overemphasizing academic interests seems to undermine the *authentic* collaborative quality of any mediating discourse (Gustavsen, 2001);
- practitioners were willing and capable of helping with qualitative data collection. On several projects, guidance was given so they could observe and report on practices of interest in their own organizations. This both generated usable data and piqued interest in outcomes. At times when preliminary qualitative data could be collected and used to stimulate reflection and discussion within the group *before* subsequent refinement of the direction of the research it established a sense of "co-creation": preliminary insights from collections of case examples, focus groups or first round interviews, provided a meaningful basis to compare and contrast practices across organizational contexts whilst developing a shared interest. It helped each participant to make sense of how his/her own context related to the research being undertaken; and
- when academics showed openness to working with the direction of practitioner interests, practitioners' energy, enthusiasm, and engagement were more sustainable, perhaps because it gave hope that the outputs would be meaningful. Academic control seemed to dampen that hope.

Further experience of "researching WITH"

Using these findings and our first years' experience, we standardized the research process maintaining it, with little variation, for a decade. Projects were only initiated based on members' interests, identified through a consultation process starting at the annual conference when the prior year's projects were being reported. We would only proceed if at least six organizations signed up to participate; more were desirable. Once members' interest in a topic was evident, we sought academic participation. We wouldn't work the other way round—an academic's "pet project" couldn't be the driver—it just didn't attract members. Repeatedly, we tried and failed to recruit a critical mass of participants for academic colleagues' proposals. The topics may have been important, but the collaborative process started on the wrong foot, without an early sense of owner-ship of its relevance. There may be several reasons why that might be:

- Practitioners may not appreciate the utility of an answer.
- They may not have the necessary knowledge foundation and hence absorp-tive capacity (Zahra & George, 2002) to recognize the problem.
- The language used to express the problem may not resonate.

Still the key concern was finding a win–win, a topic of mutual concern which they owned, because then the espousal of *collaborative* research seemed authentic.

We learned when we should coach and support academic colleagues to be more participative in research, helping them to value practitioners—most of whom were highly educated senior managers—as peers with different sets of knowledge and experience. Similarly we coached some academic speakers at our quarterly workshops to communicate and work with practitioners as peers who simply lacked an academic background rather than students to be taught. Con-sciously translating academic ideas across semantic boundaries (Carlile, 2004) was fundamental in all Forum activities, and scheduled "white space" for unstructured conversations at every event and within every project, helped participants transform knowledge (Carlile, 2004) across pragmatic contextual boundaries.

A healthy turnover of some 20 percent of members per annum until 2008, introducing challenge to refresh thinking, but continuity amongst the majority of members meant dialogue improved. Trust in closer ties allows safe explora-tion of ambiguous and ill-formed ideas, and aids meaningful knowledge exchange (Nonaka & Konno, 1998). So within three to four years, a core group of members had progressed together sufficiently to critically examine more con-ceptually demanding research topics. Then the mix of projects could safely include longer-timescale questions, such as the evolution of knowledgeable organizational forms (McKenzie & van Winkelen, 2008; van Winkelen & McKenzie, 2009), and organizational innovation capability-building (van Win-kelen & Tovstiga, 2009). Members identified numerous examples of practical value.

The academics worked hard on communication, producing four outputs from *each project*. Changing the language and style to suit different audiences:

- An academic paper which became the basis of a publication after feedback from the all member conference.
- An attractively presented "guidance document" to help practitioners apply results. Guidance documents included case studies, "hints and tips" lists, maturity models, examples, process maps, resource packs, "train the trainer" guides, coaching frameworks, templates, key points, and quick start guides. These guides were for members only (part of the proposition for attracting

new members) until 2010, when we collated them into a handbook (van Winkelen & McKenzie, 2011), with royalties from sales used to generate additional member benefits.

• A colorful four-page pamphlet—our Knowledge in Action series: short digests of key insights from a research project, written by journalists for general managers rather than knowledge managers. Any member could use these as conversation starters with colleagues to stimulate interest in organizational knowledge and learning activities.

• A short project summary with a taxonomy of all past projects so new members could navigate quickly through the growing body of research to find something useful, then dig into the more detailed academic material and guidance.

Writing several times may seem onerous, but using the language of the tribe (Gulati, 2007) cements relationships, raises the potential for research uptake, and maintains credibility within the different constituencies.

At the annual conference, research results were explained in stimulating ways, usually involving working group participants for authenticity. Like MacLean and MacIntosh (Chapter 9 in this volume), we turned to drama, art, and poetry to convey ideas, as well as using audience participation, simulations and workshops.

Ad hoc initiatives such as special interest groups, recognition for knowledge-sharing within the community, and collaborative technology for peer-to-peer interaction between quarterly workshops all supported community-building. From 2007, our consultation process evolved further to include an annual survey of member practices and priorities. This surfaced both potential research topics and themes for the quarterly events.

As global recession hit, we had to adapt the Forum model. Tighter budgets meant membership renewals fell, threatening community and knowledge continuity, and forcing us to revisit the operational model and value proposition. This, combined with constraints on academic support during the merger, led us to reduce the number of research projects to two or three per year and focus on more straightforward questions. The research process was restructured to concentrate interaction on two to three full days, rather than five or six half-days thus saving participant travel time. Less regular interactions undermined commitment. By 2010 individuals were struggling to justify time away from their desks and it was plain that short-term actionable insights were a better justification for securing organizational funding for memberships than researching long-term questions. So Forum activities focused more on capability development. We introduced facilitated peer-to-peer action learning to meet members' desires for more immediate returns, and integrated relevant prior Forum research into that process to build a foundation for future research.

Occasionally, some longstanding members engaged with bigger questions: we explored what paradoxical leadership behaviors could promote knowledge and learning (McKenzie & Aitken, 2012), and examined evaluation of complex change (Van Winkelen & McKenzie, 2013). With experience of working with research groups we modified the interactive research process and "variations on a theme" emerged. For example, some projects had more virtual interaction, one or two projects had no formal member co-champion to balance academic interests, because we had learned to recognize and work with the paradoxical demands inherent in "differing logics, time dimensions, communication styles, rigor and relevance, and interests and incentives" (Bartunek & Rynes, 2014: 1181)

We extended our insider/outsider research toolbox (Bartunek & Louis, 1996), adding action research (AR) (Bradbury, 2008) to the design options in 2014. This was a conscious move away from cross-sectional investigation towards initiating change as the research purpose to align with changing organizational interests. We still start with a substantial literature research to identify theories for organizations to draw on, then engage in cycles of application and reflection over a six- to nine-month period. Project group meetings become a reflective space for practitioners and academics to co-produce insights from applying concepts "for real." We envisage that AR will give more immediate visibility of the research impact: understanding the impact of cross-sectional research has previously required separate inquiries. Now the narrative and evidence of impact emerge during the research process, making the "relevance" argument easier to articulate to funding bodies in the form of impact case studies and internal stakeholders.

Making use of co-incidences of concern

Clearly as academics and Forum managers, we have two reasons to be interested in the dynamics of the learning community both as an object of research (see Bolisani & Scarso, 2013, for a comprehensive review) and the context for sustaining engagement in knowledge co-production. When some member organizations began experimenting with inter-organizational communities in industry we saw some research synergies. The strategy literature broadly categorized loose inter-organizational alliances with a learning objective into three structural forms: communities, networks, and technical exchanges (Johnson & Scholes, 2002), without specifying what distinguished them. The knowledge-management literature argued that inter-organizational alliances only support information and explicit knowledge exchange (Reid, Bussiere & Greenaway, 2001; Venkatramann & Henderson, 1998); only within organizations can communities produce enough sense of belonging and identification with shared interest to support tacit knowledge exchange (Wenger, 1998). Researching *with* Forum members we explored the knowledge dynamics of various types of inter-organizational relationships. Using criteria such as meaningful knowledge exchange (evidenced by tentative expression of tacit understanding); a sense of belonging, (evidenced by emotional engagement); and a locus of practice within the alliance as well as within the participating organizations (evidenced by relationship development between individuals participating on behalf of their organizations) we identified a typology of inter-organizational knowledge relationships (McKenzie, 2005) and then applied those same criteria to "research *on*" the experience of Forum membership.

Structured content analysis was applied to feedback from Forum quarterly events (the times when the whole community came together) over a four-year period. The data (900 lines were coded) offered evidence of a solid level of meaningful (including arguably tacit) knowledge exchange relationship development between individual participants, substantial engagement with shared practice primarily through research projects, and sustained (though relatively limited) evidence of a sense of belonging and identification with the Forum as a whole. This re-enforced the potential for inter-organizational tacit knowledge exchange and the importance of working hard to connect individuals through diverse activities, sustain participation in project groups, and enhance reflection and dialogue through the way events were designed.

After assessing the quality of community as the research relationship space, in 2007 we tackled the question of how members perceived research relevance— thereby joining the Mode 2 rigor–relevance debate (Gibbons, Limoges, Nowotny, Schwartzman, Scott & Trow, 1994: 3). In such research-oriented relationships the "cooperation with companies should not be perceived as a useful consequence of research but as a prerequisite for the production of actionable knowledge" (Hatcheul, 2001: S39) and simultaneous attention to both rigor and relevance is integral to the negotiation of mutual interests. Clearly, Mode 2 arguments for meeting multiple stakeholder objectives resonated. Eighteen interviews with representatives from member organizations who had participated in at least one completed research project were transcribed and analyzed by an independent colleague using Atlas.Ti and an open coding process. Results showed (McKenzie & van Winkelen, 2008) that:

- involvement in research projects brought personal benefits ranging from knowledge development, confidence, internal kudos and relationship building;
- respondents expected research to enhance organizational practices, but expectations of benefit realization ranged from immediate—effectively operational value to help achieving current objectives—to "*influencing thinking*" and satisfaction with creating potential, since one could never "*predict the value of the learning that has happened.*" "Potential" was accepted as strategically worthwhile for shaping future internal organizational direction and providing alternatives for better decision-making, suggesting that, for some, relevance was interpreted as organizational capacity building (Starkey, 2001);
- in inter-organizational collaborations, however, such as the Henley Forum, realizing potential requires representatives to have internal influence and long-term involvement. Participation on an "as needed" basis for a singular interest is insufficient.

In 2008, this "research on" relevance fed into "research with" members. The Forum became one case study in a comparative study of seven inter-organizational learning collaborations that members belonged to (van Winkelen, 2010). Our question was what features of the learning collaborations support and limit capacity building in case organizations? Building on a recent comprehensive literature review of factors affecting inter-organizational knowledge transfer (Easterby-Smith, Lyles & Tsang, 2008) we examined the characteristics of the firms involved, the nature of knowledge, and the inter-organizational dynamics. The research confirmed the pivotal role that organizational representatives play in capacity-building. Their subject-specific knowledge becomes the basis of an organization's potential absorptive capacity (Zahra & George, 2002); not all representatives saw their participation in these terms. Two reasons inter-organizational collaboration did not build organizational capacity were identified:

- individuals not translating their learning into an organizational appreciation of the need for change; and
- organizations lacking systems and processes to translate and amplify the learning they brought back.

Where capacity-building was achieved, long-term, senior leadership commitment to the inter-organizational collaboration was evident. For us, practically, this reinforced the importance of efforts to facilitate conversations between leaders and managers about research implications and giving time to enact the learning.

The latest cycle of research ON

In 2013 we started to explore the nature of belonging in academic–practitioner relationships. Seventeen interviews with past and present members of the Henley Forum combined with "insider–outsider" dialogue (Bartunek & Louis, 1996) helped explain what made belonging to a research community such as the Forum meaningful. Surprisingly we found that practitioners are not a homogeneous group. There was evidence that distinct epistemological positions affected sense-making. We had already identified different orientations towards (and pragmatic need for) immediate utility or future knowledge potential. But other epistemological predispositions in their sense-making became apparent, for example appreciating subjectivity or objectivity, preferring abstract concepts or concrete evidence, and relying on tacit or explicit knowledge. The findings led us to develop recommendations for particular academic capacities that could foster engaged scholarship in this kind of partnership (McKenzie, van Winkelen & Bartunek, 2014), in particular being able to attend to the diversity and potential contradictions in people's thinking, as well as the similarities.

Lessons learned

Having described some of the challenges of sustaining academic–practitioner relationships over 16 years and how the Forum has adapted to address them, we now summarise some learning points from our joint experience.

Recognizing and acting on salient paradoxes

Table 17.1 outlines the Forum responses to the various tensions identified by Bartunek and Rynes (2014).

Avoiding an either/or response to the differences creating the tension, we sought ways to treat them as complementary elements in the Forum model (see Jarzabkowski, Lewis and Smith in Chapter 8). The mechanisms that seem to important in the process are discussed below.

Differentiated roles and integrated processes

Having two co-champions automatically differentiates academics and practitioner logics whilst the project process integrates their interests. Equal status promotes dialogue. Similarly, in the small team of colleagues managing the Forum (typically four at any time) we recognized and deliberately turned different orientations amongst team members into complementary assets. For example, although we manage the rigor–relevance tension continually and dynamically in both the research process and the design of the Forum activities, different team members hold different priorities, which weigh into conversations: one of the chapter authors emphasizes academic concerns more, another emphasizes practitioner interests; the Forum coordinator takes a customer relationship perspective on process and the Forum Director prioritizes institutional concerns. Contradictions in our interests keep tensions to the forefront of conversation as we sense internal and external signals for re-evaluating the model. Trust, shared purpose, and process unite us. Theoretical expertise clearly matters for shaping a research agenda and designing activities and can be learnt, as we have found when colleagues without subject-specific knowledge have joined the team. Skills in facilitating the "mediating discourse" between theory and practice are equally important.

Van de Ven's (2007) diamond model of engaged scholarship (see Chapter 7, Figure 7.3) succinctly captures the iterative nature of the process we work within. It does not show the remarkable amount of time required to both remain accessible and credible to an audience of senior business practitioners and simultaneously contribute internally and remain credible within the institution. The Forum has on occasion been viewed as rather incongruous, particularly within a traditional university setting. Following the merger, adapting to the structures, processes, and governance of a public university diverted a small team's resources away from research and changed incentives for academic involvement because workload priorities and costing mechanisms altered. Certain skills for operating *within* an

Table 17.1 Working with the tensions in academic–practitioner relationships

Working with the tension created by differences in…	How the Forum design worked through the differences so they became complementary	Subsequent adaptive responses
Logics underpinning with academic and practitioner praxis	Prioritizing practitioner concerns to surface what problem to address, then using interactive research to jointly develop the research question, challenge assumptions, and co-produce knowledge. Co-champions negotiate about contradictory priorities in different logics.	Identifying intersections between theoretical developments and practice interests in a broad domain and evolving the focal phenomena (from KM to organizational learning to organizational development and change) to encompass them in a narrative arc that excites both sides.
Time horizons for useful output, i.e., short-term actionable insights answer long-term research questions	Integrating mutually supportive activities into the membership offering which both satisfy short-term interests through learning and capability development and contribute to long-term research agendas by extending organizational absorptive capacity.	In difficult times adapting the design of the space to prioritize more short-term actionable insights and reduce longer-term emphasis.
Communication styles, i.e., language of practice; theoretically precise language	Rewriting the research to fit the needs of different audiences. Using visual representations to overcome semantic differences. Iterative interaction builds understanding of scientific language.	Constantly working to develop a shared language and shared foundation for meaningful dialogue.
Interests and incentives, i.e., what motivates practitioners to belong; what motivates academics to contribute	Integrating interests through belonging to an inter-organizational CoP to which both sides develop an affiliation and derive some benefits that they can take back to their own institution.	Systematically collecting feedback to understand how processes and relationships serve different interests and how incentives change priorities in both constituencies' institutions. Reconfiguring activities to better align with different priorities on both sides.
Criteria for valuing research, i.e., rigor–relevance	Adopting a transdisciplinary approach where consideration for use occurs simultaneously with the search for understanding.	Ensuring all Forum activities develop knowledge of relevant theory, which extends capacity to do more rigorous research.

academic institution helped; for example, finding synergies between educational delivery and research, contributing to collegiate activities to cement internal relationships. We have learned that building relationships within the institution and self-funding are important defenses to our applied research model. Laura Empson (Chapter 12 in this volume) describes her approach to a similar tension.

Using evaluation research as a feedback loop to guide reconfiguration

Frequent feedback loops are important for sensing shifts in member priorities and thinking. We learned to apply developmental evaluation principles (Patton, 2011) to keep revisiting the quality of Forum experience. This form of evaluation is designed for complex social systems and has also been the subject of our own "research with" managers of knowledge and learning initiatives (Van Winkelen & McKenzie, 2013).

Attention to value creation in the relationships matters hugely for sustainability, so adjusting the format to suit changing interests is vital. We worked to ensure every event and activity re-enforced relevance and belonging—executives with limited time to build external relationships choose places where their concerns are valued. Other examples include adjusting research focus in response to an influx of people with shorter-term relevant interests. Attention to detail matters, even down to giving each organization options to send different people rather than requiring nominated employees to attend, given that individual practitioners are not a homogeneous group, so we constantly have to tailor activities and messages to different preferences.

We know most of the individuals representing their organizations at a personal level and these relationships allow early warning signs of dissatisfaction to be flagged before they become problems. Data collection after every event, the annual survey of practices and plans, and a consultation process at the annual conference, combine with the punctuation of deeper explorations through telephone interviews with members and the kinds of "research on" project described above (p. 296, p. 302). Together they give us the necessary intelligence to change. These "temperature checks" and "stock takes" are vital for working within the complexity of a multi-sector, multi-organizational environment.

Constantly sensing signals and seizing opportunities

Overall, we concur with MacLean and MacIntosh's observations (Chapter 9 in this book), that "accepting emergence and change in the research process is hallmark of any truly collaborative research." Emergence and change is equally a hallmark of sustained academic–practitioner relationships.

When the founder moved on and the range of sponsors altered, we developed different attractors for membership. When the Forum could realistically be characterized as a community we worked in one way. When that character dissipated and looser network properties disrupted the dynamics we changed the design to maintain research opportunities. This presented its own KM challenge: how to pass on the now significant body of knowledge to others? Unless we could build on this, future research opportunities would be constrained by the absorptive capacity of new members (Zahra & George, 2002). Adding complementary activities such as action learning, a course, and recorded webinars built capability for future research. Although these largely develop individuals' knowledge, our research showed the essential role they play in translating benefits back to their organization in inter-organizational communities, which builds commitment. Allowing time for networking and structuring reflective discussions also re-enforces relationship ties

What's in it for us as academics?

We have often debated whether the very nature of our research domain explains why we have both been able and motivated to work on relationships building to create a space where knowledge co-creation underpins the research agenda. On balance, we believe that academics from other business and management disciplines investigating current practices in organizations could also work this way, provided they are willing to give the same attention to process detail as they do to the content of their research. We suggest it is always possible to find a link between the academic discipline and current business and management concerns that would sustain practitioner attention and involvement.

Satisfying a concern to make a difference

Certainly having a broad research agendas at the big question level and eclectic interests at the detail level helps. The experience becomes increasingly useful as funding bodies encourage more multi-disciplinary projects. Working with practitioners develops a more critical eye on potential contribution. Learning to use a variety of insider–outsider research approaches is also stimulating.

Although translating complex academic concepts into the language of practice may seem like oversimplification, as Wendy Smith notes in her reflections on executive education (see Chapter 8), interacting with executives has benefits in terms of refining one's own reasoning and providing access to research data. Writing several times in different styles to produce deliverables from the research that suit practitioners and academic publications also refines understanding.

Assuming all of these components are in place, the approach offers easy access to major organizations to carry out a cumulative program of research. Examples from practice can also be fed into teaching activities, either as cases or through relationships that encourage speakers from the companies to participate. Relationships between the business school and the organizations are also strengthened through ongoing interaction, giving other business channels avenues to explore. Perhaps the most important thing is the feeling of excitement when you identify how to work through the various paradoxes to a mutually beneficial result and the feeling of contributing to something more valuable than an academic institution alone.

References

Adler, P. & Kwon, S. W. (2002). Social capital; Prospects for a new concept. *Academy of Management Review*, 27(1), 17–40.

Bartunek, J. M. & Louis, M. R. (1996). *Insider/Outsider Team Research* (Vol. 40). Thousand Oaks, CA: Sage Publications.

Bartunek, J. M. & Rynes, S. L. (2014). Academics and practitioners are alike and unlike: The paradoxes of academic–practitioner relationships. *Journal of Management*, 40(5), 1181–201.

Bolisani, E. & Scarso, E. (2013). The place of communities of practice in knowledge management studies: A critical review. *Journal of Knowledge Management*, 18(2), 366–81.

Bradbury, H. (2008). Quality and "actionability": What action researchers offer from the tradition of pragmatism. In Shani, A. B. R., Mohrman, S. A., Pasmore, W. A., Stymne, B. & Adler, N. (Eds.) *Handbook of Collaborative Management Research*. Thousand Oaks, CA: Sage Publications.

Carlile, P. R. (2004). Transferring, translating and transforming: An integrative framework for managing knowledge across boundaries. *Organization Science*, 15(5), 555–68.

Dixon, N. (2000). *Common Knowledge: How Companies Thrive by Sharing What They Know*. Boston, MA: Harvard Business School Press.

Easterby-Smith, M., Lyles, M. A. & Tsang, E. W. K. (2008). Inter-organizational knowledge transfer: current themes and future prospects. *Journal of Management Studies*, 45(4), 677–90.

Edvinsson, L. & Malone, M. S. (1997). *Intellectual Capital*. London: Piatkus.

Gibbons, M., Limoges, C., Nowotny, H., Schwartzman, S., Scott, P. & Trow, M. (1994). *The New Production of Knowledge: The Dynamics of Science and Research in Contemporary Societies*. London: Sage Publishing.

Granovetter, M. S. (1973). The strength of weak ties. *American Journal of Sociology*, 78(6), 1360–80.

Grant, R. M. (1996). Toward a knowledge-based theory of the firm. *Strategic Management Journal*, 17(S2), S109–S122.

Gulati, R. (2007). Tent poles, tribalism, and boundary spanning: The rigor–relevance debate in management research. *Academy of Management Journal*, 50(4), 775–82.

Gustavsen, B. (2001). Theory and practice: The mediating discourse. In Reason, P. & Bradbury, H. (Eds.) *Handbook of Action Research: Participative Inquiry and Practice*. London: Sage Publications.

Hair, J. F., Money, A. H., Samouel, P. & Page, M. (2007). *Research Methods for Business*. Chichester, UK: John Wiley and Sons.

Hatcheul, A. (2001). The two pillars of new management research. *British Journal of Management*, 12(Special Issue), S33–S39.

Johnson, G. & Scholes, K. (2002). *Exploring Corporate Strategy* (6th ed.). Harlow, UK: Pearson Education.

Liebeskind, J. P. (1996). Knowledge, strategy, and the theory of the firm. *Strategic Management Journal*, 17(S2), 93–107.

McKenzie, J. (2005). How businesses can work together. Examining the essential points of inter-organizational relationships. *KM Review*, 8(5), 16–19.

McKenzie, J. & Aitken, P. (2012). Learning to lead the knowledgeable organization: Developing leadership agility. *Strategic HR Review*, 11(6), 329–34.

McKenzie, J. & van Winkelen, C. (2004). *Understanding the Knowledgeable Organization: Nurturing Knowledge Competence.* London: Cengage Learning.

McKenzie, J. & van Winkelen, C. (2008). Knowledge management (KM) for a changing world: Challenges for third generation knowledge practice. *International Journal of Knowledge, Culture and Change Management,* 8(8), 1–14.

McKenzie, J., van Winkelen, C. & Bartunek, J. M. (2014). Elaborating from practice on the theoretical model of engaged scholarship. Paper presented at the Academy of Management Conference, Philadelphia, August.

Nahapiet, J. & Ghoshal, S. (1998). Social capital, intellectual capital and the organizational advantage. *Academy of Management Review,* 23(2), 242–67.

Nonaka, I. & Konno, N. (1998). The concept of "ba" building a foundation for knowledge creation. *California Management Review,* 40(3), 40–54.

Patton, M. Q. (2011). *Developmental Evaluation: Applying Complexity Concepts to Enhance Innovation and Use.* New York: The Guildford Press.

Reason, P. & Bradbury, H. (Eds.) (2001). *Handbook of Action Research: Participative Inquiry and Practice.* London: Sage Publishing.

Reid, D., Bussiere, D. & Greenaway, K. (2001). Alliance formation issues for knowledge based enterprises. *International Journal of Managment Reviews,* 3(1), 79–100.

Scott, A., Skea, J., Robinson, J. & Shove, E. (1999). Designing "interactive" environmental research for wider social relevance. (Special Briefing no. 3). Economic and Social Research Council, Global Environmental Change Programme, Brighton, UK.

Skea, J., Robinson, J. & Shove, E. (1998). Interactive research: Exploring the practice. Paper presented at the ESRC Global Environmental Programme, Brighton, March 2–4.

Spender, J. (1996). Making knowledge the basis of a dynamic theory of the firm. *Strategic Management Journal,* 17(Winter Special Issue), S45–S62.

Starkey, K. (2001). In defence of modes one, two and three: A response. *British Journal of Management,* 12(Special Issue), S77–S80.

Szulanski, G. (1996). Exploring internal stickiness: Impediments to the transfer of best practice within the firm. *Strategic Management Journal,* 17(S2), 27–43.

Truch, E., Ezingeard, J.-N. & Birchall, D. (2000). Developing a relevant research agenda in knowledge management: Bridging the gap between knowing and doing. *Journal of Systems and Information Technology,* 4(2), 1–11.

Van de Ven, A. H. (2007). *Engaged Scholarship: A Guide for Organizational and Social Research.* Oxford: Oxford University Press.

van Winkelen, C. (2010). Deriving value from inter-organizational learning collaborations. *The Learning Organization,* 17(1), 8–23.

van Winkelen, C. & McKenzie, J. (2009). Using scenarios to explore the potential for shifts in the relative priority of human, structural and relational capital in generating value. *EJKM Special Issue,* 7(4), S509–S516.

van Winkelen, C. & McKenzie, J. (2011). *Knowledge Works. The Handbook of Practical Ways to Identify and Solve Common Organizational Problems for Better Performance.* Chichester, UK: John Wiley & Sons.

van Winkelen, C. & McKenzie, J. (2013). From KM evaluation to developing evaluative capability for learning. Paper presented at the 14th European Conference for Knowledge Management, Kaunas University of Technology, Lithuania.

van Winkelen, C. & Tovstiga, G. (2009). Understanding and organizational's knowledge-enabled innovation capability. *International Journal of Knowledge Management Studies,* 3(1–2), 97–115.

Venkatramann, N. & Henderson, J. C. (1998). Real strategies for virtual organizing. *Sloan Management Review*, 40(1), 33–49.

Vygotsky, L. (1978). *Mind in Society: Development of Higher Psychological Processes.* Cambridge, MA: Harvard University Press.

Wenger, E. (1998). *Communities of Practice: Learning, Meaning and Identity*. Cambridge, UK: Cambridge University Press.

Zahra, S. A. & George, G. (2002). Absorptive capacity: A review, reconceptualization, and extension. *Academy of Management Review*, 27(2), 185–203.

18 Applied R&D in HR
Google's People Innovation Lab

Jennifer Kurkoski

Introduction

I run a research and development lab in HR. Yes, that's correct: a research and development lab in HR. Admittedly, the phrases "R&D" and "HR" do not typically co-occur in the same sentence, so perhaps the quizzical looks should come as no surprise. But why, really? We spend hours upon hours in organizations, working in contexts shaped by the policies and programs of HR departments. Why then are we so surprised to hear that these policies and programs might be the subjects of rigorous, thoughtful research? We do not lack for unanswered questions about people and the experience of work. Yet the existence of Google's People Innovation Lab, the PiLab, remains an oddity.

Many potential explanations for the apparent novelty come to mind, some with merit. For one, conducting research on one's own colleagues can be tricky, fraught with potential ethical (and legal) landmines and without the guidance of Institutional Review Boards. Also, objectivity may be suspect as achieving perspective on one's own organization is notoriously difficult, not to mention the absence of peer review. Furthermore, leaders may fear taking away time for "real" work in order for people to participate in studies, and employees may react negatively to being part of "experiments."

However, the opportunities presented by conducting research in organizations are at least as compelling as the challenges, if not more so. The rich contexts of real-life organizations can inspire new insights as one observes phenomena unfolding. Field testing, with the messiness and particulars of specific organizations, can provide nuance to the theories developed in the pared-down contexts of academic laboratories. When findings replicate in the "real world," we increase our confidence in their applicability, and we discover boundary conditions. And seeing those findings translate directly into action can be deeply gratifying.

In this chapter, I describe the practices and activities of Google's People Innovation Lab, the Pilab. I outline the Lab's history, discuss past projects, describe how we interact with the broader scientific community, and share some of the lessons we have learned along the way. My ultimate goal is to inspire conversation about a new model for applied social science research as a complement to the existing structures of academia, one with benefits for all involved.

A research lab in HR

When the PiLab got its start in 2008, nearly all of the data-related efforts within Google's People Operations department—Google's term for what's otherwise called Human Resources—were devoted to developing and providing critical metrics. Such data were, and continue to be, crucial for smooth operation of the business; these metrics support leaders in making important people-related decisions on the basis of data rather than instinct. But delivering metrics can be as all-consuming as it is critical. Furthermore, as the HR profession is more typically associated with intuition and gut instinct, providing data in the first place was already considered pretty innovative, and no one was asking for more. However, team members saw exceptional opportunity. Trained in social science, they knew the kinds of insight they could extract from the swirl of data surrounding them. They sensed the chance to answer questions not yet asked by senior leaders, questions that the team was willing to bet that leaders would ask soon. They just needed to carve out the time.

The PiLab was designed for precisely that purpose: creating the space to pursue answers to fundamental questions. The Lab's stated mission, unchanged since its inception, is "to conduct innovative research that transforms organizational practice at Google and beyond." Functionally, the PiLab is part of People Analytics, a larger group that continues to provide analysis and reporting for People Ops. People affiliated with the Lab typically come from research backgrounds and hold PhDs from top research institutions in fields such as Industrial & Organizational Psychology, Organizational Behavior, and Decision Science. However, neither the mission statement nor the researchers' CVs shed much light on how the Lab pursues these ends. In other words, what exactly does the Lab *do*?

The Lab's primary activities cluster into three major areas:

- infusing the wisdom of organizational science into people-related practice at Google;
- carrying out primary research when the knowledge we need does not exist, or when samples and methods spark doubt as to the applicability of existing insights to our particular environment; and
- furthering discovery by providing a living, breathing organizational laboratory to test and advance theories, often in collaboration with external researchers.

Using existing science to make HR better

When considering the work of a lab, one typically thinks about conducting new and original research. However, one of the PiLab's critical contributions within Google has been connecting Google colleagues with research already out there in the world. Many business challenges, particularly those in HR, benefit enormously from insights already available in the literature. Unfortunately, people-related decisions (e.g., hiring, promotion) are often notoriously rooted in gut instinct rather than data and analytics, despite the fact that topics as diverse as motivation, incentives, well-being, distributed work, team dynamics, fairness, decision-making, job satisfaction, and organizational citizenship are all informed by decades of scholarship. One need not reinvent the wheel—although for people who've been getting around on foot, some education on the simple existence of the wheel and its revolutionary capabilities may be in order.

In the PiLab, we regularly field requests from our colleagues in People Ops, and sometimes from the organization more broadly. Nearly every month brings some kind of inquiry. How can we make rewards and recognition more meaningful to people? What kind of screening approaches might reduce false negatives in our hiring process? How can we ensure that critical processes such as compensation planning are free from decision biases? How should we consider citizenship behaviors when evaluating performance? How many interviewers does it take to get a reliable signal of candidate quality? What are the factors that make teams effective?

In answering these questions, we certainly need not reinvent the wheel. But that wheel often needs rather a lot of alteration. The relevant literatures are rarely reported in publications beyond academic journals, with insights typically buried deep in often opaque and technical jargon. That wheel may be described as a "spherical, dynamic, resilient, physics-inspired rubber device." In addition, normal science necessitates the incremental accumulation of evidence, so insight on a general topic such as fairness or decision-making requires canvassing a large body of work in order to piece together findings. Furthermore, we must apply an especially critical eye to sample composition, experimental design, effect sizes, and boundary conditions. In short, will the findings generalize? We can't simply read an article and pass it along.

One must also consider the particulars of context. In the HR realm, a number of organizations strive to extract findings in more human-readable formats; these include The Conference Board, USC's Center for Effective Organizations (see Chapter 13 in this volume), the Society for Human Resource Management, and Cornell's Center for Advanced Human Resources Studies, among others. Publications such as *Harvard Business Review* and *Sloan Management Review* play a critical role as well. However, much of the power of PiLab's advising flows from being able to place research-backed insights within Google-specific practices and process, using Google-specific language. We can dig deeper through conversations with the authors of work of particular interest, who have almost always been generous with their time in discussing their findings. And we can augment existing work with our own analyses or even experimentation. This kind of localization reduces the organ rejection that can happen when ideas appear too foreign and thus fail to find a foothold. Applying findings and conducting secondary research also strengthens the field at large by providing further evidence of replicability, particularly at a time when studies in social science are under increasing scrutiny (Baker, 2015).

The PiLab has two powerful advantages in bringing existing research to bear on practice:

- our colleagues in People Ops actually want to know what research can teach them. They ask for our help, they listen to what we have to say, and they are willing to modify their programs based on evidence from social science. Our situation would be considerably more challenging were we having to beg people to listen; and
- we have the partnership of an enormously talented group of communications experts. The People Ops communications team helps us translate our messages to make them clear and concise, and keeps us focused on what's most important and relevant. One cannot overestimate either the importance or the difficulty of communicating to widely varying audiences. Fundamentally, the communications team helps us talk about research in ways that make people feel smart, included and energized, rather than making them feel confused and separate—or worse, ignorant and demoralized. Communication is hard work, and work for which academic writing is poor preparation.

Conducting research when existing science does not suffice

However, existing research is not always sufficient to the question at hand. Sometimes the questions are simply unanswered by science. Other times, findings exist, but they are not obviously applicable to our context at Google, so replication seems prudent. And still other times, particularly when a problem is not broadly recognized within the company or when solutions are not obvious, the research process itself provides the foundation for organizational change. When presented with rigorous data gathered in our own context, Google employees can be surprisingly eager to adopt new approaches.

One example of research informing change was work related to managers: do managers even matter? In Google's early years, the company experimented with getting rid of the people manager role entirely, thus we could not simply take on faith that managers were a necessary feature for an organization. The study, called Project Oxygen, led by Michelle Donovan and Neal Patel, aimed first to address this foundational issue and then to identify the behaviors that differentiated great managers from the merely good. Michelle and Neal's study achieved both of these goals. They found that people who reported to highly rated managers (as measured via surveys of their direct reports and via performance evaluations by their own managers) were more satisfied with their work and less likely to leave than people who reported to less highly rated managers (Bock, 2015). Interviews highlighted specific attributes shared by highly rated managers but not by the low-scoring ones. These attributes became the "Oxygen 8," a set of eight behaviors including "Don't micromanage" and "Be a good coach." These behaviors became the foundation of Google's twice-yearly Manager Feedback Survey in which everyone in the company provides their manager with feedback intended to support continued development. These behaviors also provide the framework for various learning and development programs.

A more recent example focused on teams. Much of the work done at Google, and in many organizations, is done collaboratively, but the research on teams is vast and not entirely conclusive. We wanted to understand what considerations contribute to team effectiveness in our context at Google, and so set about gathering data. Initially, we thought that composition might hold the key: find a group of rock stars, put them together, and *voilá!* However, after poring over interviews with dozens of managers and team leads, and analyzing data from 180 teams across the organization, a different story emerged. Teams' effectiveness proved most strongly related to how team members interacted with each other, and much less to who was on the team. In fact, psychological safety, a team-level perception of the consequences for taking interpersonal risks (Edmondson 1999), proved the most important and foundational of five key dynamics that characterized effective teams. The five were, in order of importance:

- psychological safety;
- dependability;
- structure and clarity;
- meaning; and
- impact.

These five dynamics now form the core of an on-demand assessment and activity available to any team within Google looking to increase its effectiveness.

A real-world laboratory for discovery

The PiLab does not only focus internally, however. Just as we learn from academic researchers and from the practices of other organizations, we seek to share insight and to provide a forum for others to do so as well, hopefully breaking down information-hoarding norms that often govern HR in the process. Our mission explicitly includes the intent to influence practice at Google "and beyond" and we pursue several paths to that end. More than that though, we seek to develop new ways to create those insights in the first place. An organizational research lab situated *within* an organization provides unique opportunities. Granted, such an arrangement presents unique challenges and constraints as well (see below, p. 317), but the advantage of within-organization research is the ability to connect constructs, events, and behaviors that span organizational life, and to do so over time.

One key way we construct opportunity for insight is through the collaborative research projects we've undertaken with university faculty. Rather than simply opening our doors for researchers to run surveys or conduct interviews, we co-define projects as full partners in the research process, from hypothesis generation to interpretation of results. As a partner on these projects, we bring to bear our deep context on the organization as well as our research training. As such, we are well-positioned to identify where a proposed intervention might be particularly well-received or provide an alternative explanation that can elucidate results (Mohrman, Gibson & Mohrman, 2001). Having trained researchers as internal partners also means never having to justify the inclusion of a control group or explain the concept of construct validity.

In collaborating with university faculty, we've sought topics with both theoretical and practical implications. But we've also tried to focus on the sorts of study made possible by working within an organization. Multimethod studies and longitudinal efforts are less daunting when one has the stability afforded by a dedicated lab. For example, one of our projects revisited the topic of organizational citizenship behaviors, or OCBs (Organ 1988), examining how modern knowledge workers conceptualize and engage in these behaviors. This project found that, while some traditional OCBs continue to exist, others were deemed irrelevant, and new ones emerged (Dekas, Bauer, Welle, Kurkoski & Sullivan, 2013). Another project, with Spencer Harrison of Boston College and David Sluss of Georgia Tech, involved a longitudinal, qualitative study of newcomer adjustment and how new hires bring external ideas to bear within the organization. This project found that people who are able to adapt their ideas to appear homegrown—and who receive support from managers and peers in doing so—are most successful in seeing those ideas through to implementation (Harrison, Sluss, Kurkoski & Wisdom, 2017). This finding stands in contrast to March's (1991) provocative argument based on simulation studies that the stubbornly slow to adapt are valuable sources of organizational change. Other projects, in process or under review, include how incentives influence habit formation and how personality traits are shaped by changes in one's network of work-related relationships.

Developing insight involves more than conducting research though. It requires ongoing exposure to new ideas and perspectives. Universities have the advantage here, given the intellectual milieu at their core. To ensure we did not become completely separated from our research roots, we started the PiLab Summit in 2009, an annual event involving a dozen or so scholars from multiple disciplines aimed at recreating some key elements of the university environment. Specifically, we designed a day of open exchange among Google HR leaders and academic researchers, batting around ideas not limited to the immediate business challenge at Google. And we kicked it off the evening before with something other than a typical sit-down dinner. Rather, leaning on the many excellent cafes that dot the Google campus, we enlisted one of the Google chefs to teach a cooking class, and then had everyone make their own meal. The experience served to level the playing field among attendees—tenured professors and junior faculty, senior vice presidents, and newly hired analysts—as it turns out that professional status and skill in the kitchen are largely uncorrelated. These dinners helped set the collegial and informal tone that shaped the following day's conversation, which has featured neither formal presentations nor paper discussions. Instead, the day has revolved around small-group conversations, loosely facilitated and focused on broad topics such as incentives, decision-making, culture, career development, and teams—topics that are relevant for Google as well as almost any organization. We've aimed to inspire new thinking, although new research[1] ideas have resulted too. Building on the spirit of the Summit—to facilitate conversations across domains and to spark new ideas—we recently hosted a larger event, in collaboration with other teams at Google. The re:Work events brought together academic researchers along with leaders from a wide range of organizations to think about how to make work better everywhere and for everyone.[2]

However, the most audacious example of the possibilities of within-organization research is gDNA, our longitudinal survey study. In 2012, the PiLab launched this project, aimed at better understanding the experience of work with the intent of improving that experience (Bock, 2014). We enrolled a randomly selected panel of employees, to which we add panelists each year, inviting those who leave Google to continue in the study if they'd like. Using scales from the academic literature, we survey the panel twice a year on topics including personality, values, beliefs, and experiences. With panelists' consent, we include other HR data (e.g., function, region, tenure, promotions, transfers) and we provide in turn customized reports to every "gDNA-er" after each survey cycle, reflecting back to panelists some of what they've shared with us. In 2016, we launched the gDNA Scholars, our first foray into sharing the data with the broader scientific community, as was intended from the start. We accepted a pilot group of promising graduate students with whom we have shared subsets of the gDNA data, based on each scholar's specific proposal. We look forward to their results, and to sharing those findings broadly.

Getting started: advice for all involved and a preview of roadblocks to come

Reflecting back on PiLab since its inception in 2008, several lessons jump out to me that may translate well for others contemplating similar endeavors:

- **Start small:** Large-scale, months-long studies are amazing, but are not good starting points. Smaller projects that can be completed in a few months help develop familiarity and trust and give people (on all sides) practice in collaborative field research. Such projects may be more opportunistic than driven by a guiding research program. For example, design a simple A/B test with an existing email campaign, randomize assignment to a training program, or analyze existing survey or archival data with more advanced statistical techniques. Maya Shankar successfully employed just such a strategy in starting the US government's Social and Behavioral Sciences Team (Shankar, 2016).
- **Be curious:** The opportunities noted above for smaller projects may not be obvious to practitioners within organizations, and they will be invisible to researchers who come in with predetermined notions of the project they

want to do. Asking questions—What challenges are you facing? What problems are you trying to solve? What are you excited about?—and then truly listening and being curious about others' worlds (Harrison, 2012) can reveal surprising opportunities for research and insight. Such small wins lay the foundation for more ambitious endeavors in the future.

- **Ask questions that matter:** As an applied R&D lab, we evaluate projects on their potential for practical application as well as for theoretical contribution. This overlap is in fact vast in the fields of HR and Organizational Behavior. However, the practical applications may not be obvious to researchers, whereas the potential for theory may not be obvious to those shaping policies and programs. For example, our retirement savings contribution reminder emails were inspired by conversation with academic researchers and the fact that, at the time, many employees were missing out on some or all of Google's matching program. We had not planned necessarily to pursue such research, but we weren't opposed. We took advantage of the opportunity, testing theories of anchoring and goal-setting along the way, and sparked hundreds of thousands of dollars of additional retirement savings (Choi, Haisley, Kurkoski & Massey, 2012).

- **Plan for action:** Research should not sit on a shelf when completed. For academics, that means publication; researchers often craft their topics and methods with that outcome in mind so as to improve the odds of achieving that goal. Similarly for practitioners, research should inform policies and programs. To ensure that action follows insight, involve from the beginning the people for whom the question is pressing, the people who should care about the findings. Partner with them when designing the study and the timeline, and work together throughout the process. Finally, consider small pilots rather than whole-scale change. For any organization, a trial run is far more palatable and a far less-risky way to try new ideas.

Inevitably, we've learned a few things over the years, from our missteps as well as from our successes. Several principles now guide our work:

- **Don't hide:** When talking about the research of the PiLab, we very deliberately describe all Google employees as partners. They are not "participants," or, worse, "subjects." Our colleagues are dedicated and insightful contributors to the Lab's work. Consequently, Googlers know what we're studying, and we tell them what we find. We've shared findings—and even non-findings—at meetings and in internal news stories targeted at the entire company. That's close to 70,000 people. In return, we get feedback about the findings, ideas for how to integrate findings into the experience of working at Google, and oftentimes requests for future research. This transparency limits some of the research we pursue (e.g., no deception studies). But, in exchange, we get the kind of trust that comes from telling people what you're doing and then telling them what you learned.

- **Play in the well-lit parts of the sandbox:** Many very important questions may not be appropriate for collaborative field research. Research involving what's known in the United States as "protected class" data (e.g., gender, ethnicity, age, disability) can create a multitude of problems for organizations, potentially from the findings themselves as well as from opportunities for discovery the studies might create. In a litigious society, ignoring such risks is irresponsible. That's not to say that companies should ignore such variables in their analyses. Rather, such work typically proceeds under attorney–client privilege. Fortunately, we have no shortage of interesting and important questions that do not depend critically on protected class data.
- **It's still really hard:** Collaborative research is not really more efficient, though it is richer. Coordination costs are real. Working across any boundary requires extra time to understand goals, elucidate norms, and define terms. When those boundaries cross significantly different institutional contexts as is the case with collaborative research, participants may not even realize what they don't know. Also, the incentives and timelines for practitioners vary wildly from those of academics. One must acknowledge and solve for the fact that businesses typically deal in months while academic timelines tend to stretch to years, and that publishing in a top-tier journal usually is of little interest to those outside of academia. Our solution has been to set key milestones in the research process and provide updates to our internal partners at each milestone. In addition, we prioritize the development of white papers or presentations that highlight key findings and implications for practice. The theoretical development and positioning within existing literature that are crucial to the often-lengthy publication process takes place in the background and after we've made the initial report.

Conclusion: inspiring change

Beyond the research, the advising, and the collaboration, I've come to believe that the PiLab plays an additional role, one I believe to be as critical to Google as the Lab's concrete activities. I hope this role may be critical to HR more generally as well. That is, I believe the PiLab serves as a symbol, one that's both normative and aspirational. The existence of the PiLab signals the expectation that academic research can—and should—be brought to bear when examining the questions that we face. Questions of incentives, of fairness in hiring practices, of leadership development, of decision-making, of organizational structure, of organizational culture—all of these topics have rich sets of findings over years of literature from which one can glean insight and inspiration. One need not rely on "best practice" when developing HR policies, programs, and processes, which really just means doing what others are doing already. Not that one should ignore best practices entirely. Google learns an enormous amount from other organizations' efforts, from SAS to Wegman's grocery. However, the world is always changing and what's "best" at one point in time and in one particular context may not be "best" in a different time and place. That's why science matters.

A useful comparison can be made to Google's famed "20 percent time" policy. This policy, which remains deliberately under-defined, allows employees to dedicate up to 20 percent of their time to a project of their own choosing. Projects should be business-relevant, which, for Google, does not overly narrow the field. And, while projects have had such high-profile results as Gmail and Google Scholar, the true power lies in the concept itself and the language it provides with which to talk about work that falls outside of one's primary responsibilities. The idea of 20 percent time sets the expectation that any employee, no matter that person's title or background, can develop a project. Not just propose an idea to senior management, but rather go out and build the proof of concept, enlist colleagues to help, and recruit internal users if applicable. Furthermore, by being able to label the endeavor "20 percent time," the organization created a mechanism for short-circuiting manager objections. An employee can always say, "Oh that? Yeah, that's my 20 percent project."

We don't have solid numbers on the amount of time actually spent on 20 percent projects, but I would argue that the number count is almost beside the point. The idea that one can, and perhaps even should, have such projects is a powerful message for the organization. I believe the PiLab communicates a related message within People Ops: applied research offers a path to insight on how one builds an organization that aims to support people in doing extraordinary work, globally, over years, and in a rapidly changing environment. HR is not about launching yet another program. It's about solving important but often complicated problems for people and organizations. Solving those problems requires asking questions about what really works, which in turn requires being able to test and measure. That is, we need science.

From time to time, we've been criticized by some in the academic community for the fact that our methods are not open for all to examine nor are our results subject to the rigor of peer review. These statements are certainly true. However, equally true is that peer review journals present a huge barrier to sharing stories like those coming out of the PiLab. If knowledge must be channeled exclusively through peer reviewed journals in order to be considered legitimate, many organizations will continue in ignorance.

Both the manager research (Bryant, 2011) and the team projects (Duhigg, 2016) were covered in hugely popular *New York Times* articles, with each article sitting on the "Most Emailed" list for weeks. The manager study was also the focus of what's become Harvard Business School's top-selling case study (Garvin, Wagonfeld & Kind, 2013). Companies need this kind of insight into others' experiments. While the popular press should in no way replace peer review, it has a role to play in the broader ecosystem of inquiry. Unfortunately, academics have no real incentive to publish in popular venues as any such effort has no bearing on obtaining the ultimate prize of tenure. And the ironically-named "impact factor" used to measure publications in no way considers real-world impact. While change to tenure and incentives in academia is a lofty goal, one can hope.

As for people working in organizations, the questions we face are far too critical to cede to researchers alone, let alone to consultants who often provide what amounts to watered-down versions of academic work. Furthermore, we cannot expect applicable answers if we're unwilling to provide the environments in which to stress-test the findings that emerge from academic labs. For the PiLab, our desire to collaborate, as well as the sheer number of interesting topics, far outstrips our capacity for such endeavors. When it comes to our mission of influencing organizational practice beyond Google, my hope is that more organizations recognize the vast, untapped value of a research-based approach to shaping organizations and that the phrase "applied R&D in HR" becomes the new normal.

Notes

1 See http://freakonomics.com/podcast/when-willpower-isnt-enough-a-new-freakonomics-radio-podcast/.
2 The re:Work event was hosted in 2014 and 2016; videos of all the talks are available by searching "videos" on the re:Work website at g.co/rework.

References

Baker, M. (2015). Over half of psychology studies fail reproducibility test. *Nature Online*. August 27.

Bock, L. (2014). Google's scientific approach to work–life balance (and much more). *Harvard Business Review*, 92(6), 18–19.

Bock, L. (2015). *Work Rules! Insights from Google That Will Transform How You Live and Lead*. New York: Hachette.

Bryant, A. (2011). Google's quest to build a better boss. *New York Times*, March 12. Retrieved August 15, 2016 from www.nytimes.com.

Choi, J. J., Haisley, E., Kurkoski, J. & Massey, C. (2012). *Small Cues Change Savings Choices*. National Bureau of Economic Research (No. w17843).

Dekas, K. H., Bauer, T. N., Welle, B., Kurkoski, J. & Sullivan, S. (2013). Organizational citizenship behavior, version 2.0: A review and qualitative investigation of OCBs for knowledge workers at Google and beyond. *The Academy of Management Perspectives*, 27(3), 219–37.

Duhigg, C. (2016). What Google learned from its quest to build the perfect team. *New York Times*, February 25. Retrieved August 15, 2016 from www.nytimes.com.

Edmondson, A. (1999). Psychological safety and learning behavior in work teams. *Administrative Science Quarterly*, 44(2), 350–83.

Garvin, D., Wagonfeld, A. & Kind, L. (2013). *Google's Project Oxygen: Do Managers Matter?* HBSP Case Study No. 313–110, Boston, MA: Harvard Business School Publishing.

Harrison, S. H. (2012). Organizing the cat? Generative aspects of curiosity in organizational life. In Cameron, K. & Spreitzer, G. (Eds.) *The Oxford Handbook of Positive Organizational Scholarship* (pp. 110–24). Oxford: Oxford University Press.

Harrison, S., Sluss, D., Kurkoski, J., & Wisdom, J. (2017). An inductive study of sharing outsider ideas while becoming an insider at Google. Google, Working paper.

March, J. G. (1991). Exploration and exploitation in organizational learning. *Organization Science*, 2(1), 71–87.

Mohrman, S. A., Gibson, C. B. & Mohrman, A. M. (2001). Doing research that is useful to practice a model and empirical exploration. *Academy of Management Journal*, 44(2), 357–75.

Organ, D. W. (1988). *Organizational Citizenship Behavior: The Good Soldier Syndrome*. Lexington, MA: Lexington Books D.C. Heath and Com.

Shankar, M. (2016). *Building a Behavioral Science Start-up at the White House* [video file]. Retrieved from https://rework.withgoogle.com/blog/rework-2016-videos/.

Index

Page numbers in *italics* denote tables, those in **bold** denote figures.

 Taylor & Francis eBooks

Helping you to choose the right eBooks for your Library

Add Routledge titles to your library's digital collection today. Taylor and Francis ebooks contains over 50,000 titles in the Humanities, Social Sciences, Behavioural Sciences, Built Environment and Law.

Choose from a range of subject packages or create your own!

Benefits for you

» Free MARC records
» COUNTER-compliant usage statistics
» Flexible purchase and pricing options
» All titles DRM-free.

 REQUEST YOUR **FREE** INSTITUTIONAL TRIAL TODAY

Free Trials Available
We offer free trials to qualifying academic, corporate and government customers.

Benefits for your user

» Off-site, anytime access via Athens or referring URL
» Print or copy pages or chapters
» Full content search
» Bookmark, highlight and annotate text
» Access to thousands of pages of quality research at the click of a button.

eCollections – Choose from over 30 subject eCollections, including:

Archaeology	Language Learning
Architecture	Law
Asian Studies	Literature
Business & Management	Media & Communication
Classical Studies	Middle East Studies
Construction	Music
Creative & Media Arts	Philosophy
Criminology & Criminal Justice	Planning
Economics	Politics
Education	Psychology & Mental Health
Energy	Religion
Engineering	Security
English Language & Linguistics	Social Work
Environment & Sustainability	Sociology
Geography	Sport
Health Studies	Theatre & Performance
History	Tourism, Hospitality & Events

For more information, pricing enquiries or to order a free trial, please contact your local sales team: **www.tandfebooks.com/page/sales**

For Product Safety Concerns and Information please contact our EU
representative GPSR@taylorandfrancis.com
Taylor & Francis Verlag GmbH, Kaufingerstraße 24, 80331 München, Germany

www.ingramcontent.com/pod-product-compliance
Ingram Content Group UK Ltd.
Pitfield, Milton Keynes, MK11 3LW, UK
UKHW021020180425
457613UK00020B/998

* 9 780367 875008 *